TUTTLE

LEARNING CHINESE CHARACTERS

A revolutionary new way to learn and remember
the 800 most basic Chinese characters

HSK Level A

Alison Matthews
Laurence Matthews

Illustrations by
Janet Jordan and Dil Roworth

TUTTLE Publishing
Tokyo | Rutland, Vermont | Singapore

Contents

Acknowledgments

First and foremost we want to thank Janet and Dil for their wonderful illustrations. From the very first day they both entered into the spirit of the enterprise with immense energy and enthusiasm, and our Friday mornings will never be so much fun again! The initial idea was to have a few pictograms for the basic building block characters — we never dreamed we would find someone who would take the task by the scruff of the neck and attempt all 219! Although we all helped at times by brainstorming possible interpretations, Janet's ability to think "outside the box" resulted in some truly inspired character pictures and many of her interpretations will never be bettered. Similarly, when Dil brought her gifts as an illustrator to bear on the story pictures, she quickly grasped that these pictures had a very specific job to do and set about developing exactly the right style for them. We will always remember her exclamations of, "Oh, I shall enjoy drawing *that*," on being presented with yet another bizarre story to illustrate. Her enthusiasm and sense of fun have produced some truly memorable pictures.

Before we sat down to write all the stories we wanted to make sure that using visualization to remember the characters would work for different ages, backgrounds and mindsets. Our search for willing volunteers resulted in a group that covered a range of ages and interests in different parts of the world. Amongst this group was a hard core who were especially helpful, and a big thank you goes out to Larry Fogg, Pat Halliwell, Marion Brumby and Nigel Maggs.

To try and ensure that the introductory text was easy to understand we prevailed upon some very good friends (most of whom have never studied any Chinese) to read it. All of them spent time going over the text and made pertinent and helpful comments and suggestions. Our thanks to Martin Adfield, John & Barbara Eastwood, Geoff & Jill Cory, and Nigel & Toby Brown. (We should add, though, that we take full responsibility for the finished result).

There are people in life who can be guaranteed to listen to your ideas no matter how off-beat they are, and encourage you to "go for it" if they think an idea will work. Debbie and Dave Russell have given unstintingly of their time in this regard. As well as talking over detailed points they have given us their unflagging support throughout. Thank you!

Inevitably there are also times in the writing of any book when you wonder why you ever got started. At times like these everyone should have a friend like Judy Landis. Quite apart from reading parts of the book, Judy has kept us straight on all things American and is our one-woman cheer-leader. Her observations are always eloquent, sound and invariably shot through with common sense and humor. Our love and thanks go to her.

For her professionalism and understanding we'd like to thank Doreen Ng at Tuttle Publishing.

Finally, it can be hard to live with two people who wander around saying things like "that's the sort of job a ghostly dwarf would do" or "what we need here is two giants from Shanghai." So our thanks go to Helen for her forbearance in not actually throwing anything at us (at least, not for these particular transgressions).

Introduction

In a dark old castle in medieval times, someone has a bright idea: "If we could find a way of putting some **fire** on a **nail** in the wall we could have a **lamp** in the room." They get the local **giant** to **dunk** twigs in candle-wax to make the first simple lamp.

If you pictured this story as you read it, you have just learned the meaning and pronunciation of a Chinese character! This book uses stories like this as well as pictures to help you to learn and remember 800 Chinese characters. This is enough to recognize about three-quarters of the characters you would come across in an average piece of Chinese text. The key features of this book are:

- it covers all 800 characters in "HSK Level A" (the first section of the vocabulary list for the HSK, the Chinese Government's Language Proficiency Test);
- it uses modern standard Chinese (*putonghua* or "Mandarin");
- simplified characters are used with pronunciations given in *Hanyu pinyin*;
- the characters are introduced in a logical way, gradually building on what you have learned;
- we arrange the characters so that the most common ones are covered early on;
- key information is given for each character, including guidance on how to write it;
- we include example compounds for the characters — in particular we include all the compounds stipulated for HSK Level A.

Basic building block characters are introduced at the start of each chapter. We use pictures to help you learn and remember them. "Fire" (火) and "nail" (丁) are examples of basic building blocks.

Composite characters come next. These are made up of the basic building blocks. For example, the characters for fire (火) and nail (丁) when squashed together make a single new composite character (灯) that means "lamp". We can picture this as follows:

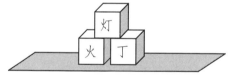

The basic building blocks "rest directly on the floor" in this picture. A composite character which is made up of two parts sits on the two blocks which support it.

Stories are provided to help you to remember these relationships: for example that the characters for "fire" and "nail" make up the character for "lamp". The story at the top of this page gives you this information in the first sentence. (The pronunciation is coded into the second sentence: more about pronunciations later).

The stories do more than encode information — they also help you *remember* it. They are based on tried and tested memory techniques which are widely recognized as being effective and long-lasting.

Everybody likes stories, and they are memorable because, without even trying, we tend to picture the scene in our mind's eye. The most memorable stories are vivid, enjoyable and/or quirky. So using stories as a memory technique not only makes learning and remembering easier, quicker and more effective than rote learning — it's also far more fun than just staring at a character and saying to yourself "this character means lamp" over and over again.

Some of our stories are illustrated with pictures, especially in the early part of the book, but as you work through the book you will find that you can visualize the stories without having any pictures — and we will give you simple tips on how to do this most effectively. But in the meantime why not test yourself: do you remember fire + nail = ?

Is this book for you?
You can learn the characters before, during, or after learning other elements of Chinese (such as grammar). It's a bit like learning to ride a bike and learning to fix the bike. You can learn to mend punctures at any point in your training (or not at all!). The point is that an expert cyclist will need to learn the same things as will a complete beginner. In the same way, the usefulness of this book to you does not depend on your knowledge of other elements of Chinese. If you want to learn Chinese characters then this book is the right book for you, whatever stage you are at in learning the Chinese language.

You can use this book if you are a complete beginner and know nothing of Chinese. If you are totally new to characters, we recommend reading Section 3: "Chinese Characters for Beginners" before you start, and as you go along you might choose to ignore some of the comments about how characters are used in practice. But the chances are, if you're reading this, that you've already learned some spoken Chinese and have at least a beginner's knowledge of the language.

Either way, whatever your level of experience, you're likely to find the idea of having to learn hundreds of characters pretty daunting — it's like a dragon lurking in the background which you know you will have to tackle sometime. You may even have tried tackling it already and have given up. But actually, this dragon is nothing to be scared of. It's just a question of taming it with the right tools, rather than trying to defeat it with brute force. Bear with us and we'll show you how. Learning Chinese characters is one of the most interesting and fun parts of learning Chinese, so don't let anyone frighten you off them!

What's different about this book?
Learning Chinese characters by breaking them down into parts is nothing new: since time immemorial students have been doing this in an effort to take some of the slog out of learning. Typically this has involved using verbal rhymes or phrases, but using imagery or visualization (seeing a picture in the mind's eye) is much stronger. Memory techniques using imagery were well known to the Romans; and a Jesuit missionary working in China called Matteo Ricci used such methods to devise a system for Chinese characters four hundred years ago. In modern times, the systematic use of imagery for learning the meanings of characters was pioneered by James Heisig (for Japanese characters, which are inherited from Chinese). So this book forms part of a long tradition in terms of the techniques it uses. But it is the first modern book to set out a consistent set of images for the meanings of Chinese characters. It also goes one step further by extending this technique to cover pronunciations too.

Learning Strategies

Which characters should you learn first?

We said that learning Chinese characters can be treated as a self-contained module that can be studied separately from other aspects of Chinese such as grammar, conversation practice, etc. Because of this you are free to learn the characters in the most sensible and logical order. The order in which we introduce the characters in this book takes into account a number of things. The main three are these:

* we build up systematically, introducing each character before it is needed as a part of other characters;
* we ease you into our system gradually, so there is not too much to learn all at once;
* we introduce the most common characters early on and the rarer ones later.

For all these reasons, it is best to work through the book "in the right order", at least for the early part of the book (Chapters 1 to 6). That way you'll be learning the most common characters first, and whenever you meet a composite character you will have already learned its component parts.

From Chapter 7 onwards, there is quite a lot of freedom to pick and choose if you want to. If there is a particular character that you would like to learn right away, then simply find it in the book (using one of the indexes), and learn it there and then. The cross references will tell you where to find any parts of the character that you haven't come across before, including any basic building blocks that it uses. You can then learn just those parts that you need to make up the character you are interested in.

How much do you need to learn about each character?

You can choose how much information you learn about a character, and when. It is perfectly OK to learn just the meanings of characters, leaving pronunciations until later. Meanings alone may satisfy your interest to begin with, and will enable you to try your hand at translating things like signs and menu items. But to learn Chinese properly you will have to learn the pronunciations too, and this is built into the stories (as you will see shortly). Your eventual aim should be to have an "integrated" view of each character:

* its meaning
* its pronunciation
* its role in words (compounds)

— only then will you fully understand all the nuances of what a character "really" means. But there's no rule to say that you have to master everything for each character before you move on to the next one.

Working with a textbook

If you are using this book in conjunction with a class textbook, you can take the characters you need for a chapter of that textbook, find them in this book (tracing their component parts using the cross references) and then use our pictures and stories to learn them.

It's not even necessary for the rest of the class to be using the same method. Learning is an individual and very private process. Nobody else even needs to know how you are learning the characters — everyone is free to use whichever method they choose.

Learning on your own

If you're working on your own, try working through a few characters a day (maybe 10–15, but it's up to you). Go at a pace that suits you; it's much better to do small but regular amounts than to do large chunks at irregular intervals.

It's a good idea to keep a note of which characters you've learned each day, and then to "test yourself" on the characters you learned the previous day, then on those from three days ago, a week ago, and a month ago. Each time you test yourself you will fix them in your memory for longer. This *expanding timescale* idea is built in to some of the "test yourself" panels in the book.

The learning environment

Find a quiet place where you can do your studying without being interrupted all the time. Bus and train journeys to and from work or college are often good times, but different things work for different people. You may find learning easier in the mornings than the evenings, or maybe it's the other way round. Whatever works best for you, try to schedule learning times for yourself accordingly. A routine where you stick to the same time of day is best of all, as your brain will get into the "habit" of being ready to learn at that time.

Take time to visualize each story in your mind's eye (there is more on this later). Write the character on a pad or in a notebook to get the "feel" of its strokes and think about its meaning and pronunciation as you write it.

Don't be too hard on yourself

Don't worry if you forget some of the characters you thought you had learned — this happens to everyone! (We give some "troubleshooting" tips later on). One encouraging fact from the research that has been done on memory is that if you learn something and then forget it, re-learning it is quicker than first time round, and makes it stick for longer.

At times it will seem as if there's a long way to go, and it's important then to remind yourself of how far you've come. At the end of many of the chapters there is a progress chart showing what percentage of written Chinese you have covered so far. Because of the way we have ordered the characters you will find that you make huge strides very quickly. For example, by the end of Chapter 4 you will already have learned 20% of the characters that you would meet in an average piece of Chinese text!

Chinese Characters for Beginners

Read this section if you are new to Chinese characters (but don't bother learning any of the characters you meet — there'll be plenty of time for that later!)

The origins of characters

Chinese characters really aren't as strange and complicated as some people try to make out — in fact they're no more mysterious than musical notation. The first characters started out as pictures:

口　mouth　　　　　　木　tree

As time went on, they were gradually simplified and abbreviated until many of them now look nothing like the original objects:

车　car　　　　　　马　horse

Then, when people wanted to describe things which weren't easy to depict, characters were "glued together" to make more complicated composite characters. We have already met the character for "lamp" which is made up of "fire" and "nail". Another example is the character 好 which means "good" or "to be fond of" and which combines 女 "woman" with 子 "child". Nowadays most characters are composites, that is, made up of two or more parts, either side by side or one on top of the other. When characters are joined together like this, they get squashed, so that the overall character is still the same size. For example, the character 日 is narrower when it is part of 时 and shorter and fatter when it is part of 星 (never mind for now what these characters mean!).

So we can divide characters into two types: *basic building blocks*, the simple characters originally based on drawings, and *composite* characters that are made up of two or more basic building blocks. We illustrated this idea by regarding a composite character as a building block which sits on the two blocks which support it, whereas basic building blocks sit "directly on the floor."

But it doesn't stop there. Composite characters can *themselves* be used as parts of yet other characters. This corresponds to building higher with our building blocks, as in the following picture:

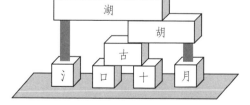

Pronunciation

The main thing you should know is that each character is pronounced in Chinese using one syllable (and it works the other way round too — each syllable of Chinese corresponds to a character).

Each syllable is fairly simple: the basic pattern consists of a consonant plus a vowel (or vowels), with the possible addition of an "n" or "ng" at the end. Some typical syllables are:

wu　　ta　　ji　　bei　　dao　　zen　　ben　　tang　　jing

In addition, each syllable is spoken using one of four *tones*. Tones indicate how the pitch of the voice varies when the syllable is spoken. There are four tones in all, and they are indicated by an accent over one of the vowels in the syllable:

1st tone	(high)	**bā**
2nd tone	(rising)	**bá**
3rd tone	(falling then rising)	**bǎ**
4th tone	(falling)	**bà**

The system we use for indicating the sounds of Chinese characters using the letters of the alphabet is called *Hanyu pinyin* (or *pinyin* for short), and is the system used in China for the benefit of foreigners (e.g. on signs in railway stations). Note that in this system many of the letters are pronounced differently from their sounds in English. There is a short description of pinyin in the Appendix, but to learn how to pronounce Chinese properly, you really need a Chinese speaking teacher (or possibly tapes). This book is about learning the pronunciations for each character (this one is "wei", that one is "tang", etc.), rather than teaching you how to say them aloud.

How characters are used in written Chinese

Chinese was traditionally written in columns, top to bottom, starting with the right hand column and working leftwards. But it can be written left to right, like English, and these days you will see both. Technical books in particular are likely to be printed left to right, like English.

Although each character has a meaning, it's not really true that characters are equivalent to "words". As you have just seen, each character corresponds to a *syllable*, and in Chinese (as in English) some words are just one syllable while other words consist of two or more syllables joined together. Some syllables (like "if" and "you" in English) are one-syllable words on their own; other syllables like ("sen" and "tence" in English) link together to form multi-syllable words. Many syllables do both: they're like the English word "light" which is happy on its own, but which also links up to form words like "headlight" or "lighthouse".

In Chinese writing, the characters are written in a long line, with no extra spaces between words. It is as if English were written like this:

If you can un der stand this sen tence you can read Chi nese too.

Compounds

A *compound* in Chinese is a word made up from two or more characters. That is, a compound is a multi-syllable word. If two characters are paired together to form a compound, they simply appear one after the other in a sentence, but are treated as a single word like "Chi" and "nese" above. Most compounds have only two characters. The flavor of a character often comes out in how it combines with other characters to make compounds, and so for many characters we give examples of compounds that they appear in.

Compounds and Composites

So what's the difference between pairing two characters to get a *compound*, and combining two characters to get a *composite character*?

A compound:	大	人	gives	大人
	dà	**rén**		**dàrén**
	big	person		adult
A composite character:	女	也	gives	她
	nǚ	**yě**		**tā**
	woman	also		she

Two characters in a *compound* are simply written one after the other, full sized, and the resulting word has a pronunciation which has two syllables — in fact it is simply the pronunciations of the two characters one after the other. Often (but not always!) you'll be able to guess the meaning of the word from the meanings of its individual characters.

On the other hand, when two characters are combined to get a new composite *character* (the process we saw with "fire" + "nail" = "lamp"), they are squashed or distorted so that the new character fits into a square the same size as each of the original two. The meaning of the new character *may* be related to the meaning of its two parts, but it frequently appears to have no connection with them at all! Finally, the new character will also have a single syllable as its pronunciation (so that if it is a word, it is a one-syllable word) and this pronunciation may, or may not, come from one of its parts.

Writing characters

Being able to read Chinese characters is satisfying, but it's also rewarding to be able to *write* them (and this is a great way to impress people who aren't learning the language!) We'll show you how to write each character, starting with basic instructions in Chapter 1. Don't worry if you're not "good at drawing" — you don't need to be. Characters these days are much more likely to be written using a ball-point pen than a calligraphy brush.

As well as being fun, writing the characters yourself is a very good way of getting to know them, and we recommend that you practice writing the characters as you learn them. You'll be learning the oldest writing system in the world which is still in use today.

You've seen that characters are often made up of two or more parts (for example 她 is made up of 女 and 也). On a more fundamental level though, each character is made up of *strokes*, where each stroke is made with a single, continuous motion of the pen: a straight line, a curve, a bent line, a line with a hook, or a dot. Each character consists of a set number of strokes, and there is a traditional, fixed order in which these strokes should be drawn. The stroke-order diagrams given with each character entry (in the line of small boxes) show you how to draw the strokes in the right order. There are also some general rules for drawing characters, which we will mention as we go along.

You might think that it doesn't really matter how the strokes are written as long as the end result looks the same. To some extent this is true, but there are some good reasons for knowing the "proper" way to write the characters. Firstly, it helps you to count strokes properly for a character which you haven't seen before (and you'll need to be able to do this to look it up in a dictionary). Secondly, it will make your characters "look right", and also help you to read other people's hand-written characters later on. In the long run it's better to learn the correct method from the start because, like with so many other things, once you get into "bad" habits it can be very hard to break them!

If you are left-handed, just use your left hand as normal, but still make sure you use the correct stroke order and direction. For example, draw your horizontal strokes left to right, even if it feels more natural to draw them right to left.

Simplified and traditional characters

In the middle of the 20th century, many characters were given simplified forms. This was to help increase literacy in China, and the simplified characters are definitely much easier to learn and use. This book uses these modern simplified characters. However, many Chinese communities around the world still use traditional characters rather than simplified ones, and of course many old documents and inscriptions were written using the traditional forms too. For this reason, if there is a traditional form of a character we give it as part of the entry for that character so that you can see what it looks like.

Types of Chinese

This book uses modern standard ("Mandarin") Chinese. The characters *mean* the same in other varieties of Chinese, for example Cantonese, but they will be pronounced completely differently (and Cantonese speakers typically use traditional characters). This means that even if two Chinese people can't understand one another when they are talking, they can usually write to each other quite happily!

Radicals

Finally, you may have heard of "radicals" (which some books call "keys" or "significs"), so we'll quickly explain what they are. Look at the following characters:

Character:	她	好	妈	姓	姐
Meaning:	she	good	mum	surname	older sister

They all have the same part on the left-hand side, 女, which means "woman". This part gives a clue to the meaning of the character, and is called the "radical". As you can see, most of these five characters have something to do with the idea of "woman". But it's not a totally reliable system and also, to make life complicated, the radical in a character is not always the left-hand part. Radicals have been used for centuries to group characters together in dictionaries, and they can still be helpful if you want to find a character in a dictionary when you don't know its pronunciation.

There is more on radicals in Chapter 24, and we will introduce some other concepts (such as a "phonetic series") as we go along. But that's all you need for now to get started.

User Guide
Essential reading before starting Chapter 1!

Here we introduce the methods we will be using in this book, and in particular how the stories and pictures work. We do this using some of the characters from Chapter 1 (which you may already know). Firstly we'll look at how to learn and remember the *meanings* of characters, and then we'll look at learning the *pronunciations*.

Learning the meanings of basic building blocks

Some characters are so simple that you hardly need any help to remember them; for example:

一　one　　　　二　two　　　三　three

Apart from some symbolic characters like these, most simple characters started off as pictures. For example:

口
mouth

There are no circles in Chinese characters, so the picture of a round mouth becomes a small square. We will supply a *character picture* like the one shown on the right for each of the simple characters which act as basic building blocks.

So far, so good. But not all characters are recognizable today as the original object they represented, or indeed still refer to the same thing as the original picture. Look at this one:

几
several

The character 几 was originally a picture of a small stool, but the character picture we have supplied is different. A drawing of a stool would remind you that 几 meant "stool" in ancient times, but not that it now means "several". It is better to see (and hence later recall) a picture of several 几-like objects. *Seeing* this picture is much more powerful, in terms of laying down a long term memory, than reading a written description.

How to use character pictures

The way to use these character pictures is as follows:

* firstly look at the picture for a short while, and see how the character's shape is used in the picture;
* then look at the character on its own, and while you are doing this, see if you can mentally superimpose the picture over the character, remembering which parts of the character correspond to which parts of the picture.

This is a good way of making sure that, when you see the character again later on, the picture (and hence the meaning) will pop into your head.

Here are two more examples:

不
not

木
tree

For 不 we have used the traditional picture of a bird flying up to the ceiling and **not** being able to escape. With 木 we are back to a straightforward drawing of an object. In modern Chinese 木 is not a hugely common character on its own, but you do need to know its meaning as it appears as a *part* of many composite characters (for example, the next two we'll meet).

But before we get on to those, how are you doing so far? Can you remember what each of these characters means?

口　　木　　不　　几

If you have a problem with any of them, go back to the character picture and study it again, and then superimpose it over the character in your mind's eye as explained above.

The meanings of composite characters

Our first composite character is made up of two basic building blocks:

机 **machine**

As you can see this character is made up of the two characters "tree" and "several" squashed together. To learn the meaning of this composite character, we relate it to the *meanings of its two parts*, by creating an *equation*:

tree 木 + **several** 几 = **machine** 机

Since most Chinese characters are composite, we will have many equations like this. Other examples are:

thread 纟 + **work** 工 = **red** 红

now 今 + **heart** 心 = **to study** 念

You can see that these equations don't really make any logical sense! However, if you can learn these equations then you can remember composite characters. For example, if you see a character which has two parts, and you recognize these simpler parts to be "thread" and "work", then you will know from the equation that the overall character means "red".

Stories and story pictures

So how do you learn these equations? This is where the stories come in. The stories are extremely short, often just a sentence, and the important thing is not just to read them but to really visualize them. To help with many of the early stories, we have illustrated them with *story pictures*.

Here is our first story, which will help you learn the equation

"**tree** 木 + **several** 几 = **machine** 机":

> It took **several tree**s to provide enough wood
> to make the parts for the huge **machine**.

How to use stories and story pictures

Have a good look at the story picture above: see how the "several trees" have indeed been felled to make the large "machine" that is taking shape. What type of trees are being used? What is the machine for? By asking yourself questions about the setting you're *paying attention* to the story picture and you will then remember it, so that when you see the character in future, the parts "tree" plus "several" will trigger the story in your mind, which will in turn trigger the word "machine".

After a while we give you stories without story pictures, but the same process applies. Read the story and visualize at least as much detail as there would be in a story picture. By doing so you will be paying attention to these details, which is what will fix the story in your memory.

You will notice that in the story for "machine" the three words from the equation are printed in **bold**. This is to remind you to pay particular attention to these words when creating the picture in your mind's eye.

Notice that in this example the equation is "**tree** 木 + **several** 几 = **machine** 机" and yet the story uses the words "tree" and "several" in the other order. We write the equation as "tree + several" because the character 机 has "tree" on the left and "several" on the right; but for the story the two parts are all we need — the order doesn't matter. So the stories combine the two words in the order that is most natural. In this case "several trees" is more natural than "a tree and several (of something else)". We are able to do this because it is very rare for A + B to form one character and B + A to form another one (we will point this out on the few occasions when it does occur).

Story pictures and character pictures

Notice that the story picture for "machine" is a completely different *type* of picture from the character pictures we have for basic building blocks. The story picture which accompanies the "**tree** 木 + **several** 几 = **machine** 机" story links the three *ideas* "tree", "several" and "machine", without any reference to the shape or appearance of the *characters* for "tree" and "several".

Character pictures, on the other hand, are based around a drawing of the character itself, and help you to remember the meaning of each basic building block directly from its shape.

More about stories

Another example will illustrate some further points about the stories:

杯 cup

tree 木 + not 不 = cup 杯

> "I said **not** the **tree** with the **cup** tied to it!" cried the horrified lumberjack to his apprentice.

Again, look at the scene. A lumberjack and his apprentice are in the forest and the apprentice is about to attack a particular tree when he is stopped in the nick of time by the lumberjack. (Why is the lumberjack horrified? What is the cup for? — Well, we shall see shortly).

Again, it is only the *meaning* you need to remember. Don't try to remember the whole story verbatim. Use the story as a bridge to get you to the meaning.

We should also stress that this story is simply an *aid to remembering* that the character 杯 means "cup"; the story does not represent the historical reason *why* 杯 has come to mean "cup". The stories are simply our way of helping you to familiarize yourself with the characters and to remember them in a simple and effective way. Often the stories will be humorous, a bit strange or bizarre, or may even seem silly, but that is just what's needed to make them stick in your memory.

If you really picture the scenes in your mind's eye, that is all the work you need to do, and the story will stick. Brute force repetition is not needed. Test it out, can you remember:

　　tree + several = ?　　　　　　　　**tree + not = ?**

At this stage it may seem quicker to simply learn the equations off by rote, but it will be a different matter when you are have covered dozens of equations and are trying to remember them without mixing them up. Using pictures (and later on, making your own vivid pictures in your mind's eye) makes it much easier to remember them all, even though on the face of it you are trying to remember "extra" information. Think about how easily you remember the basic story of a movie despite the background "richness" of hundreds of details, and compare this with how hard it is to remember isolated "bald" facts such as addresses or lists.

Two strategies for learning meanings

So we have two strategies for learning the meanings of characters:

- If the character is a basic building block, learn it from the character picture.
- If the character is composite (i.e. made up of simpler parts), remember it from the story (and story picture if there is one).

Learning the pronunciations of characters

To help you remember the pronunciations of characters, we extend the stories. The composite characters already have a story, so we'll start with them.

Pronunciations of composite characters

We simply extend the story with another sentence, whose purpose is to help you remember the pronunciation of the character. The pronunciation parts of stories are always in italics and are separated from the meaning parts of stories with a dividing line "/". (If you are interested only in the meanings of characters at this stage, then you can just ignore the parts of stories after the dividing line — although reading them will often help the stories to stick in your mind). Here are two examples:

机 machine **jī**

It took **several trees** to provide enough wood to make the parts for the huge **machine**. / *When it was finished they had to get the giant to bring his jeep to deliver it.*

杯 cup **bēi**

"I said **not** the **tree** with the **cup** tied to it!" cried the horrified lumberjack to his apprentice. / *The giant collects the sap from that one to cook his bacon in.*"

Notice that we have extended the story pictures as well as extending the stories.

Soundwords

We call "jeep" and "bacon" *soundwords*. They indicate the (approximate) pronunciations of the characters: the character 机 is pronounced somewhat like the "jee" in "jeep" and the character 杯 is pronounced like the "ba" in "bacon". Now there are several points to note immediately about soundwords:

- It is the first syllable *only* of the soundword which corresponds to the Chinese syllable; in fact we only go as far as the first vowel sound, unless it is followed by an "n" or "ng" sound.
- It is the *sound* of the English soundword which is important, *not* its English spelling.
- The sound is only *approximate*. The soundword "jeep" reminds us of the Chinese syllable **ji** (and not for example **tang** or **bei**); it does *not* mean that the Chinese syllable **ji** is pronounced *exactly* like the "jee" in "jeep".

Here are some examples of soundwords and their corresponding Chinese syllables:

Soundword	Chinese Syllable	Soundword	Chinese Syllable
pizza	**pi**	mandolin	**man**
bored	**bo**	bandit	**ban**
mouse	**mao**	mango	**mang**
tiger	**tai**	bank	**bang**
bacon	**bei**	fungus	**feng**
powder	**pao**	tongue	**teng**

Archetypes to represent tones

You may have wondered why a giant has wandered into each of the two stories above. He is there to indicate the tone! Four *archetypes* appear in the pronunciation parts of the stories, and represent the four tones of Chinese as follows:

Giant	1st tone	(high)	**bā**
Fairy	2nd tone	(rising)	**bá**
Teddy	3rd tone	(falling then rising)	**bǎ**
Dwarf	4th tone	(falling)	**bà**

So the two stories above tell you that the characters for "machine" and "cup" have 1st tone (because a giant features in each story). We have chosen these four archetypes because they are universal, familiar, timeless and distinct. If you have really pictured a story in your mind's eye, you will find that you remember which archetype featured in it.

We've said that the stories which work best for learning characters are off-beat and humorous ones, and the four archetypes we have chosen lend themselves to this. There is nothing childish about using such powerful images; they are just what you need to bypass the verbal, logical parts of your brain and plant long-lasting links in your non-verbal memory.

Now, do you remember the pronunciations of 机 and 杯?

Pronunciations of basic building blocks

Finally, what about the pronunciations of characters which are basic building blocks? For these, there is no story to extend, as there was for composite characters. Also, a story involving "mouth" by itself will tend to get mixed up with all the other stories involving "mouth".

Our solution to this is to invent a dummy object, the same one for all basic building blocks, and we have chosen the most basic piece of technology there is: a *wheel*. Thus the story to think of when you want to remember the pronunciation of "mouth" itself is the story involving "mouth + wheel".

The following examples show how this works.

口   mouth **kǒu**

*/ A large **wheel** stands across the **mouth** of the cold, dark cave, but **Teddy** simply puts on his duffel **coat** and hops between the spokes to get inside.*

几   several **jǐ**

*/ There are **several wheels** to deliver so **Teddy** offers to load them onto his **jeep**. (See him careering off down the road scattering wheels in all directions every time he hits a bump!)*

You will see that 几 is pronounced "**ji**", just like 机. But this time it is Teddy in the jeep, not the giant, so that we know that "several" is pronounced **jǐ** with the third tone, not **jī** with the first tone.

Since wheel stories are about pronunciations, they are printed in italics.

Summary

To sum up, the strategy, when you see a character you have learned and want to remember its meaning and pronunciation, is as follows:

- If it is a basic building block, remember the meaning from its character picture, and then think of the "wheel" story to get the pronunciation.
- If it is a composite character (i.e. made up of simpler parts), identify the parts and then use these to remember the story: the first part of the story gives you the meaning, and the second part gives you the pronunciation.

But rest assured that the whole process is much quicker to carry out than it is to describe!

As with any new skill, such as learning to drive, things will become automatic after a while. If you study Chinese for any length of time, you will find that you become familiar with many characters and start to read them "at a glance". When that happens, the corresponding stories presented in this book will become superfluous: like scaffolding for a building, they will have served their purpose once the building is complete. Until that time, however, the stories provide a systematic framework which can help you to hold the myriad of characters in place in your mind without mixing them up. And even much later on, when you find you have temporarily forgotten a character, you can use the parts of the character to recreate the story that ties them together, and hence "recover" the meaning and pronunciation of the character. The stories will act like a long-lasting index to the store of characters in your memory.

Key to Character Entries

See the User Guide for an explanation of the equations and stories.

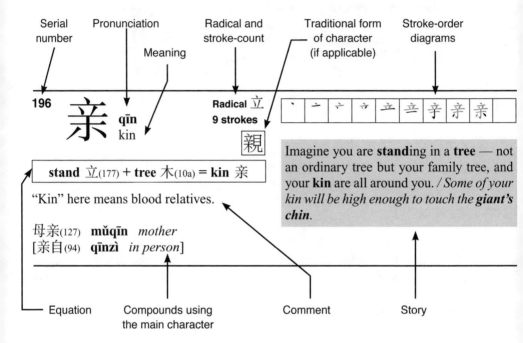

Serial number · Pronunciation · Meaning · Radical and stroke-count · Traditional form of character (if applicable) · Stroke-order diagrams

196 亲 qīn kin

Radical 立 9 strokes

親

stand 立(177) + **tree** 木(10a) = **kin** 亲

"Kin" here means blood relatives.

母亲(127) **mǔqīn** *mother*
[亲自(94) **qīnzì** *in person*]

Imagine you are **stand**ing in a **tree** — not an ordinary tree but your family tree, and your **kin** are all around you. / *Some of your kin will be high enough to touch the giant's chin.*

Equation · Compounds using the main character · Comment · Story

Serial numbers printed in black (such as **278**) refer to HSK Level A characters. Serial numbers printed in gray (such as **278a**) refer to other characters and to non-character fragments — these are included if they are needed as parts of HSK Level A characters. Pronunciations are printed in black if they are in HSK Level A, and in gray otherwise. Compounds which are not in the HSK Level A list are given in brackets [ ].

Key to icons:

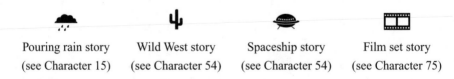

Pouring rain story (see Character 15) · Wild West story (see Character 54) · Spaceship story (see Character 54) · Film set story (see Character 75)

Story conventions: Archetypes represent tones (see User Guide):
Giant = 1, Fairy = 2, Teddy = 3, Dwarf = 4, Robot = neutral
Double archetype: i on-glide (see Character 38).
Ghostly archetype: u on-glide (see Character 59).

Chapter 1

So let's get started. We'll be taking it very gently to begin with, so there'll be rather fewer characters per chapter in the first few chapters than in the book as a whole.

Before we start, you *did* read the User Guide, didn't you? If not, go and read it now! Otherwise quite a lot of what follows won't make sense.

You've already seen four character pictures in the User Guide. The remaining ones you'll need for this chapter are given below. The first thing is to study the character pictures on this page, to learn the meaning of these basic building blocks. When you have them fixed in your mind, turn the page and start working your way through the character entries that follow. Take your time and make sure you visualize each story (the story pictures will help with this). Finally, at the end of the chapter, you can test yourself on what you have learned.

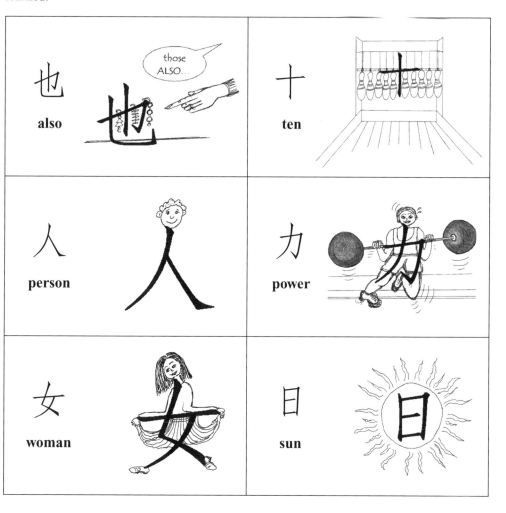

After introducing the basic building blocks and their meanings, we are now ready for the main entries for the characters in Chapter 1. For the basic building blocks we give a wheel story (for the pronunciation), and for composite characters we give the equation and two-part story.

For all characters we give the stroke order diagrams in the row of small boxes. To the left of these boxes, we give the radical for the character and its stroke-count (i.e. the total number of strokes needed to write the character).

Whenever we want to explain a general point, give you some encouragement, or tell you something interesting about the Chinese language, we will write in areas outside the character entries and across the full width of the page — exactly like we have here!

1

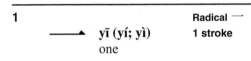

yī (yí; yì)

one

Radical ⌐

1 stroke

—									

This is the simplest character there is, and it's obviously a basic building block. As such it has a "wheel" story to help you remember the pronunciation. The soundword is "easy" so the pronunciation is "ee" (the pinyin spelling is "**yi**" but it is pronounced "ee"), and the giant in the story tells you it is pronounced using the first tone.

But, wouldn't you know it, for the very first character we have a complication with regard to the pronunciation! Essentially, the pronunciation is **yī** (1st tone), but the complication is that in practice the tone for this character varies, depending on the tone of the syllable which follows it. When it is followed by a 4th tone, it is pronounced **yí** (2nd tone), and when followed by all other tones it is pronounced **yì** (4th tone). When it is on its own, or in a string of numbers, it reverts to **yī** (1st tone). This sort of change only happens for one other character in this book, which we shall meet shortly.

For this first character a stroke order diagram seems rather superfluous! Simply

/ **One** of the huge **wheels** of the truck was stuck fast in the thick mud and the unicorn had blunted his horn trying to shift it. They called in the **giant** who took one look at it and said, "This will be **easy**."

write the stroke in a left to right direction. The large character is printed in a typical printed typeface. Don't worry about the little lump at the right-hand end of the stroke: this is like a "serif" (the small horizontal line you might find at the bottom of letters like "h" in some typefaces in English) and can be ignored. The stroke order diagrams in the boxes show you what a hand-drawn character will look like.

The word "one" isn't a very vivid word to use in stories where we need this character (it will be hard to distinguish a picture of "one tree" from simply "a tree"), so when "one" appears in an equation we will always use a *unicorn* in the story.

We shall also do this for some other numbers: for example a *biplane* will substitute for "two", a *starfish* for "five", an *octopus* for "eight". For other numbers (e.g. "four", "six") we won't need to do this as they won't appear as parts of composite characters.

2   **èr**   two   Radical 二   2 strokes

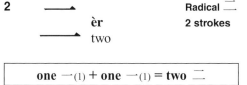

> **one** ―(1) + **one** ―(1) = **two** 二

This is a composite character, made up of "one" and "one". Hence there is an equation, and the story illustrates it. The second half of the story, separated by a slash "/", gives you the pronunciation. The soundword is "earth" and there is a dwarf in the story, so the pronunciation is **èr**.

As mentioned above, a *biplane* will substitute for "two" in future stories.

To write this character, write the top stroke before the bottom stroke, writing each stroke left to right. Note that the bottom stroke is slightly longer than the top one.

There is another character for "two" (Character 222), which we'll meet later.

The zoo had one **unicorn** so bought another **unicorn** to get a breeding pair. However they failed to check the gender of the new one so ended up with **two** of the same sex! / *The **dwarf** accountant is furious because the new unicorn had cost the **earth**.*

---

3   **sān**   three   Radical 一   3 strokes

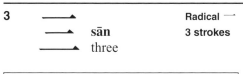

> **one** ―(1) + **two** 二(2) = **three** 三

A composite character, made up of "one" and "two". One and two are represented by the unicorn and the biplane. Take a look at the picture to fix the story in your memory: the unicorn has indeed made a nice three-point landing, but he relaxed too soon!

The soundword is "sand". Remember that with soundwords you go as far as the first vowel sound, and then see if there is an "n" or "ng" sound following it. In this case there is, so the pronunciation is **sān**, not **sā**.

When writing this character note that the second stroke is slightly shorter than the first, and the third is slightly longer.

Clearly you don't really need stories to remember the meanings of the characters

The **unicorn** lands his **biplane** on the beach perfectly so that all **three** tires touch down simultaneously. / *Unfortunately he fails to stop before he hits the **giant's** sandcastle!*

一, 二 and 三. The stories are given to help you remember the pronunciations and to get you used to how the pictures and stories work for both basic and composite characters.

4

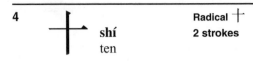

十 shí
ten

Radical 十
2 strokes

This character means "ten" (just as an X in Roman numerals means "ten"), but also represents a cross shape, such as a crossroads. Just as a unicorn substitutes for "one" in the stories, we will use a *cross* or *crossroads* as a substitute for "ten".

The soundword is the fairy's "cheroot" so the pronunciation is **shí**. (Not **ché** — it is the *sound* of the soundword, not its English spelling, that is important). There is more about the soundword system in the Appendix.

This character exemplifies another rule for writing characters: when two lines cross, a horizontal line is drawn before a vertical one.

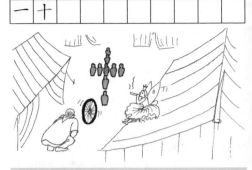

*/ At the fairground, in one game you have to roll a **wheel** and knock down **ten** skittles laid out in the shape of a cross. The **fairy**, confident of not having to pay out, sits smoking a **cheroot**.*

5

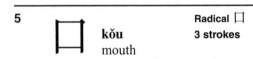

口 kǒu
mouth

Radical 口
3 strokes

This character means a person's mouth, but also more generally the mouth of a cave or river, an entrance or exit of a building, etc. We will often use *the mouth of a cave* to represent it in stories.

This character is written, not with four strokes, but with three! For the second stroke, draw the top of the square from left to right, and continue down the right-hand side of the square, without taking your pen off the paper.

*/ A large **wheel** stands across the **mouth** of the cold, dark cave, but **Teddy** simply puts on his duffel **coat** and hops between the spokes to get inside.*

6

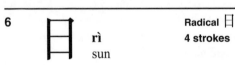

日 rì
sun

Radical 日
4 strokes

This character means "sun", but also "day", and "Japan".

*/ The **dwarf** has built a **sun**-powered **wheel**, and invites all his **relations** to come and admire it.*

We just said that 日 (Character 6) means "sun" (originally it was a picture of a round sun with a dot in the middle), but it also has several derived meanings. It can mean "day", and it's also used as an abbreviation for Japan, the "land of the rising sun". But whenever a character has several meanings like this, we will stick to a single meaning for all stories where that character appears. This single meaning is the one given in the "headline" of the character entry. So we will always use the word "sun" in stories for characters containing 日.

---

7 几 jǐ (jī) several

Radical 几
2 strokes
幾

As well as meaning "several", this character also means "how many?" (when you are asking about small numbers, say up to ten).

几 can also be pronounced **jī**, and it then has a different meaning. This extra pronunciation and meaning is included in HSK Level B, but not in Level A. Whenever a character has another meaning and pronunciation like this, we will let you know the other pronunciation so that you can look it up in a dictionary if you are interested. These extra pronunciations will be printed in gray and will be in brackets.

You will also notice that this character has a traditional form (in a box below the stroke-count) — you can ignore these tradi-

/ There are **several wheels** to deliver so **Teddy** offers to load them onto his **jeep**. *(See him careering off down the road scattering wheels in all directions every time he hits a bump!)*

tional forms for the time being if you like; we will talk about them in Chapter 27.

When drawing this character, notice that it only has two strokes.

---

8 也 yě also

Radical ⁷
3 strokes

This character is fun to draw once you get the hang of it, but watch the stroke order!

/ "This is **also** a **wheel**," Teddy claims, holding up a triangular object. "I got it from a **yeti** yesterday!"

Are you remembering to visualize the stories when you read them? Sometimes it can help if you close your eyes when you picture the scene. Don't forget that you can add in any small details that help make the scene more vivid as long as they don't distract you from remembering the meaning.

9

不
bù (bú)
not

Radical 一
4 strokes

/ *"It's **not** a **wheel**," says the **dwarf**, kicking it angrily with his **boot**.*

This is the only other character (apart from 一, Character 1) which changes tone depending on the sound which follows it. It is generally pronounced **bù** (4th tone), but this changes to **bú** (2nd tone) when followed by another 4th tone character.

When you write 不 note that the third (vertical) stroke hangs from the second stroke, so 不 is not symmetrical: that is, it is not like the bottom half of 木 (which follows).

10a

木
mù
tree

This character is printed in gray because it is not in the HSK Level A set of characters. So you can skip its pronunciation if you want to, but you *do* need to know its meaning, as it appears as a part of many composite characters (for example, the next two). We've given the pronunciation in gray, so you can look the character up in a dictionary if you want to.

We've given 木 the serial number 10a, because we are reserving the numbers 1 to

800 for the 800 HSK Level A characters covered in this book. You can easily find such characters: for example 10a appears just before Character 10. We've called it 10a and not 9a, because it is introduced because of, and hence belongs with, Character 10.

The first two strokes are like "ten" (Character 4), so the horizontal stroke is written before the vertical one. The stroke order also illustrates another general principle: you often draw a central part before drawing in small symmetrical side-pieces.

10

机
jī
machine

Radical 木
6 strokes

機

tree 木(10a) + **several 几**(7) = **machine** 机

This character is another composite character, made up of two basic building blocks, so it has an equation. The numbers in brackets refer to the building block entries.

To draw it, simply draw one part and then the other. Remember to draw each part half as wide as normal, so that the complete character fits into the same size square.

It took **several tree**s to provide enough wood to make the parts for the huge **machine**. / *When it was finished they had to get the **giant** to bring his **jeep** to deliver it. [Remember this from the User Guide?]*

11

杯
bēi
cup

Radical 木
8 strokes

---

tree 木(10a) + **not** 不(9) = **cup** 杯

You'll notice that writing a composite character usually involves simply writing the building blocks, and the building blocks you need will always have been covered earlier in the book. In cases where this does not apply, we will draw attention to it — an example is coming up in the next chapter (24a).

"I said **not** the **tree** with the **cup** tied to it!" cried the horrified lumberjack to his apprentice. / *"The **giant** collects the sap from that one to cook his **bacon** in."*

12

人
rén
person

Radical 人
2 strokes

"Person" is one of the few characters where we will not simply use the bare meaning, but a particular interpretation of it. In order to make our stories more vivid, it is best to think of a *particular* person, real or fictional, who you can easily imagine in various situations. We will call this person "Harry" — you can think of Harry Truman, Harry Houdini, Harry Potter, or any other person (called Harry or not — it could be James Bond for example) who you can easily imagine in various situations. When we mention Harry in a story, always picture this same person. At the moment all the stories have pictures with them, but later on we'll be getting you to visualize the stories yourself, and if you make objects and people *specific* and *particular* it will help to make the images you create as memorable as possible.

/ *Harry was chasing the tractor **wheel**, as fast as he could before it flattened the children. Luckily the **fairy** saw what was happening, and wrote a message "**Run!**" in the sky with her wand, so that the children scattered just in time.*

The second stroke starts just below the top of the first stroke, although in some typefaces the character looks symmetrical. There is a very similar character, "enter" (see 219a), which we'll meet much later in the book. When "person" is used as the left-hand side of a character it is compressed into the form 亻 (see 13a below).

13a

亻

person

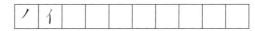

When "person" (Character 12) is used as the left-hand side of a composite character it is compressed into this form.

13   他   tā   he   Radical 亻   5 strokes

person 亻 (13a) + also 也 (8) = he 他

As explained, your chosen *particular* person is substituting for the abstract "person" here. We're calling this person "Harry" as we don't know who you've chosen — luckily this doesn't stop us drawing him as he's in a gorilla costume!

At the fancy dress party, **Harry also** came as a gorilla, but (unlike the others) **he** had a proper costume. / The **giant** arrived dressed as **Tarzan**.

---

14   力   lì   power   Radical 力   2 strokes

Make sure you practice writing this with the correct stroke order.

/ There was a **power** surge to the tram's **wheel** and it hurtled towards the **dwarf** who was crossing the road — he had to **leap** out of the way quickly before he was flattened (and he shouted angrily at the driver).

---

15   女   nǚ   woman   Radical 女   3 strokes

You might like to think of a *particular* woman when you visualize the stories with "woman" throughout the book, just as we have a particular "person" (who we're calling "Harry"). However "woman" appears as a part of far fewer characters than does "person".

The "ü" sound here is like the "ü" in German or the "u" in the French word "tu". Say "oo" and then, keeping your lips in the same position, try and say "ee". Since we don't have this sound in English, we just use an "oo" sound but have *pouring rain* in the pronunciation part of the story to indicate that it is really "**ü**" (you can think of the two dots above the "u" being rain drops). The rain-cloud icon will remind you to visualize

/ It is pouring with rain outside, so instead of going jogging the **woman** works out by running in a large treadmill **wheel**. **Teddy** uses the power it generates to cook his **noodles**!

the rain in the story. We will have more to say about these "**ü**" pronunciations later.

When drawing 女 watch the stroke order: the horizontal stroke is drawn last.

16 她 tā
she

Radical 女
6 strokes

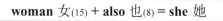

woman 女(15) + also 也(8) = she 她

The characters for "he" and "she" (Characters 13 and 16) are both pronounced **tā**, and so in *spoken* Chinese only the context makes clear which is meant. Obviously it is always clear in written Chinese.

At the fancy dress party, a **woman also** came as a gorilla! "What's **she** doing, dressed as a gorilla? / If she'd come as Jane she could have danced with the **giant** dressed as **Tarzan**."

So that was the first chapter! The 16 characters you have learned make up approximately 7% of written Chinese. As we go through the book, we will provide some charts like the one on the right to show the progress being made. By the end of the book you will have completed the whole of the HSK Level A set of characters, which as we have said covers 77% of written Chinese. (These numbers are averages taken from huge samples compiled on the internet — the actual numbers will vary from one piece of text to another of course).

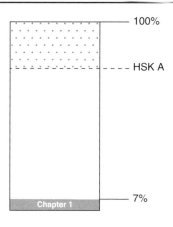

To begin with there will be a fair number of basic building blocks, but as we go on, composite characters will predominate more and more. Already, with the basic building blocks we have met, we could build the characters 什, 休, 早, 但, 查 and 唱, which are all in Level A (as well as plenty of other characters in later HSK levels). But let's not be in too much of a rush to introduce every possible character we can form from the available building blocks just yet. As well as building characters up systematically, we also want to concentrate on introducing the most frequently used characters first.

Time to see if you remembered the characters in Chapter 1! Test yourself by looking at the following block of characters — do you remember the meaning of each one? How about the pronunciations? The numbers next to the characters will let you look up any characters you've forgotten.

Test yourself: 十(4)　口(5)　不(9)　机(10)　人(12)　他(13)　女(15)
力(14)　几(7)　她(16)　日(6)　三(3)　也(8)　杯(11)

Don't worry if you don't remember all of them! If the problem is a character picture, make sure you mentally superimposed the picture over the character (as described in the User Guide). It's all too easy just to glance at a picture and move on! If the problem is a story, make sure you visualize it by having a good look at the story picture — a good idea is to imagine yourself actually being there. Use your senses — can you hear any background noises? Can you smell anything?

Chapter 2

This chapter follows the same pattern as Chapter 1. On this first page there are some new basic building blocks. Learn their meanings using the character pictures given. The "wheel stories" (for remembering their pronunciations) are in the main part of the chapter, along with some composite characters which use these basic building blocks.

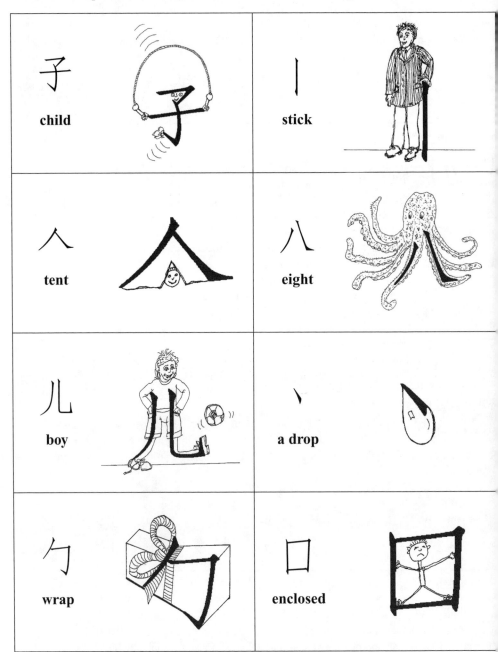

子 child

｜ stick

人 tent

八 eight

儿 boy

丶 a drop

勹 wrap

囗 enclosed

17

子
zi
child

Radical 子
3 strokes

Very occasionally characters have a "neutral" tone, and this is represented by a fifth archetype, a *robot*. There are only a few robot stories in this book.

The original meaning of this character was "child", but it is nowadays more often seen as a noun suffix (that is, attached to a noun — and not implying that the noun is small).

/ *(This story is set in the future) Imagine a small **child** playing at home, rolling **wheels** about on the floor. The **robot** babysitter emits a "zzz" sound, as though asleep, and then pretends to wake up with a start each time a wheel crashes into him.*

18

好
hǎo (hào)
good

Radical 女
6 strokes

woman 女(15) + child 子(17) = good 好

In this story and the previous one, we have added phrases in brackets. These are non-essential parts of the story we sometimes add in, to explain and expand it. They are background detail to help you visualize the scene, and they're only a means to an end. (The end is to remember the scene and hence remember the words in bold).

The gray pronunciation means that 好 can also be pronounced **hào** in HSK Level 3, with a different meaning not covered in HSK Level A (see also Character 7).

(At an art gallery) "A **woman** with a **child** represents **good**," the curator said (indicating a particularly dull picture). / *But nobody was listening, because they were all watching the **Teddy**, who was building a **house** of cards.*

19a

stick

This is a *fragment*. Fragments are only ever *parts* of characters; they never appear on their own as characters, and so they do not have pronunciations. Fragments are always printed in gray. We only give them meanings so that we can use them in equations and stories.

A vertical stroke occurs in many characters of course, but we will not treat every vertical stroke as a "stick". For example, it seems more natural to treat 十 "ten" as a basic building block, rather than trying to decompose it into "one" plus "stick". Instead, we reserve "stick" for situations where it stands on its own (as in Character 19 below).

19b

"tent"

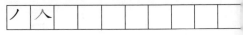

This fragment is found at the top of some characters. It has a symmetrical shape, unlike "person" (12) and "enter" (219a).

The meaning is given in quotes to indicate that the name "tent" is one we have invented for this fragment.

To draw it, draw each stroke downwards (rather than drawing a single stroke in an "up and over" movement).

19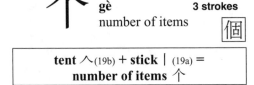

gè
number of items

Radical 人
3 strokes

個

| **tent** 人(19b) **+ stick** ｜ (19a) **=** |
| **number of items** 个 |

Notice that in this character the two building blocks are one above the other, rather than being side by side.

This is a *measure word*. In English we don't say "two breads"; we say "two loaves of bread" or "two slices of bread". Words such as "slice" are called measure words, and all nouns in Chinese have to use measure words for counting. There are dozens of measure words for different types of things (see Character 188 for an example), but 个 is an all-purpose measure word which can be used with most nouns.

He tried to keep the **tent** up with a **stick** but it fell down, so he tried a **number of items** he had lying around. / *The **dwarf** got so fed up with the tent falling on him that he went and got an iron **girder** to make sure it didn't happen again!*

20

bā
eight

Radical 八
2 strokes

In contrast to "person" and "tent", the two strokes here don't meet. The second stroke is slightly longer than the first. Both strokes are written downwards.

As with the unicorn standing in for "one", the character for "eight" is represented by an *octopus* in stories involving "eight".

/ *The octopus strapped **wheels** to all his **eight** tentacles so he could roller-skate around delivering drinks for the **giant barman**.*

21

儿 ér (r)
boy

Radical 儿
2 strokes

兒

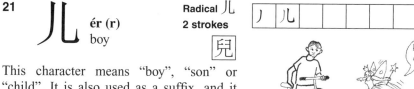

*How on **EARTH** did they get so dirty!?*

This character means "boy", "son" or "child". It is also used as a suffix, and it is then pronounced as an "**r**" sound; for example the word 好儿 is pronounced **hǎor** instead of **hǎo'ér** (see the notes on combining characters, at the end of this chapter).

Notice the hook on the second stroke, which helps to distinguish this character from the previous one.

*/ The **boy's** bicycle **wheels** were filthy. "How on **earth** did you get them so dirty?" said the **fairy**, "I only cleaned them this morning!" (You might think she's a pretty hopeless fairy if she can't keep them clean by magic!)*

Test yourself: 子(17)   日(6)   一(1)   十(4)   八(20)   机(10)   二(2)

好(18)   也(8)   杯(11)   她(16)   个(19)   女(15)   不(9)

22a

丶

a drop

A small drop that can be written in various directions in different characters (as you will see shortly). It is represented by a drop of liquid in the stories.

22

白 bái
white

Radical 白
5 strokes

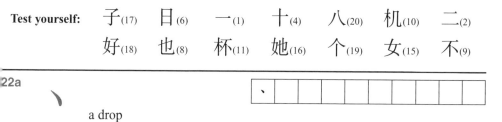

a drop 丶 (22a) + **sun** 日 (6) = **white** 白

In this character the drop is written downwards and to the left.

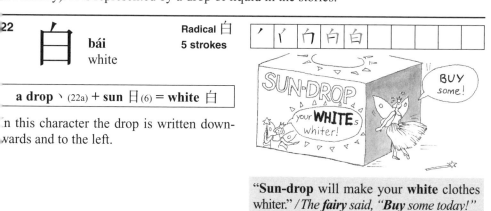

BUY some!

"**Sun-drop** will make your **white** clothes whiter." / *The **fairy** said, "**Buy** some today!"*

As a reminder, we'd like to check that you are still visualizing these stories by taking a good look at each of the story pictures. The stories and story pictures are only a means to an end — the end is to remember the meaning and pronunciation of the character. Because of this, we find that some people shortcut the process and start to learn the equations and pronunciations off by rote. Of course, you are perfectly at liberty to do this if you choose, and you will still find the structure of the book useful, in that everything is introduced in a helpful order and so on. However, you will be missing a really helpful technique which will save you untold hours in the long run. Some of the people we tested the stories on started out saying, "I'm not a visual person," but most of them found that when they gave it a try they did remember the stories after all. So give it a try — what do you have to lose?

23a

勹

wrap

| ' | 勹 | | | | | | | | |

23b

勺

sháo
ladle

| ' | 勹 | 勺 | | | | | | | |

---

wrap 勹(23a) + **a drop** 丶(22a) = **ladle** 勺

So far, composite characters have been easy to split left-right or top-bottom into two parts, but in this character "wrap" encloses the drop (or, appropriately, "wraps" around it).

This composite character is not in HSK Level A (and is therefore printed in gray), so no pronunciation part of the story is needed.

This time the drop is written upwards and to the left.

We will meet "wrap" and "ladle" again later, but they have been introduced here in order to allow you to meet the next character, which is the most common character in Chinese.

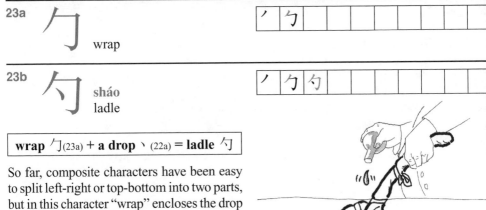

When he had **wrap**ped it up he put **a drop** of perfume on the package even though there was only a **ladle** inside. / *[No pronunciation needed]*

23

的

de (dí)
of

Radical 白
8 strokes

| ' | 亻 | 亣 | 甶 | 白 | 白' | 的 | 的 | | |

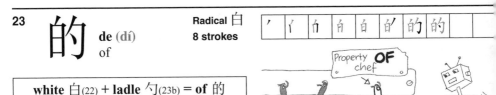

white 白(22) + **ladle** 勺(23b) = **of** 的

This is a particle which attaches to a noun or phrase to show that it is an attribute. A 的 B means "the B of A", "the B belonging to A", "the B of type A", "the B to which A refers", etc. (Particles are small words which can be hard to translate, but often give a flavor to whole phrases or sentences).

The Chef reaches for his **white ladle** — the one marked "Property **of** the Chef". / His **robot** assistant rushes over to **dust** the ladle before he uses it.

24a

口

enclosed

| 丨 | 冂 | 口 | | | | | | | |

This is like mouth, only bigger! You can always tell them apart as "mouth" never ha anything inside it, whereas "enclosed" always does.

You always delay writing the final stroke of "enclosed" until after the contents hav been drawn in. The next character demonstrates this rule in action.

24

四 sì
four

Radical 囗
5 strokes

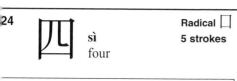

---

enclosed 囗(24a) + boy 儿(21) = four 四

We have now met several numbers — the other numbers up to ten follow shortly, in Chapter 4.

The kidnapped **boy** was **enclosed** by the force-field on all **four** sides. / *The dwarf, leading the rescue team, saluted when they found him (perhaps because he was the colonel's son).*

Here is another progress chart — you can see how much you have covered in this chapter to add to what was already achieved in Chapter 1.

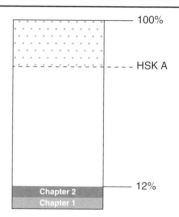

Below is another "Test Yourself" quiz block of characters. We've included these blocks of characters throughout the book. It only takes a moment to stop and work through each block, and is time well spent (and it's nice to be able to get most of them right!). There will be a mixture of recent characters and those you learned some time ago — and the same character may be tested more than once in the book.

Test yourself: 好(18)   二(2)   他(13)   儿(21)   也(8)   一(1)   几(7)

八(20)   十(4)   个(19)   人(12)   三(3)   口(5)   子(17)

Of course you may well want to test yourself systematically as well, by running through all the characters you have learned. It's a good idea at the end of a session to test yourself on the characters you've just learned, then do this again after an hour or two, then after 1 day, 3 days and a week. This repetition will really embed the characters in your long-term memory.

The characters will stay in your memory for longer after each testing. And this effect continues on after a week too. For example, if you checked a given chapter a week ago, it should last for a month, and then a monthly check will last for 3 months, etc.

We'll end this chapter with a few words about compounds. As mentioned in the introduction, characters are used together to form "compounds" or multi-syllable words. Numbers are some of the easiest examples of compounds:

十二　**shíèr**　twelve
十四　**shísì**　fourteen
三十一　**sānshíyī**　thirty one

二十　**èrshí**　twenty
四十　**sìshí**　forty

More generally, two-syllable words are formed by combining two characters:

女人　**nǚrén**　woman
杯子　**bēizi**　cup, mug, glass

儿子　**érzi**　son
女儿　**nǚ'èr**　daughter

The pronunciation of a compound is just given by the pronunciation of the characters spoken (or written) one after the other. Sometimes, in writing a compound in *pinyin*, an apostrophe is used to make it clear how to break the compound up into syllables. For example if we wrote the compound **píngān** without an apostrophe, we wouldn't know whether it was **píng'ān** or **pín'gān**.

As we've said, the meaning of many compounds can be guessed from the meanings of the characters which make it up:

人力　**rénlì**　manpower

Some compounds, however, are not at all obvious:

人口　**rénkǒu**　(human) population   日子　**rìzi**　day, date; life

From now on, we will list compounds as part of the character entries. When we do so, any compounds which are not stipulated for HSK Level A will be printed in brackets [ ]. However all compounds, whether in the HSK Level A list or not, use only HSK Level A *characters*. In fact, all compounds only use characters introduced up to that point in the book.

Of the compounds listed so far, the following are in the HSK Level A list — can you remember what they mean?

儿子　　杯子　　日子　　女儿

Chapter 3

In this chapter not all of the stories have story pictures, as we want you to start to visualize the stories yourself. Doing this should make the stories lodge in your memory more effectively than using the story pictures, as your brain will be "processing" the story more actively. We also list example words (compounds) with the characters from now on.

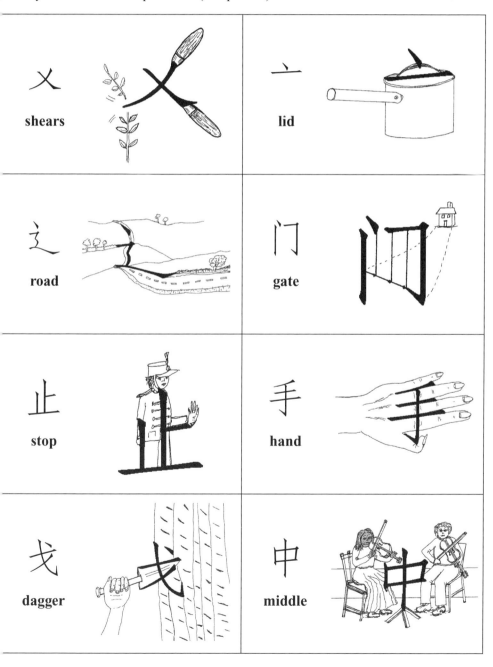

乂
shears

亠
lid

辶
road

门
gate

止
stop

手
hand

戈
dagger

中
middle

You've met all our archetype characters in action now, and as you go through the book you'll get to know them. At the end of this chapter we'll tell you a bit more about how their personalities developed.

25a   shears

Note the stroke order. This illustrates another general rule: strokes drawn downwards and to the left come before strokes drawn downwards and to the right.

25b   lid

The "drop" is written downwards and to the right in this character. In some typefaces (fonts), however, the "drop" will look like a short vertical line.

Because it is used a lot we will treat this as a basic building block, although you could regard it as being made up of "drop" plus "one".

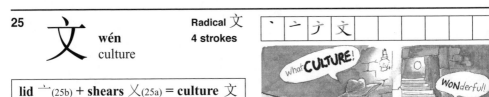

25   文   **wén**   culture   Radical 文   4 strokes

lid 一 (25b) + **shears** 乂 (25a) = **culture** 文

This character refers particularly to written language and literature.

日文 (6)   **Rìwén**   *(written) Japanese*

This is how we will list compounds from now on. The number 6 in brackets tells you that the other character in the compound (in this case, 日) is Character 6 in this book.

(Inside the ancient tomb) The archaeologist lifts the heavy **lid** and finds some beautiful ornamental **shears** — they will tell him a lot about the **culture** of the time. / *"**Wonderful**", says the **fairy**, "those are magic shears that cut the grass by themselves!"*

26a   road

This shape always encloses other characters or fragments, which nestle above the long "tail".

Note that the zigzag shape above the long "tail" is all one stroke. "Road" is always drawn last, after the character or fragment it encloses.

26

这 **zhè**
this

Radical 辶
7 strokes

這

road 辶(26a) + **culture** 文(25) = **this** 这

If you look at 这, you will probably think of it as "road" plus "culture", even though you write "culture" then "road". For this reason we will give "road" first in equations.

这个(19) **zhège** *this (one)*
这儿(21) **zhèr** *here (spoken)*

"Which **road** leads to the **culture** museum — **this** one, **this** one or **this** one?" / *The dwarf looks up from his newspaper, and says grumpily, "Follow those* ***Germans.***"

27

门 **mén**
gate

Radical 门
3 strokes

門

We regard this character as a basic building block even though it looks as if it is composed of three pieces. It was originally a picture of a door or gate. Often it acts as a three-sided enclosure (see, for example, Characters 289 and 290).

The stoke order is a relic from the traditional form of the character, and in this case overrides the left-to-right rule for drawing characters.

门口(5) **ménkǒu** *doorway*

/ *(On the canal) The lock* ***gate*** *has a* ***wheel*** *that must be turned to open it, but first you must pay* ***money*** *to the* ***fairy*** *when she flies over, and she will release the wheel.*

28

们 **men**
people

Radical 亻
5 strokes

們

person 亻(13a) + **gate** 门(27) = **people** 们

Our first story without a picture — don't just read it, visualize it!

This character is a plural ending for many nouns and pronouns which refer to people.

(The castle was being opened to the public for the first time) **Harry** opened the castle **gate** and found a long queue of **people** waiting outside. / *He programmed the* ***robot*** *to help collect the* ***money*** *so he didn't have to do it all.*

他们(13) **tāmen** *they; them*
她们(16) **tāmen** *they; them (female)*
人们(12) **rénmen** *people (in general)*

29a 止 zhǐ
stop

Sometimes this character takes the distorted form seen in 30a.

---

29 正 zhèng
upright

Radical 止
5 strokes

| **one** 一(1) + **stop** 止(29a) = **upright** 正 |

The meaning "upright" also extends to include "proper", "just so", "correct", etc.

The **unicorn**, dozing, heard someone shout "**Stop!**" and sat bolt **upright**. / *The dwarf had set up jungle tours for unicorn-watching (even though he knew the unicorn had hidden in the jungle to get a bit of peace).*

30a 𣥂 stop

This is an alternative form of 29a.

30b 疋 upright

Similarly, this is an alternative form of Character 29.

---

30 是 shì
is

Radical 日
9 strokes

| **sun** 日(6) + **upright** 疋(30b) = **is** 是 |

This is the third most common character in Chinese (after 的 and 一). Its basic meaning is "is" (but as you will know if you're learning Chinese, it's not quite as simple as that ...).

(An argument is taking place in a back garden) They are staking a **sun**flower — is it **upright**? "It **is**," says one of the gardeners; "It isn't," says the other. "**Is, is, is!**" says the first, and so on. / *The dwarf who lives next door can't stand it any longer and comes round, brandishing his shillelagh.*

31

手 **shǒu**
hand

Radical 手
4 strokes

/ **Teddy** takes one **hand** off the steering **wheel**, **showing** off his driving skills (and probably ends up in a ditch!)

When this character appears as the left-hand side of other characters it usually takes the form 扌 (152a).

This is the second story without a picture — this time it's a "wheel" story. Read the story and then shut your eyes and try to picture it. See the car Teddy is driving — what type is it? By *picturing* this scene in your mind's eye, you are using one of the most potent systems the brain uses for memory — the same process your brain carries out automatically when you are reading a novel or listening to a story on the radio. If you picture the scene vividly, then when you next think of "hand plus wheel" it will trigger the story, which will in turn trigger the soundword for the pronunciation.

The brackets [ ] round the compound show that it is not a compound included in the HSK Level A list.

[手机(10) **shǒujī** *mobile phone*]

32a

戈 **gē**
dagger

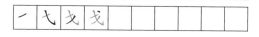

Watch the stroke order here. You finish up with the drop (after you finish writing the previous stroke downwards).

This is a picture of an ancient weapon, which was something like a cross between a dagger, an axe and a spear!

32

我 **wǒ**
I

Radical 戈
7 strokes

hand 手(31) + **dagger** 戈(32a) = **I** 我

Here "hand" and "dagger" are fused together (notice that this is built into the story) and "share" a stroke (compare this with character 152). This means the stroke order is something you have to be careful with and practice. But once you get it right you will find it is a great character to draw as your pen swoops up and down and around it.

我们(28) **wǒmen** we; us

The **dagger** was stuck in the huge stone **hand** (a bit like Excalibur) — he pulled it out and declared "**I** am the One!". / *This* **woke Teddy** *who had been asleep under the hand.*

Test yourself: 八(20)   力(14)   杯(11)   文(25)   白(22)   不(9)   机(10)

八(13)   门(27)   四(24)   好(18)   女(15)   的(23)   个(19)

33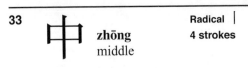

zhōng
middle

Radical │
4 strokes

A stroke which pierces through the whole character, such as the vertical one here, is generally drawn last.

This character often means "China" or "Chinese", from the Chinese way of referring to their country as the "middle kingdom".

*/ In the **middle** of each **wheel** of his car, the **giant** had etched a picture of a **jonquil**. (A jonquil is a type of small daffodil. You'll have to excuse us if we sometimes have to scratch around for soundwords — some sounds come at the start of very few English words!)*

中文(25) **zhōngwén** *(written) Chinese*

Are you getting to know the archetypes yet? In the course of writing this book, we found that they developed personalities of their own, related to the original reasons we chose them:

Giant	Slow, placid, often found working as a handyman. The high, flat 1st tone represents his size and slowness to change.
Fairy	Flits about, tends to conjure up helpful objects rather than simply granting wishes. The upward sloping accent for 2nd tone resembles her wand.
Teddy	Somewhat mischievous and irresponsible, unlikely to take things too seriously. The down-up 3rd tone represents the way he bounces around playfully.
Dwarf	Rather grumpy and officious, likely to have some responsibility, to be a janitor or foreman, and to be trying to organise things or boss people around. The downward sloping accent of the 4th tone represents his dismissive tone of voice (as well as the fact that you look down at him because of his diminutive size).
Robot	Rather mechanical and soulless — as befits a neutral tone. Likes everything logical, "just so", and is somewhat fastidious.

We have tried to keep the stories consistent with these personality traits, to help you remember which archetype features in each story.

Here is our third progress chart to show you how you're doing. From now on the light gray area will show you where you'd got to when we last showed you, and the dark gray area shows you how much you've added since then. We'll just present the progress charts from now on without further comment.

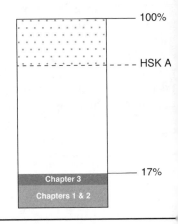

Chapter 4

As we continue, more of the stories will be given without story pictures, so that you will be visualizing the stories yourself. But this doesn't apply to character pictures — you can rest assured that there will be a character picture for every basic building block in the book.

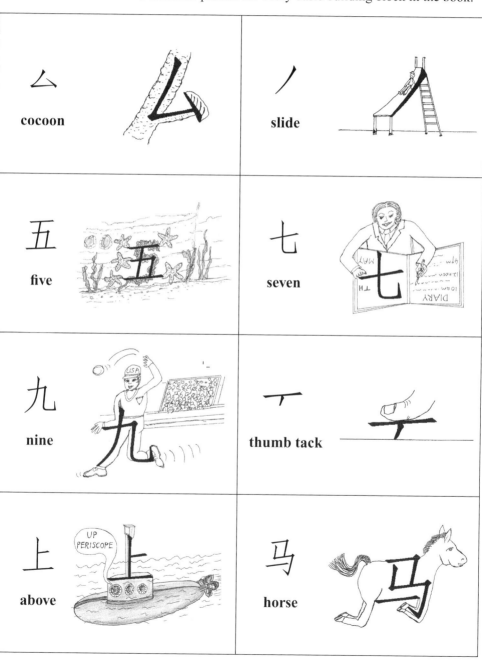

厶 cocoon

丿 slide

五 five

七 seven

九 nine

丅 thumb tack

上 above

马 horse

34a

cocoon

This character originally meant "cocoon", and from this it came to mean "to shut away", hence "self-centered" or "selfish".

34b

"slide"

We will call this stroke "slide" (think of a children's playground slide). It is much longer than a drop, and is always drawn in a downward direction.

34

me
"appendage"

Radical 丿
3 strokes

麼

slide 丿(34b) + cocoon 厶(34a) =
appendage 幺

We've called this character "appendage" because it is used as a suffix, in words like **zhème** (see below) and **shénme** (see Character 35).

You will see that we are continuing to add phrases in brackets to some of the stories. These phrases are to help you visualize (and hence remember) the scene. Of course the words in bold are all you need to remember

The **cocoon** had been fixed to the top of the children's **slide**, as an **appendage** (perhaps so that the new butterfly, when she emerges, can use the slide like a ski-jump for her first flight!) / *This throws the* **robot's** *circuits into a dreadful* **muddle** *(as he wasn't allowed to remove it when he cleaned the slide).*

in the end, but you'll remember them more easily once you recall the scene.

这幺(26) **zhème** *like this, in this manner*

35

shén
what?

Radical 亻
4 strokes

甚

person 亻(13a) + ten 十(4) = what? 什

Remember that "ten" (Character 4) is represented in stories by a cross, and "person" by "Harry" (see Character 12).

Harry stands alone at the **crossroads** but nobody else turns up. **What** is wrong? **What** has he done? / *The* **fairy** *(hovering at a safe distance) tells him everyone will* **shun** *him until he has a wash and doesn't smell any more!*

什幺(34) **shénme** *what?*
[什幺的(34, 23) **shénmede** *etc.*]

But *why*? This is a question people often ask — *why* is it that "person" plus "ten" equals "what?", o "road" plus "culture" equals "this"? There probably is a reason, if you delved deeply enough into th history of how each character evolved, but it is rarely sensible to demand explanations like this whe learning a language. The wisest course is to relax and just accept that this is how it is. It happens i English too. After all, what has a carpet got to do with a car, or a pet?

36

五 **wǔ**
five

Radical 一
4 strokes

一	丁	五	五						

You will remember that the number "eight" is represented in stories by an octopus. We will have similar representatives for the numbers 5, 7 and 9 (otherwise it would be difficult to distinguish in your mind between a story with say "7 trees" and a story with "9 trees" or "5 trees"). The character for "five" will be represented in stories by a *starfish*.

/ **Teddy** is splashing in a rock pool and sees a **five**-spoked **wheel** but when he goes to pick it up it turns out to be a starfish and it **wounds** his paw.

[五十(4) **wǔshí** *fifty*]
[十五(4) **shíwǔ** *fifteen*]
[五十五(4) **wǔshíwǔ** *fifty five*]

37

七 **qī**
seven

Radical 一
2 strokes

一	七								

The character for "seven" is represented in stories by a *diary* (a weekly planner where you look seven days ahead to see appointments, rather than a personal journal).

When writing this character, notice that the sloping stroke extends well to both sides of the hook stroke, in contrast to 匕 which we'll meet later (206a).

/ You look in your diary, and notice that in **seven** days' time your car is due for new **wheels**. The **giant** has offered to get them for you **cheap**.

[七十(4) **qīshí** *seventy*]
[十七(4) **shíqī** *seventeen*]
[七十五(4, 36) **qīshíwǔ** *seventy five*]

38

九 **jiǔ**
nine

Radical 乚
2 strokes

丿	九								

Why are there *two* teddies in this story? An explanation follows on the next page.

Compare this character with "power" (Character 14), and in particular compare the stroke orders. The character for "nine" will be represented in stories by a *baseball*.

[九十(4) **jiǔshí** *ninety*]
[十九(4) **shíjiǔ** *nineteen*]
[三十九(3, 4) **sānshíjiǔ** *thirty nine*]

/ During throwing practice each of the **nine** members of the baseball team has to throw the baseball cleanly through the spokes of a **wheel**. **Two teddies**, who are holding the wheel, keep moving it for a **joke**.

In Chinese some vowels are preceded by an "i" or "u" (these are called "on-glides"). The "i" is pronounced like the English "y" so that for example "**liang**" is pronounced "Iyang". The problem is that in general no words in English begin with these sounds. So instead what we will do is to indicate an "i" by having *two of the archetype* in the story — two giants, two dwarves, etc. Try to picture them *both* as you visualize the story. When you find two archetypes in a story, you know you have to add in the "y" sound, for example converting a "pow" sound to "pyow".

This system also helps with another problem, which is that there are no soundwords in English to distinguish between consonants such as "zh" and "j". But the i on-glide does this for us. So for example the soundwords "joke", "choker", "show" would normally indicate the syllables **zhou**, **chou**, **shou** respectively — but if there are two of the archetype in the story then they indicate **jiu**, **qiu**, **xiu** instead. (It is cheating a little to use the same soundwords for "zh" and "j", "ch" and "q", "sh" and "x", since these are different initial consonants in Chinese. But remember that the purpose of soundwords is to jog your memory as to the pronunciation of each character, rather than to reproduce it exactly, which isn't possible in English). This is why there are *two* teddies in the story for 九.

We will deal with u on-glides in the next chapter.

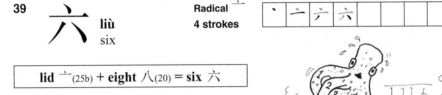

39   六   liù   six

Radical 亠
4 strokes

`丶 一 亠 六`

| **lid** 亠(25b) + **eight** 八(20) = **six** 六 |

The fact that there are *two* dwarves tells you that the "lo" sound (from the soundword) is pronounced "lyo".

This completes the numbers from one to ten. We have story substitutes (the unicorn, octopus, etc.) for some of the numbers (1, 2, 5, 7, 8 and 9). Since the characters for 3, 4 and 6 don't appear as a part of other characters, we don't need story substitutes for them.

[六十(4) **liùshí** *sixty*]
[十六(4) **shíliù** *sixteen*]

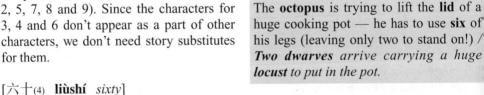

The **octopus** is trying to lift the **lid** of a huge cooking pot — he has to use **six** of his legs (leaving only two to stand on!) / *Two dwarves arrive carrying a huge locust to put in the pot.*

Test yourself: 是(30)   人(12)   文(25)   儿(21)   正(29)   她(16)   这(26)

中(33)   们(28)   我(32)   四(24)   门(27)   力(14)   手(31)

40a

┬

"thumb tack"

`一 ┬`

"Thumb tack" is our name for this shape which is found at the top of some characters, and which looks like a squashed nail which has got slightly bent.

40

bǎi
hundred

Radical 白
6 strokes

一 丆 丆 丆 百 百

> **thumb tack** 丆 (40a) + **sun** 日 (6) =
> **hundred** 百

You might feel that this character could be split into "one" plus "white", and you'd be right. There will be quite a few cases where there might seem to be a choice as to how a character can be broken down into building blocks. There is no single correct way, and if you prefer an alternative then simply

You see a **thumb tack** (on the road), glinting in the **sun**. When you look more closely, you can see there are a **hundred** of them. / *Teddy has sprinkled them on the new bypass (as a protest against it being built near his home).*

make up an alternative story to go with your choice.

[三百 (3) **sānbǎi** *three hundred*]

41

边

biān
side

Radical 辶
5 strokes

邊

フ 力 力 边 边

> **road** 辶 (26a) + **power** 力 (14) = **side** 边

Note that in Chinese the i on-glide changes an "an" sound to "yen", not "yan" (see the Appendix). This is why we use "bends" as a soundword rather than, say, "bands".

一边...一边...(1, 1) **yībiān A yībiān B**
  doing A while also doing B
[这边 (26) **zhèbiān** *this side; over here*]

A **power**ful machine is clearing a path for a new **road** by pushing everything to the **side**. / *But it can only do the straight bits so two giants have to be called on to create the bends.*

42a

卜

bǔ; bo
fortune teller

> **stick** 丨 (19a) + **a drop** 丶 (22a) =
> **fortune teller** 卜

When 卜 appears as a part of another character, "drop" sometimes turns into a short horizontal line (see Character 183 for an example).

You don't need to learn the pronunciation (as this is not an HSK Level A character), so there is no second half to the story.

丨 卜

"Dip the **stick** in this ink and let **a drop** fall on here," says the **fortune teller** (she can tell your fortune by the pattern the ink makes). / *[No pronunciation needed]*

42

上 **shàng**
above

Radical 卜
3 strokes

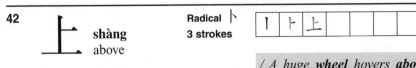

Although the basic meaning of this character is "above" or "on top of", it can also be used as a verb meaning to enter (a vehicle), attend (school), go to (work), etc.

/ *A huge **wheel** hovers **above Shanghai** with a **dwarf** sitting on it, directing the boats in the harbor.*

上边(41) **shàngbian** *above; high up*

43

下 **xià**
below

Radical 卜
3 strokes

一 丁 下

> **one** 一(1) + **fortune teller** 卜(42a) = **below** 下

In a similar way to Character 42, this character, which means "down", "below" or "under", can also be used as a verb meaning to alight (from a vehicle), finish (class or work), etc.

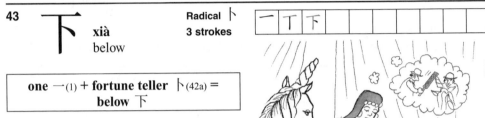

下边(41) **xiàbian** *below, under*
一下儿(1, 21) **yíxiàr** *briefly; casually*

The **unicorn** goes to see the **fortune teller**, and she looks at what is **below** the card which he points to with his hoof. / *"I see **two dwarves sharpening** your horn for you."*

44

马 **mǎ**
horse

Radical 马
3 strokes

馬

马上(42) **mǎshàng** *at once*

/ ***Teddy** has shown a **horse** how to balance on a **wheel** so they can earn money at the **market** (performing as street entertainers).*

45

吗 **ma**
question mark

Radical 口
6 strokes

嗎

> **mouth** 口(5) + **horse** 马(44) = **question mark** 吗

This is a particle which is added to the end of a sentence to turn it into a question.

Imagine looking inside the **mouth** of a **horse** you are thinking of buying, and finding a **question mark** stamped on the horse's tongue. / *Your **robot** remarks, "It's not logical to buy horses at this **market**."*

46

妈 **mā** mum

Radical 女
6 strokes

媽

woman 女(15) + horse 马(44) = mum 妈

妈妈 **māma** *mum, mom, mummy*

A teenage girl is out shopping and she turns to see a **woman** on a **horse** — naked like Lady Godiva. "**Mum**!" the teenager cries, mortified. / *Fortunately at that moment the **giant** comes bumbling through the **market** (overturning stalls and distracting everyone's attention, giving the girl a chance to lead the horse away out of sight).*

Look at the last three characters (44–46). Do you notice anything? They all contain 马 and they are all pronounced "**ma**" (with various tones). This isn't a coincidence: 马 is acting as a *phonetic* and giving a clue to how to pronounce the character. In effect 妈 is "the character which has a meaning related to 女 and sounds like 马." One reason (among many) why the equations often don't seem to make any logical sense is that sometimes one part of the character is donating its *sound* rather than its *meaning*. A series of characters like this, with a phonetic component and with the same pronunciation, is called a *phonetic series*. We will always use the same soundword for all the pronunciations in a phonetic series — in the case of Characters 44–46 we used the soundword "market". We have already seen two small examples of phonetic series (他, 她 and 门, 们), and there are many more to come. But (as you probably guessed) this is not at all a reliable system, as you will see as we go along. For example, we have already seen that 他 and 她 are pronounced **tā**, but 也 was **yě**!

Test yourself:	也(8)	个(19)	六(39)	什(35)	们(28)	九(38)	么(34)
	的(23)	子(17)	五(36)	中(33)	力(14)	七(37)	白(22)
	马(44)	女(15)	百(40)	十(4)	下(43)	不(9)	日(6)
	边(41)	四(24)	妈(46)	八(20)	上(42)	正(29)	这(26)

Did you remember all these OK? If not, are you sure you *visualized* the story in each case rather than just *reading* it? It's true that you only need to recall the meaning (and soundword/archetype), not the whole story verbatim, but picturing the story will help you to remember these vital nuggets inside the story.

As an experiment you might try really visualizing (say) three stories from the next chapter, and then for three other stories simply read them through, *not* visualizing them. Then test yourself 24 hours later and see if there is any difference. Then test yourself again 3 days and 7 days later.

Chapter 5

If there is a basic building block you are having a real problem remembering, you might try this: photocopy the character picture and color it in, making sure you trace over the character in heavy black lines. It doesn't matter whether you then tear it up or frame it on your wall; the process will have helped to embed it in your memory.

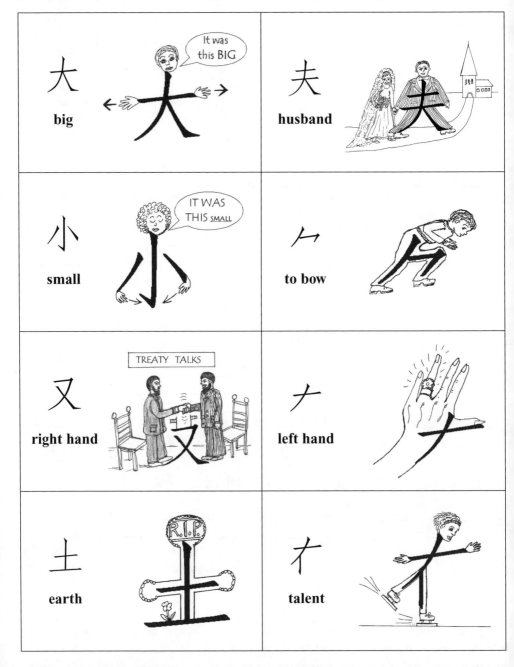

47

dà (dài)

big

Radical 大

3 strokes

The pronunciation of this character is basically **dà**, with the exception that it is pronounced **dài** in the word **dàifū** (see Character 49 below).

[大人(12) **dàrén** *adult*]

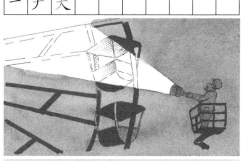

/ The **Big Wheel** at the fairground is in use all day so the **dwarf** has to do the maintenance work at night in the **dark**. (Imagine him grumbling, "How do they expect me to see what I'm doing?").

48

tài

too much

Radical 大

4 strokes

big 大(47) + a drop 丶 (22a) = too much 太

Note that the "drop" is *below* "big" — we will meet another story later (238a) which is also made up of "drop" and "big", but the "drop" is on top.

[太太 **tàitai** *wife; Mrs.*]

The fisherman throws his arms wide to show how **big** the fish was, but **a drop** of sweat falls from his brow and his friends know he is lying — they have seen **too much** of this in the past. / The **dwarf** says, disdainfully, "Are you sure it wasn't a **tiger?**"

49

fū

husband

Radical 大

4 strokes

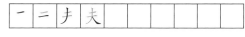

The second stroke of this character is longer than the first, just like in the character for "two" (Character 2).

/ She makes her **husband** use the exercise **wheel**. "You are fat because you eat as much **food** as the **giant**," she tells him.

大夫(47) **dàifū** *doctor (colloq.)*
夫人(12) **fūrén** *wife (formal)*

50

xiǎo
small

Radical 小
3 strokes

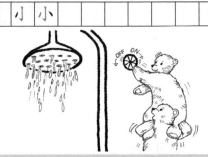

When "small" occurs at the top of other characters, it sometimes takes the form ⺌ (see Character 267). For using 小 with names, see the note on 老 **lǎo** (Character 264).

The stroke order for this character follows the "center before symmetrical sides" rule, which overrides the "left to right" rule.

[大小(47) **dàxiǎo** *size*]

/ *The small wheel has to be turned to operate the shower, but the two teddies have to stand one on top of the other to reach it.*

51a

to bow

We use this in the following character, but then we won't need it again until Chapter 18.

51b

尔 **ěr**
thou

| **bow** ⼧(51a) + **small** 小(50) = **thou** 尔 |

This is an old or literary word for "you" which we need for the next character.

Imagine two fastidious courtiers **bow**ing to each other by a **small** gap in the fence. "After **thou**," one says. "No, after **thou**!" And so on. / *[No pronunciation needed]*

51

你 **nǐ**
you

Radical 亻
7 strokes

| **person** 亻(13a) + **thou** 尔(51b) = **you** 你 |

This is the everyday, modern word for "you" (there are also various polite ways of saying "you" which we will meet later).

你们(28) **nǐmen** *you (plural)*

"**Harry, thou** art clever," says the wise man. "Why don't you just say "**you**"?" Harry replies. / *Teddy gets all excited and starts singing, "No need to kneel, no need to kneel."*

52

又 yòu
right hand

Radical 又
2 strokes

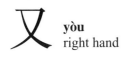

Although originally a picture of the right hand, this character now means "again" or "additionally" (there is also another word for "again"; see Character 217). We will use the old meaning "right hand" in stories, since it will be easier to create vivid stories using this than if we were to use the more abstract word "again". Moreover, we will usually use the image of shaking hands to distinguish it from stories involving "hand" in general (since this is something you do with your right hand, even if you are left-handed).

/ *Two friends on unicycles meet in the street — each extends his* **right hand** *while balancing on a single* **wheel**, *and they shake hands again and again. The* **dwarf** *comes rushing past (nearly sending them flying) — he's late for his* **yoga** *class and in no mood to be impressed.*

[又...又... **yòu A yòu B**   *both A and B*]

53a

ナ

left hand

"Left hand" forms a part of far fewer characters than "right hand".

To make "left hand" stand out from "hand" in general, we will often use stories involving wedding rings.

53

友 yǒu
friend

Radical 又
4 strokes

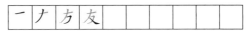

| **left hand** ナ(53a) + **right hand** 又(52) = **friend** 友 |

友好(18) **yǒuhǎo** *friendly*

They run along **(right) hand** in **(left) hand**, the best of **friends**. / *But the mischievous* **Teddy** *is waiting, and as they pass he flicks his* **yoyo** *out and they fall down in a tangle of string.*

54a

土 tǔ
earth

Once again (as in 夫, Character 49), the second stroke of this character is longer than the first. This time it really matters, for there is another character which looks just like 土, except that the first stroke is longer than the second (土, Character 487a).

When used as the left-hand side of other characters, 土 gets squashed so that the last stroke slopes upwards (see the next character for an example).

54

地 **dì; de**
1. ground 2. -ly

Radical 土
6 strokes

1.

1. **earth** 土(54a) + **also** 也(8) = **ground** 地

2. **earth** 土(54a) + **also** 也(8) = **-ly** 地

Now, here we have a character with two meanings, and two pronunciations to go with them! Whenever this happens (there are ten such characters in this book), we will simply provide two stories. However, one will be set in the Wild West, and one will be set on a large spaceship. No other characters, apart from these ten, will use either of these settings. So whenever you see a character and remember the story to go with it, if the setting is the Wild West or a spaceship, this will remind you that there is also another story (in the other setting). Of course, which meaning (and pronunciation) is appropriate will be for you to decide, depending on the context. This is like seeing the word "bow" in English: until you know the context (tying shoelaces? aboard a ship? archery?) you won't know which meaning, or which pronunciation, is appropriate.

The second meaning, "-ly", is our name for how 地 helps to qualify verbs, like the "-ly" ending of adverbs in English.

You may wonder which of the two meanings to use in future equations. Fortunately this problem doesn't arise as this character never appears as part of another character.

[地下(43) **dìxià** *underground*]

⇂ (A posse is pursuing bandits, and the sheriff dismounts to look at the spent bullets) "The **earth** has **also** been disturbed," he says, "they're heading for higher **ground**." / *His **dwarf** deputy takes a few men on a **detour** (to head them off at the pass …)*

2.

🛸 (The landing party has returned to the spaceship from the planet) "We didn't just get samples of **earth**, we **also** found some great alien artefacts, so treat them gentle." "Gent**ly**," corrects the Chief Scientist (who is a stickler for grammar). / *"And can somebody go and sort out the **robot** — he's miserable because he's got so **dusty**" (collecting the earth samples).*

55a

talent

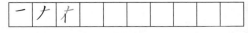

You might like to think of this as "left hand" plus "stick". But we think that our illustrator's character picture is a better and more vivid way to remember this. (We will have something else to say about this character when we get to Character 518).

55

zài
at

Radical 土
6 strokes

| talent 亻(55a) + earth 土(54a) = at 在 |

This can mean both "in/at/on" and "to be in/at/on", or "to be in the middle of " (doing something).

正在(29) **zhèngzài** *(used before a verb to denote action in progress)*

(An announcement at the flower show) "The expert gardeners, who have a special **talent** for growing things in the **earth**, will be **at** the main marquee to answer questions when the big "@" sign is displayed above it." / *The **dwarf** (who is organizing things) plays a couple of notes on his **xylophone** to end the announcement.*

56a

"swoop"

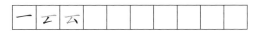

| one 一(1) + cocoon 厶(34a) = swoop 云 |

The **unicorn** finds a **cocoon** on the path, and is just about to investigate when a bird **swoops** down to pluck it from under his nose. / *[No pronunciation needed]*

56

yún
cloud

Radical 二
4 strokes

雲

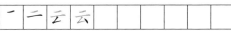

| one 一(1) + swoop 云(56a) = cloud 云 |

Alternatively, this character could be broken down into "two" plus "cocoon". If, looking at the character, this alternative seems more natural to you, then feel free to make up a story accordingly. For example, you could have a biplane pilot flying along, who sees a fluffy cocoon floating in the sky — until he realizes that it is a cloud.

A bird is teasing the **unicorn, swoop**ing under its tummy, but each time the unicorn looks round the bird hides in a **cloud**. / *The **fairy** is so impressed she makes the bird an honorary member of her aviators' **union**.*

57

yùn
transport

Radical 辶
7 strokes

運

| road 辶(26a) + cloud 云(56) = transport 运 |

The **road** is obscured by a **cloud** of dust as the big **transport** trucks roll past. / *The **dwarf** (covered in dust) calls after them, "I'll get the **union** on to you!"*

58  **dòng** move

Radical 力
6 strokes

動

cloud 云(56) + **power** 力(14) = **move** 动

A tornado **cloud** has the **power** to **move** almost anything. / *It can even knock the **dwarf** off his **donkey**.*

The previous two characters formed a mini-phonetic series, but this character breaks the pattern. This shows that phonetic series are not to be relied upon!

运动(57) **yùndòng** *(physical) exercise*
[动手(31) **dòng shǒu** *to start work*]

59a combine

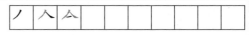

tent 人(19b) + **one** 一(1) = **combine** 合

The **unicorn** hides in his **tent**, frightened by the **combine** harvester working nearby. / *[No pronunciation needed]*

59 **huì** meeting

Radical 人
6 strokes

會

combine 合(59a) + **swoop** 乙(56a) = **meeting** 会

(The captain of the birds' aerobatic display team is speaking) "If we are going to **combine** our **swoop**ing maneuvers we need to have a **meeting** to discuss how we will do it." / *The **ghostly dwarf** (safety officer) is organizing the **hay** (to act as a safety cushion).*

Alternatively, this character could be split into "tent" plus "cloud" (see the comment for Character 56). From now on, we won't keep pointing these alternatives out.

Another meaning of this character is "to know how to".

The pronunciation of this character is something like "hway" — the u on-glide is pronounced like the English "w". See the remarks after this character entry.

机会(10) **jīhuì** *chance, opportunity*
[大会(47) **dàhuì** *congress, assembly*]
一会儿(1, 21) **yíhuìr** *(in) a moment*

To signal a u on-glide, as in Character 59, we have a *ghostly* archetype. We try to give ghostly figures a guarding or protecting role in the stories. When you find a ghostly archetype, add in the "w" sound, e.g. converting a "go" sound to "gwo". (Recall our discussion of i on-glides after Character 38).

Test yourself: 你(51) 我(32) 大(47) 正(29) 小(50) 手(31) 运(57)
太(48) 口(5) 吗(45) 夫(49) 几(7) 们(28) 是(30)

60a

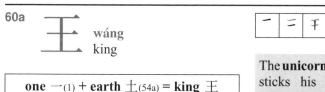

王 wáng
king

| 一 | 三 | 干 | 王 | | | | | | |

one 一 (1) + **earth** 土 (54a) = **king** 王

The **unicorn** (telling the story of Excalibur) sticks his horn into the **earth**, then withdraws it with a flourish to demonstrate how the young Arthur became **king**. / *[No pronunciation needed]*

60b

玉 yù
jade

| 一 | 三 | 干 | 王 | 玉 | | | | | |

king 王 (60a) + **a drop** 丶 (22a) = **jade** 玉

This is similar to the situation for 太 (Character 48). In 玉 the drop is low down in the character, and the story reflects this. This is to keep it distinct in your mind from

The **king** is out jogging and as each **drop** of sweat touches the ground it turns to **jade**. / *[No pronunciation needed]*

another character you'll meet later (主, Character 297), which has a drop *on top of* a king.

60

国 guó
country

Radical 囗
8 strokes

國

| 丨 | 冂 | 冂 | 月 | 囗 | 国 | 国 | 国 | | |

enclosed 囗 (24a) + **jade** 玉 (60b) = **country** 国

Here is another ghostly archetype, indicating the pronunciation is closer to "gwo" than "go" (see the text following Character 59).

The **jade** crown is **enclosed** in a theft-proof case at the exhibition as it is a very important part of the **country**'s heritage. / *The legendary **ghostly fairy** who came from the **Gobi** desert guards it.*

[中国 (33) **zhōngguó** *China*]

Because we are covering the most common characters early on in the book, we've already covered almost a quarter of the characters you'll find in an average piece of Chinese text! Of course, you won't be able to understand the average piece of text yet — in English the most common words are "and", "the" and so on, and knowing these wouldn't enable you to read English either. However, you are on your way now and most of the "mystery" and "fear of the unknown" should be gone. By now we hope you'll agree that there is actually nothing to stop you learning as many characters as you like!

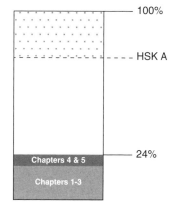

100%

HSK A

Chapters 4 & 5

24%

Chapters 1-3

Chapter 6

Some characters have minor variations between typefaces which are not significant. For example, in the character for "moon" below, the two small horizontal lines almost meet the far side of the character, but in the main character entry (next page) the lines *do* reach the whole way across. The characters on these "basics pages" are also slightly "italic" compared with the main character entries. This will help you to recognize characters in these different fonts.

月

moon

未

not yet

\ /

horns

了

complete

讠

words

夕

evening

刀

knife

61 月 **yuè**
moon

Radical 月
4 strokes

| 丿 | 刀 | 月 | 月 | | | | | |

We would normally class this as a DIY pronunciation (one you have to memorize on your own as there is no reasonable soundword available in English). For most of these, it will be simplest if you just learn the pronunciation, rather than us inventing a new trick each time. But we'll try to give you some help when we can.

We saw that the character for "sun" also means "day" (Character 6), and in a similar way the character for "moon" also means "month".

*/ You are out walking at night when the **moon**light falling on a **wheel** lights up the **dwarf** who is sitting on it. "That **you, eh?**" he whispers gruffly.*

Occasionally 月 is distorted into 夕 (but we won't see this happening until much later, in Chapter 16).

[二月(2) **èryuè** *February*]
[三月(3) **sānyuè** *March*]
[三个月(3, 19) **sān ge yuè** *three months*]

---

62 朋 **péng**
companion

Radical 月
8 strokes

| 丿 | 刀 | 月 | 月 | 刖 | 刖 | 朋 | 朋 | |

moon 月(61) + **moon** 月(61) =
companion 朋

朋友(53) **péngyǒu** *friend*
朋友们(53, 28) **péngyǒumen** *friends*

"Why did you buy two moon-shaped balloons?" her mother asks. "Because the first **moon** needed another **moon** as a **companion**," the little girl says. */ But just then one of the moons gets **punctured**, but (before the child can start to cry) the **fairy** quickly flies over, flicks her wand, and it's as good as new.*

---

63 有 **yǒu**
have

Radical 月
6 strokes

| 一 | ナ | 才 | 有 | 有 | 有 | | | |

left hand ナ(53a) + **moon** 月(61) = **have** 有

This means both "have", "possess" and the impersonal "there is" or "there exists".

有的(23) **yǒude** *some*
[有力(14) **yǒulì** *strong, forceful*]

"Why is there a **moon** on the **left hand** side of every picture?" the girl's mother asks. "Because I only **have** a moon stencil," the girl replies. */ **Teddy** practices his favorite **yoga** posture (and says "Why not draw me instead?")*

64a  wèi
not yet

Yet again, as in 夫 (49) and 土 (54a), the second stroke of this character is longer than the first. This is another occasion where it *does* matter, because we shall be meeting the character 末 (793a) later.

It is unfortunately true that some small details like this do matter, whereas other small differences don't — as mentioned at the start of this chapter. We will do our best to draw attention to the differences that matter and you will soon get used to these; you will also soon be routinely recognizing minor variants of the same character.

---

64 mèi
younger sister

Radical 女
8 strokes

woman 女(15) + **not yet** 未(64a) =
younger sister 妹

There is no character in Chinese for "sister"; instead we have this character for "younger sister" and another one (Character 444) for "older sister". The same thing happens for brothers.

(Two lads in the pub) "What about that **woman** over there — she's **not yet** married," says one. "You can't fancy her, she's my **younger sister**!" his mate replies. / *"Anyway the **dwarf** has his eye on her, and he's a **Major**."*

妹妹 **mèimei** *younger sister*

65a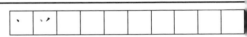
horns

The "horns" usually come at the top of a character (but not always — see the following character).

---

65 lái
come

Radical 一
7 strokes

來

horns ∨ (65a) + **not yet** 未(64a) = **come** 来

上来(42) **shànglái** *come up*
下来(43) **xiàlái** *come down*

The stags are going off on their hunt, but the fawn is too young. "Your **horns** are **not yet** grown so you cannot **come** yet," he is told. / *The **fairy** (who comes to babysit him) fixes up **lights** to amuse him and guide the returning hunters.*

Test yourself: 么(34)   子(17)   妈(46)   又(52)   在(55)   他(13)   个(19)

友(53)   云(56)   十(4)   会(59)   地(54)   日(6)   动(58)

66　了　**le; liǎo**　　Radical 亅
　　　　1. transition　　2 strokes
　　　　2. complete

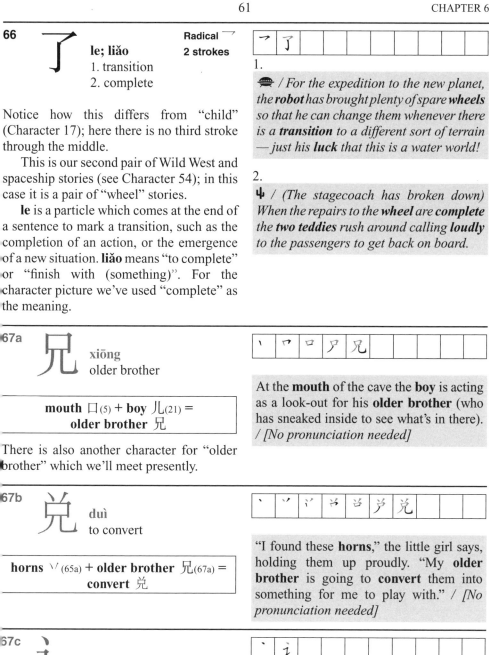

1.

🚀 / *For the expedition to the new planet, the **robot** has brought plenty of spare **wheels** so that he can change them whenever there is a **transition** to a different sort of terrain — just his **luck** that this is a water world!*

Notice how this differs from "child" (Character 17); here there is no third stroke through the middle.

　　This is our second pair of Wild West and spaceship stories (see Character 54); in this case it is a pair of "wheel" stories.

　　le is a particle which comes at the end of a sentence to mark a transition, such as the completion of an action, or the emergence of a new situation. **liǎo** means "to complete" or "finish with (something)". For the character picture we've used "complete" as the meaning.

2.

🛞 / *(The stagecoach has broken down) When the repairs to the **wheel** are **complete** the **two teddies** rush around calling **loudly** to the passengers to get back on board.*

67a　兄　**xiōng**　older brother

mouth 口 (5) + **boy** 儿 (21) = **older brother** 兄

There is also another character for "older brother" which we'll meet presently.

At the **mouth** of the cave the **boy** is acting as a look-out for his **older brother** (who has sneaked inside to see what's in there). / *[No pronunciation needed]*

67b　兑　**duì**　to convert

horns ⌄ (65a) + **older brother** 兄 (67a) = **convert** 兑

"I found these **horns**," the little girl says, holding them up proudly. "My **older brother** is going to **convert** them into something for me to play with." / *[No pronunciation needed]*

67c　讠　words

This common component, which appears on the left-hand side of characters, is a simplification of the character 言 which we'll meet later (Character 375). In our stories we usually refer to words which are written down rather than spoken.

67 shuō
say

Radical 讠
9 strokes

words 讠 (67c) + convert 兑(67b) = say 说

Another ghostly archetype (see the text after Character 59), which means "sho" from the soundword is changed into "**shuo**". We won't mention this every time it occurs from now on.

(A new aid for blind people has been invented) "All you have to do is run this gadget over the written **words** and it will **convert** them into signals which it can then **say** out loud." / *The **ghostly giant** (who is the guardian of this new device) **shows** the blind people how to use it.*

[小说(50) **xiǎoshuō** *a novel*]

68a 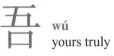 wú
yours truly

five 五(36) + mouth 口(5) = **yours truly** 吾

A literary character for "I" or "we".

The **starfish** puts the pen nib in his **mouth** to lick it, and signs off the letter with a flourish, "**Yours truly.**" / *[No pronunciation needed]*

68 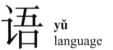 yǔ
language

Radical 讠
9 strokes

words 讠 (67c) + yours truly 吾(68a) =
language 语

Notice the pouring rain: the "u" sound in "yu" is really "ü" (see Character 15).

口语(5) **kǒuyǔ** *spoken language*
日语(6) **Rìyǔ** *Japanese (language)*

☔ (Writing a letter to your bank manager) You try to think of the correct **words** to finish with, and eventually write "**Yours truly**" — thinking that this is the sort of **language** that is expected. / *Teddy, realizing that the letter is finally finished, cries "**Eureka!**" (although it's pouring with rain so he'll get soaking wet posting it).*

69a 夕 **xī** evening

| ノ | ク | 夕 | | | | | | |

The final stroke is written in a downwards direction.

69 多 **duō** many
Radical 夕
6 strokes

| ノ | ク | 夕 | 夕 | 多 | 多 | | | |

evening 夕(69a) + evening 夕(69a) = many 多

多么(34) **duōme** *How ..?; How ..!*
[多云(56) **duōyún** *cloudy*]

(Walking along the pier each night) The friendly policeman says "**Evening, evening**" to the **many** couples he passes. / *He even stops to call "Good evening" to the **ghostly giant** who guards the **dome** at the end of the pier.*

70 名 **míng** name
Radical 夕
6 strokes

| ノ | ク | 夕 | 夕 | 名 | 名 | | | |

evening 夕(69a) + mouth 口(5) = name 名

This means "name" in the normal sense of someone's name, but also in the sense of "fame" or "repute".

有名(63) **yǒumíng** *famous, well known*

(The worried young man is looking for his girlfriend) By **evening** he had reached the **mouth** of the cave and called out her **name**. / *The **fairy** brought her out, having conjured up a **mink** coat to keep her warm.*

71 外 **wài** outside
Radical 夕
5 strokes

| ノ | ク | 夕 | 夕 | 外 | | | | |

evening 夕(69a) + fortune teller 卜(42a) = outside 外

外边(41) **wàibian** *outside*
外语(68) **wàiyǔ** *foreign language*
外文(25) **wàiwén** *foreign (written) language*
外国(60) **wàiguó** *foreign country*
[在外(55) **zàiwài** *excluded*]
[外人(12) **wàirén** *outsider, stranger*]
[外国人(60, 12) **wàiguórén** *foreigner*]

In the **evening** (after a hard day's work) the **fortune teller** likes to sit **outside** (and enjoy the fresh air). / *The **dwarf** from the next stall comes over to share her bottle of **wine** (he's too stingy to buy his own!)*

72 刀 dāo knife

Radical 刀
2 strokes

㇅	刀							

When appearing on the right-hand side of composite characters, this takes the form 刂 (see 74a).

*/ The **giant** fixed a **knife** to the **wheel** as instructed, but he had grave **doubts** about whether it would really cut the crops as it rolled along.*

[刀子(17) **dāozi** *knife*]

73 分 fēn (fèn) division

Radical 八
4 strokes

ノ	八	今	分					

eight 八(20) + **knife** 刀(72) = **division** 分

This can be a verb, "to divide", or a noun meaning a small division of something — it is used for a hundredth of a yuan or a minute (of time).

The **octopus**, with a **knife** in each tentacle, **divides** the huge pizzas into lots of equal pieces. / *The **giant** (who is on his tea break) finds it great **fun** to watch.*

十分(4) **shífēn** *totally, 100%*

74a 刂 knife

丨	刂							

When "knife" appears as the right-hand side of composite characters, it takes this form.

74b 至 zhì until

一	エ	云	云	至	至			

swoop 云(56a) + **earth** 土(54a) = **until** 至

The birds (following the farmer sowing his seeds) **swoop** down to the **earth** one after another **until** there are no seeds left. / *[No pronunciation needed]*

74 到 dào arrive

Radical 刂
8 strokes

一	エ	云	云	至	至	到	到	

until 至(74b) + **knife** 刂(74a) = **arrive** 到

Until the magic **knife** has finished trimming the decorations it is not safe for the guests to **arrive**. / *The **dwarf** says, "I have grave **doubts** about the safety of using magic knives."*

75

倒

dǎo; dào

topple; invert

Radical 亻
10 strokes

| 丿 | 亻 | 亻 | 仁 | 佢 | 佢 | 佢 | 佢 | 倒 | 倒 |

---

person 亻 (13a) + **arrive** 到 (74) =
topple; invert 倒

Here we have two meanings, and two pronunciations, but the pronunciations differ only in tone — so they share the same soundword but have different archetypes. As with Wild West/spaceship characters, the choice of which meaning/pronunciation is appropriate will depend on the context.

For this type of character (there are nine in this book) we will use *film set* stories. Each one takes place on the film set of a particular movie, and has two parts. The first part is a normal story, leading to a meaning, soundword and archetype as usual.

📽️ **Harry arrives** on the film set of a "Harry Potter" film, just as a burning candle **topples** over (and threatens to set light to everything). / *Teddy tries to douse the flames by flicking water from a fire bucket. But the dwarf shows him how to douse it properly.* \ "**Invert** the whole bucket over the fire, like this," he says.

In the second part the second archetype introduces the second meaning (remember, the soundword is the same). So if, when you see a character and the story you recall based on its parts takes place on a film set, then you know that the character has two possible meanings, with pronunciations that differ only in tone.

You may feel that with Wild West stories, ghostly dwarves and so on, and now film set stories, this is all getting too complicated. But film set stories are the last complication (honest!) and only apply to a few characters anyway. After this you can just sit back for the rest of the book.

You have already learned 75 characters, including all 20 of the "Top 20" most frequent characters in Chinese. The initial feeling of characters being "impenetrable squiggles" is behind you, and characters won't be scary ever again. Now you are into your stride, all you need to do is to keep going, slowly and steadily. Resist the temptation to race ahead; instead choose a modest schedule and stick to it, and remember to visualize the stories rather than just reading them and passing on.

At this stage, if you were learning characters by rote, you would be running into the "too many and yet too few" problem: you would know too few characters as yet to read Chinese, but at the same time too many to keep them clear in your head. Well, the first part of this is still true for you, but the second part shouldn't be, if you have been visualizing the stories. Think about it — how many hundreds of movies have you seen and yet you can still remember which is which, and what happens in each?

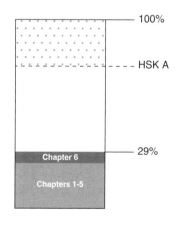

Test yourself: 妹(64) 门(27) 国(60) 白(22) 是(30) 有(63) 中(33)

朋(62) 儿(21) 她(16) 来(65) 月(61) 了(66) 好(18)

Chapter 7

On this page (as on the "basics" pages at the start of previous chapters) we have a mixure of "obvious" character pictures (such as "nail" and "cover") and others which are not (such as "car"). For the non-obvious ones, pay particular attention to what the various strokes correspond to in the character picture, so that when you see the character on its own you can imagine the character picture drawn around it.

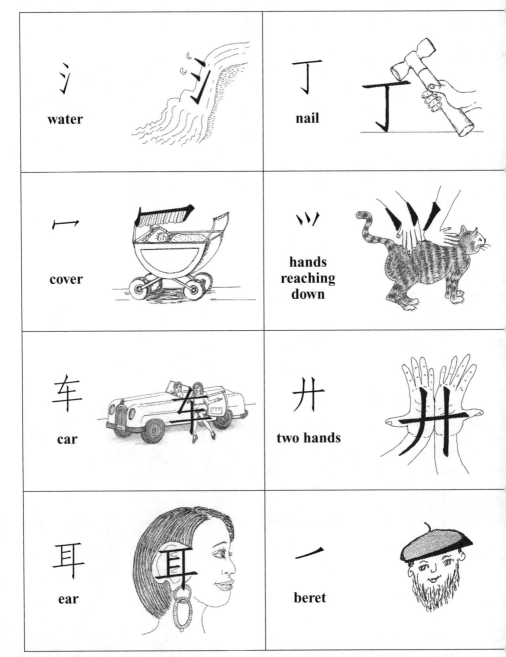

氵 water	丁 nail
cover	丷 hands reaching down
车 car	廾 two hands
耳 ear	一 beret

76

天   **tiān**   heaven

Radical 一
4 strokes

one 一(1) + big 大(47) = heaven 天

Other common meanings for this character are "sky", "day" and "weather".

The **unicorn** was so **big** that his horn seemed to touch the **heaven**s. / *But he made an ideal umpire for the two giants playing tennis (as he was tall enough to see clearly what was going on).*

白天(22)   **báitiān**   *daytime*]
天天   **tiāntiān**   *every day*]

77

明   **míng**   bright

Radical 日
8 strokes

sun 日(6) + moon 月(61) = bright 明

It's the **sun** shining on the **moon** that makes it **bright**. / *The fairy likes to wear her mink shawl in the bright moonlight.*

明天(76)   **míngtiān**   *tomorrow*
说明(67)   **shuōmíng**   *explain, explanation*

78a

water

This very common fragment is an abbreviation of the character 水 which we'll meet later (Character 523) — it takes this form when appearing as the left-hand part of composite characters. Note that the final stroke is written in an upwards direction.

78

汉   **hàn**   Han Chinese

Radical 氵
5 strokes

漢

water 氵 (78a) + right hand 又(52) = Han Chinese 汉

The Han Chinese are the majority ethnic group in China.

汉语(68)   **Hànyǔ**   *Chinese (language)*

They sprinkle **water** on their right hands before **shaking hands** to demonstrate that they are **Han Chinese**. / *The dwarf is reaching up his hand so that he can be included (because he doesn't like to miss out on things).*

79a 另 **lìng** other

mouth 口(5) + **power** 力(14) = **other** 另

Sometimes (in older typefaces) you may see the "power" part of this character replaced by "knife" (Character 72).

"Man has two types of power: physical strength is one, but "**mouth power**", the power of persuasion, is the **other**." / *[No pronunciation needed]*

---

79 别 **bié** don't — Radical 刂, 7 strokes

other 另(79a) + **knife** 刂(74a) = **don't** 别

This character is another one meaning "other", but it is also used colloquially as a negative imperative, in phrases such as "Don't touch!".

别的(23) **biéde** *other*
别人(12) **biérén** *other people*

"Use the **other knife**, **don't** use that one, we haven't sharpened it yet." / ***Two fairies*** *hold a* ***belt*** *between them to sharpen the knives on.*

---

80 如 **rú** if — Radical 女, 6 strokes

woman 女(15) + **mouth** 口(5) = **if** 如

不如(9) **bùrú** *not as (good) as*

The **woman** stands at the **mouth** of the cave, hesitating, "it looks **if**fy to me" she says. / *The* ***fairy*** *flutters over and gives her a magic* ***ruby*** *to keep her safe.*

81a 彳 step forward

slide ノ(34b) + **person** 亻(13a) = **step forward** 彳

Harry is standing at the bottom of the **slide** ready to **step forward** and catch any children who are going too fast. / *[No pronunciation needed]*

81b 丁　dīng　nail

You will also see this used to mean fourth in a sequence, much as (d) or (iv) are used in English.

81c 于　footstep

one 一 (1) + nail 丁 (81b) = footstep 于

This is a distorted form of 81a (step forward) and combines with it to form the next character.

The **unicorn** has a **nail** stuck in his hoof so you can hear his **footsteps** clattering when he's walking along the road. / *[No pronunciation needed]*

81 行　xíng; háng　Radical 彳　6 strokes
1. OK　2. line

1. step forward 彳 (81a) + footstep 于 (81c) = OK 行

2. step forward 彳 (81a) + footstep 于 (81c) = line 行

See Character 54 if you need reminding about the significance of Wild West and spaceship stories.

The two halves of this character can bracket other characters between them (see Character 710 for an example).

不行 (9)　**bùxíng**　*not allowed, not OK]*
行动 (58)　**xíngdòng**　*to move; behavior]*

1.

🔱 The sheriff looks up and down the street before he dares to **step forward**, but then he thinks he hears a **footstep** behind him. He whirls round … but it's **OK**. / *It's just the fairy fixing up a shingle at the doctor's house (and she'd dropped it).*

2.

🛸 (Outside the sickbay, the morning after the planet-leaving party). You are about to **step forward** into the sickbay when you hear a **footstep** behind you. You look back and see a long **line** of people queueing up. / *The fairy is well known for her hangover cures!*

82a 　cover

Notice the difference between this and "to bow" (51a): "cover" is much flatter.

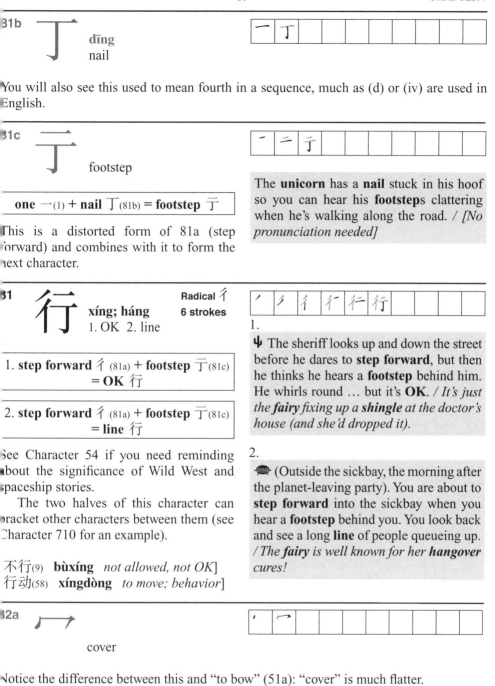

82b ⟍⟍⟋

hands reaching down

82c ⟍⟍⟋

"unveil"

hands reaching down ⟍⟍⟋ (82b) +
cover ⌒ (82a) = **unveil** ⟍⟍⟋

Imagine a row of people lined up along the roof of a new building — the band strikes up below then their **hands reach down** to pull on a **cover** to **unveil** the company's name on its new headquarters. / *[No pronunciation needed]*

82 学   **xué**   Radical 子
study   8 strokes

學

unveil ⟍⟍⟋ (82c) + **child** 子 (17) = **study** 学

大学(47)	**dàxué**	*university*
中学(33)	**zhōngxué**	*high school*
上学(42)	**shàngxué**	*attend class*
文学(25)	**wénxué**	*literature*

(At the opening of the new college) a local celebrity **unveils** a statue of a **child** in front of the main building — the child is **study**ing a book. / *[DIY pronunciation]*

83 车   **chē**   Radical 车
car   4 strokes

車

This character can mean any vehicle: a car, bus, train, etc.

*/ The **giant** is changing the **wheel** on his car, but he is careless when he takes the old wheel off and it rolls down the hill and demolishes the **church**!*

84 连   **lián**   Radical 辶
linked up   7 strokes

連

road 辶 (26a) + **car** 车 (83) = **linked up** 连

连...也...(8)   **lián A yě B**   *even A is/does B*

Imagine an isolated stretch of **road** with a single **car** on it that can't go anywhere because the road isn't **linked up** to the highway system yet. / *The **two fairies** take pity on the owner and magic up some dried **lentils** to use as gravel to make a temporary road surface.*

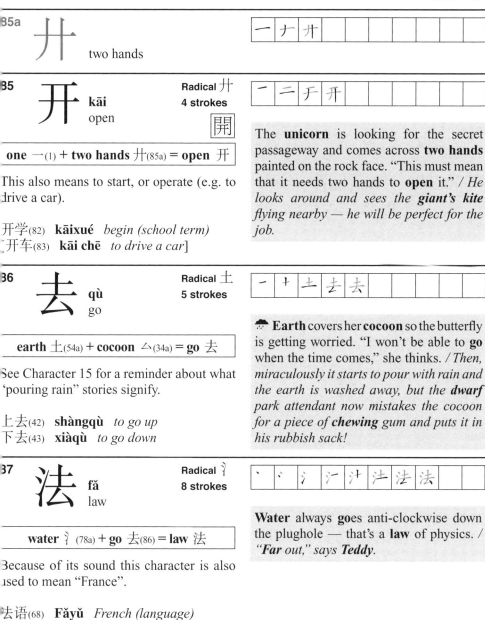

85a 廾 two hands

一 ナ 廾

---

85 开 **kāi** open

Radical 廾
4 strokes

開

一 二 干 开

one 一(1) + two hands 廾(85a) = open 开

This also means to start, or operate (e.g. to drive a car).

开学(82) **kāixué** *begin (school term)*
[开车(83) **kāi chē** *to drive a car*]

The **unicorn** is looking for the secret passageway and comes across **two hands** painted on the rock face. "This must mean that it needs two hands to **open** it." / *He looks around and sees the giant's kite flying nearby — he will be perfect for the job.*

---

86 去 **qù** go

Radical 土
5 strokes

一 十 土 去 去

earth 土(54a) + cocoon 厶(34a) = go 去

See Character 15 for a reminder about what "pouring rain" stories signify.

上去(42) **shàngqù** *to go up*
下去(43) **xiàqù** *to go down*

☂ **Earth** covers her **cocoon** so the butterfly is getting worried. "I won't be able to **go** when the time comes," she thinks. / *Then, miraculously it starts to pour with rain and the earth is washed away, but the dwarf park attendant now mistakes the cocoon for a piece of chewing gum and puts it in his rubbish sack!*

---

87 法 **fǎ** law

Radical 氵
8 strokes

丶 丶 氵 氵 氵 注 法 法

water 氵 (78a) + go 去(86) = law 法

Because of its sound this character is also used to mean "France".

法语(68) **Fǎyǔ** *French (language)*
法文(25) **Fǎwén** *(written) French*
语法(68) **yǔfǎ** *grammar*

Water always **go**es anti-clockwise down the plughole — that's a **law** of physics. / *"Far out," says Teddy.*

88a  ěr
ear

Note the stroke order here — it often seems to catch people out.

88 qǔ
acquire

Radical 耳
8 strokes

ear 耳(88a) + right hand 又(52) =
acquire 取

☂ (The secret agent has been waiting for ages for his contact to show up). When the contact finally arrives they **shake hands** and he whispers in the agent's **ear**, "You must **acquire** the secret plans to the military base," and then he walks away. / *It starts to pour with rain so* ***Teddy*** *is keen to go, because he's getting soaking wet and his* ***chewing*** *gum has run out.*

89a

"beret"

This is our name for the gently slanting stroke found at the top of some characters, such as the next one. The stroke is drawn from right to left.

89 千 qiān
thousand

Radical 十
3 strokes

beret ⌐(89a) + ten 十(4) = thousand 千

This is also used in a general sense to mean "numerous".

This is another "Do It Yourself" (DIY) pronunciation. There are something like fifty DIY pronunciations scattered through the book.

If you do want to construct a pronunciation part of this story for yourself then you will need a soundword for "chen". If it helps, the nearest we can find is "Chennai" (the city

(Picture a war-grave cemetery at the site of a commando landing) — rows and rows of **cross**es with a regimental **beret** on each one — a **thousand** in neat rows. / *[DIY pronunciation]*

in India which used to be called Madras). I you have two giants from Chennai, mak sure to give them some distinctive clothes o some other memorable features!

[三千(3) **sānqiān** *three thousand*]

90a

ﾍ丷

"feet"

丶	丷	丷							

horns ﾍ丷 (65a) + **one** 一 (1) = **feet** 丷

Sneaking up on a **unicorn** in the forest, he sees **horns**. "I thought unicorns only had one horn?" he says under his breath. But when he gets closer he realises that the unicorn is asleep on its back and what he'd seen was its **feet**! / *[No pronunciation needed]*

90b

刖 canoe

丿	冂	月	月	刖'	刖				

moon 月 (61) + **knife** 刂 (74a) = **canoe** 刖

The **moon**light glinting on his **knife** shows him where he had dropped it — in his **canoe**! / *[No pronunciation needed]*

90

前 qián
in front of

Radical 丷
9 strokes

丶	丷	丷	丷	前	前	前	前	前	

feet 丷 (90a) + **canoe** 刖 (90b) =
in front of 前

Your **feet** in a **canoe** are out **in front of** you! / *[DIY pronunciation]*

Another DIY pronunciation (see Character 9).

前边 (41) **qiánbiān** *front, in front of*

Test yourself: 外 (71)   去 (86)   名 (70)   这 (26)   倒 (75)   说 (67)   别 (79)

的 (23)   语 (68)   连 (84)   多 (69)   手 (31)   天 (76)   我 (32)

We've had a few characters now where we've said that alternative stories are possible — in one case (Character 56) we've even given one. Alternative stories are fine, and not only where there is an alternative way of breaking a character down into basic building blocks. They are also perfectly acceptable if you simply don't like one of the stories for any reason — and in particular if you have problems visualizing or remembering it. At the end of the book we will give some hints for making up your own stories (for characters beyond this book) — but the main tips are to make the stories as vivid and quirky as you can — bizarre or silly even — and to make sure the parts of the story interact together (rather than just sitting there side by side, as it were).

Chapter 8

Quite often there will be pairs of basic building blocks which are very similar to one another. An example is the pair "west" and "whisky bottle" below. So that you can compare them, we have tried to put such pairs together in the same chapter. Clearly it's a good idea when you are learning these to pay particular attention to the parts of the characters where any differences lie, so that you will remember which is which.

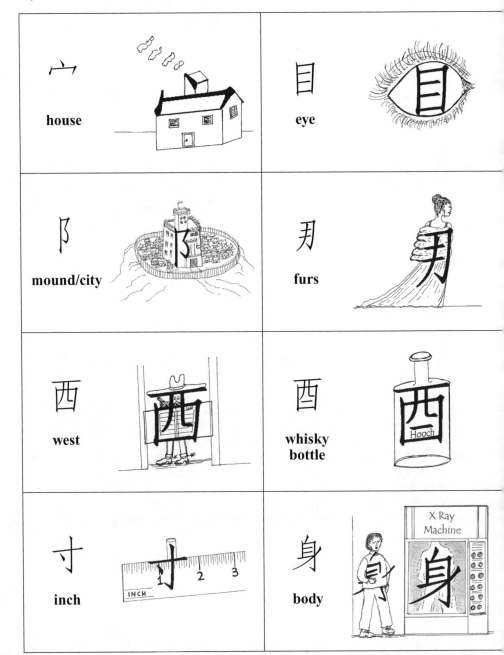

宀	eye
house	目

阝	爿
mound/city	furs

西	酉
west	whisky bottle

寸	身
inch	body

91a 宀

house

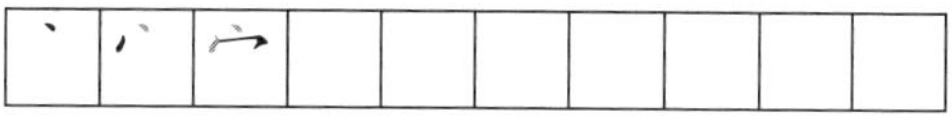

---

91 安 **ān** peace

Radical 宀
6 strokes

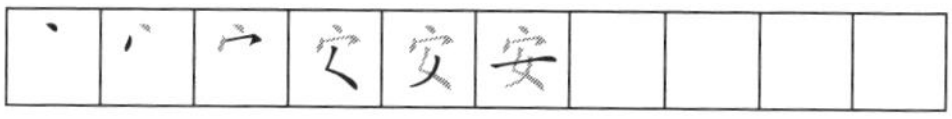

house 宀(91a) + **woman** 女(15) = **peace** 安

[天安门(76, 27) **Tiān'ānmén** *Tiananmen (Gate of Heavenly Peace) in Beijing*]

The **woman** is alone in the **house** at last, and looking forward to some **peace** and quiet. / *But the* ***giant*** *starts working on his* ***anvil*** *next door, and there is peace no more!*

---

92 字 **zì** Chinese character

Radical 宀
6 strokes

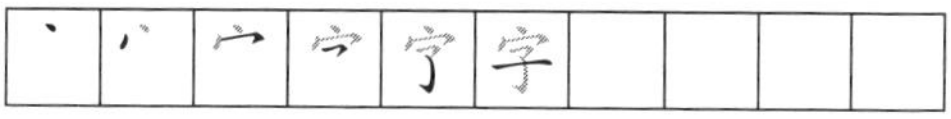

house 宀(91a) + **child** 子(17) = **Chinese character** 字

汉字(78) **Hànzì** *Chinese character*
名字(70) **míngzì** *name, given name*

The **child** has to stay in the **house** to learn her **Chinese characters**. / *She recites them out loud until the* ***dwarf*** *babysitter dozes off, and when she hears the "zzz" sounds she sneaks out to play.*

---

93 目 **mù** eye

Radical 目
5 strokes

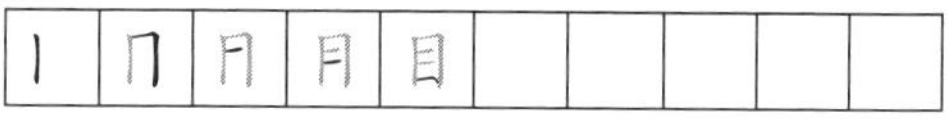

目前(90) **mùqián** *at present*

/ *In the factory the* ***dwarf*** *keeps his* ***eye*** *on the* ***wheel****. He's in a bad* ***mood*** *(because the relief shift hasn't turned up yet).*

---

94 自 **zì** self

Radical 自
6 strokes

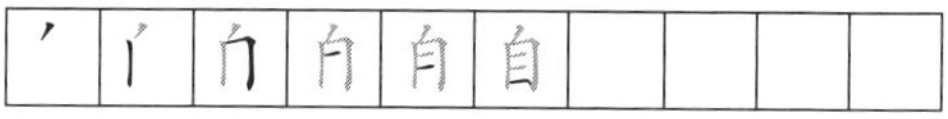

a drop 丶(22a) + **eye** 目(93) = **self** 自

Take care not to confuse this character with "white" (Character 22).

[自动(58) **zìdòng** *automatic*]
自行车(81, 83) **zìxíngchē** *bicycle*

"You'll need to put **a drop** of this in your **eye**," the doctor said, "but you'll have to do it your**self**. / *I can hear from the "zzz" sound that my* ***dwarf*** *assistant is asleep again."*

95 咱 zán we

Radical 口
9 strokes

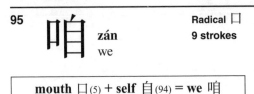

mound 口 (5) + self 自 (94) = we 咱

This is used in situations where "we" includes both the speaker and the person being spoken to.

The two friends stand at the **mouth** of the cave. "I'm not going in there by my**self**," she says. "You don't have to, **we**'ll go together," says her friend. / *"If we don't go in, we won't find out what the fairy has brought back from Zanzibar for us."*

咱们 (28) **zánmen** *we (including you)*

96a 阝 mound; city

This is the only component whose meaning depends on where it appears in a character. When it's on the left it means "mound", but when it's on the right it means "city". Examples of each follow in the next few characters. We realise that this is confusing but because everyone else observes this distinction, we will too. The situation arose because 阝 is an abbreviation of two completely different older characters, one which always appeared on the left and another which always appeared on the right. A similar situation applies to a few other characters, but modern Chinese doesn't distinguish between them so you don't have to worry about those!

Nowadays this fragment is regarded as being written with only two stokes, but traditionally it was classed as having three strokes.

96 阳 yáng in the open

Radical 阝
6 strokes

陽

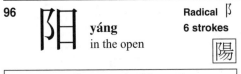

mound 阝(96a) + sun 日 (6) = in the open 阳

It's best to read this and the next story together. Yin and yang (this character and the following one) are the two opposing forces in Taoist philosophy. Yang is the force associated with being overt, in the sun, positive and masculine; and yin with things hidden or occult, cloudy, negative or feminine (insert here a comment of your

When the **sun** shines, the creatures that live in the **mound** come out **into the open**. / *The fairy visits the mound in the day-time to develop her yang side.*

choice about male chauvinism!). In the stories the fairy and the giant are getting in touch with their masculine and feminine sides, respectively.

太阳 (48) **tàiyáng** *the sun; sunshine*

97 阴 **yīn** hidden

Radical 阝
6 strokes

陰

mound 阝(96a) + moon 月(61) = hidden 阴

[阴天(76) **yīntiān** *a cloudy day*]

When the **moon** is up, the creatures burrow into the **mound** so that they are **hidden**. / *The giant now comes at night-time, to develop his yin side.*

98a 月 furs

---

98 那 **nà** that

Radical 阝
6 strokes

furs 月(98a) + city 阝(96a) = that 那

This character can (colloquially) also be pronounced **nèi**.

Every time she sees a **fur** coat in a shop window in the **city** she says, "That one, I want **that** one." / *The dwarf is well and truly fed up with this. "It's enough to drive you to narcotics," he grumbles.*

那个(19) **nàge** *that one*
那么(34) **nàme** *so, in that manner*
那儿(21) **nàr** *there (spoken)*
[那边(41) **nàbiān** *that side*]

---

99 哪 **nǎ (na)** which?

Radical 口
9 strokes

mouth 口(5) + that 那(98) = which? 哪

This character can also (colloquially) be pronounced **něi**.

It also has another role, for which the pronunciation is **na** with neutral tone. This is explained later (see 啊, Character 143).

[那儿(21) **nǎr** *where (spoken)*
哪个(19) **nǎge** *which*]

(At the dentist) She opens her **mouth** and points to a tooth, "It's **that** one which hurts." "Which?" asks the dentist (peering more closely). / *Teddy, trying to be helpful, has brought along some narcotics in case she needs some...*

100 西 xī — west

Radical 西
6 strokes

一 丆 冂 币 西 西

When this character appears at the top of other characters, the central two strokes are compressed into short vertical lines: this happens in the next character.

/ *The enormous* **wheel** *that hangs on the* **west** *gate of the city is the perfect size for the* **giant** *to use as a* **shield** *(so he pinches it!)*

西边(41) **xībiān** *the west side*
[西安(91) **Xī'ān** *Xian (the city)*]

101 要 yào; yāo — want; ask for

Radical 西
9 strokes

一 丆 冂 币 西 西 覀 要 要

west 西(100) + woman 女(15) =
want; ask for 要

This is the second example of a character with two pronunciations, which share the same spelling and differ only in tone. Recall that this is signalled by a film set story: so the two meanings are associated with two different archetypes (see Character 75).

When it uses the fourth tone this character can sometimes be used with another verb, it then means "must" or "have to".

 As a **West**ern **woman** alone in an Eastern culture, think of the King of Siam's tutor in "The King and I" — so this is a film set story. As the director calls "Cut!" for the umpteenth time, the actress playing the leading role shouts, "What do you **want** from me?" / *She storms off stepping on the* **dwarf's** *foot, causing him to shout "Yeow!" For good measure she also kicks the* **giant's** *foot and he says "Yeow!" too — (but more in surprise than pain).* \ "All I did was **ask for** her autograph!" he complains.

不要(9) **búyào** *Don't ...*
要是(30) **yàoshì** *if*

102a 酉 yǒu — whisky bottle

一 丆 冂 币 西 西 酉

102 酒 jiǔ — liquor

Radical 氵
10 strokes

丶 冫 氵 沪 汀 沔 沔 洒 酒 酒

water 氵 (78a) + whisky bottle 酉(102a) =
liquor 酒

They had put **water** in the **whisky bottle**, pretending it was **liquor**. / *The two teddies passed the bottle between them (pretending to be drunk) and thought this was a great joke.*

[酒杯(11) **jiǔbēi** *wine glass*]

103 从 cóng from

Radical 人
4 strokes

從

person 人(12) + person 人(12) = from 从

Note the second stroke, which is truncated into a drop. This is a rare occasion when "person" on the left-hand side of a character does not take the form 亻.

For pronunciations beginning with "c" see the note for Character 104 below.

Harry unwraps the large parcel — and inside is a statue of Harry himself. He looks through the packaging to see who it's **from**. / *[DIY pronunciation]*

从...到...(74) **cóng A dào B** *from A to B*
从前(90) **cóngqián** *the past*
自从(94) **zìcóng** *since (a time/date)*

104a 寸 cùn inch

Note that the vertical stroke is off center and has a hook at the end.

---

104 村 cūn village

Radical 木
7 strokes

tree 木(10a) + inch 寸(104a) = village 村

Pronunciations begining with "c" (unless they begin "ch") give us a problem: the letter "c" in the Pinyin system stands for the sound "ts", but hardly any English words begin with "ts". Our solution to this problem is to use soundwords which begin "st" instead. So if a soundword begins "st" you must reverse the s and t to get the

They have to measure the girth of the **tree** in **inch**es, to check that it will be the right size for the **village** square. / *The giant has offered to erect it for them and it will look stunning once it is decorated.*

pronunciation. There are 14 such characters in the book; the next one isn't until Chapter 15.

[村子(17) **cūnzi** *village*]

---

105 时 shí time

Radical 日
7 strokes

時

sun 日(6) + inch 寸(104a) = time 时

The **sun**dial is marked out in **inch**es to tell the **time**. / *The fairy is sitting on it smoking a cheroot!*

小时(50) **xiǎoshí** *hour*
有时(63) **yǒushí** *sometimes*]

106  **guò**
to cross

Radical 辶
6 strokes

road 辶(26a) + inch 寸(104a) = cross 过

过来(65) **guòlái** *come across*
过去(86) **guòqù** *in the past*

The snail on the **road** can only travel an **inch** every hour so it takes all day **to cross** the road. / *The **ghostly dwarf**, who's been assigned to protect him, urges him on, "**Go**, go, go!" (he wants to get home for his tea).*

---

107 身 **shēn**
body

Radical 身
7 strokes

It is worth writing this character a few times to get the hang of the stroke order.

[动身(58) **dòng shēn** *set off (on journey)*]
[身边(41) **shēnbiān** *on one's person*]

/ *(The railway has been attacked and there is a gap in the tracks over the bridge). The **giant** lets the **wheels** of the train run over his **body** and saves the day — but he's now too tired to go back to his usual job of **shunting** carriages.*

108a **shè**
to shoot

body 身(107) + inch 寸(104a) = shoot 射

Note that the final stroke of "body" gets truncated here.

The sniper moves his **body** forward an **inch** at a time until he has a clear view and can **shoot** at his target. / *[No pronunciation needed]*

---

108 谢 **xiè**
thank

Radical 讠
12 strokes

謝

words 讠 (67c) + shoot 射(108a) = thank 谢

[谢谢你(51) **xièxie nǐ** *thank you*]

The bank robbers had used their guns to **shoot** holes in the bank's door spelling out the words "**thank** you" before they left. / *The **two dwarves** agree to let them stash the money in their **shed** until the heat is off. (Try to visualize both of the dwarves — maybe one is holding open the shed door, while the other one keeps a look out for the cops!)*

Chapter 9

The character picture for "of" on this page is a great example of how character pictures can work their magic.

  If you just look at the shape of the character 之 on its own, does it suggest "of"? No, it doesn't. But if you look at the character picture for a moment, and then look back to the character itself, don't you now immediately see the prow of a ship and the swell of a wave on the ocean? This image is now probably with you for life, reminding you of the ship's name "Pride **of** the Seas". If this works for you, then the character picture has done its job! The fact that the character doesn't actually have anything to do with ships doesn't matter at all.

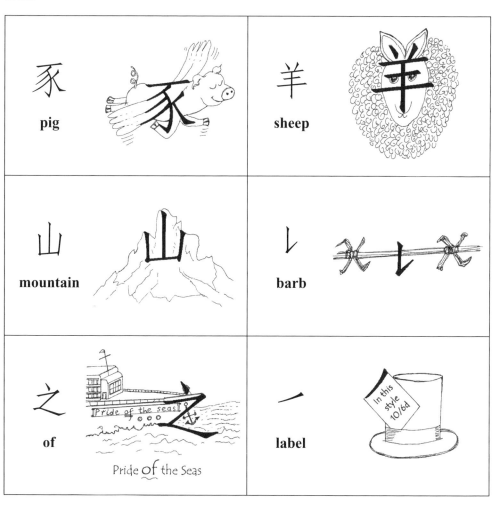

109a 豕 pig

| 一 | 丆 | 丂 | 亐 | 豸 | 豕 | 豕 | | | |

---

109 家 jiā household — Radical 宀 10 strokes

| 丶 | 丷 | 宀 | 宀 | 宀 | 宁 | 宇 | 宁 | 宏 | 家 |

house 宀(91a) + pig 豕(109a) = household 家

"If you have a **pig** in your **house** it must be included in your **household**." / *The **two giants** debate the meaning of the **jargon** on the census form.*

大家(47) **dàjiā** *everyone*
国家(60) **guójiā** *nation state*

---

110 山 shān mountain — Radical 山 3 strokes

| 丨 | 屮 | 山 | | | | | | | |

/ *Taking a break from pushing the huge **wheel** up the **mountain**, the **giant** stops for a swig of **shandy**.*

---

111 羊 yáng sheep — Radical 羊 6 strokes

| 丶 | 丷 | 兰 | 半 | 兰 | 羊 | | | | |

We treat this as a basic building block as it is traditionally a picture.

/ *The stupid **sheep** has got his head stuck in the spokes of the wagon **wheel**. The **fairy** has to come and **yank** him out.*

[小羊(50) **xiǎoyáng** *lamb*]
[山羊(110) **shānyáng** *goat*]

---

112 样 yàng appearance — Radical 木 10 strokes 樣

| 一 | 十 | 才 | 木 | 术 | 杧 | 栏 | 样 | 样 | 样 |

tree 木(10a) + sheep 羊(111) = appearance 样

那样(98) **nàyàng** *so, in that manner*
样子(17) **yàngzi** *appearance, manner*
一样(1) **yíyàng** *same, identical*
这样(26) **zhèyàng** *like this*

The **tree** is a good place for the escaped **sheep** to hide while he changes his **appearance**. / *But the **dwarf** (shepherd) finds him and **yanks** him off back to the flock.*

113 班 bān team

Radical 王
10 strokes

| 一 | 二 | 丬 | 王 | 五 | 玑 | 玌 | 玨 | 玔 | 班 |

king 王(60a) + **knife** 刂(74a) + **king** 王(60a)
= **team** 班

You will see that we have broken this character down into three parts, and so the equation and story have three components to them. We will only do this for a few characters where it seems "natural" to do so. When a character is made up of three parts ABC, it usually splits most naturally into A and BC, because the combination BC already means something. Examples are 倒, 哪, 谢 (Characters 75, 99 and 108).

At the inter-kingdom quiz, the **two kings** sit on either side of the beautiful jewelled **knife** that will be presented to the winning **team**. / *For the final deciding question the teams have to identify a picture of the* **giant** *in a* **bandanna**.

Note that the final stroke of the first "king" slopes upwards (compare 54a).

[上班(42) **shàng bān** *to go to work*]
[下班(43) **xià bān** *leave/finish work*]

114 出 chū exit

Radical 山
5 strokes

| 乚 | 屮 | 屮 | 出 | 出 | | | | | |

mountain 山(110) + **mountain** 山(110) =
exit 出

The stroke order shows that, despite appearances, this character is not *really* two mountains!

(Arriving in the train station in Switzerland) You can see **mountain** upon **mountain** out of each **exit**. / *The* **giant** *is sitting on one of them* **chewing** *gum.*

出来(65) **chūlái** *come out*
出去(86) **chūqù** *go out*
[出口(5) **chūkǒu** *exit; to export*]

Test yourself: 友(53) 行(81) 汉(78) 刀(72) 如(80) 身(107) 分(73)
机(10) 阴(97) 明(77) 到(74) 法(87) 谢(108) 四(24)

115a 石 shí stone

| 一 | 丆 | 丆 | 石 | 石 | | | | | |

thumb tack ⌐(40a) + **mouth** 口(5) =
stone 石

Notice how the thumb tack has slid off to the side — it is not fixed to the top of the character (as in, for example, 百, Character 40).

You're trying to fix up a notice saying "Slippery Stones" with a **thumb tack** at the **mouth** of the cave, but (ironically) it keeps slipping on the **stone**. / *[No pronunciation needed]*

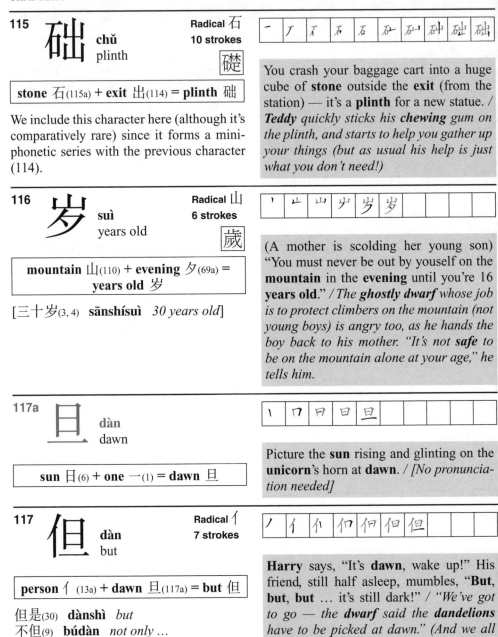

115   础   chǔ   plinth   Radical 石   10 strokes   礎

stone 石(115a) + exit 出(114) = **plinth** 础

We include this character here (although it's comparatively rare) since it forms a mini-phonetic series with the previous character (114).

You crash your baggage cart into a huge cube of **stone** outside the **exit** (from the station) — it's a **plinth** for a new statue. / *Teddy quickly sticks his chewing gum on the plinth, and starts to help you gather up your things (but as usual his help is just what you don't need!)*

116   岁   suì   years old   Radical 山   6 strokes   歲

mountain 山(110) + evening 夕(69a) = **years old** 岁

[三十岁(3, 4)   **sānshísuì**   *30 years old*]

(A mother is scolding her young son) "You must never be out by youself on the **mountain** in the **evening** until you're 16 **years old**." / *The ghostly dwarf whose job is to protect climbers on the mountain (not young boys) is angry too, as he hands the boy back to his mother. "It's not* **safe** *to be on the mountain alone at your age," he tells him.*

117a   旦   dàn   dawn

sun 日(6) + one 一(1) = **dawn** 旦

Picture the **sun** rising and glinting on the **unicorn**'s horn at **dawn**. / *[No pronunciation needed]*

117   但   dàn   but   Radical 亻   7 strokes

person 亻 (13a) + dawn 旦(117a) = **but** 但

但是(30)   **dànshì**   *but*
不但(9)   **búdàn**   *not only …*

Harry says, "It's **dawn**, wake up!" His friend, still half asleep, mumbles, "**But, but, but** … it's still dark!" / *"We've got to go — the dwarf said the dandelions have to be picked at dawn." (And we all know how cross he'll be if they don't do it right…)*

118a 导 get

| ╲ | 冖 | 彐 | 日 | 旦 | 旦 | 寻 | 导 | | |

dawn 旦(117a) + **inch** 寸(104a) = **get** 导

She wakes up at **dawn** and sees beautiful icicles an **inch** long at the window. "**Get** a camera, we must **get** a picture of these before the sun melts them," she says. / *[No pronunciation needed]*

118 得 dé; de; děi — Radical 彳 — **11 strokes**
1. obtain 2. way
3. must

| ╱ | ╱ | 彳 | 个 | 彳 | 彳 | 彳 | 得 | 得 | 得 |
| 得 | | | | | | | | | |

1. **step forward** 彳 (81a) + **get** 导(118a) = **obtain** 得

2. **step forward** 彳 (81a) + **get** 导(118a) = **way** 得

3. **step forward** 彳 (81a) + **get** 导(118a) = **must** 得

This is the one and only character in HSK Level A which has *three* pronunciations — and three meanings to go with them. When 得 is pronounced **dé** it means "to obtain"; pronounced **de** it means "in such a way that", and pronounced **děi** it means "have to".

To keep these straight we have a special story with three parts: the setting is the medal presentation ceremony at the Olympic games (you can decide for yourself which event they have all taken part in or just make one up — the sillier it is, the better!) Now, whenever you see this character and break it down into "step forward" plus "get", picture the medal ceremony, and then you can run through the story for each of the medals, Gold, Silver and Bronze and recall each of the three meanings which go with them. You have to look at the context to see which of these is appropriate in each case — as you have to with characters which have *two*

1.

He **steps forward** to **get** the gold medal — he had won by **obtain**ing the best overall score. / *But there was a dearth of gold so the fairy had conjured up a temporary medal until a proper one could be made.*

2.

He **steps forward** to **get** the silver medal — the **way** he had performed had been the best (but he had lost technical marks). / *The robot polishes the medal as it's dusty and he likes all silver things (like himself) to be shiny.*

3.

He **steps forward** to **get** the bronze medal — he had done all the bits he **must** do (the compulsory bits) but nothing more. / *Teddy puts the bronze medal on a daisy chain to try and cheer up the third place competitor.*

pronunciations (and which have Wild West/ spaceship or film set stories). Of course you'll get used to seeing this character and knowing the pronunciation automatically before long.

得到(74) **dédào** *get, obtain*
取得(88) **qǔdé** *achieve, obtain*

Test yourself: 前(90) 过(106) 开(85) 咱(95) 车(83) 文(25) 村(104)

取(88) 样(112) 阳(96) 时(105) 千(89) 学(82) 哪(99)

119

公　gōng
public

Radical 八
4 strokes

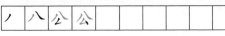

eight 八(20) + cocoon 厶(34a) = **public** 公

[公开(85) **gōngkāi** *open, public*]

The **octopus** lives in a **cocoon** which he is so proud of that he throws it open to the **public**. / *The giant sounds a gong to attract visitors.*

120a

"barb"

This is used in the following character and we will see it again later in the book. Note that the downward vertical line and the hook together count as only one stroke.

120

以　yǐ
using

Radical 人
4 strokes

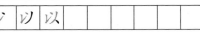

barb レ (120a) + a drop 丶 (22a) +
person 人 (12) = **using** 以

Harry puts a **drop** of colored wax on the **barb** of his fish-hook, **using** the bright colors of the wax to attract the fish. / *Teddy tries it too, and catches an eel.*

The meaning of this character is hard to pin down in English: depending on how it is used, it could be translated by words such as "using", "by means of", "according to", "in order to", etc. It is also used in "positional" compounds such as the two given here.

以前(90)　**yǐqián**　*before; a while ago*
以外(71)　**yǐwài**　*apart from, except*

121

之　zhī
of

Radical 丶
3 strokes

/ *The giant is playing the Wheel Of Fortune and wins a trip to Japan (he has always wanted to see Mount Fuji).*

This character is a literary equivalent of "of" (Character 23) and is found in certain fixed expressions.

分之(73)　**fēnzhī**　*fraction of*
[之前(90)　**A zhīqián**　*before A*]
[之下(43)　**A zhīxià**　*below A*]
[之中(33)　**A zhīzhōng**　*among A*]

122

为 **wéi; wèi**
act as; for

Radical 丶
4 strokes

為

| 丶 | ノ | 力 | 为 | | | | | | |

power 力(14) + a drop 丶 (22a) +
a drop 丶 (22a) = act as; for 为

By now you'll be familiar with the idea of using film set stories for characters with two meanings and two pronunciations (which differ only in tone). In future we'll rely on the film icon to signal them for you.

Note that the stroke order for the "power" part of this character is non-standard. This is because it is inherited from the traditional form (shown in the box). Compare this with the stroke order for Character 123 which follows.

🎬 The potion which confers great **power** from only a **couple of drops** is the Gauls' magic potion in the film of "Asterix". On the film set the main actor has to **act as** if he is strong. / *The fairy conjures up fake **weights** for him to lift. The dwarf grumbles as he carries the **weights**.* \ "Why does somebody have to carry these things around **for** him?"

为了(66) **wèile** *for, because of*
以为(120) **yǐwéi** *think (wrongly)*
为什么(35, 34) **wèishénme** *why, what for*

123

办 **bàn**
manage

Radical 力
4 strokes

辦

| 了 | 力 | 办 | 办 | | | | | | |

power 力(14) + eight 八(20) = manage 办

Both this and the previous character consist of "power" plus a couple of drops. To distinguish between them, we have cheated slightly here, and think of this one as being "power" plus "eight".

The "**power-octopus**" is a big eight-armed machine in the factory, so complicated that it needs someone to **manage** it full-time. / *The dwarf banishes everyone else from the vicinity.*

办法(87) **bànfǎ** *method*
[办公(119) **bàngōng** *(office) work*]

Test yourself: 行(81) 子(17) 西(100) 安(91) 班(113) 自(94) 正(29)
那(98) 家(109) 字(92) 力(14) 要(101) 口(5) 吗(45)

124a

"label"

| 丿 | | | | | | | | | |

The "label" is always attached to a horizontal stroke, as in the following character. Compare this with "beret" (89a) which is a longer, more gently sloping stroke (usually attached to a vertical stroke), and "a drop" (22a) which is not attached to anything (unless sitting on top of something).

124b

"clouds"

label ╱ (124a) + one 一(1) = clouds ㇒

There's a **label** on the side of the **unicorn** in the safari park (saying "unicorn"), because he usually has his head in the **clouds**. (People kept mistaking him for a horse because they couldn't see his horn when it was in the clouds). / *[No pronunciation needed]*

---

124 干

gān; gàn
dry; work

Radical 一
3 strokes

one 一(1) + ten 十(4) = dry; work 干

干 **gàn** also means the trunk or main part of something. **Gān** and **gàn** were once two separate characters (which is why there are two traditional forms).

When 干 appears as part of another character, we will use the meaning "dry" in the equation and the story.

[干杯(11) **gān bēi** *Bottoms up! (on drinking a toast)*]
[干吗(45) **gàn ma** *what (are you) doing?*]

▭ Picture the **unicorn** standing on a white **cross** on the floor, which is his mark on the film set of "The Wizard of Oz" — they are filming in the Emerald City. Everything is ready but they must wait for **dry** weather. / *Then the giant can erect the lighting gantry. The dwarf kicks the gantry poles angrily.* \ "When are we going to get any **work** done?"

---

125 午

wǔ
noon

Radical ノ
4 strokes

clouds ㇒(124b) + ten 十(4) = noon 午

Another way of looking at this character is to see it as "label" plus "dry". Our rule, for deciding when to use clouds and when to use label, will be: if we can see clouds on the top of a character we will use clouds, otherwise we use label.

上午(42) **shàngwǔ** *morning*
中午(33) **zhōngwǔ** *noon*
下午(43) **xiàwǔ** *afternoon*

The morning **clouds** go in one direction, the afternoon clouds go in another direction, so when the clouds **cross** it must be **noon**. / *Teddy whoops with delight, as this means it's lunchtime.*

126a
hé
grain

| 一 | 二 | 千 | 千 | 禾 | | | | |

beret 一 (89a) + **tree** 木 (10a) = **grain** 禾

Notice how "beret" differs from "label".

The meaning of "grain" embraces all cereal plants, including rice.

The **beret** (that they'd been using as a frisbee) is now stuck in a **tree** and they won't be able to retrieve it without trampling the **grain** growing around the tree. (Who's going to be the one to ask the farmer if they can get it?) / *[No pronunciation needed]*

126
hé; huó
1. with 2. mix

Radical 禾
8 strokes

| 一 | 二 | 千 | 千 | 禾 | 禾 | 禾 | 和 | 和 | |

1. **grain** 禾 (126a) + **mouth** 口 (5) = **with** 和

2. **grain** 禾 (126a) + **mouth** 口 (5) = **mix** 和

1.

↓ The cowboy rolls the **grain** around in his **mouth** and says, "This needs something to go **with** it." / *The **fairy** says, "Try it with some of my **herbs**."*

hé means "with" in the sense of "along ... nd is often translated simply as

... become reconciled]

2.

(A baby alien has sneaked aboard the spaceship) They find it sitting on the storeroom floor, stuffing **grain** in its **mouth** and getting all the carefully-labeled grain samples **mixed** up. / *The **ghostly fairy** who protects the planet comes to fetch the alien and take it **home**.*

...his progress so that you don't "lose" ...ed. One way is to keep up with ...uch as the one below, whenever ...ou can also test yourself on the ...ly by writing out the characters f... ...of paper or card (good writing pr...

...cter (it happens), go back and visu... ...will almost certainly find you had ... ...ly without letting it sink in. Visua... ...add one or two details to the scene t...

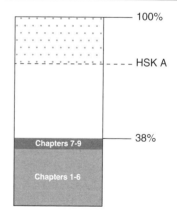

Chapter 10

You will see that "plant" on this page is the same as "earth" (10a) with an additional stroke. Similarly, "use" is the same as "moon" (61) with an extra stroke. As a refresher quiz, see if you can remember the meanings of these characters and fragments — in each pair the difference is a single stroke:

大　夫　　　上　止
了　子　　　大　天
十　千　　　木　禾
木　未　　　西　酉
日　白　　　目　自

母　mother

十　criminal

用　to use

生　plant

工　to work

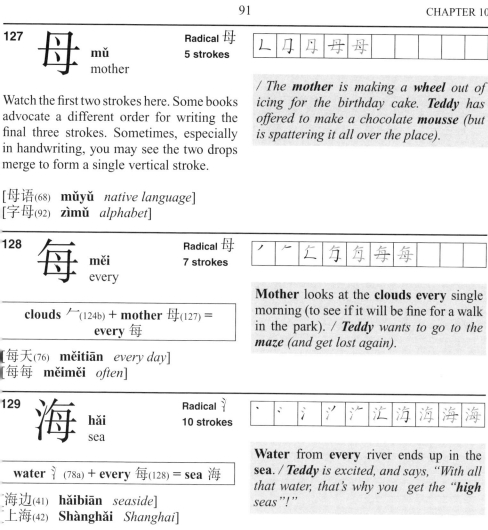

127 母 mǔ mother

Radical 母
5 strokes

Watch the first two strokes here. Some books advocate a different order for writing the final three strokes. Sometimes, especially in handwriting, you may see the two drops merge to form a single vertical stroke.

/ The **mother** is making a **wheel** out of icing for the birthday cake. **Teddy** has offered to make a chocolate **mousse** (but is spattering it all over the place).

[母语(68) **mǔyǔ** *native language*]
[字母(92) **zìmǔ** *alphabet*]

128 每 měi every

Radical 母
7 strokes

clouds 宀(124b) + mother 母(127) = every 每

Mother looks at the **clouds every** single morning (to see if it will be fine for a walk in the park). / *Teddy* wants to go to the *maze (and get lost again).*

[每天(76) **měitiān** *every day*]
[每每 **měiměi** *often*]

129 海 hǎi sea

Radical 氵
10 strokes

water 氵(78a) + every 每(128) = sea 海

Water from **every** river ends up in the **sea**. / *Teddy* is excited, and says, "With all that water, that's why you get the "**high seas**"!"

[海边(41) **hǎibiān** *seaside*]
[上海(42) **Shànghǎi** *Shanghai*]

130a 十 "criminal"

130 用 yòng to use

Radical 冂
5 strokes

Try to visualize a particular setting for this story — what type of wheel are we talking about here?

/ The **dwarf** says, "You're too **young** to **use** the **wheel**."

[不用(9) **búyòng** *don't have to*]
[有用(63) **yǒuyòng** *useful*]

131  **bàn** half

Radical 丨
5 strokes

---

horns ∨ (65a) + criminal 丰 (130a) =
half 半

半天(76) **bàntiān** *a long time*
[多半(69) **duōbàn** *more often than not*]

(At the prison Christmas pantomime) The toughest **criminal** grabbed the **horns** as he wanted to be the front **half** of the pantomime bull. / *The dwarf governor (who suspected trouble) made them put **bandages** over the horns so that nobody could get hurt.*

---

132   **lì** benefit

Radical 禾
7 strokes

---

grain 禾(126a) + knife 刂(74a) = benefit 利

利用(130) **lìyòng** *make use of*
[有利(63) **yǒulì** *advantageous*]

Each **grain** must be split open with a **knife** to get the full **benefit** of the nutrients. / *The dwarf cooks it in a liter of water and leaves it to soak.*

133a   plant

一 二 丰 主

---

133 生 **shēng** life

Radical 丿
5 strokes

丿 一 匕 牛 生

---

label ∕ (124a) + plant 主 (133a) = life 生

Recall the discussion (Character 125) about labels and clouds. Although you could see "clouds" in this character, they are not at the top of the character (which is where clouds rightfully belong), so we use label instead.

This character has various meanings connected with life, in particular birth and growth; it can also mean unripe, uncooked.

生日(6) **shēngrì** *birthday*
[出生(114) **chūshēng** *to be born*]
学生(82) **xuéshēng** *student, pupil*
[女生(15) **nǚshēng** *female student*]

Every house in the village has **plant**s with **labels** displayed in the windows. It's the custom that when a new child is born, a plant is chosen to symbolize their **life** (and labeled with the child's name). / *[DIY pronunciation]*

134 胜 shèng triumph

Radical 月
9 strokes

勝

| ノ | 刀 | 月 | 月 | 月 | 肝 | 胖 | 胖 | 胜 |

moon 月(61) + life 生(133) = triumph 胜

The astronauts who first discover **moon life** will return in **triumph**. / [DIY pronunciation]

胜利(132) **shènglì** win; victory

[名胜(70) **míngshèng** a famous scenic spot]

---

135 姓 xìng surname

Radical 女
8 strokes

| し | 女 | 女 | 女 | 姓 | 姓 | 姓 | 姓 |

woman 女(15) + life 生(133) = surname 姓

(A group of women are talking together) "Even though it's the **woman** who gives birth to **life**, the baby still gets the man's **surname**." / They have been watching the **dwarf** across the road putting up his name on a **shingle**.

[姓名(70) **xìngmíng** full name]

---

136 星 xīng star

Radical 日
9 strokes

| ヽ | 口 | 日 | 日 | 戸 | 旦 | 早 | 星 | 星 |

sun 日(6) + life 生(133) = star 星

"Our **sun** is vital to all **life** on our planet, yet it is just a **star**." / The **giant**, lying on his back on the **shingle** on the beach, looks up at the night sky and ponders.

So here we have two mini phonetic series: Characters 133, 134 ("**sheng**"), and 135, 136 ("**xing**"). You can see from the similarity of these two sounds that they had a common origin.

[星星 **xīngxīng** star]

[明星(77) **míngxīng** (movie) star]

137a 生 "calf"

| ノ | 仁 | 仕 | 生 |

label ノ(124a) + earth 土(54a) = calf 生

You see a **label** lying on the **earth** — the **calf** has been newly tagged on its ear (but has managed to dislodge his label by rubbing his ear on the ground). / [No pronunciation needed]

If you take the tail off the character for cow (Character 384) this is what you get!

137 先 **xiān** ahead

Radical 儿 6 strokes

calf 牛(137a) + **boy** 儿(21) = **ahead** 先

先生(133) **xiānshēng** *sir, Mr.; husband*

It looks as if the **calf** is taking the **boy** to market (rather than vice versa) because the calf keeps walking **ahead**. / *[DIY pronunciation]*

138 告 **gào** inform

Radical 口 7 strokes

calf 牛(137a) + **mouth** 口(5) = **inform** 告

[告别(79) **gàobié** *to part with*]

(The cattle are all falling sick — only a calf is left standing) The **calf** goes to the **mouth** of the cave to **inform** the vet. / *The **dwarf** assistant listens to the symptoms and says dismissively, "All this fuss, it's probably only **gout**."*

139 洗 **xǐ** wash

Radical 氵 9 strokes

water 氵(78a) + **ahead** 先(137) = **wash** 洗

[干洗(124) **gānxǐ** *dry cleaning*]

There's only limited hot **water** in the rooming house so she races to get to the bathroom **ahead** of everyone else and have a good **wash**. / *But Teddy has beaten her to it, and is washing his **sheets** in the sink.*

A word about how you can make use of the compounds we give with the characters. The compounds show you how the character in question combines to make words, when used together with other characters you've already learned. So you can use compounds as a revision aid for characters you've already learned: look at the compound and see if you can remember what the component characters mean. Sometimes it's interesting and instructive to see how the meaning of the compound as a whole relates to the meanings of the characters which make it up. A good example is that the literal meaning of 先生 is "ahead [in] life" (i.e. "senior").

You can also turn this around and use compounds as another way of remembering how to *pronounce* characters. You will probably recognize many words (such as **xiānshēng**) which you've come across in your Chinese language lessons. If you now realize that 先 is the first character in **xiānshēng** then you know it is pronounced **xiān**. Of course the soundwords are there to help you with pronunciations, but there's no such thing as too much help!

140

可 kě
     may

Radical 口
5 strokes

---

mouth 口 (5) + nail 丁 (81b) = may 可

The meaning is "may" in the sense of "being permitted to", but since this is a bit abstract we will cheat here and use a play on words: we will associate this character with Mayday celebrations in an English village, where children dance round a Maypole.

Note that the shaft of the nail is displaced to the right to make room for the mouth.

Some books advocate a different stroke order, where the whole of "nail" is drawn first, and then "mouth". Occasionally we point out alternative stroke orders (we already mentioned alternatives for Character 127). Sometimes the different versions exist because one is more firmly grounded in the "traditional" way of doing things and one is more "modern", but in other cases there simply seem to be two accepted ways of writing the character. Where we point out

The carpenter holds **nails** in his **mouth** while fixing up the **May**pole for the May celebrations. / *Teddy cuts up strips of **curtains** for the streamers.*

alternatives, either will produce a perfectly well-drawn character and so you can choose which to adopt. All this doesn't alter the fact that for the overwhelming majority of characters there is a single stroke order which is accepted as being "correct".

可以(120) **kěyǐ** *may, be allowed*
可是(30) **kěshì** *but (colloq)*

141

河 hé
     river

Radical 氵
8 strokes

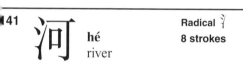

---

water 氵 (78a) + may 可 (140) = river 河

There is also another character for "river" (Character 148) at the end of this chapter.

Water for the dunking stool at the **May** celebrations has to be brought from the **river**. / *The **fairy** puts **herbs** into it to hide the smell!*

运河(57) **yùnhé** *canal]*
星河(136) **xīnghé** *the Milky Way]*

142

何 hé
     what

Radical 亻
7 strokes

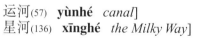

---

person 亻 (13a) + may 可 (140) = what 何

Harry arrives at the **May** celebrations, and a drink is pressed into his hand. He drinks, but splutters, "**What** is this stuff?" / *It's the **fairy's** new **herbal** drink (and the fairy looks piqued).*

143a 阿 ā ah

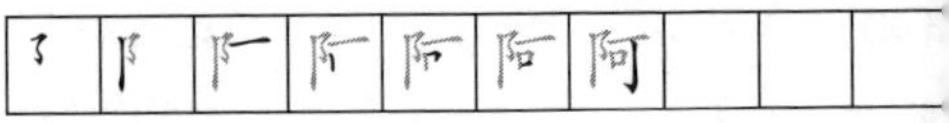

mound 阝(96a) + **may** 可(140) = **ah** 阿

Up on the **mound** sits the **May** queen on her throne. Everyone goes "**Ah**" when they see her, she looks so splendid. / *[No pronunciation needed]*

143 啊 **ā (a)** eh! **Radical 口** **10 strokes**

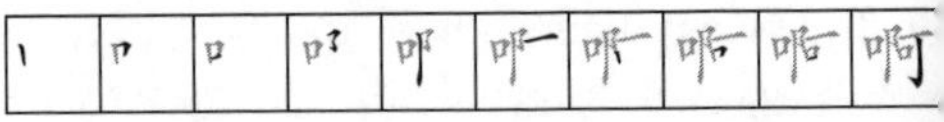

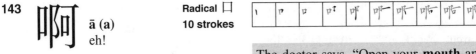

mouth 口(5) + **ah** 阿(143a) = **eh!** 啊

This character is used as an exclamation, added to a sentence to express surprise, admiration, regret, etc. depending on the context. When at the end of a sentence, it has a neutral tone; if the preceding word ends in -n or -ng it changes into 哪 (Character 99) and is pronounced **na**.

The doctor says, "Open your **mouth** and say "**ah**" — yes, these tonsils will have to come out." "That bad, **eh**?" the patient says in surprise. / *The **giant** says "**Ah**" in sympathy (he had to have his tonsils out as a child and he'd cried!)*

144 首 **shǒu** head **Radical 八** **9 strokes**

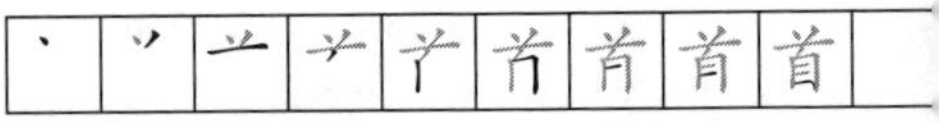

feet 䒑(90a) + **self** 自(94) = **head** 首

[首先(137) **shǒuxiān** *first of all*]

You need to lift your **feet** right above the rest of your**self** if you're going to be able to stand on your **head**. / ***Teddy shows you** how … show-off!*

145 道 **dào** way **Radical 辶** **12 strokes**

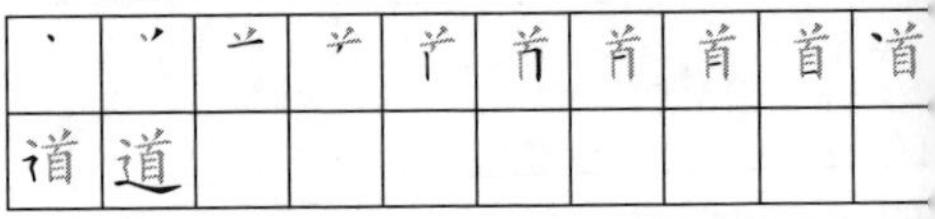

road 辶(26a) + **head** 首(144) = **way** 道

[一道(1) **yídào** *together*]
[人行道 (12, 81) **rénxíngdào** *pedestrian crossing*]

You emerge from the forest to find a **road** at last, but scratch your **head**: which **way** should you walk? / *The **dwarf** grumbles, "Whichever way we go, I **doubt** it will be the right one."*

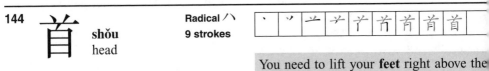

146 **fā** (fà)
send out

Radical 又
5 strokes

發

一 ナ 方 发 发

a drop 丶 (22a) + **friend** 友 (53) =
send out 发

This looks like a "drop" added to a modification of "friend" (Character 53) so we have used the idea of a "special friend" in the story to acknowledge this. Notice the unusual first stroke.

Pronounced **fā** this character means "to emit, send out, develop". With the other pronunciation **fà** (and another traditional form) it also means "hair".

She is writing her Christmas cards and puts **a drop** of perfume on the cards to her **special friend**s before **send**ing them **out**. / *The giant gets a large drop on his as he lives far, far away (and the perfume has to last until the card gets there).*

出发(114)   **chūfā**   *set out (on journey)*
[发出(114)   **fāchū**   *send out, emit*]
[发明(77)   **fāmíng**   *invent, invention*]
发生(133)   **fāshēng**   *happen, take place*

---

147 工 **gōng**
to work

Radical 工
3 strokes

一 丁 工

工人(12)   **gōngrén**   *worker*
[工会 (59)   **gōnghuì**   *trade union*]

/ *You trudge off every day to **work** at the **wheel** factory, and the only thing you look forward to is the **giant** sounding his **gong** for tea breaks and for the end of the shift.*

---

148 江 **jiāng**
river

Radical 氵
6 strokes

丶 冫 氵 氵 汀 江

water 氵 (78a) + **work** 工 (147) = **river** 江

We have already seen the other character for river (Character 142).

江山 (110)   **jiāngshān**   *landscape, scenery; country*]

They needed **water** to **work** the mill so they built it by the **river**. / *Two giants do a rain dance with jangling keys and chains to keep the river flowing.*

Test yourself: 我(32)   百(40)   会(59)   但(117)   和(126)   胜(134)   边(41)
公(119)   午(125)   之(121)   得(118)   生(133)   个(19)   先(137)

Chapter 11

Ten chapters out of forty done now!

cliff

drag

comb

field

electricity

outer limits

heart

knee

49 厂

chǎng
cliff

Radical 厂
2 strokes

廠

This character, whose basic meaning is "cliff", appears in quite a few composite characters. On its own, however, the character nowadays means "factory".

工厂 (147) **gōngchǎng** *factory*

/ *[DIY Pronunciation]. This is one of the very few basic building blocks that has a DIY pronunciation, so you can choose simply to learn the pronunciation, or make up a wheel story. Perhaps Teddy is rolling a large wheel off a cliff, almost hitting Mr Chang (Chang later tells this tale to his grandson, who we will meet in the next chapter working on the spaceship).*

50a 厂

drag

"Drag" is different from "cliff" — the first stroke is a sloping line, and the angle between the lines is more than 90 degrees.

50b 口

"piled up"

one 一(1) + **mouth** 口(5) = **piled up** 口

The **unicorn** has to use his **mouth** to pick up things to **pile** them **up** on the trash heap. / *[No pronunciation needed]*

---

50 后

hòu
rear

Radical 丿
6 strokes

後

drag 厂(150a) + **piled up** 口(150b) = **rear** 后

Breaking up this character into "drag" and "piled up" is cheating a bit, as the horizontal stroke joined on to drag is actually something else.

This character originally meant "empress" but has also taken on the role of the simplified form of 後 and is now mostly used in this sense.

"We must **drag** all the old furniture out and **pile** it **up** at the **rear** of the house. / *The dwarf is going to turn the house into a hotel.*"

后边(41) **hòubiān** *rear, at the back*
以后(120) **yǐhòu** *after, later*
[后天(76) **hòutiān** *the day after tomorrow*]

51a 川

"comb"

151 而　ér
and yet

Radical 一
6 strokes

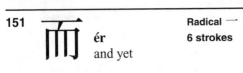

---
thumb tack 一 (40a) + comb 丌 (151a) =
and yet 而

This character occasionally means simply
"and", but usually indicates a contrast and
so might be translated as "but", "yet", or
"on the other hand".

(Using a comb as a musical instrument)
He had marked his notes on the **comb**
with **thumb tacks, and yet** it still sounded
awful. / *The **fairy** fled, saying "I've
remembered an **urgent** appointment
elsewhere!"*

[从而(103) **cóng'ér** *thus, thereby*]
[而后(150) **érhòu** *after that; and then*]

152a 扌
hand

This is the form which 手 "hand" (Character 31) usually takes when it forms the left-hand
side of a character. Note the stroke order (compared with that for 手), and also note that
the final stroke is drawn upwards.

---

152 找　zhǎo
look for

Radical 扌
7 strokes

---
hand 扌 (152a) + dagger 戈(32a) =
look for 找

Compare 找 with the far more common
character 我 meaning "I" (Character 32).
Here the hand and dagger are separate,
whereas in Character 32 they were fused
together; a difference reflected in the stories
for these two characters.

At the crime scene the detective pulls the
policeman's **hand** away from the **dagger**
saying, "We must **look for** fingerprints
first." / *Teddy's alibi is that he was watching the **jousting** on TV.*

[找到(74) **zhǎodào** *to find*]

---

153 打　dǎ
hit

Radical 扌
5 strokes

---
hand 扌 (152a) + nail 丁 (81b) = hit 打

He uses his **hand** to steady the **nail** before
he **hit**s it. / *It is difficult to get on with the
work because Teddy keeps **darting** in and
out between his legs.*

[打动(58) **dǎdòng** *to touch; move*]
[打倒(75) **dǎdǎo** *overthrow; Down with...!*]

154 对 **duì** correct

Radical 又
5 strokes

對

right hand 又(52) + **inch** 寸(104a) = **correct** 对

The basic meaning of this character is "facing towards" and it has also come to mean "line up", "match up", "to be correct" and "to treat" (a person in a certain way). It is also used as a measure word for pairs of objects.

If, when you **shake hands**, you have your right hands lined up to the nearest **inch**, you will be doing it in the **correct** way. / *The* **ghostly** *etiquette-guarding* **dwarf** *makes the class practice* **daily**.

对手(31) **duìshǒu** *opponent*]
对了(66) **duì le** *correct (at last); aha!*]

155 树 **shù** tree

Radical 木
9 strokes

樹

tree 木(10a) + **correct** 对(154) = **tree** 树

This is the modern character for "a tree", rather than using 10a on its own.

(A little girl is insistently pointing to objects and naming them) "**Tree**!" "Yes, **correct**, it's a **tree**." / *Now* **shoo**,*" says the* **dwarf** *grumpily, "and let me get on with my work."*

树干(124) **shùgàn** *a tree trunk*]

Test yourself: 几(7)   外(71)   姓(135)   母(127)   半(131)   办(123)   发(146)
星(136)   为(122)   利(132)   江(148)   干(124)   告(138)   们(28)

156a 田 **tián** field

156 男 **nán** male

Radical 田
7 strokes

field 田(156a) + **power** 力(14) = **male** 男

This and 女 (Character 15) are useful characters to know when identifying toilets!

Out in the **field** the farmer needs more **power** to work the churn. "I'll need another **male**," he says. / *The* **fairy** *flicks her wand and a* **nanny** *goat appears! ("Oops—wrong sort!" she says).*

男人(12) **nánrén** *man (i.e. not woman)*]

157

里 **lǐ** (li)
in

Radical 里
7 strokes

裏　裡

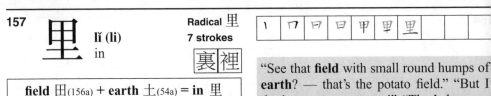

field 田(156a) + **earth** 土(54a) = **in** 里

Although this looks like "field" plus "earth", the stroke order shows that it isn't, really. (The same situation occurred for "exit", Character 114). In writing the character some books suggest writing the fifth and sixth strokes in the other order.

This character means "in", and is usually a suffix (i.e. it comes after a noun), where it often loses its tone. There are two variants of the traditional form. A 里 is also an old measure of distance (roughly half a mile).

"See that **field** with small round humps of **earth**? — that's the potato field." "But I don't see any potatoes!" "That's because they're **in** the humps!" / *Teddy runs to leap on the humps (crying, "Let's make mashed potatoes!")*

里边(41) **lǐbiān** *inside, in*
这里(26) **zhèli** *here*
哪里(99) **nǎlǐ** *where*
公里(119) **gōnglǐ** *kilometer*

158

理 **lǐ**
reason

Radical 王
11 strokes

king 王(60a) + **in** 里(157) = **reason** 理

道理(145) **dàolǐ** *principle, reason*

(The king's mother-in-law is visiting yet again) "Is the **king in**?" she asks the guard, and the guard has to think up a new **reason** each time why the king can't see her. / *Teddy peeks out to let the king know when she leaves (and the coast is clear).*

159

电 **diàn**
electricity

Radical 日
5 strokes

電

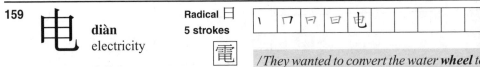

电车(83) **diànchē** *streetcar, tram*

/ *They wanted to convert the water **wheel** to run on **electricity** — the **two dwarf** experts from **Denmark** were called in (each connecting up one of the two wires).*

160a

冂

outer limits

丨	冂								

This usually forms a 3-sided enclosure, with another character inside it. Note the hook at the bottom of the second stroke. For the stories, think of the "outer limits of the kingdom" — a desolate, dangerous area of rocky hills, probably inhabited by bandits.

160

同

tóng
same

Radical 冂
6 strokes

outer limits 冂(160a) + **piled up** 口(150b) =
same 同

This also means "together with", "along with".

同时(105)　**tóngshí**　*simultaneously*
同学(82)　**tóngxué**　*classmate*
不同(9)　**bùtóng**　*different*
同样(112)　**tóngyàng**　*same*]

At the **outer limits** of the kingdom were **piled up** heaps of discarded boxes, all the **same**. / The **fairy** used her magic **tongs** to arrange them in neat piles.

161

心

xīn
heart

Radical 心
4 strokes

This appears at the bottom of a large number of characters, when it takes a slightly squashed form. It can also take the form 忄 when appearing on the left-hand side of characters (see 339a).

Just like the English word "heart", it means not just the heart in your body, but also "core", "center", and "feelings".

/ The **heart** of the **wheel** (its hub) is as big as the **giant's shin** bone.

[安心(91)　**ānxīn**　*to be content*]
[中心(33)　**zhōngxīn**　*center (often used in phrases like "shopping center")*]
[用心(130)　**yòngxīn**　*to apply oneself to*]
[小心(50)　**xiǎoxīn**　*cautious*]

162

必

bì
inevitably

Radical 丶
5 strokes

heart 心(161) + **slide** 丿(34b) =
inevitably 必

It is natural to think of this as "heart" together with an extra stroke, but watch the stroke order.

必要(101)　**bìyào**　*necessary*]
不必(9)　**búbì**　*don't need to*]

In the theme park there is a huge **slide** through the **heart** of the forest — **inevitably** it gets clogged up (with twigs and leaves). / Each day the **dwarf** has to send his **beaver** down the slide to clean it out.

163 相

xiāng; xiàng
mutual; appearance

Radical 木
9 strokes

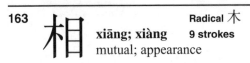

| 一 | 十 | 才 | 木 | 朹 | 朾 | 相 | 相 | 相 |

---

tree 木(10a) + eye 目(93) = mutual; appearance 相

When this character appears as part of another character (for example in Character 164 which follows this one), we will use "mutual" (and not "appearance") in the equation and story.

[相同(160) **xiāngtóng** *identical, same*]

▦ **Eye**s peering out from behind all the **trees** suggest Sherwood Forest, and the film set of "Robin Hood" — but this is a Chinese remake! At the auditions the actors are milling about, profuse with their **mutual** praise. / *Particularly two giants from Shanghai, auditioning for the part of Little John. Two dwarves from Shanghai are also competing for the role (sadly not having understood that the role of Little John calls for a giant rather than a dwarf).* \ They won't be told and are spending ages perfecting their **appearance**.

164 想

xiǎng
think about

Radical 心
13 strokes

| 一 | 十 | 才 | 木 | 朹 | 朾 | 相 | 相 | 相 | 相 |
| 想 | 想 | 想 | | | | | | | |

---

mutual 相(163) + heart 心(161) = think about 想

[理想(158) **lǐxiǎng** *an ideal, aspiration*]
[想法(87) **xiǎngfǎ** *(one's) opinions*]
[想一下(1, 43) **xiǎng yíxià** *give it some thought*]

The conjoined twins share a **mutual heart**. The surgeon has to **think about** how best to separate them. / *Fortunately he's practiced on two teddies in Shanghai!*

165 思

sǐ
think

Radical 田
9 strokes

| 丶 | 冂 | 冂 | 甲 | 田 | 甲 | 思 | 思 | 思 |

---

field 田(156a) + heart 心(161) = think 思

思想(164) **sīxiǎng** *thought, thinking*

One of the farmer's **fields** is **heart**-shaped and he always goes there to **think**. / *The giant had brought a (giant!) sequoia so that the farmer could sit under it (with his back against the trunk) to do his thinking.*

166a 7

"knee"

| 7 | | | | | | | | | |

166  今 **jīn**
now

Radical 人
4 strokes

丿 人 人 今

combine 人 (59a) + knee ㄱ (166a) = now 今

今天 (76) **jīntiān** *today*
今后 (150) **jīnhòu** *from now on*]

It needs the **combined** strength of everyone in the operating theater to pull the **knee** back into position. The surgeon gets everyone ready and then says, "Ready, Steady … **Now!**" / *The **giant** had been drinking too much **gin** (so fell over and dislocated his knee).*

167 念 **niàn**
to study

Radical 心
8 strokes

丿 人 人 今 今 念 念 念

now 今 (166) + heart 心 (161) = study 念

想念 (164) **xiǎngniàn** *to miss, long for*]

"**Now** I think it is time for the **heart**," said the surgeon, as he turned to **study** his "Heart Transplant Manual" (imagine him with his nose in this blood-spattered book) / [DIY pronunciation]

What can you do when you find that you've forgotten a composite character (apart from resolving to go back at the first opportunity and visualize the story again)?

In the equation A+B=C you will know A and B, but can't remember C. The first step is to try to get the *scene*, that is, the setting for the story. What do A and B together evoke? Logic may help here: try combining A and B in different ways. Try A in B, A hits B, A uses B for something, etc. (and also the other way round: B in A as well as A in B — usually one will make sense much more than the other). We've tried to make the stories recoverable like this, as far as possible. Once you have the scene, C will follow. It is this second stage (getting from the scene to C) that is often bizarre, silly or illogical.

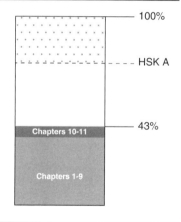

Test yourself: 后 (150)   工 (147)   用 (130)   对 (154)   可 (140)   里 (157)   海 (129)
夫 (49)   洗 (139)   同 (160)   每 (128)   理 (158)   打 (153)   首 (144)

Chapter 12

Notice how similar the character for "shelter" is to the character for "cliff" (in Chapter 11), and see how the character pictures help you remember which is which. The drop in the character for "shelter" is a drop of rain, which is much more relevant to "shelter" than it would be to "cliff".

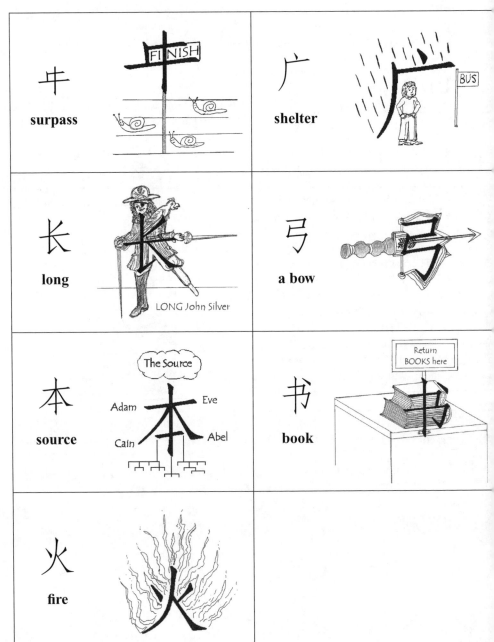

牛

surpass

广

shelter

长

long

弓

a bow

本

source

书

book

火

fire

168a

中

surpass

| 一 | ㄏ | 二 | 牛 | | | | | |

We use this fragment in the following character and will see it again much later, in Character 787.

168

年

nián

year

Radical 丿
6 strokes

| 丿 | 二 | 二 | 二 | 年 | 年 | | | |

clouds 亠(124b) + surpass 中 (168a) = year 年

今年(166) **jīnnián** *this year*
去年(86) **qùnián** *last year*
明年(77) **míngnián** *next year*

"These **clouds surpass** anything we've seen all **year**." (Picture a group of glider pilots looking at the sky and judging which clouds will give the best thermal up-currents). / *[DIY pronunciation]*

169a

殳

to strike

| 丿 | 几 | 𠬛 | 殳 | | | | | |

several 几(7) + right hand 又(52) = strike 殳

Think of striking something forcefully with a long pole (see 190a below).

(An attempt at a world record) The challenger **shakes hands** with **several** of the dignitaries who wish him luck, and then sees how many garden gnomes he can knock over with a single **strike** with his long pole. / *[No pronunciation needed]*

169

没

méi

not

Radical 氵
7 strokes

| 丶 | 冫 | 氵 | 氵 | 沪 | 没 | 没 | | |

water 氵 (78a) + strike 殳(169a) = not 没

Although the literal meaning is "to sink" or "submerge", this is more commonly seen as a negator for **yǒu** (Character 63). "Not" for most other verbs is conveyed by Character 9.

没有(63) **méiyǒu** *have not, does not*
没用(130) **méiyòng** *useless*]

(At the funfair) At one sideshow he had to **strike**, with a pole, anything that appeared out of the **water**, but everything stayed submerged and he complained, "There is **not** a thing to hit!" / *The fairy suggested to him that he should try his luck at the maze instead.*

170 广 guǎng shelter

Radical 广
3 strokes

廣

This character, whose basic meaning was a shelter (it is a picture of a lean-to structure), appears in quite a few characters, usually as an enclosure. On its own, however, the character nowadays means "broad". (Notice how "broad" also appears in the story).

/ (At the Formula 1 team's secret test track) They have to build a **shelter** for the spare **wheels** and other equipment, broad enough to accommodate the **ghostly teddy** and his **gang** (who guard it all).

[广大(47) **guǎngdà** *vast; extreme*]
[广告(138) **guǎnggào** *advertisement*]

171 床 chuáng bed

Radical 广
7 strokes

林

shelter 广(170) + **tree** 木(10a) = **bed** 床

He took a **tree** into the **shelter** to make a **bed**. / [DIY pronunciation]

[河床(141) **héchuáng** *riverbed*]
[机床(10) **jīchuáng** *machine tool*]
[床上(42) **chuángshang** *in bed*]

Test yourself: 手(31) 上(42) 正(29) 工(147) 不(9) 儿(21) 文(25)
何(142) 地(54) 厂(149) 河(141) 啊(143) 今(166) 道(145)

172 长 cháng; zhǎng 1. long 2. chief

Radical ノ
4 strokes

長

1.

 / On the bridge of the spaceship the captain looked at the **long** row of **wheels** on the engineer's desk. He had no idea which one to turn, so sent the **fairy** flitting off to find Mr **Chang**, the engineer.

Normally "chang" would be a DIY pronunciation, but we need a spaceship story here!

When 长 appears as part of another character we will use "long" in the equation and story.

2.

↯ / "Big **Chief Wheel**" was so called because he collected wagon wheels from raids on the passing wagon trains. **Teddy** made **jangling** wind chimes out of the wheel bolts (so that the wind proclaimed how many wagons the Chief had raided).

[长江(148) **chángjiāng** *the Yangtse River*]
[长大(47) **zhǎngdà** *to grow up*]
[生长(133) **shēngzhǎng** *to grow, grow up*]
[班长(113) **bānzhǎng** *leader (of team)*]

173a 弓   **gōng**   a bow

This is a (stringed) bow, for a violin or for archery.

173 张   **zhāng**   sheet (of paper)

Radical 弓
7 strokes

張

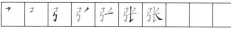

a bow 弓 (173a) + **long** 长 (172) = **sheet** 张

This is another character which can act as a measure word, as shown by the following compound.

[一张床 (1, 171)   **yì zhāng chuáng**   *a bed*]

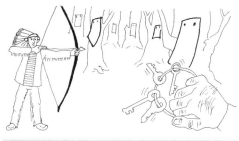

(In archery practice) The chief tries to show off by taking his **long bow** and aiming at **sheet**s of paper pinned to trees in the forest. / *The giant tries to put him off by jangling his keys loudly.*

174 本   **běn**   source

Radical 木
5 strokes

Originally this meant "root" of a tree, then "source" or "basis", hence "book". It can be used to mean "this", and is the measure word for books. This is a good illustration of the way in which characters can come to mean various things down the years.

/ *The source of the wheel* (i.e. where it was made) *was written round its edge, so Teddy looked to see where his bun was made!*

本子 (17)   **běnzi**   *notebook*
[本来 (65)   **běnlái**   *originally, at first*]
[本地 (54)   **běndì**   *local*]
[日本 (6)   **Rìběn**   *Japan*]

175 体   **tǐ**   body

Radical 亻
7 strokes

體

person 亻 (13a) + **source** 本 (174) = **body** 体

身体 (107)   **shēntǐ**   *human body; health*
个体 (19)   **gètǐ**   *(a person's) build*]

Harry was reading the **source** book on anatomy and when he opened it a hologram of a **body** floated out from the pages. / *Then Teddy hopped out dressed up as a teacher and started pointing out all the different body parts.*

176 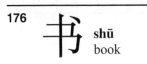 **shū** book

Radical 丨
4 strokes

書

| ㄱ | ㄢ | 书 | 书 | | | | | |

[书法(87) **shūfǎ** *calligraphy*]
[一本书(1, 174) **yì běn shū** *a book*]

/ *The giant balanced his book on the wheel but the wheel turned and the book fell on his shoe-polish.*

---

177 **lì** to stand

Radical 立
5 strokes

| 丶 | 亠 | 立 | 立 | 立 | | | | |

lid 亠 (25b) + **feet** ⺌ (90a) = **stand** 立

This can also mean "at once".

[自立(94) **zìlì** *stand on one's own feet; support oneself*]
[树立(155) **shùlì** *to erect, set up*]

He was trying to close the **lid** of his bulging suitcase, but in the end he had to use his **feet** and **stand** on it. / *When he got home, the dwarf realized he'd crushed his sun-cream, which had leaked out (and ruined his hat).*

---

178 位 **wèi** place

Radical 亻
7 strokes

| 丿 | 亻 | 亻 | 位 | 位 | 位 | 位 | | |

person 亻 (13a) + **stand** 立(177) = **place** 位

Literally a place or seat, this character is more commonly used as a polite measure word for people.

[地位(54) **dìwèi** *status, position*]

(At a group photo) **Harry** asks where to **stand** and they find him a **place**. / *"Wait!" cries the dwarf photographer, "I'll find him a place when I'm ready."*

---

179 **lā (lǎ)** pull

Radical 扌
8 strokes

| 一 | 丨 | 扌 | 扌 | 扩 | 扩 | 拉 | 拉 | |

hand 扌 (152a) + **stand** 立(177) = **pull** 拉

(On the slopes of a volcano) A huge **hand** appears and helps the boy to **stand**, giving him a strong **pull**. / *The giant points to the approaching lava (which the boy hadn't seen).*

180

啦 la
exclamation

Radical 口
11 strokes

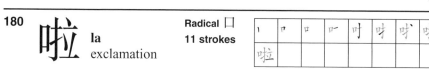

mouth 口(5) + **pull** 拉(179) =
exclamation 啦

This is an abbreviation for 了啊 ("le" plus
"a", Characters 66 and 143).

(Think of this as a continuation of the
previous story) The boy points at the
mouth of the cave, **pull**ing at his rescuer's
sleeve. "Over there! Look!" he **exclaims**.
/ *The robot, covered in bits of lava, has
reached the safety of the cave and is trying
to clean himself up.*

181

火 huǒ
fire

Radical 火
4 strokes

/ *The wheel is on fire but the ghostly teddy
(who was supposed to be guarding it)
can't put out the flames because when he
tries to pick up the hose his paw passes
straight through it!*

Supposedly a picture of a flame with two
sparks, but you may prefer to think of it as
a person running, hands in the air, shouting
"fire!" It takes a severely squashed form
when appearing at the bottom of characters
(see 185a). Some books give a different
stroke order.

火车(83) **huǒchē** *a train*

182

灯 dēng
lamp

Radical 火
6 strokes

燈

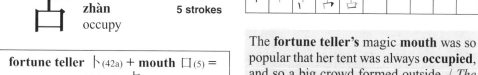

fire 火(181) + **nail** 丁(81b) = **lamp** 灯

电灯(159) **diàndēng** *electric light*

(In an old castle) "If we could find a way
of putting some **fire** on a **nail** in the wall
we could have a **lamp** in the room." / *The
giant dunks twigs in candle-wax to make
the first rudimentary lamp. (Does this
story sound familiar?)*

183

占 zhàn
occupy

Radical 卜
5 strokes

丨　卜　卢　占　占

fortune teller 卜(42a) + **mouth** 口(5) =
occupy 占

The fortune teller's "drop" is a short horizontal line here (see the note for 42a).

The **fortune teller's** magic **mouth** was so
popular that her tent was always **occupied**,
and so a big crowd formed outside. / *The
dwarf janitor had to be called to clear
them away.*

184 站 zhàn station

Radical 立
10 strokes

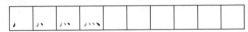

stand 立(177) **+ occupy 占**(183) =
station 站

This also means a (bus) "stop", or "to stand".

Notice the final stroke of "stand" has a definite slope (compare the note for 54a).

You're **stand**ing impatiently outside the **occupied** toilets at the train **station** (and your train is due any minute). / *The **dwarf** is sitting in the **janitor's** office (and is in no mood to be helpful).*

车站(83) **chēzhàn**   *(bus) stop, station*

185a

ノ丷丷丷   fire

This is the form taken by "fire" when appearing as the bottom part of other characters.

---

185 点 diǎn speck

Radical 灬
9 strokes

點

occupy 占(183) **+ fire 灬**(185a) **= speck 点**

This is used for any dot, point or speck, including the marks on a clock face, hence it also means "o'clock".

All the places round the camp **fire** were **occupied**, except two seats with white **speck**s on them. / *It was toothpaste left by the **two teddies** who'd gone off to the **dentist**.*

点心(161) **diǎnxīn** *dim sum, snack*
[地点(54) **dìdiǎn** *venue*]
一点儿(1, 21) **yìdiǎnr** *a bit, a tiny amount*
[有点儿(63, 21) **yǒudiǎnr** *slightly; somewhat*]

---

186 店 diàn store

Radical 广
8 strokes

shelter 广(170) **+ occupy 占**(183) =
store 店

This "store" is a shop where you buy things, not a place where you stash things away.

If you **occupy** the **shelter** for a certain length of time, you are allowed to turn it into a **store**. / *The **two dwarves** set up a shop selling **dentist's** supplies (picture them surrounded by false teeth, drills, etc.)*

[书店(176) **shūdiàn** *bookstore*]
[酒店 (102) **jiǔdiàn** *liquor store; pub*]

Chapter 13

There are no new building blocks needed for the characters in this chapter — you have already met and learned all the building blocks you will need.

187

果
guǒ
fruit

Radical 木
8 strokes

---

field 田(156a) + tree 木(10a) = fruit 果

Note that you don't simply write "field" then "tree" (this also happened for Character 157).

The developers want to dig up the **field** with the **tree** in it, but can't because the tree produces a rare **fruit**. / *The ghostly teddy who looks after the tree says, "Go away, Go away!"*

[如果(80) **rúguǒ** *if*]
[后果(150) **hòuguǒ** *consequence*]

188

棵
kē
number of trees

Radical 木
12 strokes

---

tree 木(10a) + fruit 果(187) = number of trees 棵

A measure word for trees and plants. When the primary use of a character is as a measure word, we will give its meaning as "number of" something (we did this for Character 19 and another example is coming up: Character 223 in the next chapter).

Each **tree** only bore a few **fruits** so it took **a number of trees** to produce enough fruit for a pot of jam. / *The giant used the whole crop to make his lemon curd.*

[三棵树(3, 155) **sān kē shù** *three trees*]

189

课
kè
lesson

Radical 讠
10 strokes

课

---

words 讠(67c) + fruit 果(187) = lesson 课

课文(25) **kèwén** *(piece of) text*
上课(42) **shàngkè** *attend class*
课本(174) **kèběn** *textbook*
下课(43) **xiàkè** *finish class*

(In school) Next to their pictures, the **words** for the **fruit**s are written up during the **lesson**. / *In the next lesson the dwarf teaches them how to make lemon curd (and is irritated at having to sit in for the cookery teacher).*

190a

to tap

| clouds 宀(124b) + shears ㄨ(25a) = tap 攵 |

This component always appears as the right-hand side of a character.

Compare it with "pursue" (506a) which looks similar but has one less stroke.

The meaning is "to tap" with a stick — think of it as tapping lightly, in the way

The topiarist was dreaming of trimming **clouds** with his **shears** (creating wonderful shapes) — until he felt a **tap** on his shoulder (waking him up as his lunch break was over). / *[No pronunciation needed]*

that a magician might tap with a wand; as opposed to the heavy swiping motion of "to strike" (169a).

190

zhèng
government

Radical 攵
9 strokes

| upright 正(29) + tap 攵(190a) = government 政 |

A ranger stands by the **upright** stone and **tap**s it, saying, "You can't come in here — this is an area protected by the **government**." / *The dwarf has to take his jungle tours elsewhere.*

191a

古
gǔ
old

| ten 十(4) + mouth 口(5) = old 古 |

A big **cross** has been painted above the **mouth** of one of the caves, to remind the forgetful **old** woman who lives there which cave is hers! / *[No pronunciation needed]*

191

gù
former

Radical 攵
9 strokes

| old 古(191a) + tap 攵(190a) = former 故 |

(The finale of the conjuror's act) "This time I'm going to use this very **old** wand to **tap** the hat, because it belonged to my **former** magic teacher." / *The dwarf assistant wondered what the conjuror would say when he pulled a goose from the hat (as the dwarf hadn't been able to find a rabbit).*

192 姑 gū aunt

Radical 女
8 strokes

| ㇀ | ㇖ | 女 | 女 | 女 | 奼 | 姑 | 姑 | |

woman 女(15) + old 古(191a) = aunt 姑

[姑姑 **gūgu** *aunt (father's sister)*]

"Why does that **woman** look so **old**?" asks the little girl. "Shh! She's your **Aunt**!" her mother replies in a whisper. / *"If you're rude about her the giant will come and fill your mouth with sticky goo."*

193a 胡 hú beard

髥

old 古(191a) + moon 月(61) = beard 胡

| 一 | 十 | 十 | 古 | 古 | 刮 | 胡 | 胡 | 胡 |

This can also mean "reckless" or "crazy" (in which case it acts as its own traditional form).

The **old moon** has become reckless and has let his **beard** grow. / *[No pronunciation needed]*

193 湖 hú lake

Radical 氵
12 strokes

| 丶 | 丶 | 氵 | 汁 | 汁 | 汁 | 湖 | 湖 | 湖 |
| 湖 | 湖 | | | | | | | |

water 氵(78a) + beard 胡(193a) = lake 湖

The **water** gets in the wizard's **beard** as he drinks from the **lake**. / *The lake fairy appears and says, "Who's that? Who's there?"*

194 克 kè gram

Radical 十
7 strokes

| 一 | 十 | 十 | 古 | 古 | 声 | 克 | | |

old 古(191a) + boy 儿(21) = gram 克

[马克(44) **mǎkè** *mark (in exam)*]

In school the **old boy**s are being taught about **gram**s (they'd learned to use ounces when they were younger). / *The dwarf teacher curses the newfangled metric system.*

Test yourself: 七(37) 车(83) 有(63) 没(169) 而(151) 念(167) 心(161)
张(173) 男(156) 找(152) 电(159) 必(162) 体(175) 树(155)

195

辛 xīn
spicy

Radical 辛
7 strokes

stand 立(177) + **ten** 十(4) = **spicy** 辛

This also means "bitter" or "acrid" and hence also "hardship".

(At the children's party) The children have to **stand** on the **cross** painted on the ground until they get the signal to start, then they must follow the **spicy** smell trail. / *The **giant** had laid the trail by strapping a bag of curry powder to his **shin**!*

196

亲 qīn
kin

Radical 立
9 strokes

stand 立(177) + **tree** 木(10a) = **kin** 亲

"Kin" here means blood relatives.

母亲(127) **mǔqīn** *mother*
[亲自(94) **qīnzì** *in person*]

Imagine you are **stand**ing in a **tree** — not an ordinary tree but your family tree, and your **kin** are all around you. / *Some of your kin will be high enough to touch the **giant's** chin.*

197

产 chǎn
to produce

Radical 亠
6 strokes

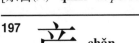

stand 立(177) + **cliff** 厂(149) =
produce 产

Notice that the bottom stroke of "to stand" has merged with the first stroke of "cliff". We will see this happening again in a couple of instances (Characters 295 and 640), but it doesn't always happen (see for example Character 257).

    This is an example of the sort of decision we have had to make all the way through writing this book. Do we invent a new fragment made up of "lid" plus "horns", or do we use "stand" but point out when something slightly non-standard happens? In the end we have done the latter, for three

Imagine **stand**ing on a **cliff** overlooking the sea — it's the ideal spot for a factory to **produce** buckets and spades. / *Teddy buys the first ones and slides down the **channel** leading to the beach.*

reasons — we want to keep the number of fragments to a minimum, everyone else calls this "stand", and it *is* where the character 产 came from. But if you prefer (as always) you can make up stories to go with the other choice.

生产(133) **shēngchǎn** *to manufacture*
[产生(133) **chǎnshēng** *to produce, give rise to*]

198

卡
kǎ
card

Radical 卜
5 strokes

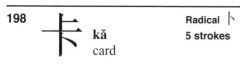

| above 上(42) + fortune teller 卜(42a) = card 卡 |

This character is actually the characters "above" and "below" (Characters 42 and 43), sharing the central horizontal stroke.

The compound below was coined because the sound **kǎ** resembles the English word "car".

Above the fortune teller's head floats her business **card**. / *Teddy secretly borrows her magic **carpet** to fly up behind her and get a closer look.*

卡车(83) **kǎchē** *truck, lorry*

199

还
hái; huán
1. still
2. give back

Radical 辶
7 strokes

還

| 1. road 辶(26a) + not 不(9) = still 还 |

| 2. road 辶(26a) + not 不(9) = give back 还 |

还是(30) **háishì** *still, yet; or*

1.

 The spaceship driving instructor says: "It's **not** a **road**, you don't have to observe the speed limits here." The pupil replies, "I'm **still** a bit nervous." / *"Just wait till the **fairy** shows you how to use the **hyper drive**!"*

2.

 (The bandits have robbed a bank and are fleeing the posse) "Let's **not** use the **road** — we might meet the posse and we'd have to **give back** the gold." / *But the **ghostly fairy** who guards the bank catches up with them and calls out, "**Hands up!**"*

200

看
kàn
look at

Radical 目
9 strokes

| hand 手(31) + eye 目(93) = look at 看 |

Note the slightly deformed form of "hand". Be careful not to confuse this character with Character 205 below.

(On an old sailing ship) The Captain raises a **hand** to shade his **eyes** to **look at** the enemy ship. / *He sees the **dwarf** loading a **cannon**.*

好看(18) **hǎokàn** *good-looking; interesting*
[看来(65) **kànlái** *it looks as if*]
[看法(87) **kànfǎ** *(negative) opinion*]

201 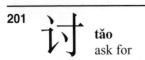 **tǎo** ask for

Radical 讠
5 strokes

words 讠 (67c) + **inch** 寸 (104a) = **ask for** 讨

This also means "to explore".

The young child is learning to read, and traces her finger along the **words inch** by **inch** — but has to **ask for** help when any big words crop up. / *Teddy has to keep quiet, and is building a **tower** of blocks in the corner (but every now and again there is a loud crashing sound!)*

202 **huí** return

Radical 囗
6 strokes

enclosed 囗 (24a) + **mouth** 口 (5) = **return** 回

This means to return to a place; hence also "to come back" in the sense of to respond or reply; or the number of times an action is repeated.

回来(65) **huílái** *to return (here)*
回去(86) **huíqù** *to return (there)*
[来回(65) **láihuí** *return (journey), there and back*]

The tribe's oracle **mouth** is displayed in the museum in an **enclosed** area; people keep **return**ing to see it (because it's so unusual). / *The **ghostly fairy** conjures up a shimmering **halo** to protect it.*

203a 妾 concubine

stand 立 (177) + **woman** 女 (15) = **concubine** 妾

(In the old days) You had to **stand** with a foot on a **woman** to claim her as your **concubine**. / *[No pronunciation needed]*

203 **jiē** receive

Radical 扌
11 strokes

hand 扌 (152a) + **concubine** 妾 (203a) = **receive** 接

He stretches out his **hand** to the new **concubine** to **receive** her into his household. / *She has brought a huge plate of **jelly** as a gift which it took **two giants** to carry!*

204a

羊
sheep

This modified form of "sheep" (Character 111) has the tail swept off to one side to make room for another character underneath. The vertical stroke remains one stroke when it is drawn at an angle, even though in some older fonts it looks as if it is broken into two.

204

差
chà
fall short

Radical 羊
9 strokes

sheep 羊(204a) + **work** 工(147) =
fall short 差

[差不多(9, 69) **chàbuduō** *more or less*]
[差点儿(185, 21) **chàdiǎnr** *almost, nearly*]

The **sheep** keep **work**ing at their long-jump practice by trying to jump across the river, but keep **falling short**. / *Their dwarf coach keeps a chart of their progress and he's not impressed!*

205

着
zháo; zhe (zhāo)   11 strokes
1. to catch
2. -ing

Radical 羊

1. **sheep** 羊(204a) + **eye** 目(93) = **catch** 着

2. **sheep** 羊(204a) + **eye** 目(93) = **-ing** 着

Don't confuse this character with "look at" (看, Character 200 above).

Pronounced as **zháo**, this character can have a variety of meanings. "To catch" means "touch", "come into contact with", as in "catch a cold". Pronounced as **zhe**, it is used after a verb to indicate an action in progress, hence our choice "-ing" for the meaning.

接着(203) **jiēzhe** *and then; to catch*

1.
In the cowboy town they were keeping an **eye** on the **sheep**, hoping **to catch** the sheep rustlers. / *The fairy is teaching the posse jousting skills (ready for the confrontation with the sheep rustlers).*

2.
In the spaceship the **sheep** is patrolling the corridors, putting his **eye** to each door to see if he can catch anything funny go**ing** on. / *Imagine his surprise when he sees the robot practicing his juggling!*

Test yourself: 从(103) 刀(72) 政(190) 思(165) 广(170) 儿(21) 想(164)
书(176) 灯(182) 年(168) 相(163) 辛(195) 在(55) 点(185)

Chapter 14

Abstract words such as "suddenly" and "again" are very hard to evoke directly with pictures. What we can do, though, is to use the shape of the character to remind you of something tangible and solid — and then link that with the abstract word. Look at the character picture for "suddenly" for example — hopefully in future when you see the fragment 乍 you will "see" the start of the running track, and hence remember that sprint races start "suddenly".

With "again", the shape of the character reminded us of the plunger used to detonate explosives, and so we used this in the character picture. You just have to remember that the particular thing being blown up is an old factory chimney, and the youngster is keen to see this demolition happen again — and again!

If you find that a basic building block strongly suggests to you a different object, then by all means use that image instead of our character picture. All you need to do is conjure up a (vivid!) situation to link this object with the meaning of the basic building block.

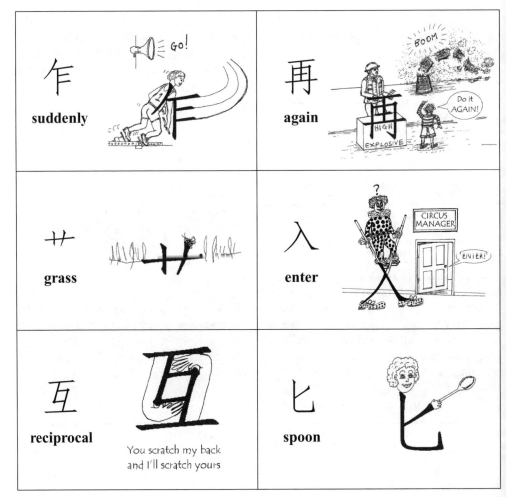

206a 匕 spoon

Notice how this differs from "seven" (Character 37) where the sloping stroke extends to both sides of the hook stroke. Many books give the stroke order as the other way round.

206 能 néng
able to

Radical 厶
10 strokes

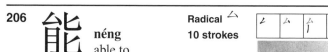

cocoon 厶 (34a) + **moon** 月 (61) + **two spoons** 匕 (206a) = **able to** 能

The one and only example in this book where a character is broken down into *four* parts which are then combined in a story.

可能 (140) **kěnéng** *may, possible*
[能干 (124) **nénggàn** *capable*]
[能力 (14) **nénglì** *ability*]

You see someone picking up a **cocoon** in the **moon**light … it's a waiter practicing picking things up using **two spoons** held in one hand — he has to be **able to** do this before he can pass his waitering exams. / *[DIY pronunciation]*

207a 乍 zhà
suddenly

207 作 zuò
do

Radical 亻
7 strokes

In a blinding flash, **Harry suddenly** knew what he had to **do**. / *[DIY pronunciation]*

person 亻 (13a) + **suddenly** 乍 (207a) = **do** 作

A general-purpose character meaning to do or make (see also Character 210 below).

We've gathered together here the 6 characters with pronunciation "zuo". Two pairs of these characters form mini phonetic series. You might like to have a go at constructing the pronunciation parts of stories for these six. You will need a ghostly archetype each time. If it is any help, the name "Zodiac" has been given to a make of car,

and an inflatable boat. If you find this hard work, relax — normal service is resumed after the next six characters (and spare a thought for us as we tried to come up with well over 800 of these stories so that each of them would be memorable!)

工作 (147) **gōngzuò** *work, job*
[作文 (25) **zuòwén** *essay*]

208 昨 **zuó** yesterday

Radical 日
9 strokes

sun 日(6) + suddenly 乍(207a) = yesterday 昨

昨天(76) **zuótiān** *yesterday*

(At the all night birthday party) She sees the **sun** coming up and **suddenly** realizes it is a new day. It isn't her birthday any more — that was now **yesterday**. / *[DIY pronunciation]*

---

209 左 **zuǒ** left (hand)

Radical 工
5 strokes

left hand 𠂇(53a) + work 工(147) = left 左

This means the left-hand side, on the left, etc. (rather than the actual hand with fingers).

[左边(41) **zuǒbiān** *left-hand side*]
[左手(31) **zuǒshǒu** *the left hand*]

(Showing a new employee how to work the big machine in the factory) "Use your **left hand**, your wedding ring hand, to **work** the controls as they are all on the **left** side of the machine." / *[DIY pronunciation]*

---

210 做 **zuò** do

Radical 亻
11 strokes

person 亻(13a) + former 故(191) = do 做

To do or make; the same meaning as Character 207 but more commonly used.

[做法(87) **zuòfǎ** *method*]

Harry's **former** wife runs into the church during the wedding ceremony just as he is saying, "I **do**." / *[DIY pronunciation]*

Test yourself: 同(160) 店(186) 床(171) 差(204) 位(178) 站(184) 张(173)
亲(196) 棵(188) 立(177) 讨(201) 火(181) 产(197) 长(172)

Character 210 is actually a fairly complicated character, but by now you are probably looking at characters like this and breaking them up automatically into parts without thinking. This just serves to show how far you've come. It may in fact be quite hard now to recall how you felt back at the beginning when characters were all "squiggles".

211 坐 zuò
sit

Radical 土
7 strokes

from 从(103) + earth 土(54a) = sit 坐

From the **earth** rises a beautiful throne to **sit** on. / [DIY pronunciation]

This character doesn't split neatly left-right or top-bottom into its two parts; you could also see this as two people sitting on the earth.

[坐班(113) **zuò bān** *keep office hours*]

212 座 zuò
seat

Radical 广
10 strokes

shelter 广(170) + sit 坐(211) = seat 座

You run into the **shelter** to **sit** out the storm — fortunately there's a **seat** to sit on. / [DIY pronunciation]

This is also used as a measure word for buildings and other large objects.

[座位(178) **zuòwèi** *a seat*]

213 右 yòu
right (hand)

Radical 口
5 strokes

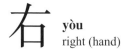

left hand ナ(53a) + mouth 口(5) = right 右

"Put your **left hand**, the one with your wedding ring on it, over your **mouth** and stretch your other hand out to the floor so that you lean to the **right**." / *The dwarf demonstrates how this yoga posture looks (Imagine what he looks like!)*

This is the opposite of "left" (Character 209), not the right hand with fingers.

[右边(41) **yòubiān** *right-hand side*]
[右手(31) **yòushǒu** *the right hand*]
[左右(209) **zuǒyòu** *approximately*]

Sorry to keep on about this, but you are remembering to visualize the stories properly, aren't you?
    For Character 211, for example, what is the situation? Who is present and what have they done to provoke the throne to rise out of the earth? Are they in a palace, in a clearing in a forest, or where? For Character 212, where are you? Can you "see" the shelter? What sort of shelter is it? Is the sky dark or light? Imagine you are telling a story to a small child who you are trying to keep amused — what details might you add to catch their interest?

214 **jiàn**
see

Radical 见
4 strokes

見

outer limits 冂(160a) + boy 儿(21) = see 见

Note that the top part of this character is not really "outer limits" (it is narrower and has no hook) — so we are cheating a bit here.

(On a bus tour of the outer limits) In the **outer limits** the **boy** wants to go to the loo but won't go behind a bush. "Someone might **see** me!". [Notice the boy's legs are held together in the character!] / *The two dwarf passengers decide that gentlemen don't go in the bushes, so they will try to wait until the toilets at the next stop.*

看见(200) **kànjiàn** *see, catch sight of*
[会见(59) **huìjiàn** *to meet (formally)*]
[接见(203) **jiējiàn** *grant an audience*]

---

215 现 **xiàn**
the present

Radical 王
8 strokes

現

king 王(60a) + see 见(214) =
the present 现

This means "the present time", "now", "current", or "ready to hand".

The **king** has special powers and can **see** everything going on at **the present** time in his kingdom. / *[DIY pronunciation]*

出现(114) **chūxiàn** *to appear*
现在(55) **xiànzài** *now*
发现(146) **fāxiàn** *discover*

---

216 观 **guān**
observe

Radical 又
6 strokes

觀

right hand 又(52) + see 见(214) =
observe 观

[观点(185) **guāndiǎn** *point of view*]

(In the evening you meet an old friend in the street) You **shake hands** and **see** that he's wearing a special watch, and he tells you he's off to **observe** the stars. / *In the observatory the ghostly giant will be up on the gantry readying the big telescopes and looking after them until your friend gets there.*

Test yourself: 还(199) 故(191) 果(187) 拉(179) 坐(211) 左(209) 姑(192)
吗(45) 啦(180) 课(189) 卡(198) 个(19) 做(210) 占(183)

217 再 **zài** again
Radical 一
6 strokes

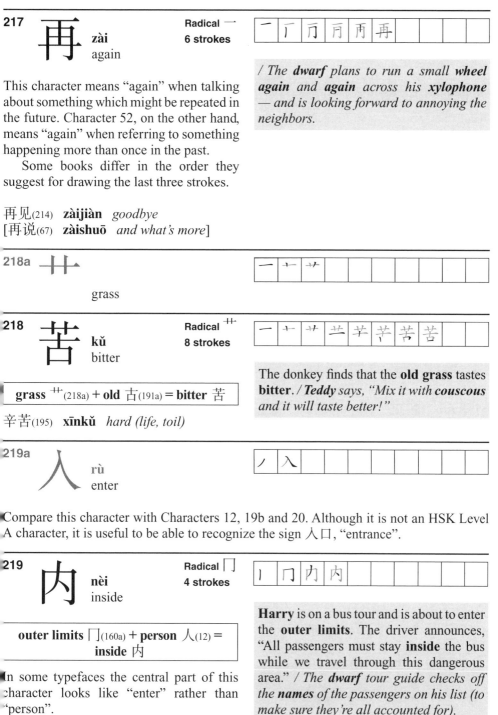

This character means "again" when talking about something which might be repeated in the future. Character 52, on the other hand, means "again" when referring to something happening more than once in the past.

Some books differ in the order they suggest for drawing the last three strokes.

/ *The **dwarf** plans to run a small **wheel** **again** and **again** across his **xylophone** — and is looking forward to annoying the neighbors.*

再见(214) **zàijiàn** *goodbye*
[再说(67) **zàishuō** *and what's more*]

218a 卄 grass

218 苦 **kǔ** bitter
Radical 卄
8 strokes

grass 卄(218a) + old 古(191a) = bitter 苦

The donkey finds that the **old grass** tastes **bitter**. / ***Teddy*** *says, "Mix it with **couscous** and it will taste better!"*

辛苦(195) **xīnkǔ** *hard (life, toil)*

219a 入 **rù** enter

Compare this character with Characters 12, 19b and 20. Although it is not an HSK Level A character, it is useful to be able to recognize the sign 入口, "entrance".

219 内 **nèi** inside
Radical 冂
4 strokes

outer limits 冂(160a) + person 人(12) = inside 内

In some typefaces the central part of this character looks like "enter" rather than "person".

Harry is on a bus tour and is about to enter the **outer limits**. The driver announces, "All passengers must stay **inside** the bus while we travel through this dangerous area." / *The **dwarf** tour guide checks off the **names** of the passengers on his list (to make sure they're all accounted for).*

[以内(120) **yǐnèi** *during, within*]
[在内(55) **zàinèi** *included*]

220 呐
nà (na)
[shout]

Radical 口
7 strokes

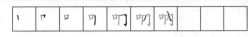

mouth 口(5) + inside 内(219) = shout 呐

Recall that we use square brackets [ ] for the meaning of characters which you are only ever likely to see in compounds (see Character 557 for the compound in question, but it's not an important one).

呐 can also be used as a particle at the end of questions, in the same way as 呢 (see Character 268), and in this guise it is pronounced **na** with a neutral tone.

(A drugs bust) They are standing at the **mouth** of the cave when, from **inside**, comes a **shout**. / *"The dwarf has found a stash of narcotics!"*

The main reason we've introduced this character here is to show you what it looks like when "person" is replaced by "enter" (see the comment for Character 219). This only happens for Characters 219 and 220: it does not happen for any of the following characters (221–225).

---

221 肉
ròu
meat

Radical 冂
6 strokes

outer limits 冂(160a) + person 人(12) + person 人(12) = meat 肉

Several characters containing "moon" are actually derived from this character instead.

[羊肉(111) **yángròu** *mutton*]

In the **outer limits** stands a totem pole made from one statue of **Harry** on top of another **Harry**: it's advertising Harry's **meat** stall. / *The dwarf ignores the rules and sneaks off the tour bus to buy meat for his Sunday roast.*

---

222 两
liǎng
a couple

Radical 一
7 strokes

one 一(1) + from 从(103) + outer limits 冂(160a) = couple 两

二 (Character 2) is used in writing numbers, in isolation or in a telephone number for example. But 两 is used with measure words, when talking about "two of" something.

[两个人(19, 12) **liǎng ge rén** *two people*]
[两棵树(188, 155) **liǎng kē shù** *two trees*]

The zoo gets a **unicorn from** the **outer limits**, to obtain a **couple** of unicorns which they hope might breed (where have we heard this before?!) / *The two teddies are set the task of watching the unicorns' body language, to see if they are getting on!*

223 辆 liàng number of cars

Radical 车
11 strokes

辆

car 车(83) + couple 两(222) = **number of cars** 辆

A measure word for vehicles.

[三辆车(3, 83) **sān liàng chē** *three vehicles*]

(In the car showroom) The elderly **couple** sit in the **car** that they like most, tired after having been shown a **number of cars**. / *The two dwarf salesmen had talked and talked, but the technical language (about big ends etc.) had been incomprehensible to them.*

---

224 俩 liǎ two people

Radical 亻
9 strokes

俩

person 亻(13a) + couple 两(222) = **two people** 俩

[他们俩(13, 28) **tāmen liǎ** *the two of them (people)*]

Harry only invited **couple**s to his party, so that every time the doorbell rang, there were **two people** standing there. / *Two teddies tried to gatecrash the party as a lark.*

225a 两 scales

grass ⁺⁺(218a) + couple 两(222) = **scales** 两

The recipe calls for a **couple** of handfuls of **grass** — it is difficult to weigh it on **scales** as it is so light. / *[No pronunciation needed]*

---

225 满 mǎn full

Radical 氵
13 strokes

满

water 氵(78a) + scales 两(225a) = **full** 满

[满分(73) **mǎnfēn** *full marks*]

She has to measure the **water** on the **scales**, as her measuring jug is already **full** (of something else). / *Teddy doesn't know how to use the scales and has to read the manual.*

226   互   **hù**   reciprocal   Radical 一   4 strokes

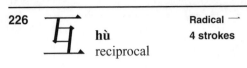

互相(163) **hùxiāng** *mutually, each other*
[相互(163) **xiānghù** *mutual, each other*]

/ *(In the past a friend gave you their spare wheel when you had a flat tire) You now see this friend with a flat tire and stop to give them your spare* **wheel** *as a* **reciprocal** *favor. Behind you a* **dwarf** **hoots** *impatiently, wanting to get past.*

---

227   它   **tā**   it   Radical 宀   5 strokes

house 宀(91a) + **spoon** 匕(206a) = **it** 它

This is the neuter form of he/she (Characters 13 and 16) — all three are pronounced **tā**.

它们(28) **tāmen** *they, them (neuter)*

He builds a small **house** to accommodate his silver **spoon**. "Why does **it** get all the attention?" asks his pet dog jealously. / *"Because spoons* **tarnish** *and dogs don't!" replies the* **giant**.

---

228   比   **bǐ**   compared with   Radical 比   4 strokes

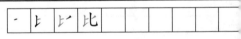

spoon 匕(206a) + **spoon** 匕(206a) = **compared with** 比

Notice that the left-hand spoon has been squashed so that its hook has turned into a "barb" (see 120a).

[比如(80) **bǐrú** *for example*]
[对比(154) **duìbǐ** *compare & contrast*]

He took one **spoon**, then another **spoon**, and **compared** one **with** the other. / *Teddy didn't care which one he had, as long as he got to eat his* **beans**.

---

229   批   **pī**   criticize   Radical 扌   7 strokes

hand 扌(152a) + **compared with** 比(228) = **criticize** 批

[大批(47) **dàpī** *lots of*]

The teacher looked at the **hand**s of the children and **compared** them **with** her own — she **criticize**d any failings such as dirty nails. / *The ones with clean hands were allowed to take the* **pizza** *to the* **Giant**.

230

切

qiè (qiē)
to cut

Radical 刀
4 strokes

一	圡	切	切						

seven 七(37) + **knife 刀**(72) = **cut 切**

We've included this character here so you can compare it with Character 228. The left-hand side of Character 230 is "seven", not "spoon" (although it too has been squashed and has a "barb"). The telling detail is that the cross stroke in Character 230 extends to both sides of the vertical stroke.

You look in your **diary** and see that seven days ago you met with the murder victim, so you use a **knife** to **cut** out the incriminating page. / *The **two dwarves** are going round **checking** on everyone's alibis.*

一切(1) **yíqiè** *all, everything*

[亲切(196) **qīnqiè** *cordial*]

Test yourself:

日 (6)	接(203)	能(206)	几 (7)	座(212)	国(60)	湖(193)
看(200)	这(26)	也(8)	回(202)	克(194)	再(217)	运(57)
内(219)	右(213)	下(43)	辆(223)	着(205)	六(39)	昨(208)
它(227)	苦(218)	动(58)	白(22)	见(214)	作(207)	明(77)

You will have realized by now that the concept of "basic building block" is a little fuzzy at the edges. This is not a major problem: the concepts of "animal" and "plant" in biology are also fuzzy at the edges (what are algae?) but in everyday life we all know what animals and plants are. Similarly, most of the time it is clear whether a character is composite or a basic building block: either it is "obviously" composed of two parts, or it is "obviously" a single entity. But there are gray areas at the boundaries.

A particular case in point is when to regard "one" (a single horizontal stroke) as a separate part. When the stroke is completely "free floating" (not joined on at all) we always regard the character as composite. Thus 二 , 云 and 旦 are composite. When the horizontal line is joined on, we have a gray area. The general rule we have adopted is to regard such characters as basic building blocks, unless there is a horizontal line at the *top* of the character *and* when you remove this line you get something recognizable. Thus 干, 王 and 下 are composite but 工 and 不 are basic building blocks. We don't try to detach a horizontal line at the *bottom* of a character unless it is completely free-floating. So 旦 is composite but 土 and 上 are basic building blocks.

Sticking to a rule like this (even if the choice of rule is somewhat arbitrary) makes it easier to decide confidently whether a character is a basic building block or composite.

Chapter 15

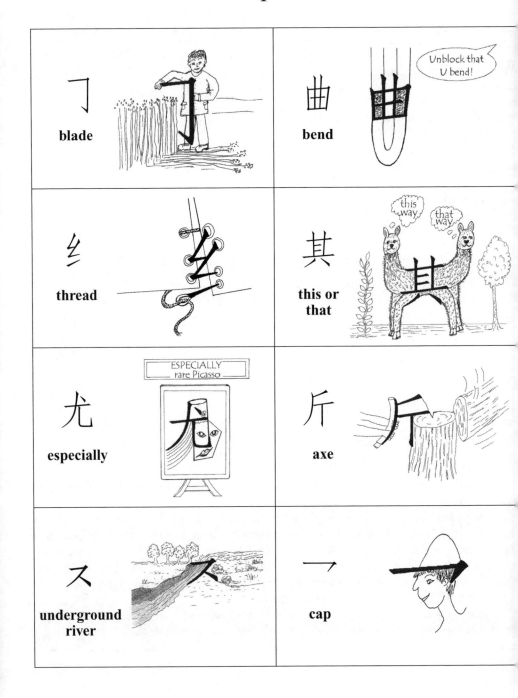

blade

bend

thread

this or that

especially

axe

underground river

cap

231a 丁 "blade"

231b 司 **sī** department

piled up 口 (150b) + blade 丁 (231a) = department 司

The **blades** were **piled up** in the production **department** because the sales department couldn't sell them fast enough. / *[No pronunciation needed]*

31 词 **cí** word

Radical 讠
7 strokes

词

words 讠 (67c) + department 司 (231b) = word 词

(A new boy is being shown round the factory) "The **words department** makes the words, so whenever you need a **word** they will supply it. / *The fairy keeps statistics on which words are being requested most often.*"

Recall that soundwords which begin "st" signal pronunciations which start with "ts" written as "c" in the Pinyin system — see Character 104).

主词 (133)   **shēngcí**   *a new word (in a language lesson)*
名词 (70)   **míngcí**   *noun]*
动词 (58)   **dòngcí**   *verb]*

232a 曲 bend

232 典 **diǎn** reference book

Radical 八
8 strokes

bend 曲 (232a) + eight 八 (20) = reference book 典

Note that the horizontal line at the base of "bend" is extended on both sides.

One of the **octopus'** tentacles has a permanent **bend** in it, so he puts a heavy **reference book** on it to try to straighten it out. / *The two teddies try using the same method to get rid of the dent in their frisbee!*

司典 (231)   **cídiǎn**   *dictionary*
字典 (92)   **zìdiǎn**   *character dictionary]*

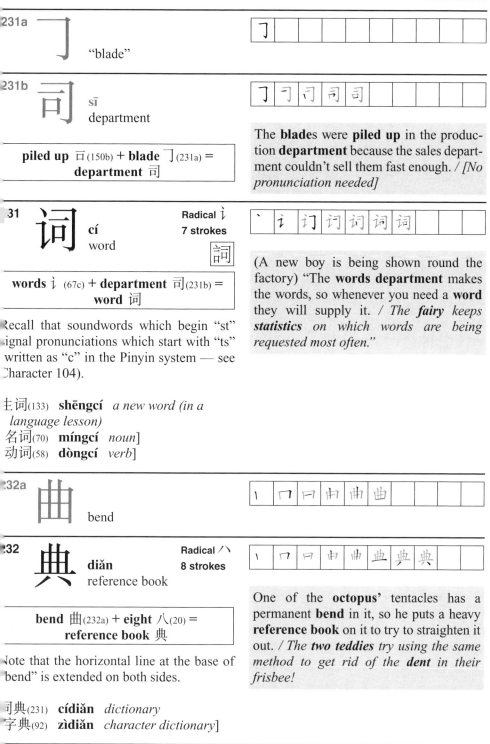

233a

丝   thread

This fragment always appears as the left-hand side of composite characters. We will meet another form of it later (607b).

233 红 hóng   red

Radical 丝
6 strokes

thread 丝 (233a) + work 工 (147) = red 红

[红海(129) **Hónghǎi** *the Red Sea*]

(A young girl is sewing a quilt) She rests for a moment with the **thread** trailing across her **work**. Then she looks down and sees a **red** stain spreading across the fabric — she has pricked her finger without realizing. / *Luckily the **fairy** knows a magic stain-removing spell that she learnt in **Hong Kong**!*

234 细 xì   slender

Radical 丝
8 strokes

thread 丝 (233a) + field 田 (156a) = slender 细

[细心(161) **xìxīn** *meticulous*]

He strung the **thread** backwards and forwards across the **field** (to protect the crops from the birds). It was very **slender** so it would do the job without blocking the light. / *The **dwarf** was satisfied as this would **shield** the crops from the birds (and save him from trying to keep them away).*

Test yourself: 子(17) 点(185) 我(32) 比(228) 观(216) 俩(224) 批(229) 两(222) 本(174) 现(215) 又(52) 肉(221) 切(230) 的(23)

235 其 qí   "this or that"

Radical 八
8 strokes

This character corresponds to a wide range of English words (this, that, he, she, it, etc.), depending on the context.

/ *"Do you want **this or that wheel**?" asked the salesman. "Whichever is **cheaper**," the **fairy** said.*

[其他(13) **qítā** *other*]

236 期 qī *due*

Radical 月
12 strokes

this or that 其(235) + **moon** 月(61) =
due 期

This means due (as in "due for an appointment"); an appointed time; or a period of time. It appears in the names for days of the week (note that there are two words for Sunday).

星期(136)　**xīngqī**　*week*
日期(6)　**rìqī**　*date (of event)]*
长期(172)　**chángqī**　*a long time]*
学期(82)　**xuéqī**　*term, semester]*
星期日(136, 6)　**Xīngqīrì**　*Sunday*
星期一(136, 1)　**Xīngqīyī**　*Monday]*

(Two telescopes are set up to watch the lunar eclipse) The curator says, "You can use **this or that** one to see the **moon** — but hurry, the eclipse is almost **due**." / *But clouds obscure the view, so the giant, on a nearby hill, holds up a lump of cheese with a bite out of it for them to look at instead!*

[星期二(136, 2)　**Xīngqī'èr**　*Tuesday*]
[星期三(136, 3)　**Xīngqīsān**　*Wednesday*]
[星期四(136, 24)　**Xīngqīsì**　*Thursday*]
[星期五(136, 36)　**Xīngqīwǔ**　*Friday*]
[星期六(136, 39)　**Xīngqīliù**　*Saturday*]
星期天(136, 76)　**Xīngqītiān**　*Sunday*

237 基 jī *foundation*

Radical 土
11 strokes

this or that 其(235) + **earth** 土(54a) =
foundation 基

基本(174)　**jīběn**　*basic, fundamental*
基础(115)　**jīchǔ**　*base, foundation*

"Do you want to use **this or that earth** for the **foundation**?" the builder asks, pointing. / *"In either case we'll need so much that it'll take the giant and his jeep to transport it."*

238a 犬 quǎn *dog*

big 大(47) + **a drop** 丶(22a) = **dog** 犬

Compare this character with "too much" (Character 48), which was also formed out of "drop" and "big". It's the same fisherman, but notice how in the stories the drop is on top of him, or falling from him, as appropriate. When appearing on the left as a radical, this character uses the distorted form 犭 (see 263a), in which the drop disappears.

The **big** fisherman felt **a drop** of water on his arm (but there was no cloud in the sky). The **dog** was shaking itself after having been in the river. / *[No pronunciation needed]*

238 尤 **yóu** especially

Radical 尤
4 strokes

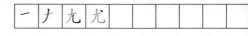

This is a deformation of the previous character.

*/ The **fairy** found the **wheel** useful, especially in her **yoga** class.*

尤其(235) **yóuqí** *especially*

239a 亠 "tall"

lid 亠(25b) + **mouth** 口(5) = **tall** 亠

A wooden **lid** fits across the **mouth** of the cave, but (since it is hinged at the top) you need to be very **tall** to open and close it. / *[No pronunciation needed]*

239b 京 **jīng** capital

tall 亠(239a) + **small** 小(50) = **capital** 京

There were both **tall** and **small** buildings in the **capital**. / *[No pronunciation needed]*

That is, a capital city. This is not an HSK A character but you will see it in 北京, "Beijing".

---

239 就 **jiù** right away

Radical 亠
12 strokes

capital 京(239b) + **especially** 尤(238) = **right away** 就

This character can also mean "regarding, concerning".

In the **capital** it is **especially** important to get on the train **right away**. / *The two dwarf attendants don't like people joking around (as everyone's in a rush).*

一...就...(1) **yī A jiù B** *no sooner A than B*
[就是(30) **jiùshì** *even if; exactly; precisely*]

Test yourself: 厂(149) 么(34) 门(27) 了(66) 又(52) 互(226) 朋(62)

词(231) 大(47) 国(60) 满(225) 村(104) 比(228) 妈(46)

240

jīn
axe

Radical 斤
4 strokes

Often used to mean a unit of weight (equivalent to 500 grams).

公斤(119) **gōngjīn** *kilogram*

*/ The **giant** is sharpening his **axe** on the grinding **wheel**, and has a swig of **gin** every so often to keep up his strength!*

241

近

jìn
close

Radical 辶
7 strokes

road 辶(26a) + axe 斤(240) = close 近

近来(65) **jìnlái** *recently, nowadays*]
接近(203) **jiējìn** *be close to*]

An **axe** was lying in the **road** and he swerved dramatically to avoid it. "That was **close**!" / *In the passenger seat the **dwarf** had a swift swig of his **gin** to recover!*

242

听

tīng
listen

Radical 口
7 strokes

聽

mouth 口(5) + axe 斤(240) = listen 听

听见(214) **tīngjiàn** *to hear*
听说(67) **tīngshuō** *to hear of; people say (that)*

At the **mouth** of the cave he was working away with an **axe** (to clear the trees which had blocked it) when he thought he heard something and stopped to **listen**. / *A tingle ran up the **giant's** spine.*

243

新

xīn
new

Radical 斤
13 strokes

kin 亲(196) + axe 斤(240) = new 新

新年(168) **xīnnián** *New Year*

He was so fed up with his **kin** that he felt like taking an **axe** to them and finding a **new** lot. / *The **giant** chuckled to himself as he thought of the **shindig** that would create.*

244a 又

underground river

244b 圣

channel

underground river 又(244a) + **work**
工(147) = **channel** 圣

The **underground river** had become silted up so they had to **work** hard to clear a **channel** (so that the flood waters could drain away). / *[No pronunciation needed]*

244 经 **jīng**
go through

Radical 纟
8 strokes

經

thread 纟 (233a) + **channel** 圣(244b) =
go through 经

This means "to go through" in the sense of "to experience"; also "to manage"; and there are other derived meanings such as "scriptures" and "longitude".

(On a potholing expedition) The leader tied a **thread** around his waist and swam along the **channel** to the next cave; this made it easier for the others to **go through** in turn after him. / *Sitting in the final cave was a giant who jingled some bells (to lead them to him). [Note that we will distinguish jingling (bells) from jangling (coins, keys, chains and all other objects)].*

经过(106) **jīngguò** *go through, pass by*
[经理(158) **jīnglǐ** *manager*]

245 轻 **qīng**
lightweight

Radical 车
9 strokes

輕

car 车(83) + **channel** 圣(244b) =
lightweight 轻

年轻(168) **niánqīng** *young*

Cars are being allowed along the drainage **channel** but only **lightweight** ones. / *The giant who maintains the channel, has spotted a chink in the channel floor (and so has imposed a weight restriction).*

246a 冫

ice crystals

a drop 丶 (22a) + **a drop** 丶 (22a) =
ice crystals 冫

Drop after **drop** of water in the icy cave slowly builds up a stalagmite of **ice crystals**. / *[No pronunciation needed]*

246

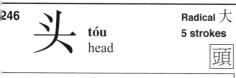

头
tóu
head

Radical 大
5 strokes

頭

ice crystals ⟍(246a) + **big** 大(47) = **head** 头

This means both literally a "head" and also more figuratively "chief" or "foremost".

Note that the last stroke is a drop; this character is not really "ice crystals" plus "big", but we've used this breakdown since this is what the character looks like at first glance.

In the cavern, the **ice crystals** were so **big** that he hit his **head** on one. / *The **fairy** conjured up a lamp for him to see by, just as he was about to stub his **toe** on another one.*

[点头(185) **diǎntóu** *to nod one's head*]

247a

"cap"

Compare this with "knee" (166a): this is a much longer stroke with a short hook at the end.

247

买
mǎi
buy

Radical ⟍
6 strokes

買

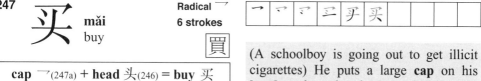

cap ⟍(247a) + **head** 头(246) = **buy** 买

买不到(9, 74) **mǎibudào** *out of stock*]

(A schoolboy is going out to get illicit cigarettes) He puts a large **cap** on his **head** so that when he **buys** them he can smuggle them back in it. / *Teddy puts on a bishop's **miter** (trying to help, but only drawing attention to the two of them).*

248

卖
mài
sell

Radical 十
8 strokes

賣

ten 十(4) + **buy** 买(247) = **sell** 卖

Careful: the top looks a bit like "earth" (54a), but it isn't!

买卖(247) **mǎimài** *trade, business*]

(At the cathedral in Rome) The pilgrim wants to **buy** a **cross** — and there's no shortage of people to **sell** him one! / *One trinket seller, a dwarf, is wearing a bishop's **miter** in the hope that people will think his goods are more authentic.*

249 **dú** to read

Radical 讠
10 strokes

讀

words 讠 (67c) + **sell** 卖(248) = **read** 读

[读书(176) **dú shū** *to read, study*]

She has **words** written on flash cards, which she **sells** to schools to help children learn to **read**. / *The **fairy** sits on the children's **duvets** and listens to them reading at bedtime.*

250 **shí** real

Radical 宀
8 strokes

實

house 宀(91a) + **head** 头(246) = **real** 实

实现(215) **shíxiàn** *to materialize*
[实用(130) **shíyòng** *useful, practical*]
[实行(81) **shíxíng** *put into practice*]
[实在(55) **shízài** *honest; indeed*]

He dreamt that the **house** was falling on his **head**; he woke up and thought it was **real**, because his bed was covered in dust. / *But it was only ash — the **fairy** had been chain-smoking **cheroots**!*

Congratulations! Learning 250 characters is a real achievement. Did you really believe, right at the beginning, that you'd actually be able to get this far?

The flash cards mentioned in the story for Character 249 are actually a very good idea. They are small cards for testing yourself (say credit card sized) with the character on one side and its meaning and pronunciation on the other. Use them to test yourself at odd moments, in supermarket check-out lines for example. You can buy these cards in ready-made sets or make a set yourself. If you mix the cards together, adding the cards for each chapter as you go along, you will be creating the same effect as the Test Yourself panels in this book. Speaking of which:

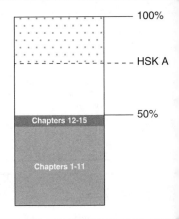

Test yourself: 语(68) 近(241) 五(36) 月(61) 典(232) 倒(75) 机(10)

这(26) 斤(240) 她(16) 汉(78) 妹(64) 啊(143) 轻(245)

Chapter 16

Once again, you have already learned all the basic building blocks you will need for this chapter.

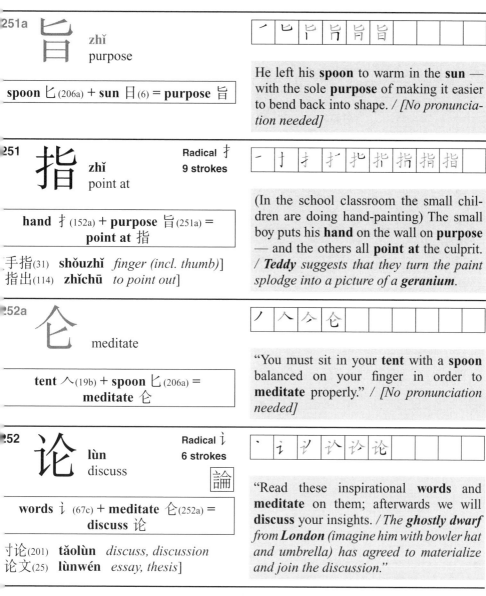

251a 旨 zhǐ purpose

spoon 匕 (206a) + sun 日 (6) = purpose 旨

He left his **spoon** to warm in the **sun** — with the sole **purpose** of making it easier to bend back into shape. / *[No pronunciation needed]*

251 指 zhǐ point at

Radical 扌
9 strokes

hand 扌 (152a) + purpose 旨 (251a) = point at 指

[手指 (31) **shǒuzhǐ** *finger (incl. thumb)*]
[指出 (114) **zhǐchū** *to point out*]

(In the school classroom the small children are doing hand-painting) The small boy puts his **hand** on the wall on **purpose** — and the others all **point at** the culprit. / *Teddy suggests that they turn the paint splodge into a picture of a geranium.*

252a 仑 meditate

tent 人 (19b) + spoon 匕 (206a) = meditate 仑

"You must sit in your **tent** with a **spoon** balanced on your finger in order to **meditate** properly." / *[No pronunciation needed]*

252 论 lùn discuss

Radical 讠
6 strokes

論

words 讠 (67c) + meditate 仑 (252a) = discuss 论

[讨论 (201) **tǎolùn** *discuss, discussion*]
[论文 (25) **lùnwén** *essay, thesis*]

"Read these inspirational **words** and **meditate** on them; afterwards we will **discuss** your insights. / *The ghostly dwarf from London (imagine him with bowler hat and umbrella) has agreed to materialize and join the discussion.*"

253 认 rèn recognize

Radical 讠
4 strokes

認

| ` | 讠 | 讠 | 认 | | | | |

words 讠 (67c) + **person** 人(12) =
recognize 认

认为(122) **rènwéi** *think (that)*
[认得(118) **rènde** *know, understand*]

Words have been scrawled up around the school, saying "Harry go home!" — but everyone **recognizes** the handwriting. / *The dwarf teacher finally spots the culprit in action and runs to apprehend him.*

254 只 zhǐ; zhī only; one of a pair

Radical 口
5 strokes

祇隻

| 丶 | 冂 | 口 | 尸 | 只 | | | |

mouth 口(5) + **eight** 八(20) =
only; one of a pair 只

The two traditional forms 祇 and 隻 correspond to **zhǐ** and **zhī** respectively. **zhī** is a measure word, and is also used to refer to things which usually come in pairs.

When this character appears as part of another character we will use the meaning "only" in the equation and the story.

只好(18) **zhǐhǎo** *have to*
[只要(101) **zhǐyào** *provided that*]
[只是(30) **zhǐshì** *only, just, merely*]
[只有(63) **zhǐyǒu** *only if; have to*]
[一只手(1, 31) **yì zhī shǒu** *a hand*]

 The **octopus** is at the **mouth** of the cave (it is an underwater cave and we are on the film set for "20,000 Leagues under the Sea"). The main scene will **only** work if they can film lots of swirling water. / *Teddy suggests using a jacuzzi. They go to see if they can film in the giant's jacuzzi.* \ He gives them **one of a pair** of his old gloves to make a squid costume out of!

255 织 zhī weave

Radical 纟
8 strokes

織

| ㄥ | 纟 | 纟 | 纟 | 纟 | 纟 | 纟 | 织 |

thread 纟 (233a) + **only** 只(254) =
weave 织

THREAD ONLY for WEAVING

"This **thread** can **only** be used for **weav**ing, not knitting." / *The giant likes to relax in his jacuzzi and passes the time knitting (but finds this message written on the new thread he has just bought).*

Test yourself: 我(32) 得(118) 和(126) 正(29) 实(250) 了(66) 来(65)
别(79) 理(158) 细(234) 就(239) 时(105) 经(244) 名(70)

---

256 识 **shí**
knowledge

Radical 讠
7 strokes

識

| 丶 | 讠 | 讣 | 识 | 识 | 识 | 识 | | | |

words 讠 (67c) + only 只(254) =
knowledge 识

认识(253) **rènshí** *know, understand*

(A cookery program on TV) "The **words** of a recipe **only** mean something if you have some **knowledge** of how to cook." / *The fairy holds up a shallot (and adds, "You have to know your onions!")*

---

257 音 **yīn**
sound

Radical 音
9 strokes

| 丶 | 一 | 立 | 立 | 立 | 音 | 音 | 音 | | |

stand 立(177) + sun 日(6) = sound 音

[语音(68) **yǔyīn** *pronunciation*]
[口音(5) **kǒuyīn** *accent*]

"If you **stand** this in the **sun** for a while it will make a deep, resonant **sound**. / *But the giant won't like it because it upsets his yin!*"

---

258 意 **yì**
idea

Radical 音
13 strokes

| 丶 | 一 | 亠 | 立 | 立 | 音 | 音 | 音 | 音 | |
| 意 | 意 | 意 | | | | | | | |

sound 音(257) + heart 心(161) = idea 意

满意(225) **mǎnyì** *satisfactory*
意见(214) **yìjiàn** *opinion, view*
同意(160) **tóngyì** *agree, approve*
意思(165) **yìsī** *meaning*
有意思(63, 165) **yǒu yìsi** *interesting*
没意思(169, 165) **méi yìsi** *uninteresting*

"If we listen to the **sound** of your **heart**, this will give us a better **idea** of what is going on," the surgeon said. / *The dwarf stands by with ether for anesthetic.*

259a 戊 **wù**
fifth

| 一 | 厂 | 仄 | 戊 | 戊 | | | | | |

cliff 厂 (149) + dagger 戈(32a) = fifth 戊

"Dagger" and "cliff" are fused together here (similar to the situation for 我, Character 32).

He embeds the **dagger** in the **cliff**, in the middle of the painted star, to indicate that he is of the **fifth** generation. / *[No pronunciation needed]*

259 成 chéng turn into

Radical 戈
6 strokes

一 厂 厈 成 成 成

blade 丁(231a) + fifth 戊(259a) =
turn into 成

The **blade** of the **fifth** lord's dagger **turned into** chocolate. / *He looked around and there was a **chunky fairy** smiling mischievously — clearly she had done it.*

[成长(172) **chéngzhǎng** *to grow up*]
[成就(239) **chéngjiù** *great achievement*]
[成果(187) **chéngguǒ** *positive outcome*]
[成立(177) **chénglì** *set up, establish*]

260 城 chéng town

Radical 土
9 strokes

一 十 土 圠 圤 坊 城 城 城

earth 土(54a) + turn into 成(259) =
town 城

Originally this character meant "city wall", hence its appearance in the name for the Great Wall of China.

(A property developer shows investors a site) "This whole expanse of **earth** will **turn into** a **town**," he says. / *The **chunky fairy** lands heavily at his feet and says, "Over my dead body."*

[长城(172) **chángchéng** *the Great Wall*]
[城里(157) **chénglǐ** *in town*]

261a 耂 old man

一 十 土 耂

earth 土(54a) + slide ノ(34b) = old man 耂

The children arrive at the park to find **earth** on their **slide**. It was the **old man** (who lives near the park and objects to the noise). / *[No pronunciation needed]*

261 者 zhě specialist

Radical 耂
8 strokes

一 十 土 耂 耂 者 者 者

old man 耂(261a) + sun 日(6) =
specialist 者

This is used as a suffix meaning -ist or -er, i.e. the person doing something.

The **old man** has been out in the **sun** for too long (and has a sunburnt head) — so he has to go and see a **specialist**. / *Teddy gives him a **jersey** to put over his bald head.*

[作者(207) **zuòzhě** *author*]
[读者(249) **dúzhě** *reader (eg of newspaper)*]

262

都

dōu; dū

1. all
2. metropolis

Radical 阝
10 strokes

1. **specialist** 者(261) + **city** 阝(96a) = **all** 都

2. **specialist** 者(261) + **city** 阝(96a) = **metropolis** 都

首都(144) **shǒudū** *capital city*

连...都...(84) **lián A dōu B** *even A is/does B*

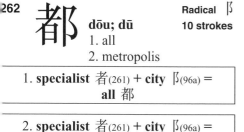

1.

☠ The sheriff was wounded in the gunfight and had to go back East to the **specialist** in the **city** — **all** the people in the town clubbed together to pay for the treatment. / *The **giant** carried him so that the sheriff could **doze** on the way to the hospital.*

2.

🛸 The spaceship crew land on the planet looking for a **specialist** in the **city** — but get directed to the **metropolis**. / *The **giant** carries the sick alien wrapped up in a **duvet**.*

263a

犭

dog

Recall that this is a distorted form of 犬 "dog" (238a).

263

猪

zhū
pig

猪

Radical 犭
11 strokes

dog 犭(263a) + **specialist** 者(261) = **pig** 猪

Character 263 means "pig", but you probably remember that we already had a character for "pig" (109a). We have seen this happen already a number of times — for example, there were two characters for "river".

This isn't a problem, as we are always working in the Chinese to English direction. If you see Character 263 and remember the story, then you will remember that the

The **dog specialist** (in the poodle parlor) looked up, astonished, as a customer brought a **pig** into the shop. / *The **giant** wanted a **jeweled** collar (for his pet pig).*

character means "pig" (however many other characters there are that also mean "pig").

This is just as well, as a third pig will be coming along in Chapter 27!

[猪肉(221) **zhūròu** *pork*]

Test yourself: 干(124)   中(33)   每(128)   以(120)   是(30)   红(233)   咱(95)

分(73)   好(18)   新(243)   月(61)   小(50)   织(255)   克(194)

264

老 **lǎo**
old

Radical 耂
6 strokes

一 十 土 耂 耂 老

| old man 耂(261a) + spoon ヒ(206a) = |
| old 老 |

"Old" here can mean either "elderly" or "long-standing". It can be used with an older person's surname (e.g. 老王, Lǎo Wáng) as a term of friendly respect. Conversely, xiǎo (Character 50) can be used as a casual, friendly way of talking about (or to) someone younger than you (e.g. 小李, Xiǎo Lǐ).

The **old man** ate everything with a **spoon**. He said, "You can do what you like when you are as **old** as I am." / *Teddy copies him, slurping **loudly***.

老二(2) **lǎo èr** *second child*
[老实(250) **lǎoshí** *honest*]
[老人(12) **lǎorén** *elderly person*]
[老百姓(40, 135) **lǎobǎixìng** *the common people*]

265a

孝 **xiào**
filial piety

一 十 土 耂 耂 孝 孝

| old man 耂(261a) + child 子(17) = |
| filial piety 孝 |

This strange-sounding phrase means respect for parents and ancestors, which is a powerful tradition in China.

The **old man** was delighted to see that the **child** had been brought up to show **filial piety** ("Unlike most of the youth of today," he mutters). / *[No pronunciation needed]*

265

教 **jiāo; jiào**
teach

Radical 攵
11 strokes

一 十 土 耂 耂 孝 孝 孝 孝
教

| filial piety 孝(265a) + tap 攵 (190a) = |
| teach 教 |

This character has two pronunciations but it means "teach" regardless! So (just this once) we have two different archetypes sharing the same story — except that as we are talking about an i- onglide, there are two of each, and so we end up with four altogether!

The **filial piety** teacher **tap**s impatiently on his desk — he wants to get on and **teach** the lesson. / *But the pupils are all distracted, listening to the sounds of the **jousting** tournament next door — **two dwarves** and **two giants** are in the semifinals.*

[教学(82) **jiàoxué** *teaching*]

266a moon

| ノ | 勹 | 夕 | 夕 | | | | | | |

You may recall that this is a distorted form of 月, "moon" (Character 61).

266b "dog food"

| ノ | 勹 | 夕 | 夕 | 夕⼀ | 夕丿 | 犾 | 犾 | | |

moon 夕(266a) + **dog** 犬(238a) = **dog food** 犾

During the fasting season even the **dog** has to wait until the **moon** is up, before he can have his **dog food**. / *[No pronunciation needed]*

266 然 **rán** however

Radical 灬
12 strokes

| ノ | 勹 | 夕 | 夕 | 夕⼀ | 夕丿 | 犾 | 犾 | 犾丿 | 然 |
| 然 | 然 | | | | | | | | |

dog food 犾(266b) + **fire** 灬(185a) = **however** 然

The **dog food** has gone bad so they throw it on the **fire** — **however**, the fire then goes out. / *The fairy can't bear the rancid smell (so conjures the fire into life again).*

This character also means "correct"; "but"; "so"; "this"; "-ly", depending on the context.

然后(150) **ránhòu** *after, and then*
[自然(94) **zìrán** *nature; natural*]
[必然(162) **bìrán** *inevitable, bound to*]
[不然(9) **bùrán** *or, otherwise*]

Test yourself: 如(80) 听(242) 期(236) 外(71) 读(249) 指(251) 过(106) 头(246) 时(105) 只(254) 连(84) 细(234) 在(55) 买(247)

If you are practicing writing characters (as you should), your first attempts will have been awkward, but as with most things you'll be getting better with practice. Try drawing large (1 inch or 2 cm) squares on a piece of paper and practice drawing the characters to fill these squares. What commonly happens otherwise is that your characters get smaller and smaller as you write a line of them.

Don't be too hard on yourself (we all draw gawky-looking characters when we start). Even now, you'll be able to look back at your early attempts and compare them with your most recent ones, and see just how much you've improved.

Finally, try writing out sentences, or just lines of characters, on ordinary paper. To begin with you can mark out squares to write in if you want to, but after that simply imagine the squares and try to keep your characters all equally sized and equally spaced.

Chapter 17

The three characters 己 已 巳 are very similar but distinct. Look at their three character pictures — you might think of the first character as being a bit **self** conscious because he can feel himself turning into a **snake** — by the 已 stage he's **already** halfway there!

Also on this page, notice the small differences between the important fragments "gold" and "food".

彐 **snout**	尸 **corpse**
己 **self**	已 **already** *already half snake...*
巳 **snake**	釒 **gold**
艮 **stubborn**	飠 **food**

267a

彐　snout

＼コ彐｜｜｜｜｜｜｜

267

当
dāng (dàng)
act as

Radical 小
6 strokes

當

丨丶丷彑当当｜｜｜

small 小(50) + snout 彐(267a) = act as 当

They look like **small snout**s, but **act as** gasmasks. / *The **giant** is handing them out; he has them all **dangling** from his fingers.*

The top three strokes are a distorted version of "small" (Character 50).

The character means "to act as" and also "to regard as".

当然(266)　**dāngrán**　*of course*
[当前(90)　**dāngqián**　*now, at present*]
[当地(54)　**dāngdì**　*local; at that place*]
[当做(210)　**dāngzuò**　*regard as, treat as*]
[当时(105)　**dāngshí**　*at that time*]
[当年(168)　**dāngnián**　*then; in those years*]

268a

尸　shī
corpse

屍

｜コ尸｜｜｜｜｜｜

268b

尼
ní
nun

｜コ尸尸尼｜｜｜｜

corpse 尸(268a) + spoon 匕(206a) = nun 尼

In the convent hospital each **corpse** is sprinkled with holy water from a **spoon** by the senior **nun**. / *[No pronunciation needed]*

268

呢
ne
as for

Radical 口
8 strokes

丨口口口口口尸呢呢｜｜

mouth 口(5) + nun 尼(268b) = as for 呢

A particle, used at the end of questions. One use is to repeat the question, but now referring to a new subject. It can also be used in a rhetorical way, or to soften the tone of a question or sentence.

The **nun**'s **mouth** dropped open in disbelief. **As for** the other nuns, what about them? Had they noticed it? / *No — which was just as well, as they'd go **nuts** if they realized there was a **robot** creeping up behind them!*

269

户 **hù** door

Radical 户
4 strokes

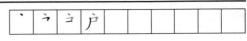

a drop 丶(22a) + **corpse** 尸(268a) = **door** 户

They put **a drop** of oil on the **corpse** so that they could squeeze it through the **door**. / *The **dwarf**, outraged, said, "Remember **who** that is!"*

270 所 **suǒ** building

Radical 斤
8 strokes

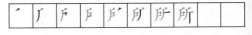

door 户(269) + **axe** 斤(240) = **building** 所

The left-hand side is an older version of "door" (Character 269), and does not appear in any other character in this book. Some books suggest writing the left-hand side of Character 270 by following the stroke-order used for Character 269.

所以(120) **suǒyǐ** *therefore, so*
所有(63) **suǒyǒu** *all*

The burglars broke down the **door** with an **axe** to gain access to the **building**. / *The **ghostly teddy** who guarded the building threw bars of **soap** at the intruders.*

271 己 **jǐ** self

Radical 己
3 strokes

This, and the characters 274 and 275a, are all very similar — use the character pictures for the basic building blocks at the beginning of the chapter to help you remember which is which.

自己(94) **zìjǐ** *self; one's own*

/ ***Teddy** is fitting new special **self**-cleaning **wheels** to his **jeep** (and ends up in need of some cleaning, himself!).*

272 记 **jì** note down

Radical 讠
5 strokes

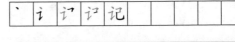

words 讠(67c) + **self** 己(271) = **note down** 记

[记者(261) **jìzhě** *reporter*]
[日记(6) **rìjì** *diary*]

(Stuck in a traffic jam) He has no paper, so has to write the **words** down on himself, as he wants to **note down** what has occurred. / *In particular, he wants to report the **dwarf** who has blocked the road with his **jeep**.*

273 纪 jì
discipline

Radical 纟
6 strokes

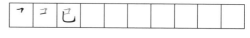

thread 纟 (233a) + **self** 己 (271) =
discipline 纪

This character also means an "age" or "era".

(A driver is trying to develop good habits) He ties some color-coded **thread**s round the controls to encourage him to be more **self-disciplin**ed with his driving. / *The **dwarf** won't rent him a **jeep** until his driving improves.*

年纪(168) **niánjì** *age*

[纪念(167) **jìniàn** *commemorate*]

---

274 已 yǐ
already

Radical 已
3 strokes

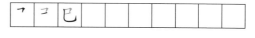

Here the last stroke half-closes the box at the top of the character; this is a halfway house between "self" and "snake" (271 and 275a).

/ *When they got to the fair, there was **already** a long queue for the Big **Wheel**. **Teddy** sat in the queue eating **Easter** eggs (getting chocolate everywhere).*

已经(244) **yǐjīng** *already*

275a 巳 sì
snake

Both this and Character 271 began as a picture of a snake. In fact "self" and "snake" tend to be used somewhat interchangeably in some composite characters.

---

275 走 zǒu
walk

Radical 走
7 strokes

earth 土 (54a) + **stop** 止 (30a) = **walk** 走

We could also break this up into "ten" plus "upright"; make up a story for this alternative if you prefer.

(On a mountain path there is a landslide and soil is pouring down across the path) He had to wait for the **earth** to **stop** moving before he could **walk** any further. / *Teddy was bouncing around, saying, "I should have come with someone who had the right **zodiac** sign!"*

[走道(145) **zǒudào** *footpath; sidewalk*]
[走动(58) **zǒudòng** *stretch one's legs*]

276  **qǐ** rise up

Radical 走
10 strokes

walk 走(275) + snake 巳(275a) = rise up 起

This is an example of a character where "snake" is often replaced by "self" (see 275a). In fact, using "self" is more usual nowadays (as shown in the main character entry here), but "snake" makes for a more memorable story!

You take your pet **snake** for a **walk** — you've trained it to **rise up** to greet your friends. / *Teddy wants to take a photo of it. "Say **Cheese**!" he says.*

起床(171) **qǐ chuáng** *to get up (from bed)*
一起(1) **yìqǐ** *together*
起来(65) **qǐlái** *stand up, rise up*
从...起(103) **cóng A qǐ** *starting from A*
对不起(154, 9) **duìbuqǐ** *excuse me, sorry*

---

277 导 **dǎo** guide

Radical 巳
6 strokes
導

snake 巳(275a) + inch 寸(104a) = guide 导

[指导(251) **zhǐdǎo** *supervise, direct*]

(A guided tour in the desert) Nobody saw the **snake inch**ing along the ground behind the tour **guide**. / *That is, until Teddy ran up and **doused** it with a bucket of water (and chaos ensued).*

278a 钅 gold

We will treat this as a basic building block. It is the form taken by the character 金 (which is in HSK Level B) when acting as the left-hand side of another character.

---

278 钟 **zhōng** clock

Radical 钅
9 strokes
鐘

gold 钅(278a) + middle 中(33) = clock 钟

In the **middle** of a **gold** block is set a **clock**. / *The giant who made it had also etched his jonquil design into the gold. (Remember jonquils? See Character 33).*

点钟(185) **diǎnzhōng** *o'clock*
钟头(246) **zhōngtóu** *hour (spoken Chinese)*
分钟(73) **fēnzhōng** *a minute*

279 种
zhǒng (zhòng)　　Radical 禾
species　　　　　　9 strokes

種

grain 禾(126a) + middle 中(33) = species 种

Also more generally "a kind, type, sort"; also "a seed" and "to plant or cultivate".

The teacher says, "In the **middle** of the **grain** is the DNA which defines the **species**." / *Teddy jumps up waving a jonquil asking, "Does it work for this too?"*

[种子(17) **zhǒngzi** *seed*]

280 足
zú　　　　　Radical 足
foot　　　　7 strokes

mouth 口(5) + stop 止(30a) = foot 足

When foot appears as the left-hand side of another character, the bottom is distorted (and looks more like 29a than 30a — see Character 283 below for an example).

At the **mouth** of the cave they all **stop**ped — nobody dared put a **foot** inside. / *Only when the fairy zoomed in to check it out did they relax.*

[满足(225) **mǎnzú** *satisfy*]

Test yourself:　儿(21)　阴(97)　上(42)　走(275)　四(24)　者(261)　其(235)

什(35)　到(74)　当(267)　杯(11)　卖(248)　山(110)　洗(139)

281a 艮
stubborn

Note the stroke order!

281 很
hěn　　　　Radical 彳
very　　　　9 strokes

step forward 彳(81a) + stubborn 艮(281a) = very 很

(Volunteers are sought for a dangerous mission to capture the dragon) Sir Galahad **stepped forward stubborn**ly; he was **very** sure he wanted to do it. / *Teddy jumps around excitedly singing, "A dragon hunt, a dragon hunt!"*

得很(118)　**A dehěn**　*very A*

282 根 gēn root

Radical 木
10 strokes

一 十 十 木 术 村 村 村 枳 根 根

tree 木(10a) + **stubborn** 艮(281a) = **root** 根

[根本(174) **gēnběn** *essence; basic*]

The **tree stubborn**ly refused to move a single **root**. / *The **giant** went to get his **gunpowder** to shift it.*

283 跟 gēn with

Radical 足
13 strokes

丶 ㄇ 口 ㅂ ㅂ 卫 足 跟 跟 跟
跟 跟 跟

foot 足(280) + **stubborn** 艮(281a) = **with** 跟

This means "with" in the sense of "together with" (not as in "writing with a pen").

[跟前(90) **gēnqián** *in front of; close to*]

(Think of this as a continuation of the previous story) The landowner puts his **foot stubborn**ly in the door (at the police station). "I'm going to stay here until you come **with** me. / *There's a **giant** on my land threatening to blow things up with **gunpowder!**"*

284 眼 yǎn eye

Radical 目
11 strokes

丨 冂 冃 目 目 目 眊 眊 眊 眼
眼

eye 目(93) + **stubborn** 艮(281a) = **eye** 眼

This is the normal character for a person's eye, rather than simply 目.

[眼前(90) **yǎnqián** *before one's eyes; at this very moment*]

The little girl plucked at the stuffed donkey's one remaining **eye** but it **stubborn**ly refused to budge. "I can't have a donkey with one **eye**!" / *Teddy had always had a **yen** to be a surgeon and found a new pair of eyes for it.*

285 银 yín silver

Radical 钅
11 strokes

丿 ㇏ 牛 钅 钅 钅 钅 钅 银 银
银

gold 钅(278a) + **stubborn** 艮(281a) = **silver** 银

银行(81) **yínháng** *bank (for money)*

(At a retirement ceremony) "I want a **gold** watch," he says **stubborn**ly, "**Silver** is for wimps." / *The **fairy** whispers, "Don't get stressed, it will upset your **yin**."*

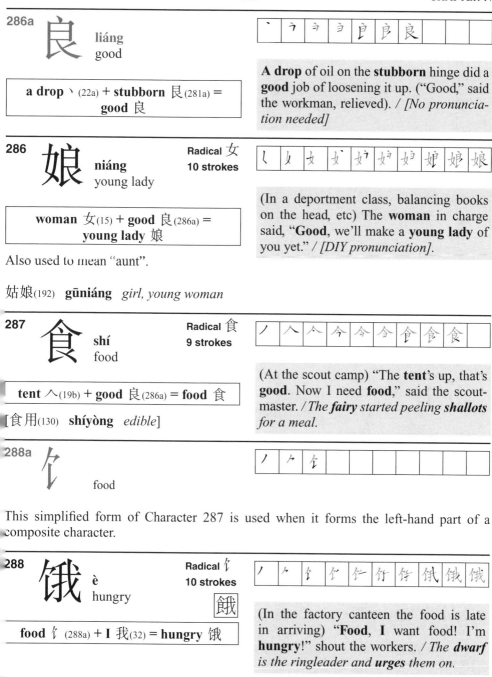

286a 良 liáng good

` ㇇ ㇆ ㇆ 自 自 良

a drop 丶 (22a) + stubborn 艮 (281a) = good 良

A drop of oil on the **stubborn** hinge did a **good** job of loosening it up. ("Good," said the workman, relieved). / *[No pronunciation needed]*

286 娘 niáng young lady

Radical 女
10 strokes

乚 女 女 女 女ㄱ 女ㄱ 妒 娘 娘

woman 女 (15) + good 良 (286a) = young lady 娘

(In a deportment class, balancing books on the head, etc) The **woman** in charge said, "**Good**, we'll make a **young lady** of you yet." / *[DIY pronunciation]*.

Also used to mean "aunt".

姑娘 (192) **gūniáng** *girl, young woman*

287 食 shí food

Radical 食
9 strokes

丿 人 人 今 今 今 食 食 食

tent 人 (19b) + good 良 (286a) = food 食

(At the scout camp) "The **tent**'s up, that's **good**. Now I need **food**," said the scout-master. / *The fairy started peeling shallots for a meal.*

[食用 (130) **shíyòng** *edible*]

288a 饣 food

丿 𠂉 饣

This simplified form of Character 287 is used when it forms the left-hand part of a composite character.

288 饿 è hungry

Radical 饣
10 strokes

餓

丿 𠂉 饣 饣 饣 饦 饳 饿 饿 饿

food 饣 (288a) + I 我 (32) = hungry 饿

(In the factory canteen the food is late in arriving) "**Food, I** want food! I'm **hungry**!" shout the workers. / *The dwarf is the ringleader and urges them on.*

Chapter 18

Time to take stock. By now, not only do you understand how all the systems work, but you'll also have a good feel for your own habits and preferences, and what works best for you.

If you look back you'll see that some character pictures and some stories have worked particularly well for you, and you've got them for life. Others you will have tried to learn a few times and keep forgetting. Try looking to see if those that you remember easily have anything in common. It is valuable to know this, because you can tailor the character pictures and stories to suit your own style of learning. We do keep saying that you can replace any story or character picture with one of your own devising, and if you do then it is likely to be memorable, both because of the effort you have put into it, and because it will be personalized to you.

What next? You've learned enough characters now to be able to pick any character further on in the book and learn it straight away. The most you will need to do is learn a basic building block or two if the character uses parts you haven't learned yet. But if you can, then simply carry on, and you will be adding to your knowledge with each character. It will still seem a long way to go to get to 800, but all you need to do is persevere, keeping up a slow, steady routine.

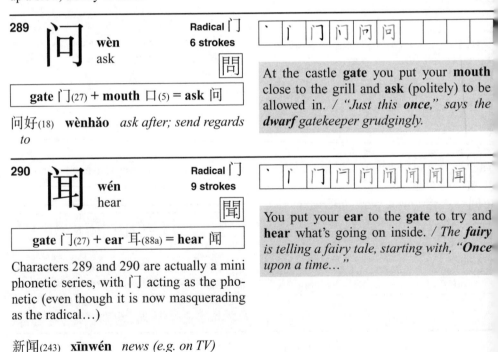

289 问 **wèn** ask

Radical 门
6 strokes

问

gate 门(27) + mouth 口(5) = ask 问

问好(18) **wènhǎo** *ask after; send regards to*

At the castle **gate** you put your **mouth** close to the grill and **ask** (politely) to be allowed in. / *"Just this once," says the* ***dwarf*** *gatekeeper grudgingly.*

290 闻 **wén** hear

Radical 门
9 strokes

聞

gate 门(27) + ear 耳(88a) = hear 闻

Characters 289 and 290 are actually a mini phonetic series, with 门 acting as the phonetic (even though it is now masquerading as the radical…)

新闻(243) **xīnwén** *news (e.g. on TV)*

You put your **ear** to the **gate** to try and **hear** what's going on inside. / *The* ***fairy*** *is telling a fairy tale, starting with, "****Once*** *upon a time…"*

Test yourself: 门(27) 取(88) 然(266) 识(256) 运(57) 人(12) 跟(283)
其(235) 音(257) 已(274) 尤(238) 们(28) 都(262) 法(87)

291 方 **fāng** direction

Radical 方
4 strokes

lid 亠(25b) + bow ㇒(51a) = direction 方

We have called the bottom part of this character "bow", but you might like to think of it as a form of "wrap" (23a) instead, in which case you can modify the story accordingly.

As well as "direction", this character also means "square (shape)". It gives rise to another good phonetic series, represented by Fang the dog.

Some books advocate writing the final two strokes in the reverse order.

方法(87) **fāngfǎ** *method*
[四方(24) **sìfāng** *square*]
[西方(100) **xīfāng** *the West*]
[对方(154) **duìfāng** *the other side/party*]
[地方(54) **dìfāng** *place; aspect*]
[立方(177) **lìfāng** *cubic (e.g. meters)*]
[比方(228) **bǐfāng** *analogy*]

(The vet stops to ask the way from a strange old man who is sitting outside his house) The old man has a **lid** on his head (instead of a hat) and silently **bows** to show which **direction** the vet must go. / *The vet is off to meet the giant to attend to his dog, Fang. [Fang will appear in the next few stories: picture him as a huge soppy dog].*

---

292 访 **fǎng** visit

Radical 讠
6 strokes

訪

words 讠 (67c) + direction 方(291) = visit 访

访问(289) **fǎngwèn** *visit, interview*

The **words** on the card are **direction**s, as this is your first **visit** to these friends. / *Teddy and Fang (the dog) are mucking about in the back seat of the car.*

---

293 房 **fáng** house

Radical 户
8 strokes

door 户(269) + direction 方(291) = house 房

This can also mean a room, as well as referring to a complete building.

房子(17) **fángzi** *house*]

You knock on the **door** to ask **direction**s to your friend's **house**. / *The fairy opens the door and casts a spell on Fang the dog to enable him to show you the way.*

294

放 **fàng**
release

Radical 方
8 strokes

丶 亠 方 方 方 方 放 放

direction 方(291) + **tap** 攵(190a) =
release 放

The convicts communicate **direction**s to their accomplice by **tap**ping (on the pipes in Morse code), so that he can carry out the plan to **release** them. / *The dwarf jailor sets **Fang** the dog to chase them as they try to escape.*

295

旁 **páng**
beside

Radical 方
10 strokes

丶 亠 亠 立 立 立 旁 旁

stand 立(177) + **cover** ⼍(82a) +
direction 方(291) = **beside** 旁

He had to **stand** up tall to put the **cover** over the **direction** sign, and set up a new sign **beside** it. / *The **fairy** had asked him to divert passing traffic past her new **pancake** stall.*

The last stroke of "to stand" has merged with "cover" (we saw something similar in 产, Character 197).

旁边(41) **pángbiān** *side*
[两旁(222) **liǎngpáng** *both sides*]

296

万 **wàn**
ten thousand

Radical 一
3 strokes

萬

一 丆 万

one 一(1) + **bow** ⼇(51a) =
ten thousand 万

As well as the exact amount of "ten thousand", this is used to mean "very many" in a more general sense.

As with Character 291, you might like to think of the bottom of this character as "wrap" instead of "bow". The same comment on stroke order applies: some books suggest writing the last two strokes in the other order.

The village elder goes on a pilgrimage to see the fabled **unicorn**, **bows** to him and explains the plight of the village. "**Ten thousand** blessings will fall upon your village as a reward for your courage," says the unicorn magnanimously. / *[DIY pronunciation]*

[百万(40) **bǎiwàn** *million*]
[万能(206) **wànnéng** *multi-purpose; all-powerful*]
[万岁(116) **A wànsuì** *Long live A!*]

Test yourself: 马(44)   而(151)   岁(116)   开(85)   论(252)   基(237)   你(51)

有(63)   谢(108)   地(54)   边(41)   起(276)   六(39)   呢(268)

297

主
zhǔ
lord

Radical 王
5 strokes

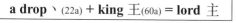

a drop 丶 (22a) + king 王 (60a) = lord 主

Don't confuse this with "plant" (133a).

You will recall that "jade" (60b) was also formed out of "king" and "a drop". Notice how in this story for "lord" the drop is on top of the king, whereas in the story for "jade" the drop was falling from the king. If you keep this in mind you won't get the stories mixed up.

(At the ceremony) **A drop** of the special oil fell on the **king** when the man was presented, indicating that the man is to be made a **lord**. / *Teddy is playing around twirling the jewel of office until it's needed for the ceremony.*

主要 (101) **zhǔyào** *main, major, chief*
主意 (258) **zhǔyi** *idea, view*]
主观 (216) **zhǔguān** *subjective*]
主动 (58) **zhǔdòng** *of one's own accord, on one's own initiative*]
主人 (12) **zhǔrén** *host; proprietor*]
买主 (247) **mǎizhǔ** *customer, buyer*]

298

住
zhù
to live in

Radical 亻
7 strokes

person 亻 (13a) + lord 主 (297) = live in 住

This character means to reside or live in a place (not simply to be alive).

Harry is made a **lord** and given an official house to **live in**. / *The dwarf supervises the placing of the lordly jewel above the front door.*

住口 (5) **zhùkǒu** *Shut up!*]

299

注
zhù
pour

Radical 氵
8 strokes

water 氵 (78a) + lord 主 (297) = pour 注

This also means "to pay heed", "pay attention", "take notes".

Water is brought to the new **lord** who **pours** it into the ceremonial urn. / *The dwarf dips the lordly jewel into the urn to turn the water into wine.*

注意 (258) **zhùyì** *pay attention to*

300 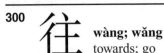 **wàng; wǎng**   Radical 彳   8 strokes

towards; go

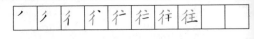

> step forward 彳 (81a) + lord 主(297) = towards; go 往

[往往 **wǎngwǎng** *often*]
[已往(274) **yǐwǎng** *in the past*]

🎬 "**Step forward, Lord** Vader, and walk **towards** the ewok," said the director (on the film set of "Star Wars"). But there is no ewok! / *"Wang! Where's **Wang** the **dwarf**?" calls the director. **Teddy** starts running around calling, "**Wang! Wang!** \ Somebody **go, go** and find him!"*

301a

"pedestal"

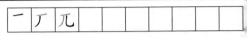

> one 一(1) + boy 儿(21) = pedestal 兀

The **unicorn** uses his horn to lift the small **boy** onto the **pedestal** (so that people can see the new "chosen one"). / *[No pronunciation needed].*

---

301 **yuán**   Radical 二   4 strokes

yuan

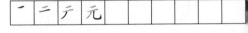

> one 一(1) + pedestal 兀(301a) = yuan 元

This has several meanings: "first"; "chief"; "unit"; "yuan". The last of these is the unit of currency in China, and we will use "yuan" as the soundword in the resulting phonetic series.

Clearly we could also regard this character as "two" plus "boy". We will be meeting "pedestal" again in Chapter 39.

[公元(119) **gōngyuán** *A.D.*]
[日元(6) **Rìyuán** *(Japanese) yen*]

In the town square there is a statue of a **unicorn** on a **pedestal**; people throw **yuan** coins onto the pedestal for good luck. / *At night the **fairy** comes to collect the **yuan** coins for charity.*

---

302 **yuán**   Radical 囗   7 strokes

garden

 園

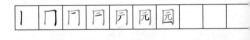

> enclosed 囗(24a) + yuan 元(301) = garden 园

公园(119) **gōngyuán** *park, public garden*

The historic **yuan** coin is **enclosed** in a display case in the memorial Chinese **garden**. / *The fairy sets up a souvenir stall to sell replica **yuan** coins.*

303

远 **yuǎn**
distant

Radical ⻌
7 strokes

遠

| road ⻌(26a) + yuan 元(301) = distant 远 |

[远亲(196) **yuǎnqīn** *distant relatives*]
[远近(241) **yuǎnjìn** *distance*]

一 二 テ 元 元 远 远

You can see the **yuan** coins lying on the **road** sparkling into the **distance** like cat's eyes. / *Teddy tries to pick up all the yuan coins but can't hold them all.*

304

玩 **wán**
play

Radical 王
8 strokes

| king 王(60a) + yuan 元(301) = play 玩 |

玩儿(21) **wánr** *play, have fun*
[好玩儿(18, 21) **hǎowánr** *great fun*]

一 二 チ 王 玓 珏 玕 玩

The **king** likes to sneak out with his pockets full of **yuan** coins and **play** the slot machines! / *[DIY pronunciation]*

305

完 **wán**
finish

Radical ⼧
7 strokes

| house ⼧(91a) + yuan 元(301) = finish 完 |

完成(259) **wánchéng** *fulfil, accomplish*
用完(130) **yòngwán** *use up*]

丶 丷 宀 宀 宇 完 完

The high-class building firm has a custom, when building a new **house**, to cement a **yuan** coin to the roof when the work is **finish**ed (to show that they don't penny-pinch). / *[DIY pronunciation]*

306

院 **yuàn**
institute

Radical 阝
9 strokes

| mound 阝(96a) + finish 完(305) = institute 院 |

学院(82) **xuéyuàn** *college*
住院(298) **zhùyuàn** *to stay in hospital*]
院子(17) **yuànzi** *courtyard, compound*]

了 阝 阝 阝 阝 阠 陉 陉 院

They built a temporary **mound** in front when they had **finish**ed building the **Institute**. / *The dwarf stood on it to place the commemorative yuan coin above the door, to declare the Institute for Dwarf Studies open.*

307a

 offend

| ` | `´ | ⸜ | ⸝ | 羊 | | | | |

horns ⸜ (65a) + **dry** 干(124) = **offend** 羊

The ram left his **horns** to **dry** so that there would be no smell to **offend** anyone. / *[No pronunciation needed]*

307

 nán
south

Radical 十
9 strokes

| 一 | 十 | 广 | 内 | 内 | 南 | 肉 | 南 | 南 |

ten 十(4) + **outer limits** 冂(160a) + **offend** 羊(307a) = **south** 南

南边(41) **nánbiān** *the south side*
[南海(129) **Nán Hǎi** *the South China Sea*]

If you **offend** against the rules in the **outer limits**, by going in areas marked with a **cross**, you'll be sent to the **South** Pole (to help count the penguins). / *The **fairy** will conjure up a flying **nanny** goat to take you there!*

308

 xìng
good fortune

Radical 土
8 strokes

| 一 | 十 | 土 | 坴 | 查 | 查 | 查 | 幸 | |

earth 土(54a) + **offend** 羊(307a) = **good fortune** 幸

You take a pot of **earth** to the housewarming party, which seems to **offend** the new householder — this mystifies you as in your own culture it brings **good fortune**. / *The **dwarf** behind you has brought a pot of **shingle** (and wonders how this will be received ...)*

309

 píng
level

Radical 一
5 strokes

| 一 | 一 | 一 | 立 | 平 | | | | |

dry 干(124) + **horns** ⸜ (65a) = **level** 平

Note the "horns" are inside "dry" rather than on top (as in "offend", 307a) and notice once again that this difference is built into the story.

As well as "level", this character also means "flat" or "calm".

[平安(91) **píng'ān** *safe, safe and sound*]
[和平(126) **hépíng** *peace*]
[平方(291) **píngfāng** *square (e.g. meters)*]
[不平(9) **bùpíng** *unfair; resent*]

The cow put her **horns** inside the tumble **dry**er — which were such a weight that she had to check it was **level** before she could switch it on. / *The **fairy** used the level surface as a **ping-pong** table.*

310 苹 **píng** [apple]

Radical 艹
8 strokes

蘋

| 一 | 十 | 艹 | 艹 | 艾 | 芦 | 苸 | 苹 | | |

grass 艹(218a) + **level** 平(309) = **apple** 苹

苹果(187) **píngguǒ** *apple*

To test whether the **grass** is **level** he uses an **apple** (seeing if it rolls around). / *The fairy suggests using a ping-pong ball instead (so she can eat the apple!)*

---

311 评 **píng** comment on

Radical 讠
7 strokes

評

| 丶 | 讠 | 讠 | 讠 | 评 | 评 | 评 | | | |

words 讠 (67c) + **level** 平(309) = **comment on** 评

批评 (229) **pīpíng** *criticize; criticism*

A sign-writer trying to get his **words level** (on a shop sign) asks people across the street to **comment on** how he's doing. / *The fairy gives a definitive view by using her ping-pong ball as a spirit level.*

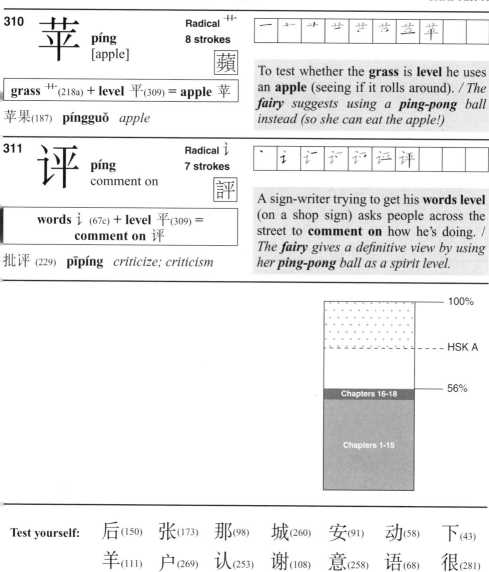

100%

HSK A

56%

Chapters 16-18

Chapters 1-15

Test yourself: 后(150) 张(173) 那(98) 城(260) 安(91) 动(58) 下(43)

羊(111) 户(269) 认(253) 谢(108) 意(258) 语(68) 很(281)

Chapter 19

dexterity

affair

firewood

east

music

bamboo

sequence

5..4..3..2..1....

un-

Un connected

312a  手

dexterity

312 事 **shì** affair

Radical 一
8 strokes

This is a rather complex "basic" character! You can think of a story involving "piled up" (Character 150b) and "dexterity" for it if you prefer.

/ "The **Affair** of the **Wheel**" is the title of a slushy romance between two cyclists. After a few pages the **dwarf** throws the book down in disgust, saying, "What a **charade**!"

故事(191) **gùshì** story, tale
做事(210) **zuòshì** to work]
办事(123) **bàn shì** to handle matters]
事实(250) **shìshí** a fact]
没事儿(169, 21) **méishìr** it doesn't matter, it's nothing; to have nothing to do]

313 面 **miàn** face

Radical 一
9 strokes

 麵

thumb tack ⌐ (40a) + **enclosed** 口 (24a) + **eye** 目 (93) = **face** 面

This character has two completely separate meanings: "face" or "surface"; and "flour" or "noodles". The traditional form only applies to the second meaning.

To write the character, notice that the "eye" touches the box of "enclosed" and so the stroke-order changes accordingly.

(The children had been throwing flour at each other and some went in the girl's eye) They used a **thumb tack** to secure the bandages **enclosing** the **eye**, which made her **face** look very odd! / The **two dwarves** grumbled to each other, "These children are a right **menace**," as they cleaned up the mess.

见面(214) **jiànmiàn** to meet
方面(291) **fāngmiàn** side, aspect
外面(71) **wàimiàn** the outside]
前面(90) **qiánmiàn** the front]
对面(154) **duìmiàn** the opposite side]
地面(54) **dìmiàn** the earth's surface]

314a 此 **cǐ** this

stop 止 (29a) + **spoon** 匕 (206a) = **this** 此

"**Stop** using that **spoon** to eat your soup — use **this** one!" / [No pronunciation needed]

314

此 xiē
a few

Radical 二
8 strokes

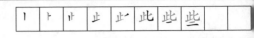

this 此(314a) + two 二(2) = few 些

那些(98) **nàxiē** *those*
一些(1) **yìxiē** *a small amount of*
这些(26) **zhèxiē** *these*
有些(63) **yǒuxiē** *some (items)*

(Air show commentary) "**This biplane** is one of the **few** of its type remaining. / *The **two giants** kindly carried it all the way from their **shed** so it can be here today.*"

315a

音 spit

` ⊃ ⊃ ⊃ 立 ⊃ 音 音

stand 立(177) + mouth 口(5) = spit 音

Not only "to spit" but also "to vomit" — a pleasant character all round!

He had to **stand** on the creature's **mouth** to stop it **spit**ting. / *[No pronunciation needed]*

315

倍 bèi
multiple

Radical 亻
10 strokes

丿 亻 亻 亻 亻 伫 伫 倍 倍 倍

person 亻 (13a) + spit 音(315a) = multiple 倍

[四倍(24) **sìbèi** *four-fold*]

Harry had to **spit** to get rid of the vile taste — but as the spit hit the floor it turned into a tiny version of him. He kept spitting until there were **multiple** versions of him everywhere. / *The **dwarf** had to be called on to take the **baby** Harry's away!*

316

部 bù
section

Radical 阝
10 strokes

` ⊃ ⊃ ⊃ 立 ⊃ 音 音 音⊃ 部

spit 音(315a) + city 阝(96a) = section 部

部分(73) **bùfen** *portion, part*
干部(124) **gànbù** *cadre, party official*
[部门(27) **bùmén** *department*]
[内部(219) **nèibù** *the interior, inside*]
[部长(172) **bùzhǎng** *(govt.) minister*]
[南部(307) **nánbù** *southern part*]

Spitting was not allowed in many parts of the **city** but the bylaw varied from **section** to section. / *The **dwarf** could **boot** out anyone found breaking the law.*

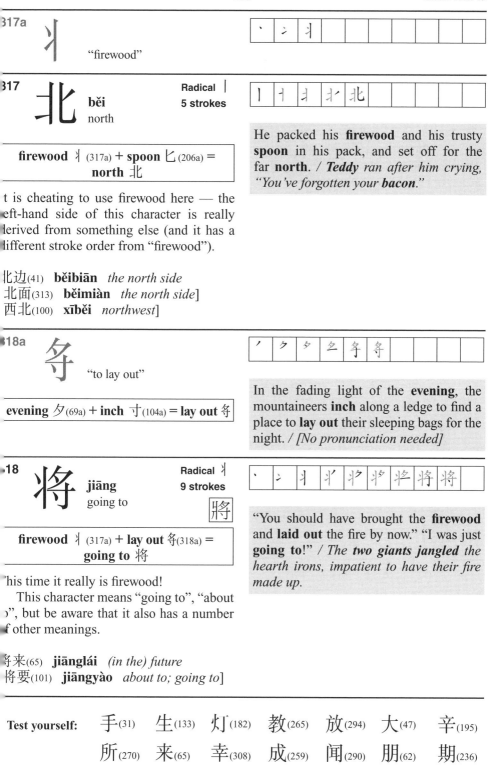

317a 丬 "firewood"

317 北 **běi** north

Radical 丨
5 strokes

firewood 丬 (317a) + spoon 匕 (206a) = north 北

He packed his **firewood** and his trusty **spoon** in his pack, and set off for the far **north**. / *Teddy ran after him crying, "You've forgotten your **bacon**."*

It is cheating to use firewood here — the left-hand side of this character is really derived from something else (and it has a different stroke order from "firewood").

北边(41) **běibiān** *the north side*
北面(313) **běimiàn** *the north side*]
西北(100) **xīběi** *northwest*]

318a 夅 "to lay out"

evening 夕(69a) + inch 寸(104a) = lay out 夅

In the fading light of the **evening**, the mountaineers **inch** along a ledge to find a place to **lay out** their sleeping bags for the night. / *[No pronunciation needed]*

318 将 **jiāng** going to

Radical 丬
9 strokes

將

firewood 丬 (317a) + lay out 夅(318a) = going to 将

"You should have brought the **firewood** and **laid out** the fire by now." "I was just **going to**!" / *The two giants jangled the hearth irons, impatient to have their fire made up.*

This time it really is firewood!
This character means "going to", "about to", but be aware that it also has a number of other meanings.

将来(65) **jiānglái** *(in the) future*
将要(101) **jiāngyào** *about to; going to*]

Test yourself: 手(31) 生(133) 灯(182) 教(265) 放(294) 大(47) 辛(195)
所(270) 来(65) 幸(308) 成(259) 闻(290) 朋(62) 期(236)

319 东 dōng east

Radical 一
5 strokes

東

Notice how similar this character is to "car" (Character 83), "music" (Character 320 below), and especially to "select" (713a).

东边(41) **dōngbiān** *the east side*
东西(100) **dōngxi** *thing*
[东北(317) **dōngběi** *northeast*]
[东方(291) **dōngfāng** *the East, Orient*]

/ *The **giant** took the big **wheel** from the **east** gate of the city (to fix his cart) and made a quick getaway on his **donkey**!*

320 乐 yuè (lè) music

Radical 丿
5 strokes

樂

This story is attempting to give you some help with what is really a DIY pronunciation.

With the pronunciation **lè**, 乐 also means "happy", as in the phrase "Happy Birthday".

/ *The **music** box on **wheels** (that is, a barrel organ) has been set up outside the **dwarf**'s house again, and he comes out to complain: "**You, eh**? I've told you before, go and play somewhere else!"*

音乐(257) **yīnyuè** *music*

321a 竹 bamboo

321 算 suàn reckon

Radical 竹
14 strokes

| **bamboo** 竹 (321a) + **eye** 目 (93) + **two hands** 廾 (85a) = **reckon** 算 |

打算(153) **dǎsuàn** *plan; intend*

The pirate captain raised the **bamboo** telescope to his **eye** and steadied it with **two hands**. "**I reckon** I'll need fifty men to storm that castle," he said to his crew. *But it was actually a **sand** castle that the **ghostly dwarf**, who guarded the island, had built to deter pirates.*

322a 弟 sequence

| ㄱ | 一 | 弓 | 弗 | 弟 | | | | | |

---

322 第 **dì** Number Radical ⺮ 11 strokes

| ノ | ⺈ | ⺊ | ⺮ | ⺮ | 竹 | 竺 | 竿 | 笃 | 第 |
| 第 | | | | | | | | | |

bamboo ⺮ (321a) + **sequence** 弟 (322a) = **Number** 第

第一 (1) **dìyī** *Number 1*

(In the panpipes factory) The **bamboo** pipes have to be sorted into the right **sequence** and labeled **Number** 1, **Number** 2, and so on. / *The dwarf has been demoted (so is given this job, which he thinks is beneath him).*

---

323 弟 **dì** younger brother Radical ⅤⅠ 7 strokes

| 丶 | 丷 | 丷 | 弎 | 弟 | 弟 | 弟 | | | |

horns ⅤⅠ (65a) + **sequence** 弟 (322a) = **younger brother** 弟

弟弟 **dìdi** *younger brother*

The goats were all being lined up, the size of their **horns** determining their place in the **sequence**. One goat noticed that his **younger brother** had sneaked in above him. / *He told the dwarf (organizing the line-up), so that his brother was demoted.*

324a 芇 glowing

| 一 | 十 | 艹 | 芇 | 芇 | | | | | |

grass 艹 (218a) + **cover** ⼍ (82a) = **glowing** 芇

They tried to hide the radioactive waste by putting a **cover** over it and putting **grass** on top of that, but it soon started **glowing**, which gave the game away. / *[No pronunciation needed]*

---

324 劳 **láo** toil Radical 艹 7 strokes 勞

| 一 | 十 | 艹 | 芇 | 芇 | 劳 | 劳 | | | |

glowing 芇 (324a) + **power** 力 (14) = **toil** 劳

劳动 (58) **láodòng** *do (manual) work*

Keeping the furnaces **glowing** at the **power** station was hard **toil**. / *The fairy played loud music for the workers (so that they could hear it over the roar of the furnaces while they worked).*

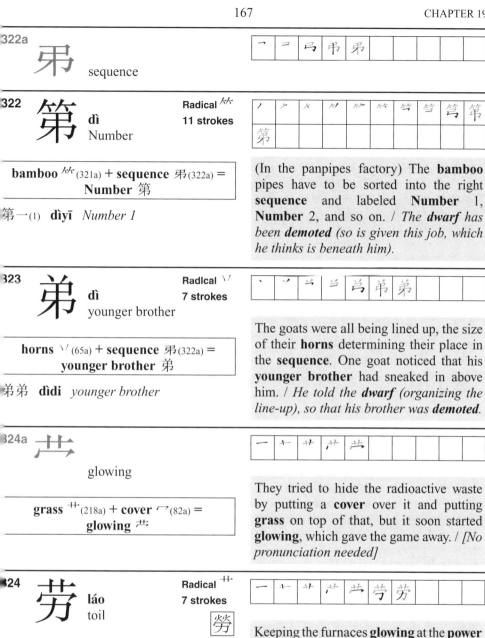

325 加 jiā
add

Radical 力
5 strokes

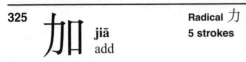

power 力(14) + **mouth** 口(5) = **add** 加

[加以(120) **jiāyǐ** *moreover; ought to*]
[加工(147) **jiā gōng** *to process (unfinished products)*]

A **power** socket has been installed by the **mouth** of each cave, to **add** the cave dwelling area to the electricity grid. / *Two giant workmen arrive, carrying a huge jar of plugs and switches between them.*

326 驾 jià
drive (a vehicle)

Radical 马
8 strokes

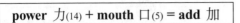

add 加(325) + **horse** 马(44) = **drive** 驾

劳驾(324) **láojià** *may I trouble you?*

The cart salesman says, "All you have to do is **add** a **horse** and you can **drive** it away!" / *The two dwarves who are thinking of buying the cart are now arguing over who should smash the jar against the side to "launch" it (like a boat) and who should drive it away.*

327 咖 kā
[coffee]

Radical 口
8 strokes

mouth 口(5) + **add** 加(325) = **coffee** 咖

This character, and Character 329 below, are both used for their sound. You will only ever see them when they appear together in the word 咖啡 (**kāfēi**, "coffee").

As he put the mug to his **mouth** he remembered that he must **add** milk to his **coffee**. / *The giant got a carton of milk from his fridge.*

328 非 fēi
un-

Radical 非
8 strokes

[非法(87) **fēifǎ** *unlawful, illegal*]

/ *"It's **un-wheel**" was the catch-phrase of the **famous giant** with the speech impediment!*

329 啡 **fēi** [coffee]

Radical 口
11 strokes

丶	丨	口	叮	叮	唎	唎	唎	啡
啡								

mouth 口(5) + un- 非(328) = coffee 啡

咖啡(327)　**kāfēi**　*coffee*

As he put the mug to his **mouth** he realized it was **un**sweetened **coffee**. / *The famous giant pulled a face.*

330 排 **pái** line

Radical 扌
11 strokes

一	丨	扌	扌	扌	扌	扌	排	排
排								

hand 扌(152a) + un- 非(328) = line 排

安排(91)　**ānpái**　*arrange*

He had to use his bare **hand**s to **un**couple the **line** of rail cars. / *The fairy whispered to him to disconnect the pipes too.*

Test yourself:　就(239)　饿(288)　今(166)　妹(64)　眼(284)　云(56)　名(70)
五(36)　根(282)　夫(49)　导(277)　猪(263)　为(122)　足(280)

Chapter 20

With this chapter you will have completed half the chapters in the book. Once again, we already have available all the basic building blocks we will need.

331

反 **fǎn** oppose

Radical 又
4 strokes

| ノ | 厂 | 反 | 反 | | | | | | |

drag 厂(150a) + **right hand** 又(52) = **oppose** 反

The older form of this character uses "cliff" instead of "drag" and you will still see this form around.

It is often translated as "anti-", "counter-".

The young prince has to be **drag**ged along to **shake hands** with all the dignitaries, but is **oppose**d to all the pomp and circumstance (and vows to do things differently when he is king). / *Teddy is happy though, as he gets to play fanfares on his trumpet.*

反对(154) **fǎnduì** *oppose, object to*
[反动(58) **fǎndòng** *reactionary*]

332

饭 **fàn** meal

Radical 饣
7 strokes

飯

| ノ | ㇆ | 饣 | 饣 | 饣 | 饭 | 饭 | | | |

food 饣 (288a) + **oppose** 反(331) = **meal** 饭

Used to mean "cooked rice", or more generally, "a meal".

There were so many types of **food** that the fussy guest was **oppose**d to (on ideological grounds) that it was difficult to put together a **meal** for him. / *The dwarf chef demands that a fanfare be played (to accompany his entrance with the resulting meal, after all the trouble he's gone to).*

午饭(125) **wǔfàn** *lunch*
饭店(186) **fàndiàn** *hotel; restaurant*

333

板 **bǎn** board

Radical 木
8 strokes

| 一 | 十 | 才 | 木 | 朾 | 朾 | 板 | 板 | | |

tree 木(10a) + **oppose** 反(331) = **board** 板

The **tree** is **oppose**d to the new highway and he is certainly opposed to them nailing a **board** to him announcing the development. / *Teddy pulls the board off and bandages up the holes.*

[老板(264) **lǎobǎn** *boss, proprietor*]

334

米 **mǐ**
rice

Radical 米
6 strokes

`丶　丷　二　半　兴　米`

horns 丷 (65a) + **tree** 木(10a) = **rice** 米

Also means "meter", the unit of length; (see also 777a for another character for "meter").

(A party game) "Animal **horns** have been hidden in the **tree**, with **rice** inside — you have to climb up, find a horn and bring it down without spilling any rice. Who wants to try it?" / *"Me", says Teddy, "me, me, me!"*

[大米(47) **dàmǐ** *rice*]
米饭(332) **mǐfàn** *cooked rice*

Test yourself: 己 (271)　政(190)　学(82)　问(289)　首(144)　太(48)　老(264)
目 (93)　他(13)　部(316)　院(306)　第(322)　房(293)　店(186)

335

青 **qīng**
blue-green

Radical 青
8 strokes

`一　二　丰　圭　丰　青　青　青`

plant 主 (133a) + **moon** 月(61) = **blue-green** 青

The character means either "blue" or "green" (though there are also separate characters for each of these two colors) so we have called it both!

This character gives rise to a good phonetic series, coming right up. In fact we have *two* phonetic series, one pronounced "qing" and the other "jing". We have already seen something like this with Characters 133 to 136.

(On a cliff face) The **plant** in the moonlight looks **blue**, but it's actually **green**. / *Only the giant is tall enough to see into the chink of rock where the plant is growing.*

This situation arose because the pronunciations have gradually changed down the centuries (although you can see that the two sounds are still very similar), while the characters stayed the same.

青年(168) **qīngnián** *a youth*
[年青(168) **niánqīng** *young*]

336

请 **qǐng**
please

Radical 讠
10 strokes

請

`丶　讠　讠́　讠̄　计　请　请　请　请`

words 讠 (67c) + **blue-green** 青(335) = **please** 请

This is used in various phrases such as "Please come in", and also means "to invite".

The **words** are written in big **blue-green** metal letters on the cliff face: "**Please** don't disturb the plants." / *Teddy clambers up on the letters to peer into the chink.*

请问(289) **qǐngwèn** *Excuse me, …*

337 清 **qīng** transparent **Radical** 氵 **11 strokes**

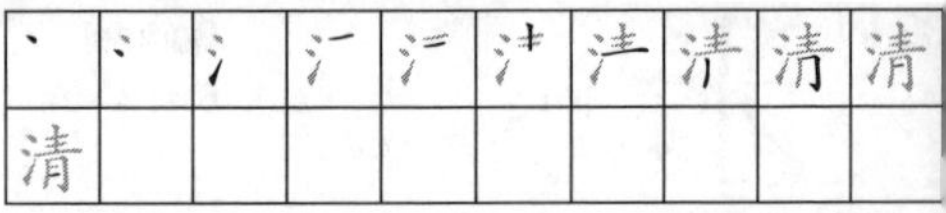

water 氵 (78a) + **blue-green** 青 (335) = **transparent** 清

[清理(158) **qīnglǐ** *to put in order, sort out*]

When **water** falls on the **blue-green** plant it turns it **transparent**. / *The **giant** verifies this by peeping into the **chink** in the rock.*

---

338 晴 **qíng** fine weather **Radical** 日 **12 strokes**

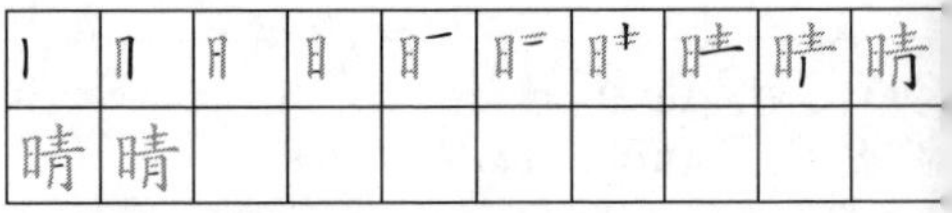

sun 日 (6) + **blue-green** 青 (335) = **fine weather** 晴

[晴天(76) **qíngtiān** *a sunny day*]

The **sun** turning the plant **blue-green** again is the first sign of **fine weather**. / *The **fairy** keeps flitting up to the **chink** to check out this natural barometer.*

339a 忄 heart

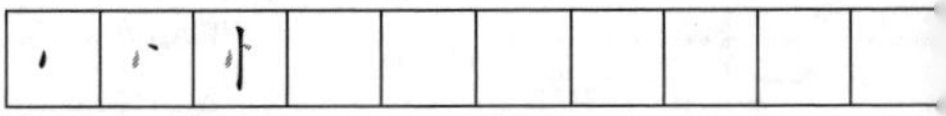

This is the form taken by Character 161 when it appears as the left-hand side of a character.

Some books suggest writing the strokes in the order left to right.

---

339 情 **qíng** state of affairs **Radical** 忄 **11 strokes**

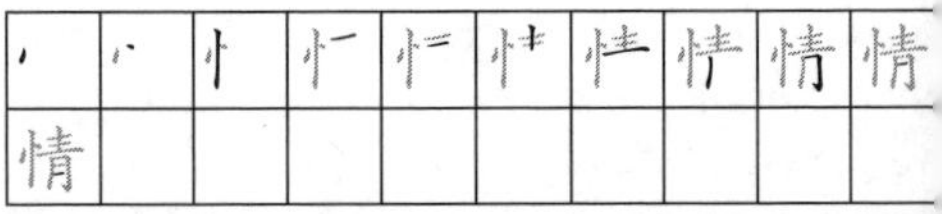

heart 忄 (339a) + **blue-green** 青 (335) = **state of affairs** 情

This and the previous four characters form a phonetic series based on 青 (Character 335). The following two characters form a second series based on the same character but with a different pronunciation.

事情(312) **shìqíng** *affair, matter*
[同情(160) **tóngqíng** *sympathy*]
[心情(161) **xīnqíng** *mood, state of mind*]

The **heart** of the plant only turns **blue-green** when this **state of affairs** (the fine weather) persists. / *Only the **fairy** can get right inside the **chink** to see the color change.*

340 睛 jīng
pupil (of eye)

Radical 目
13 strokes

丨	冂	冂	月	目	目⌐	目⌐	目扌	睊	睛
睛	睛	睛							

eye 目(93) + blue-green 青(335) =
pupil 睛

眼睛(284) **yǎnjīng** *eye*

"Color your **eyes** with **blue-green** eye shadow to set off your **pupils**!" / *The giant fancies a job in advertising and is trying to write **jingles** (this is his first effort, for a cosmetics company).*

---

341 精 jīng
splendid

Radical 米
14 strokes

丶	丶	二	斗	米	米	米	粁	精
精	精	精	精					

rice 米(334) + blue-green 青(335) =
splendid 精

[精力(14) **jīnglì** *energy, vigor*]

"**Blue-green rice** is **splendid**!" / *Another of the giant's advertising jingles.*

Test yourself: 友(53) 说(67) 利(132) 平(309) 分(73) 倍(315) 样(112)

己(271) 本(174) 纪(273) 倒(75) 近(241) 种(279) 弟(323)

342a 亭
"gazebo"

丶	二	六	亠	古	亠	亭		

tall 古(239a) + cover ⌒(82a) = gazebo 亭

Erect **tall** poles and sling a **cover** over the top, and you have a **gazebo**! / *[No pronunciation needed]*

---

342 亮 liàng
shining

Radical 亠
9 strokes

丶	二	六	亠	古	亠	亭	亮	亮

gazebo 亭(342a) + several 几(7) =
shining 亮

In some older typefaces "several" is replaced by "boy" (Character 21) in this character.

月亮(61) **yuèliàng** *the moon*

In the **gazebo** were **several** golden statues of a young boy, **shining** so brightly in the sun that they were dazzling passers by. / *The **two dwarves** had found the statues languishing in a back room at the museum and had polished them up (rather too well it seems!)*

343a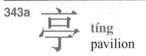
亭 tíng
pavilion

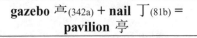

gazebo 亳(342a) + nail 丁(81b) =
pavilion 亭

This character is also used for a small kiosk or stall.

Inside the **gazebo** is a box of **nail**s so the carpenter can convert it into a **pavilion** (by nailing up walls to it). / *[No pronunciation needed]*

343
停 tíng
halt

Radical 亻
11 strokes

person 亻(13a) + pavilion 亭(343a) =
halt 停

Harry wanders into the **pavilion** and **halt**s in his tracks. / *A beautiful **fairy** hovering near the ceiling sends a **tingle** down his spine.*

344
单 dān
single

Radical 丷
8 strokes

單

horns 丷(65a) + field 田(156a) + ten 十(4)
= single 单

[单位(178) **dānwèi** *work unit*]
[单词(231) **dāncí** *a word*]
[单人床(12, 171) **dānrénchuáng** *single bed*]

They carried **horns** into the **field** and tied them to a **cross** which marked where the **single** rare flower would bloom. / *Unfortunately the **giant** came along and picked it, thinking it was a **dandelion**!*

345
间 jiān
room

Radical 门
7 strokes

間

gate 门(27) + sun 日(6) = room 间

This also means "between".

The huge city **gate**s blocked the **sun** from the **room**. / *The two **giants** set up a **generator** to provide lighting.*

房间(293) **fángjiān** *a room*
中间(33) **zhōngjiān** *center; among*
时间(105) **shíjiān** *a period of time*
之间(121) **A B zhījiān** *between A and B*
[洗手间(139, 31) **xǐshǒujiān** *washroom, toilet*]

346

简 **jiǎn**
simple

Radical ⺮
13 strokes

簡

| ノ | ト | ⺊ | ⺊丿 | ⺮ | ⺮ | ⺮ | 竹 | 竹 | 简 |
| 简 | 简 | 简 | | | | | | | |

> **bamboo** ⺮ (321a) + **room** 间(345) =
> **simple** 简

简单(344) **jiǎndān** *simple*

The **bamboo** stands ready in the **room** and a piece of paper headed "**Simple** Instructions" is pinned to the wall. / *The two teddies (rather optimistically) set about building their own generator.*

Test yourself: 算(321) 住(298) 记(272) 银(285) 理(158) 方(291) 排(330)

南(307) 钟(278) 亲(196) 娘(286) 访(292) 字(92) 完(305)

347

合 **hé**
join together

Radical 人
6 strokes

| ノ | 人 | 人 | 合 | 合 | 合 | | | | |

> **combine** 人(59a) + **mouth** 口(5) =
> **join together** 合

This means "to join together" or "combine"; hence also "to suit" or "suitable".

[合理(158) **hélǐ** *logical, reasonable*]

[合作(207) **hézuò** *co-operation*]

[合同(160) **hétong** *agreement, contract*]

(At the end of the marriage ceremony) They **combine**d **mouth**s in a kiss for so long that they found they had become **joined together**. / *All very embarrassing, as they had to shuffle along to the fairy who brewed up a herbal remedy to separate them.*

348

拿 **ná**
using

Radical 手
10 strokes

| ノ | 人 | 人 | 人 | 合 | 合 | 合 | 盒 | 盒 | 拿 |

> **join together** 合(347) + **hand** 手(31) =
> **using** 拿

This character means "to grasp" or "hold in the hand"; hence "using".

To make a long table the carpenter **joined together** two pieces of wood — with a **hand** underneath to support them while **using** a screwdriver in the other hand. / *The fairy had supplied wood with a beautiful swirling grain from the gnarled tree.*

拿去(86) **náqù** *to take (away)*]

349 **shí** pick up

Radical 扌
9 strokes

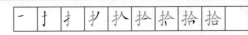

hand 扌(152a) + **join together** 合(347) = **pick up** 拾

This character and the previous one are another pair of characters made up from the same components. Notice that in the previous story the hand is *underneath*, to reflect this difference.

拾 is used for "ten" (instead of 十) on bank checks, to prevent alterations.

(The king says to the princess) "You must accept the **hand** of the winning suitor and **join together** with him in matrimony. Each suitor will **pick up** the marital plate. / *The fairy will sit on the plate with a **shallot** balanced on her head, and the one who keeps it balanced there the longest will be the winner."*

350 哈 **hā** laugh

Radical 口
9 strokes

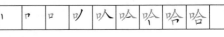

mouth 口(5) + **join together** 合(347) = **laugh** 哈

哈哈 **hāhā** *(sound of laughter)*

At the **mouth** of the cave the potholers are **joined together** with ropes so nobody can get lost, when they hear a **laugh** booming round the cave. / *They run in all directions, falling over the ropes, and the **giant** laughs even **harder**.*

351 **gěi (jǐ)** for (someone)

Radical 纟
9 strokes

給

thread 纟(233a) + **join together** 合(347) = **for** 给

He took colored **thread**s which he **joined together**, plaiting them into a bracelet. But who is it **for**? / *For **Teddy's** new girlfriend, the **geisha**.*

352 答 **dá (dā)** answer

Radical 竹
12 strokes

bamboo 竹(321a) + **join together** 合(347) = **answer** 答

回答(202) **huídá** *to reply, answer*

In the old days a couple had to ask the village **bamboo** pipe if they were suitable to **join together** in marriage — a lot depended on the **answer** it gave. / *But it was really only the **fairy** in the **dark** who was whispering the answers.*

Chapter 21

And so, after the first twenty chapters, onwards into the second twenty. This is where you need to keep to your routine, slowly and steadily, and after a few more chapters it will be all downhill.

片 **slice**	丩 **entangle**
卑 **inferior**	井 **a well**
冫 **ice**	久 **long time**
爪 **claw**	巴 **wait for**

353 片 **piàn**
slice

Radical 片
4 strokes

丿 丿' 丿- 片

[片面(313) **piànmiàn** *onesided, unilateral*]

*/ (It's the racing driver's birthday) They all want a **slice** of the birthday cake, which is in the shape of a steering **wheel**. The **two dwarf** chefs carry the cake up to the **penthouse** where the party is in full swing.*

354a 丩
"entangle"

ㄴ 丩

---

354 叫 **jiào**
call

Radical 口
5 strokes

丨 口 口 口ㄴ 叫

mouth 口(5) + **entangle** 丩(354a) = **call** 叫

This can mean both "to call" and "to be called" (as in "I'm called Joe.")

[叫做(210) **jiàozuò** *be called, be known as*]
[叫门(27) **jiàomén** *call at the door*]

At the **mouth** of the cave you have become **entangle**d in the brambles and **call** for help. / *Unfortunately the **two** mountain rescue **dwarves** are watching the **jousting** on TV (and can't hear you calling as they are too busy arguing over which is the better team).*

---

355 收 **shōu**
accept

Radical 攵
6 strokes

ㄐ 丩 丩' 丩- 收 收

entangle 丩(354a) + **tap** 攵(190a) = **accept** 收

收拾(349) **shōushi** *put in order, tidy up*
[收音机(257, 10) **shōuyīnjī** *radio set (receiver)*]

(In a mountaineeering contest) A climber gets **entangle**d in his ropes and has to **tap** on the rocks to attract attention — he has to **accept** help from his bitter rival. / *The **giant**, who would normally do the rescues, is away watching the **show-jumping**.*

356a 卑 **bēi**
inferior

丿 丿' 白 白 白 卑 卑 卑

You could think of this as "drop" plus "field" plus a distorted form of "entangle".

356 啤 pí
[beer]

Radical 口
11 strokes

| 丨 | 口 | 口 | 口ノ | 口八 | 哨 | 哨 | 哨 | 啤 |
| 啤 | | | | | | | | |

mouth 口 (5) + **inferior** 卑 (356a) = **beer** 啤

啤酒 (102) **píjiǔ** beer

"Normally I don't let anything **inferior** into my **mouth**, but what I really fancy right now is a **beer**. / It's just what I need to go with my **pizza**," said the **fairy** (slumming it a bit).

357a 井 jǐng
a well

| 一 | 二 | 𠃌 | 井 | | | | |

357 讲 jiǎng
talk

Radical 讠
6 strokes

講

| 丶 | 讠 | 讠一 | 讠二 | 讲 | 讲 | | |

words 讠 (67c) + **a well** 井 (357a) = **talk** 讲

[讲座 (212) **jiǎngzuò** lecture, lecture course]

Mysterious **words** have appeared, etched around the inside of the village **well**, and the villagers can **talk** about nothing else. / The **two teddies**, eager to investigate down the well, **jangle** the chain as one lowers the other down in the bucket.

358 进 jìn
proceed

Radical 辶
7 strokes

進

| 一 | 二 | 𠃌 | 井 | 井丶 | 讲 | 进 | |

road 辶 (26a) + **a well** 井 (357a) = **proceed** 进

进去 (86) **jìnqù** go in
进来 (65) **jìnlái** come in
进行 (81) **jìnxíng** to conduct, carry out
[前进 (90) **qiánjìn** to advance]
[请进 (336) **qǐng jìn** please come in]
[先进 (137) **xiānjìn** advanced]

The **road** to the well was so full of people that you could only **proceed** slowly along it. / The **dwarf**, stuck in the queue, was glad that he had brought his hip flask full of **gin**.

Test yourself: 可 (140) 七 (37) 取 (88) 听 (242) 饿 (288) 苹 (310) 请 (336)
站 (184) 旁 (295) 班 (113) 劳 (324) 食 (287) 纪 (273) 北 (317)

359 **gǎi**
alter

Radical 攵
7 strokes

self 己(271) + tap 攵(190a) = alter 改

[改进(358) **gǎijìn** *improvement*]
[改期(236) **gǎiqī** *to change the date (of a meeting etc.)*]
[改日(6) **gǎirì** *another day (than today)*]
[改正(29) **gǎizhèng** *rectify*]

The magician needed merely to **tap** him**self** with his wand to **alter** his appearance completely. / *Teddy (dressed up as his assistant) cries, "Will you look at this **guy**!"*

360a ice

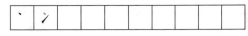

This is "water" (80a), but with one less drop.

---

360 **kuàng**
situation

Radical 氵
7 strokes

ice 氵 (360a) + older brother 兄(67a) = situation 况

OK, so kangaroo may not be the best idea on ice, but how many choices for a soundword did we have?!

His **older brother** fell head-first through the **ice**. "That's another fine **situation** you've got me into," he spluttered. / *The ghostly ice-guardian **dwarf** bounds across on his **kangaroo** to investigate.*

情况(339) **qíngkuàng** *situation*

361a **qiàn**
lacking

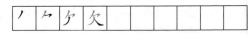

bow 𠂉(51a) + person 人(12) = lacking 欠

This HSK Level B character also means "to owe".

As he watched the man **bowing** to him, **Harry** found it difficult not to laugh as the man's trousers fell down, **lacking** a belt to keep them up! / *[No pronunciation needed]*

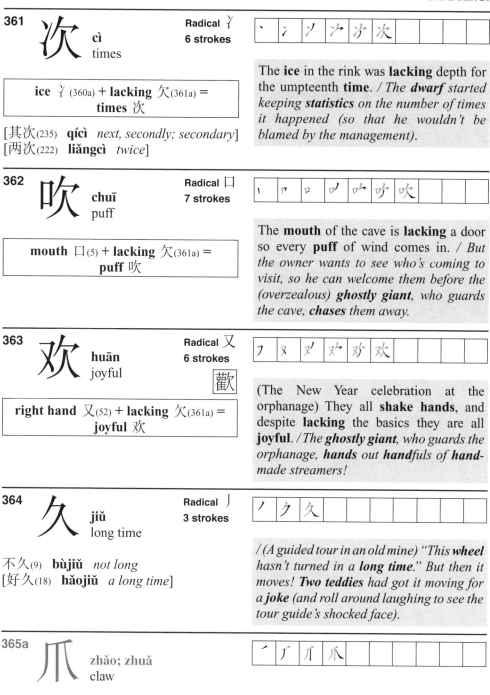

361
次
cì
times

Radical 冫
6 strokes

ice 冫(360a) + lacking 欠(361a) =
times 次

[其次(235) **qícì** *next, secondly; secondary*]
[两次(222) **liǎngcì** *twice*]

The **ice** in the rink was **lacking** depth for the umpteenth **time**. / *The **dwarf** started keeping **statistics** on the number of times it happened (so that he wouldn't be blamed by the management).*

362
吹
chuī
puff

Radical 口
7 strokes

mouth 口(5) + lacking 欠(361a) =
puff 吹

The **mouth** of the cave is **lacking** a door so every **puff** of wind comes in. / *But the owner wants to see who's coming to visit, so he can welcome them before the (overzealous) **ghostly giant**, who guards the cave, **chases** them away.*

363
欢
huān
joyful

Radical 又
6 strokes

歡

right hand 又(52) + lacking 欠(361a) =
joyful 欢

(The New Year celebration at the orphanage) They all **shake hands**, and despite **lacking** the basics they are all **joyful**. / *The **ghostly giant**, who guards the orphanage, **hands** out **handfuls** of **hand-made streamers!***

364
久
jiǔ
long time

Radical 丿
3 strokes

不久(9) **bùjiǔ** *not long*
[好久(18) **hǎojiǔ** *a long time*]

/ *(A guided tour in an old mine) "This **wheel** hasn't turned in a **long time**." But then it moves! **Two teddies** had got it moving for a **joke** (and roll around laughing to see the tour guide's shocked face).*

365a
爪
zhǎo; zhuǎ
claw

When it is used as the top of a composite character, "claw" takes the form 365b below.

365b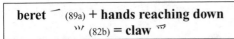

claw

| beret ¯ (89a) + **hands reaching down** ʷ (82b) = **claw** ˯ |

The old lady always puts a **beret** over her **hands** when she **reaches down** for something, so that nobody can see that her hand looks like a **claw**. / *[No pronunciation needed]*

365c 丞

hand down

| **claw** ˯ (365b) + **cover** ⌐(82a) = **hand down** 丞 |

(The old crone is in the attic) She lifts the **cover** of the chest with her **claw**ed hand and **hands down** the precious heirloom (to her granddaughter waiting below). / *[No pronunciation needed]*

365 爱 **ài** love

Radical 爪
10 strokes

愛

| **hand down** 丞(365c) + **friend** 友(53) = **love** 爱 |

爱人(12) **àirén** *spouse*
[爱情(339) **àiqíng** *(romantic) love*]
[可爱(140) **kě'ài** *lovely, lovable*]
[亲爱(196) **qī'nài** *darling, beloved*]

The dying duke says, "I intend to **hand down** all my possessions to you when I die; you have been a true **friend** to me and shown me the only **love** I've ever known." / *The dwarf butler actually smiles: this had melted the ice in his heart.*

366 暖 **nuǎn** warm

Radical 日
13 strokes

| **sun** 日(6) + **love** 爱(365) = **warm** 暖 |

If you look very closely, you will see that the "cover" in the middle of the right-hand side of this character has been abbreviated into a simple horizontal line.

暖和(126) **nuǎnhuo** *warm (weather)*

The holidaymakers lie in the **sun** and **love** the feeling of being so **warm**. / *The ghostly teddy (who guards their well-being) rides up and down the beach on a nanny goat (to warn people against getting sun burnt).*

367 父 fù *father*

Radical 父
4 strokes

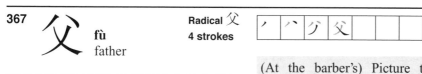

eight 八(20) + shears ㄨ(25a) = father 父

父亲(196) **fùqīn** *father*

(At the barber's) Picture the **octopus** wielding a pair of **shears**, giving a haircut to your **father**! / *In the next chair along, a dwarf is grumpily trimming the beard of Fu Manchu (he doesn't hold with all this personal vanity).*

Test yourself: 车(83) 生(133) 必(162) 将(318) 完(305) 万(296) 阳(96)

玩(304) 答(352) 青(335) 想(164) 停(343) 评(311) 主(297)

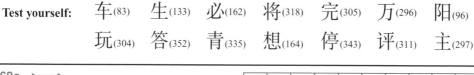

368a 巴 bā *wait for*

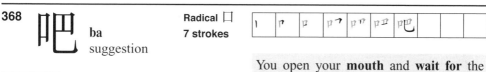

This means "to wait for" but also "to hope for".

---

368 吧 ba *suggestion*

Radical 口
7 strokes

mouth 口(5) + wait for 巴(368a) = suggestion 吧

This is a particle put at the end of a sentence to indicate a suggestion or a supposition. 吧 is also used for its sound, often with 1st tone, as in the following compound.

[酒吧(102) **jiǔbā** *bar (a place serving drinks)*]

You open your **mouth** and **wait for** the dentist to start work, but instead he says, "I have a **suggestion**. / *Perhaps you'd like to try my robot assistant — he can do this work at a bargain price.*"

---

369 把 bǎ *handle*

Radical 扌
7 strokes

hand 扌(152a) + wait for 巴(368a) = handle 把

This character is also used to mark a direct object in a sentence.

[一把刀(1, 72) **yì bǎ dāo** *a knife*]

(There's a queue for the sale at the department store) You are at the front of the queue **wait**ing **for** the shop to open, your **hand** ready to grab the door **handle** as soon as the door is unlocked. / *Behind you, Teddy excitedly hops around, hoping to bag a bargain.*

370 爸 **bà**
dad

Radical 父
8 strokes

---

father 父(367) + **wait for** 巴(368a) =
dad 爸

爸爸 **bàba** *dad, daddy, papa*

(In the queue for the sale at the department store) Imagine **wait**ing **for** your **father** to come (so that you will be allowed in). When he arrives you shout, "**Dad!**" / *You both race off to stop the **dwarf** grabbing all the **bargains**.*

---

371 爬 **pá**
climb

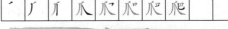

Radical 爪
8 strokes

---

claw 爪(365a) + **wait for** 巴(368a) =
climb 爬

This also means "to crawl".

[爬山(110) **pá shān** *to climb a mountain*]

The cat sits with its **claw**s at the ready, and **waits for** the mouse to come through the hole in the fence — but the mouse **climb**s over the fence instead. / *Nothing will stop him getting to one of the **fairy**'s legendary **parties**.*

Test yourself: 厂(149) 天(76) 先(137) 足(280) 注(299) 出(114) 单(344)
起(276) 进(358) 片(353) 加(325) 往(300) 欢(363) 清(337)

Chapter 22

This is another chapter where you've already learned all the basic building blocks you will need.

---

372 关 **guān** switch off

Radical 丷
6 strokes

關

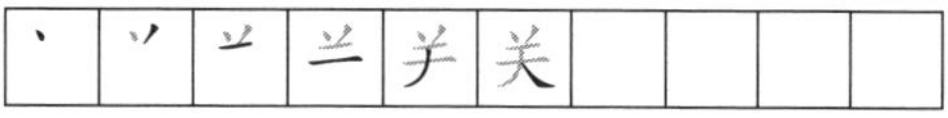

horns 丷(65a) + **heaven** 天(76) = **switch off** 关

This originally meant "a guarded mountain pass", which explains why today it can also mean "to shut" or "a barrier", but also "a connection".

关心(161) **guānxīn** *care for, care about*
[海关(129) **hǎiguān** *(frontier) customs*]

(Arriving at a fancy dress party in Heaven) "You shouldn't wear **horns** in **Heaven** — especially not plastic ones with flashing lights — **switch** them **off** at once!" / *The voice came from a **ghostly giant** sitting on a **gantry** above the Pearly Gates.*

---

373 送 **sòng** deliver

Radical 辶
9 strokes

road 辶(26a) + **switch off** 关(372) = **deliver** 送

This also means "to give" (as a gift).

[送行(81) **sòngxíng** *see off (visitors)*]
[欢送(363) **huānsòng** *see off (visitors)*]

The delivery van driver's instructions read: "Park on the **road**, and **switch off** your engine before you **deliver** the packet. / *Otherwise the **dwarf** will make a **song** and dance about the fumes."*

---

374 联 **lián** connect

Radical 耳
12 strokes

聯

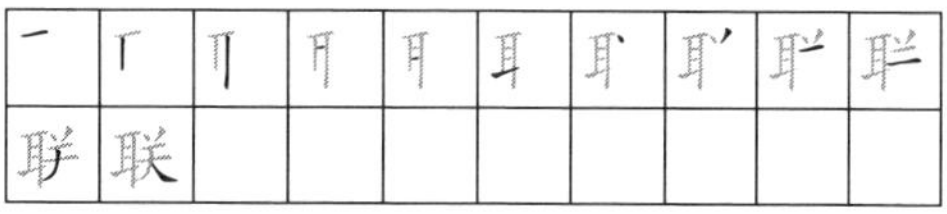

ear 耳(88a) + **switch off** 关(372) = **connect** 联

[联合(347) **liánhé** *unite, get together*]

(The bomb disposal expert has been called to deal with an old unexploded bomb) He puts his **ear** to the casing until he hears the mechanism **switch off**, then he can **connect** up the two wires to make it safe. / ***Two fairies** fly in with a bowl of **lentil** soup (to relax with, afterwards).*

375 言 yán
words

Radical 言
7 strokes

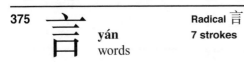

| 丶 | 一 | 亠 | 言 | 言 | 言 | 言 | | |

lid 亠(25b) + two 二(2) + mouth 口(5) = words 言

When this character appears as the left-hand part of other characters, it has the simplified form 讠, which we have already met (67c).

In the **biplane** you can see your co-pilot's **mouth** moving but can't hear what she's saying (because of the wind noise), so you fit a canopy or **lid** on top so you can hear each other's **words**. / *The **fairy** has a **yen** to go for a ride (and might do so now that the canopy will protect her hairdo!)*

语言(68) **yǔyán** *language*
[发言(146) **fā yán** *(make a) speech*]

376 信 xìn
letter

Radical 亻
9 strokes

| 丿 | 亻 | 仁 | 仁 | 信 | 信 | 信 | 信 | 信 |

person 亻(13a) + words 言(375) = letter 信

Notice that we have already met a character made up from "person" and "words" in the other order: 认 (Character 253). If you read the previous sentence and recognized the two forms of "person" and "words" without thinking about it, it just shows how familiar you are getting with Chinese characters!

Harry is good at reading documents written using old **words**, and people often bring him old **letter**s to decipher. / *The **dwarf** brings him an old **shin** bone with writing on it (hoping to catch him out).*

相信(163) **xiāngxìn** *believe (in, that)*
[来信(65) **láixìn** *incoming letter*]
[回信(202) **huí xìn** *a reply*]
[信心(161) **xìnxīn** *confidence*]

Test yourself: 千(89) 见(214) 里(157) 础(115) 是(30) 情(339) 学(82)
园(302) 南(307) 久(364) 驾(326) 间(345) 事(312) 男(156)

---

377 少 shǎo (shào)
few

Radical 小
4 strokes

| 丨 | 丿 | 小 | 少 | | | | | |

small 小(50) + slide 丿(34b) = few 少

This can also mean "seldom", "to be missing/lacking" or "young".

The **small slide** is for small children only — but there are only a **few** slides like this in the whole country. / ***Teddy** clambers up and **shouts** with joy as he slides down. (Teddies are allowed on too as they're very light.)*

多少(69) **duōshǎo** *how many?*
[不少(9) **bùshǎo** *quite a few*]

378 步 **bù**
step

Radical 止
7 strokes

stop 止(29a) + few 少(377) = step 步

Note that the third stroke of "few" disappears in this character.

"**Stop!** — only a **few** may walk in the master's foot**steps**." / *The **dwarf** carefully removes his **boots** to lead the chosen few (placing his feet in the footprints).*

[进步(358) **jìnbù** *make progress*]

---

379 省 **shěng**
province

Radical 小
9 strokes

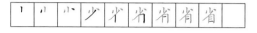

few 少(377) + eye 目(93) = **province** 省

The governor chooses a **few** trusted officials to keep an **eye** on the **province** while he is away on his next foreign trip. / *[DIY pronunciation]*

[省力(14) **shěnglì** *to save effort*]
[省会(59) **shěnghuì** *provincial capital*]

---

380 交 **jiāo**
pay

Radical 宀
6 strokes

lid 宀(25b) + father 父(367) = **pay** 交

The basic meaning is to "hand over" or "transfer"; hence "exchange" and (social) "intercourse".

The boy bangs a saucepan **lid** by his **father**'s ear. "**Pay** me my pocket money!" / *But the father only grunts — he's watching the **two giants jousting** on TV.*

[外交(71) **wàijiāo** *foreign affairs*]

---

381 饺 **jiǎo**
dumpling

Radical 饣
9 strokes

餃

food 饣 (288a) + pay 交(380) = dumpling 饺

(In the canteen) "The **food** is a disgrace, you have to **pay** so much, and then all you get is **dumpling**s." / *The **two teddies** (the cooks) are watching the **jousting** on TV (so haven't bothered to cook anything else).*

饺子(17) **jiǎozi** *stuffed dumpling*

382 较 jiào comparison

Radical 车
10 strokes

較

car 车(83) + **pay** 交(380) = **comparison** 较

比较(228) **bǐjiào** *comparatively*

(At the freeway toll booths) The **cars** are queuing up to **pay**, with the drivers in the two queues making **comparison**s about how long they had been there. / *The queues are building up because the two dwarves, who man the two toll booths, are both watching the jousting on their TV sets.*

383 校 xiào school

Radical 木
10 strokes

tree 木(10a) + **pay** 交(380) = **school** 校

学校(82) **xuéxiào** *school*
[校园(302) **xiàoyuán** *campus*]

In the village there is a special **tree**, and the villagers make people **pay** to see it, using the money to build a **school**. / *Two dwarves go round the local area like town criers, shouting out news about the tree and drumming up business.*

384 牛 niú cow

Radical 牛
4 strokes

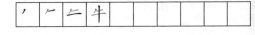

label ノ (124a) + **criminal** 十(130a) = **cow** 牛

When this forms the left-hand part of a composite character, the lower horizontal stroke is slanted, and drawn last (see Character 466 for an example).

[牛肉(221) **niúròu** *beef*]
[吹牛(362) **chuīniú** *to boast, brag*]

While the **criminal** was on parole he had to wear a **label** with a picture of a **cow** on it — to show that his job was to look after the cows. / *It took two fairies (working in shifts) to keep an eye on this notorious criminal.*

385 件 jiàn number of things

Radical 亻
6 strokes

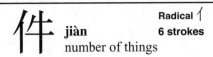

person 亻 (13a) + **cow** 牛(384) = **number of things** 件

This is a fairly general measure word for various objects such as items of clothing or pieces of furniture.

(In the "Best Trained Cow" competition at the village fete) **Harry** trains his **cow** to do a **number of things** (juggling, standing on its head, etc.) / *It finishes by genuflecting to the two dwarf adjudicators.*

386 哥 gē older brother

Radical 口
10 strokes

一 | 一 | 一 | 口 | 可 | 可 | 哥 | 哥 | 哥 | 哥

may 可(140) + **may** 可(140) =
older brother 哥

哥哥 **gēgē** *older brother*
[大哥(47) **dàgē** *eldest brother*]

At the May celebrations there are **two** **May**poles, one for the older children and one for the smaller children. A small boy dances round the smaller pole and looks across to where his **older brother** is dancing round the other one. / *The **giant** accompanies the dance with a tune on chimes made out of **girders**.*

387 歌 gē song

Radical 欠
14 strokes

一 | 一 | 一 | 口 | 可 | 可 | 哥 | 哥 | 哥 | 哥
哥 | 歌 | 歌 | 歌

older brother 哥(386) + **lacking** 欠(361a)
= **song** 歌

[歌手(31) **gēshǒu** *(professional) singer*]
[儿歌(21) **érgē** *nursery rhyme*]

Your **older brother** is totally **lacking** in talent but insists on singing his favorite **song**. / *The **giant** accompanies him on the chimes made out of **girders** (but unfortunately can't quite drown him out).*

388a 业 "haul up"

丶 | 丷 | 业 | 业

hands reaching down ''' (82b) +
one 一(1) = **haul up** 业

The **unicorn** has fallen overboard from the Ark but there are soon friendly **hands reaching down** to **haul** it **up** onboard again. / *[No pronunciation needed]*

388 应 yīng (yìng) should

Radical 广
7 strokes

應

丶 | 一 | 广 | 广 | 广 | 应 | 应

shelter 广(170) + **haul up** 业(388a) =
should 应

应当(267) **yīngdāng** *should, ought to*]

The hermit who lives in the mountains **hauls up** his supplies (in a basket on a rope) and stores them in a **shelter** next to his hut. Each delivery **should** be enough to last a month (but he always eats them up early). / *[DIY pronunciation]*

389a 问 "skylight"

outer limits 冂(160a) + **mouth** 口(5) = **skylight** 问

At the **outer limits** of the kingdom there is a special cave: from the **mouth** of the cave you can see daylight as this cave has a **skylight**! / *[No pronunciation needed]*

---

389 向 **xiàng** towards

Radical 丿
6 strokes
嚮

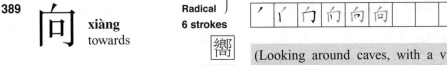

a drop 丶 (22a) + **skylight** 问(389a) = **towards** 向

(Looking around caves, with a view to buying one) **A drop** of rain falls on the **skylight** and they realize it faces **towards** the prevailing winds. / *The two dwarves argue back and forth for a while but finally decide this is a small price to pay to live in Shanghai.*

This character has various shades of meaning and the traditional form only applies to some of these.

方向(291) **fāngxiàng** *direction*

---

390 响 **xiǎng** noisy

Radical 口
9 strokes
響

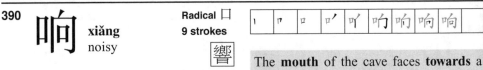

mouth 口(5) + **towards** 向(389) = **noisy** 响

The **mouth** of the cave faces **towards** a **noisy** part of town. / *The two teddies, though, are excited: "We'll be able to see all the Shanghai goings-on."*

---

391 化 **huà** to change

Radical 亻
4 strokes

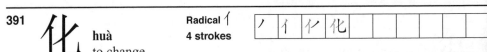

person 亻 (13a) + **seven** 七(37) = **change** 化

Harry looks in his **diary** and sees that in seven days he has to **change** the clock on the church tower (to daylight saving time). / *Last time he had forgotten and the ghostly dwarf who guards the tower had given him a hard time.*

This also means "to alter" and can sometimes be translated by using word endings such as "-ize" or "-ify".

化学(82) **huàxué** *chemistry*
文化(25) **wénhuà** *culture*

Test yourself: 晴(338)   元(301)   暖(366)   叫(354)   家(109)   反(331)   果(187)
关(372)   东(319)   何(142)   面(313)   灯(182)   哪(99)   咖(327)

392

花 huā
flower

Radical ⁺⁺
7 strokes

| 一 | 十 | 艹 | 艼 | 艻 | 花 | 花 | | | |

grass ⁺⁺(218a) + change 化(391) = flower 花

[花园(302) **huā yuán** *garden*]
[种花(279) **zhòng huā** *to grow flowers*]

Rather than just having **grass**, she wants to **change** part of her garden into a **flower** bed. / *She employs the **ghostly giant** to look after the flowers, and he uses his **hard** hat to protect them from frost.*

393

历 lì
experience

Radical 厂
4 strokes

歷 曆

| 一 | 厂 | 历 | 历 | | | | | | |

cliff 厂(149) + power 力(14) = experience 历

This also means "calendar" (and if so the second traditional form applies).

[经历(244) **jīnglì** *experience*]

He builds the **power** plant at the bottom of the **cliff** — **experience** has taught him that this is a good place for a hydroelectric plant. / *The **dwarf** has to go round checking for **leaks** in the pipes.*

394

旧 jiù
outdated

Radical 日
5 strokes

舊

| 丨 | 刂 | 卪 | 旧 | 旧 | | | | | |

stick 丨(19a) + sun 日(6) = outdated 旧

Another character for "old", which often means "traditional".

[旧历(393) **jiùlì** *lunar calendar*]

(In a town park) Using a **stick** and the **sun** is a very **outdated** way of telling the time. / *The **two dwarf** park keepers mutter to each other — they think it is a **joke** that something so outdated is still used, and in their park too.*

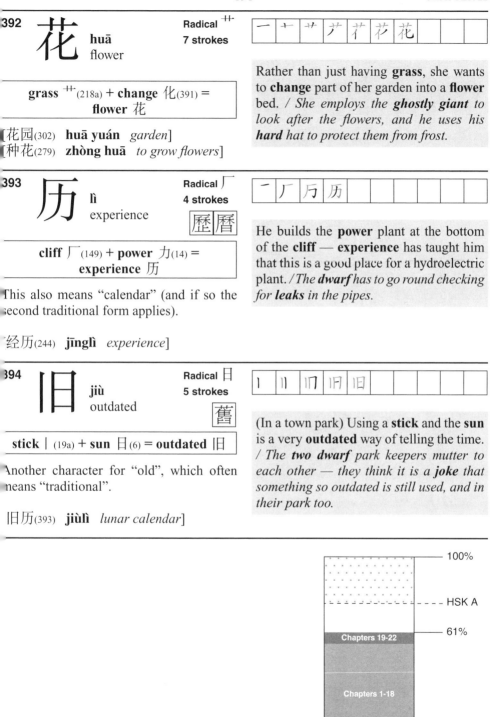

100%

HSK A

61%

Chapters 19-22

Chapters 1-18

Chapter 23

Once again there are a few pairs of basic building blocks where it is worth paying particular attention to the small differences:

史 and 吏; 夫 and 央; 垂 and 重

史 history

吏 an official

更 even more

央 center

夬 to separate

重 heavy

垂 droop

业 industry

395 业 **yè** industry

Radical 业
5 strokes

業

| 丨 | 丨丨 | 丷丨 | 业丨 | 业 | | | | | |

工业(147) **gōngyè** *(manufacturing)*
  industry
作业(207) **zuòyè** *homework, assignment*
[事业(312) **shìyè** *career; cause,*
  undertaking]

/ The **dwarf** had created a whole **industry** out of making **wheels**, employing **yetis** to do the work.

396a 亚 **yà** Asia

亞

| 一 | 丆 | 亓 | 亓 | 亚 | 亚 | | | | |

one 一(1) + **industry** 业(395) = **Asia** 亚

The **unicorn industry** churns out plastic unicorns, each with "Made in **Asia**" stamped underneath. / *[No pronunciation needed]*

396b 並 stand side by side

| 丶 | 丷 | 亠 | 䒑 | 丷 | 兯 | 並 | 並 | | |

horns 丷 (65a) + **Asia** 亚(396a) =
stand side by side 並

In the high plateaus of **Asia** they play tunes on animal **horns** — **stand**ing **side by side** (like a huge set of pan-pipes). / *[No pronunciation needed]*

---

396 碰 **pèng** bump into

Radical 石
13 strokes

| 一 | 丆 | 石 | 石 | 石 | 石 | 石゙ | 石ˊ | 矿 | 矿 |
| 碰 | 碰 | 碰 | | | | | | | |

stone 石(115a) + **stand side by side**
並(396b) = **bump into** 碰

This can mean "to encounter", or to literally "bump into" something.

Imagine setting up large (Stonehenge-type) **stone**s like a huge domino run — they **stand side by side** so that when each one falls it will **bump into** the next one. / *The dwarf warns people to be punctual or they will miss this big event.*

---

397 史 **shǐ** history

Radical 口
5 strokes

| 丶 | 丩 | 口 | 少 | 史 | | | | | |

历史(393) **lìshǐ** *history*

/ The **history** lesson was about the invention of the **wheel**. **Teddy** is bored by this class and sits munching **shallots** at the back. (Smell his breath!)

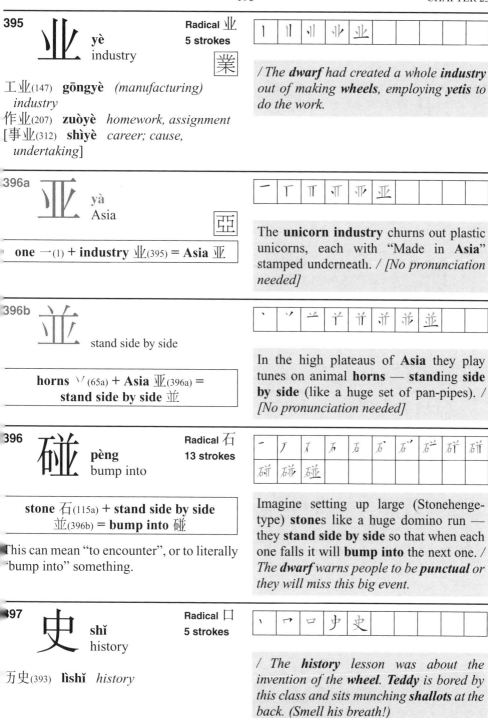

398a 吏 an official

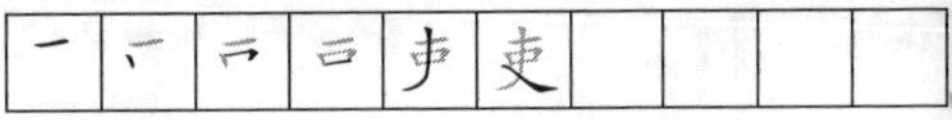

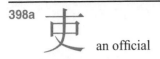

398 使 **shǐ** use — **Radical 亻 8 strokes**

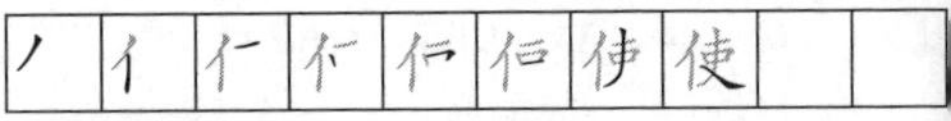

person 亻 (13a) + **an official** 吏(398a) = **use** 使

This also means "to send" or "an envoy".

使用(130) **shǐyòng** *use, apply*

(In the gallery of modern art) **Harry** asks the **official** if he can **use** his camera. / *He wants a picture of the sculpture "**Teddy** sitting on a pile of **shallots**".*

399 更 **gèng** even more — **Radical 一 7 strokes**

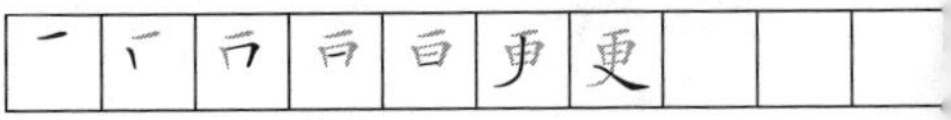

[更加(325) **gèngjiā** *still more, even more*]

*/ (At the tire shop) **Even more wheels** than yesterday are being returned by the customers. The **dwarf** orders them to be coated with **gunk** and resold ...*

400 便 **pián; biàn** 1. advantageous 2. convenient — **Radical 亻 9 strokes**

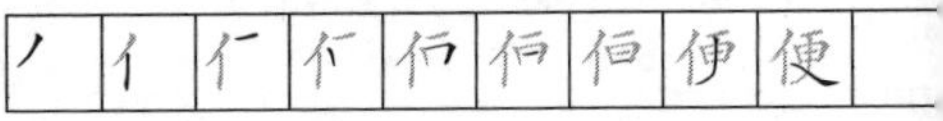

1. **person** 亻 (13a) + **even more** 更(399) = **advantageous** 便

2. **person** 亻 (13a) + **even more** 更(399) = **convenient** 便

方便(291) **fāngbiàn** *convenient, handy*
[便利(132) **biànlì** *convenient*]

1.
In the saloon **Harry** had had a lot to drink, but his opponent had drunk **even more** — Harry would find this **advantageous** if it came to a gunfight. / *The **two fairies** wanted to avoid bloodshed so each conjured up a bullet-proof vest so that any bullets wouldn't **penetrate**.*

2.
On the spaceship **Harry** has **even more** room in his cabin than the Captain, which is **convenient** (as he can accommodate large aliens and get to know them). / *The **two dwarves** complain that they have to share a cabin, with barely enough room for a **bench**.*

Test yourself: 太(48) 些(314) 很(281) 电(159) 情(339) 非(328) 简(346)
饺(381) 远(303) 爱(365) 新(243) 亮(342) 再(217) 啤(356)

401a 央 yāng center

〡　冂　므　央　央

401 英 yīng hero

Radical ⧻
8 strokes

一　十　艹　艻　苨　英　英

grass ⧻(218a) + center 央(401a) = hero 英

This character is also (from its sound) used to mean "England" or "English". By the way, 美 **měi** (not in HSK Level A) is the corresponding character for America or the USA.

英语(68)　**yīngyǔ**　*English (language)*
英文(25)　**yīngwén**　*(written) English*
英里(157)　**yīnglǐ**　*a mile*]

Who's that standing in the **center** of the **grass**? It's a statue of the English **hero**, Nelson. / *[DIY pronunciation]*

402a 夬 to separate

フ　ユ　므　夬

402 块 kuài lump

Radical 土
7 strokes

塊

一　十　土　圩　坢　块　块

earth 土(54a) + separate 夬(402a) = lump 块

Also (colloquially) used to refer to a yuan, the unit of currency in China.

一块儿(1, 21)　**yíkuàir**　*together*

(Someone sneaks into the vegetable gardens) He **separates** the good **earth** from the **lump**s which he dumps on a neighboring plot. / *The ghostly dwarf, who looks after the gardens, hoists a red kite to alert the authorities.*

403 快 kuài quick

Radical 忄
7 strokes

丶　丷　忄　忙　忙　快　快

heart 忄(339a) + separate 夬(402a) = quick 快

If conjoined twins are joined near the **heart** then the operation to **separate** them has to be **quick**. / *The ghostly dwarf (who has been assigned to protect the twins) decides that he can't be expected to hang around and watch so goes outside to fly his kite during the operation.*

404 决   **jué**   decide

Radical 冫
6 strokes

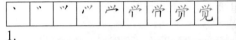

> **ice** 冫 (360a) + **separate** 夬 (402a) = **decide** 决

This is a DIY pronunciation. In this book the pronunciation "jue" only applies to this character and the following one.

[决心(161) **juéxīn** *be determined, make up one's mind*]

(You're out skating on a frozen lake) The **ice** starts to **separate**, and you have one foot on each side of the gap so have to **decide** very quickly which way you're going to jump! / *[DIY pronunciation]*

---

405 觉   **jué; jiào**   1. feel 2. sleep

Radical 见
9 strokes

覺

> 1. **unveil** 龸 (82c) + **see** 见 (214) = **feel** 觉

> 2. **unveil** 龸 (82c) + **see** 见 (214) = **sleep** 觉

觉得(118) **juéde** *feel, think (that)*
[自觉(94) **zìjué** *being aware of; voluntary*]

1.

 They **unveil**ed the new name on the front of the saloon so that everyone could **see** — it had been named after the local outlaw. But how would this make the relatives of the outlaw's victims **feel**? (Picture a widow bursting into tears). / *[DIY pronunciation]*

2.

 The spaceship captain **unveil**ed the statue (to be left behind on the planet) and wondered why everyone was laughing — they could **see** the sculptor who had been **sleep**ing under the cover. / *The crew wondered why a statue of **two dwarves jousting** was appropriate.*

---

406 定   **dìng**   decide on

Radical 宀
8 strokes

> **house** 宀 (91a) + **upright** 疋 (30b) = **decide on** 定

决定(404) **juédìng** *decide; decision*
一定(1) **yídìng** *fixed, specified*

Since the **house** was on a riverbank he checked carefully that it was **upright** before **deciding on** whether to buy it. / *The dwarf was happy that he could tie up his dinghy alongside.*

Test yourself: 火(181)   取(88)   乐(320)   合(347)   送(373)   样(112)   啡(329)

较(382)   父(367)   要(101)   睛(340)   板(333)   化(391)   饺(381)

407 重
zhòng (chóng)   Radical ノ   9 strokes
heavy

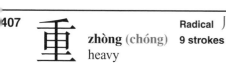

This is another character where there is a choice — we can regard it as a somewhat complicated basic building block, or try to split it up into parts. We've chosen to regard it as a basic building block, but you can regard it as "thousand" plus "in" (Characters 89 and 157) if you like: a bag with a thousand pebbles in it would be heavy!

/ "The **heavy wheel** on your tractor squashed this rare **jonquil**," said the policeman. The **dwarf** can't see what the fuss is about ("It was only a flower, for goodness' sake," he mutters).

重要(101) **zhòngyào** *important*
重点(185) **zhòngdiǎn** *main point, emphasis*]
重大(47) **zhòngdà** *major, great*]

408a 董
dǒng
director

grass ⁺⁺(218a) + **heavy** 重(407) = **director** 董

(The young office workers have sneaked into the washrooms for a "cigarette" break) "This **grass** is **heavy**, man," says one. But the other one sees that the **director** is coming! / [No pronunciation needed]

---

408 懂
dǒng   Radical 忄
understand   15 strokes

heart 忄(339a) + **director** 董(408a) = **understand** 懂

The **heart director** (head of the cardiac unit) is trying to get his students to **understand** irregular heartbeats. / He gets **Teddy** to lead a **donkey** round the lecture hall (so that the hoofbeats drum out an irregular rhythm).

懂得(118) **dǒngde** *understand, grasp*]

409a 垂
chuí
droop

Notice how this differs from 重 (Character 407 above), and be careful with the stroke order.

The two small vertical strokes on either side are joined on at the top and bottom in some typefaces (this is shown in the large character here) and not in others (as shown in the stroke-order diagrams).

409 　睡　shuì　　　**Radical** 目　　｜　冂　冂　日　目　目′　日˝　旷　旷　旷
　　　　　　sleep　　　　**13 strokes**　　　睅　睡　睡

---

eye 目 (93) + droop 垂 (409a) = sleep 睡

睡觉 (405)　**shuìjiào**　*sleep; go to bed*
[睡着 (205)　**shuìzháo**　*to fall asleep*]

His **eyes** began to **droop** and all he wanted to do was **sleep**. / *Fortunately the* ***ghostly dwarf*** *(guarding the emperor's palace) was wearing* ***shades****, so nobody could see his eyes close.*

Test yourself:　用 (130)　年 (168)　爬 (371)　化 (391)　饭 (332)　响 (390)　拿 (348)

但 (117)　收 (355)　课 (189)　联 (374)　湖 (193)　精 (341)　经 (244)

At the end of Chapter 11 we gave you some tips for what to try when you have forgotten the meaning of a character. What if you can't remember the pronunciation? Here are some suggestions:

First, can you remember the archetype? Sometimes you will find that you can, and then you can ask yourself — what would a dwarf (fairy, etc.) do here? If you can picture the scene, with the archetype in that scene, this may be enough to trigger the soundword.

If you can't remember the archetype, try using the personality traits. Does a mischievous or grumpy archetype seem to belong in this story? Were there two archetypes? (Does the story seem to need two — e.g. were they arguing or holding each end of something?) Is the archetype ghostly? (Was it guarding or protecting something?) One particular point to bear in mind is that two archetypes are never ghostly — an archetype can be ghostly, or duplicated, but not both (that would be silly!). If you really can't remember the archetype, don't worry too much — the tone is the least important part to remember, less important than the meaning and pronunciation.

Another avenue is to go back to the first half of the story for clues which we have sometimes been able to put in (for example when we had the soundword "tandoori" we had an Indian theme to the first half of the story).

Can you remember the pronunciation of other similar characters? It's possible that the character you're thinking of is part of a phonetic series (see the comments after Character 46).

Finally, try saying the story, or the part of the story which you remember, to yourself out loud — this sometimes brings back other details of the story, including the soundword (we tried this ourselves a number of times, and were surprised how much easier it was to remember things about the story when we started relating it out loud).

Chapter 24

Note that while "thirty" is simply three tens, "twenty" is not simply two tens. The extra stroke in "twenty" is necessary to distinguish it from "grass" (218a in Chapter 14).

乁 **bird's wing**	飞 **to fly**
乙 **2nd**	与 **with**
丂 **choke**	廿 **twenty** — two tens joined together make 20!
巾 **towel**	卅 **thirty** — 3 × 10 = 30

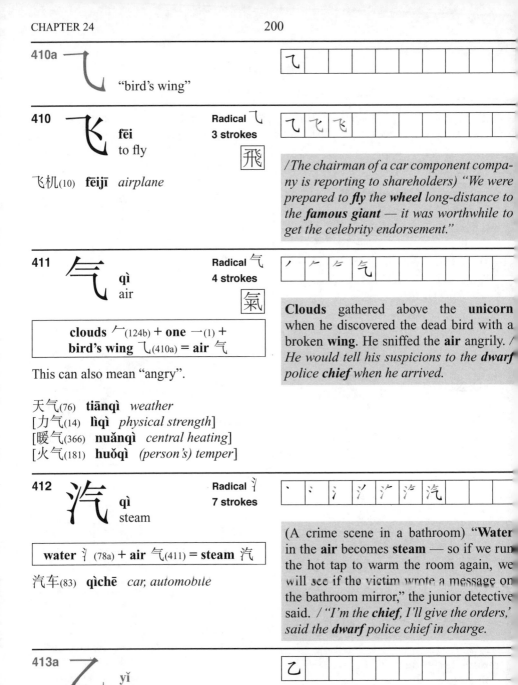

410a   "bird's wing"

410   **fēi**   to fly

Radical 乁
3 strokes

飞机(10) **fēijī** *airplane*

*/The chairman of a car component company is reporting to shareholders) "We were prepared to **fly** the **wheel** long-distance to the **famous giant** — it was worthwhile to get the celebrity endorsement."*

411   **qì**   air

Radical 气
4 strokes

clouds 〳(124b) + **one** 一(1) +
bird's wing 乁(410a) = **air** 气

This can also mean "angry".

Clouds gathered above the **unicorn** when he discovered the dead bird with a broken **wing**. He sniffed the **air** angrily. / *He would tell his suspicions to the **dwarf** police **chief** when he arrived.*

天气(76) **tiānqì** *weather*
[力气(14) **lìqì** *physical strength*]
[暖气(366) **nuǎnqì** *central heating*]
[火气(181) **huǒqì** *(person's) temper*]

412   **qì**   steam

Radical 氵
7 strokes

water 氵(78a) + **air** 气(411) = **steam** 汽

汽车(83) **qìchē** *car, automobile*

(A crime scene in a bathroom) "**Water** in the **air** becomes **steam** — so if we run the hot tap to warm the room again, we will see if the victim wrote a message on the bathroom mirror," the junior detective said. / *"I'm the **chief**, I'll give the orders,' said the **dwarf** police chief in charge.*

413a   **yǐ**   second

Be careful not to confuse this with "bird's wing" (410a).

The character 丁 ("nail", 81b) is also used to mean "fourth", and we will meet 丙 "third" later (510a). Strangely, 甲 "first" does not appear in HSK Level A, even as a fragment.

413 亿 **yì** hundred million   Radical 亻 3 strokes 億

person 亻 (13a) + second 乙(413a) = hundred million 亿

[十亿(4) **shíyì** *a billion*]

Harry came **second** in the contest to guess the distance from the Earth to the Sun. He said a **hundred million** miles. / *The dwarf logged the guesses on a blackboard set up on an easel.*

414 艺 **yì** art   Radical 卄 4 strokes 藝

grass 卄 (218a) + second 乙(413a) = art 艺

文艺(25) **wényì** *the arts*

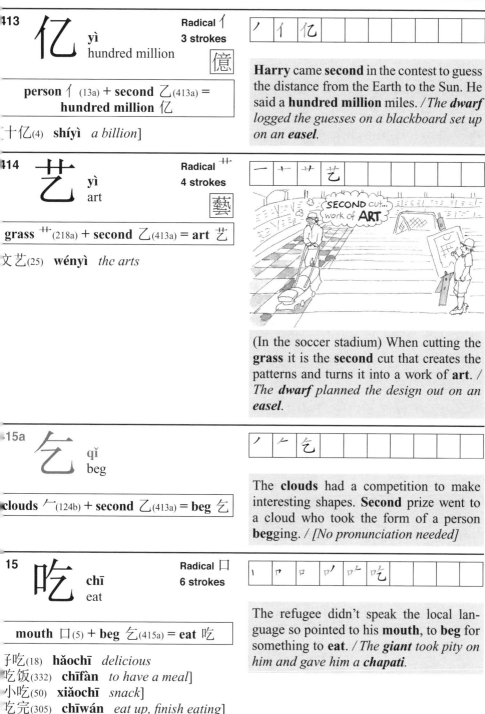

(In the soccer stadium) When cutting the **grass** it is the **second** cut that creates the patterns and turns it into a work of **art**. / *The dwarf planned the design out on an easel.*

415a 乞 **qǐ** beg

clouds 𠂉(124b) + second 乙(413a) = beg 乞

The **clouds** had a competition to make interesting shapes. **Second** prize went to a cloud who took the form of a person **beg**ging. / *[No pronunciation needed]*

415 吃 **chī** eat   Radical 口 6 strokes

mouth 口(5) + beg 乞(415a) = eat 吃

[好吃(18) **hǎochī** *delicious*
吃饭(332) **chīfàn** *to have a meal*]
[小吃(50) **xiǎochī** *snack*]
[吃完(305) **chīwán** *eat up, finish eating*]

The refugee didn't speak the local language so pointed to his **mouth**, to beg for something to **eat**. / *The giant took pity on him and gave him a chapati.*

416

全   **quán**   whole

Radical 人
6 strokes

The **king** sat in his **tent** — he was so plump that he took up the **whole** space. / *[DIY pronunciation]*

| **tent** 人(19b) + **king** 王(60a) = **whole** 全 |

This is a unique DIY pronunciation; in other words it is the only character in the book with this pronunciation.

完全(305)   **wánquán**   *complete*
全部(316)   **quánbù**   *all, without exception*
全体(175)   **quántǐ**   *all (of a group of people)*
[安全(91)   **ānquán**   *safety, security*]

417

色   **sè**   color

Radical 刀
6 strokes

The monk was **bow**ing at the pedestrian crossing, **wait**ing **for** the lights to change **color**. / *His dwarf servant (fed up of this) impatiently pressed the button!*

| **bow** 勹(51a) + **wait for** 巴(368a) = **color** 色 |

This may also mean "scene" or (someone's) "looks".

[红色(233)   **hóngsè**   *the color red*]

418

角   **jiǎo**   "dime"

Radical 角
7 strokes

The beggar **bows** to passers by and says, "Buddy, I could **use** a **dime**." / *He's a bit miffed as further down the sidewalk two teddies are jousting to amuse the crowds (and raking it in).*

| **bow** 勹(51a) + **use** 用(130) = **dime** 角 |

You will sometimes see this character in an older form where the middle vertical line does not extend beyond the bottom horizontal line (so the inside part looks like "earth" rather than "criminal").

    This character means 1/10 of a yuan, or ten cents — another character (毛, Character 453) is used colloquially for the same thing. Other meanings for 角 are "angle", "corner" or (actor's) "role".

[九角五分(38, 36, 73)   **jiǔ jiǎo wǔ fēn**
  ninety five cents]
[三角(3)   **sānjiǎo**   *triangle*]

419 确 **què** certain

Radical 石
12 strokes

確

一	ｒ	石	石	石	石ʼ	矿	矿	确	确
确	确								

stone 石(115a) + dime 角(418) = certain 确

Another unique DIY pronunciation.

(They tossed for it) The **dime** landed on the **stone**. "Heads — I win!" "Let me see — are you **certain**?" / [DIY pronunciation]

确实(250) **quèshí** *indeed, veritably*
正确(29) **zhèngquè** *correct, accurate*

420a 觜 heron

｜	┝	｜├	止	止	此	此	此	觜ʼ	觜
觜	觜	觜							

this 此(314a) + dime 角(418) = heron 觜

(A zookeeper is showing off his collection of strange objects) "**This** is the **dime** I found in the stomach of a **heron**." / [No pronunciation needed]

---

420 嘴 **zuǐ** mouth

Radical 口
16 strokes

｜	冂	口	口ʼ	口ᵗ	口ᵗ	口止	口止	口此	口此
嘴	嘴	嘴	嘴	嘴	嘴				

mouth 口(5) + heron 觜(420a) = mouth 嘴

An almost-unique DIY pronunciation, shared only by this character and the next one.

This is the character which is usually used to refer to a person's mouth (rather than 口).

The **heron** had a fish in its **mouth**, which it took back to its nest to put into the **mouth** of its young chick. / [DIY pronunciation]

---

421 最 **zuì** utmost

Radical 日
12 strokes

｜	冂	日	日	旦	昌	昌	昇	最	最
最	最								

sun 日(6) + acquire 取(88) = utmost 最

最后(150) **zuìhòu** *finally, final stage*
最近(241) **zuìjìn** *recently, recent time*

"I would **acquire** the **sun** for you if I could, to prove my **utmost** love," he said (while she reached for the sick bag!). / [DIY pronunciation]

Test yourself: 不(9) 刀(72) 种(279) 读(249) 言(375) 座(212) 便(400)

吧(368) 河(141) 米(334) 织(255) 哈(350) 校(383) 岁(116)

422a 炎 yán
inflammation

fire 火(181) + fire 火(181) =
inflammation 炎

"I can't believe it — a **fire** on top of last week's **fire**, now the **inflammation** on my burnt hand is even worse." / *[No pronunciation needed]*

---

422 谈 tán
talk over

Radical 讠
10 strokes

談

words 讠 (67c) + inflammation 炎(422a) =
talk over 谈

[会谈(59) **huìtán** *hold (formal) talks*]
[座谈(212) **zuòtán** *have an informal meeting/discussion*]

(In a hospital) The nurse said, "I've written down a few **words** for you about this **inflammation** but our burns expert can **talk over** the details with you. / *I'll get the fairy to fly off and arrange a tannoy call for him.*"

423a 与 yǔ; yù
with

與

---

423 写 xiě
write

Radical 冖
5 strokes

寫

cover 冖(82a) + with 与(423a) = write 写

听写(242) **tīngxiě** *dictation*
[写作(207) **xiězuò** *to write; writing*]
[书写(176) **shūxiě** *to write; handwriting*]
[大写(47) **dàixiě** *uppercase letter; capital letters*]

(In the school exam) The boy **cover**s his paper **with** his hand so that his neighbor can't see what he **writes**. / *The two teddies have been put one at each end of the shelf (so that they can't distract anyone during the exam).*

424a 丂
"choke"

424

号 hào date

Radical 口
5 strokes

號

| 号 | 口 | 口 | 乛 | 丨 | | | | |

mouth 口 (5) + **choke** 丂 (424a) = **date** 号

Also used more generally to mean "Number" (as in "Number 3") or "symbol".

[单号 (344) **dānhào** *an odd number*]
[口号 (5) **kǒuhào** *slogan*]

(Reading the newspaper at breakfast) He's just put a spoonful of cereal in his **mouth**, and **choke**s when he spots the **date** on the newspaper (he's forgotten their wedding anniversary!) / *The **dwarf** butler is very **houseproud**, and mutters as he sweeps up the cornflakes from the floor.*

425a

廿 niàn twenty

| 一 | 十 | 廿 | 廿 | | | | | |

Notice the stroke order (and number of strokes) — this is not "pit" (see 626a) plus "one".

425

度 dù degrees

Radical 广
9 strokes

| 丶 | 一 | 广 | 广 | 庐 | 庐 | 庐 | 度 | 度 |

shelter 广 (170) + **twenty** 廿 (425a) + **right hand** 又 (52) = **degrees** 度

"Degrees" can refer to temperatures or to angles.

[度过 (106) **dùguò** *spend (time)*]

The farmer agrees to buy **twenty shelter**s for his cows and **shakes hands** on the deal; under the agreement they'll be delivered when the temperature drops to twenty **degrees**. / *The **dwarf** salesman says he'll also throw in a **duvet** jacket for the cowherd.*

426

态 tài attitude

Radical 心
8 strokes

態

| 一 | 丆 | 大 | 太 | 太 | 态 | 态 | 态 | |

too much 太 (48) + **heart** 心 (161) = **attitude** 态

态度 (425) **tàidu** *attitude, approach*

(At the vet's surgery) "**Too much** food is bad for your **heart** — you need to develop a more healthy **attitude** to eating." / *The **dwarf** tells the **tiger** to eat smaller portions (not noticing the tiger sizing him up …)*

Test yourself: 西 (100) 青 (335) 况 (360) 气 (411) 食 (287) 吹 (362) 历 (393)
拾 (349) 公 (119) 啦 (180) 讲 (357) 平 (309) 牛 (384) 重 (407)

427a

巾 jīn towel

Radical 巾
3 strokes

| 丨 | 冂 | 巾 | | | | | | |

427 市 shì market

Radical ⼇
5 strokes

`、 一 亠 方 市`

---

lid ⼇(25b) + towel 巾(427a) = market 市

Take care to distinguish between this character, "encompass" (428a) and "sash" (429b).

城市(260) **chéngshì** *city*
[都市(262) **dūshì** *city*]

He puts a **lid** on the box of **towel**s (before loading it onto the cart) to take it to **market**. / *Last time the towels had got wet and the* ***dwarf*** *had hit him with a* ***shillelagh****!*

428a 帀 "encompass"

`一 丆 冂 帀`

---

one 一(1) + towel 巾(427a) = encompass 帀

The grateful villagers made the **unicorn** a large **towel** which was big enough to **encompass** him (even his horn). / *[No pronunciation needed]*

---

428 师 shī master

Radical ｜
6 strokes

師

`丿 刀 丬 牜 师 师`

---

knife ⺉(74a) + encompass 帀(428a) = master 师

老师(264) **lǎoshī** *teacher*
[教师(265) **jiàoshī** *teacher*]

(At the murder crime scene) They drew a chalk line round the body which **encompass**ed the **knife** he was holding — they would need a **master** detective to solve this. / *The* ***giant*** *spotted a blood-soaked* ***shillelagh*** *on top of a wardrobe ("I didn't need to be a master detective to spot this," he said).*

429a 卅 thirty

`一 卄 卅 卅`

429b 帍 sash

`丶 冖 冖 冖 帍`

---

cover ⼍(82a) + towel 巾(427a) = sash 帍

The ambassador had just had a shower, and so was **cover**ed only in a **towel** when the doorbell rang. But at least he put on his **sash** before answering the door! / *[No pronunciation needed]*

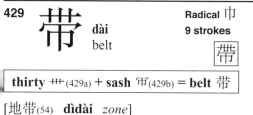

429 带 dài belt

Radical 巾
9 strokes

一 十 卄 丗 卅 丗 带 带 带

thirty 卅 (429a) + sash 帀 (429b) = belt 带

[地带(54) **dìdài** *zone*]

(In the embassy laundry) At the end of each month they had to wash **thirty sash**es for the ambassador, a different one for each day. "Why can't he just wear a **belt**?" the laundry worker complained. / *The **dwarf** (supervisor) told him that they were all **dyed** different colors (and it was important for protocol reasons to have the right one for each occasion).*

You probably know at least vaguely what a radical is (see the User Guide, and the comments about "phonetic series" at the end of Chapter 4). The radical often gives a clue to the meaning of a character. For example the heart radical suggests something to do with feelings or emotions, the water radical something to do with liquids, and so on. Thus it is more a classification device than an insight into the root meaning of individual characters. Many authors feel that the word "radical" (from the Latin for "root") is misleading, and use other words such as "classifier" or "signific". But radical is by far the most commonly used word.

The radical doesn't always appear on the left-hand side of a character. Sometimes it's on the right, or on the top or on the bottom. Here are some examples:

Character	Radical	Position of radical
都	阝	right
星	日	top
您	心	bottom
这	辶	left and bottom

Because it's not always easy to tell what the radical is for a particular character, the radical is listed for each of the characters in this book. As you learn more characters, you'll find you can often guess the radical just by looking at a character. If you've been looking at the radicals as you worked through this book, you'll probably already have a good feel for this.

Why bother with radicals? The main use of radicals if for grouping characters together so that they can be organized in dictionaries. For hundreds of years Chinese dictionaries have used the radical components of the characters as a way of grouping them. All characters, even the really simple ones, are assigned one radical or another (mainly just for the purpose of placing them within the index of a dictionary). We will say more about looking up characters in dictionaries at the end of Chapter 27.

Traditional characters all had a universally agreed (although sometimes not at all obvious) radical from a set of 214. For simplified characters the situation has been much more fluid, with dictionaries adopting their own lists of radicals which vary from about 180 to around 230. More recently there has been some convergence towards a set of 189 and this is the set which we have used in this book. However, note that there are plenty of characters where two (or more) choices for the radical are possible (and dictionaries might then list them under both).

Chapter 25

The basic building blocks "bookcase" and "treasure" are very similar. Clearly one has an extra stroke; but how do you remember which is which? Think of ordering your books by the color of their covers — you put red, white and blue books on the top, middle and bottom shelves respectively. Color in the picture of the bookcase like this, with red and blue pens or pencils. You'll then remember that "bookcase" has three shelves, not four.

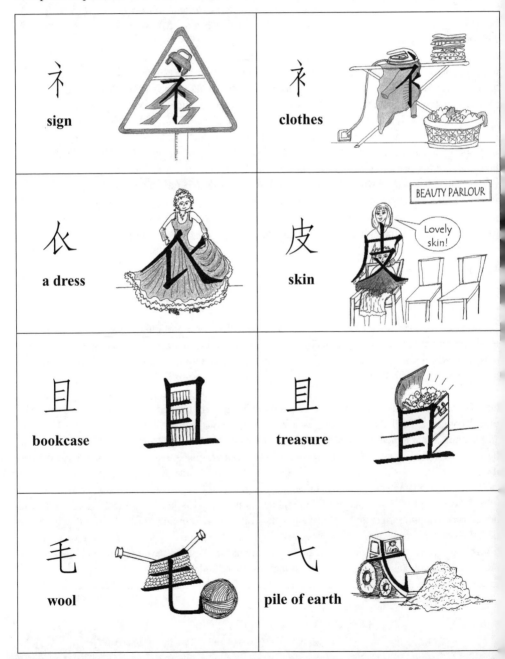

sign

clothes

a dress

skin

bookcase

treasure

wool

pile of earth

430 示 **shì** sign

Radical 示
5 strokes

two 二(2) + **small** 小(50) = **sign** 示

When this appears as the left-hand side of other characters it takes the form 礻 (see 433a below).

A **small** (remote-control model) **biplane** is flying around, doing **sign** writing in the sky. / *The **dwarf** smokes his **cheroot** (and sulks now that nobody's interested in his smoke rings any more).*

[示意(258) **shìyì** *to signal, hint*]

---

431 票 **piào** ticket

Radical 西
11 strokes

west 西(100) + **sign** 示(430) = **ticket** 票

[票子(17) **piàozi** *banknote, bill*]
[门票(27) **ménpiào** *admission ticket*]
[飞机票(410, 10) **fēijī piào** *airplane ticket*]
[火车票(181, 83) **huǒchē piào** *train ticket*]

(Tours of the White House) At the entrance to the **West** Wing, the **sign** says "Special **tickets** beyond this point". / *The **two dwarves** see a ticket on the ground and both **pounce** on it.*

---

432 漂 **piào** pretty

Radical 氵
14 strokes

water 氵 (78a) + **ticket** 票(431) = **pretty** 漂

漂亮(342) **piàoliàng** *pretty, good-looking*

On the **water** floats a **ticket** to see the "**Pretty** Maids" dancing troupe. / *The **two dwarves** both **pounce** on this ticket too.*

433a 礻 sign

This is the form which Character 430 takes when appearing as the left-hand side of other characters. This is easy to mistake for "clothes" 衤 (439a), which has one more stroke.

433

社 **shè**
society

Radical 礻
7 strokes

| **sign** 礻(433a) + **earth** 土(54a) = **society** 社 |

This can mean a club or association, as well as society in general.

社会(59) **shèhuì** *society (in general)*

"Look for the **sign** on the building depicting little heaps of **earth** — that's the house where the mole-fanciers' **society** meets. / *The **dwarf sherpa** is giving a talk tonight on 'Mountains and Mole-hills'.*"

434

祝 **zhù**
best wishes

Radical 礻
9 strokes

| **sign** 礻(433a) + **older brother** 兄(67a) = **best wishes** 祝 |

A **sign** in the sky — his **older brother** had organized a skywriting airplane to send him **best wishes** for his birthday. / *The **dwarf** said it was **juvenile** (probably because he hadn't thought of it).*

435

视 **shì**
to watch

Radical 礻
8 strokes

| **sign** 礻(433a) + **see** 见(214) = **to watch** 视 |

电视(159) **diànshì** *television*
[近视(241) **jìnshì** *near-sighted*]

(At the zoo) The **sign** says, "This is the place to **see** the feeding of the tigger" — so all the children stop **to watch**. / *The **dwarf** feeds it **shallots** (for this is what tiggers like best) whilst grumbling to himself that people in his position shouldn't have to feed the animals that are there purely for entertainment.*

Test yourself: 米(334) 几(7) 云(56) 父(367) 面(313) 向(389) 最(421)

件(385) 把(369) 汽(412) 英(401) 给(351) 花(392) 看(200)

436a

 "a dress"

Notice that the second stroke has a "barb" (120a), and notice the order for writing the last two strokes.

436

biǎo
indicator

Radical 衣
8 strokes

錶

---

plant 主 (133a) + dress 𧘇 (436a) =
indicator 表

This character can mean "to show" or "a surface", and is used for any chart such as a timetable; also for an instrument such as a gauge, meter or wristwatch (only for the last of these meanings does the traditional form apply).

The little girl puts an old **dress** on a **plant** in her front garden, as an **indicator** of which house is holding the birthday party. / *Two teddies stand on either side of the front gate, bowing to guests as they arrive.*

表示(430) **biǎoshì** *show, indicate*
手表(31) **shǒubiǎo** *wrist watch*
表现(215) **biǎoxiàn** *display, show*
[发表(146) **fābiǎo** *publish, publicize*]
[表面(313) **biǎomiàn** *a surface*]
[表明(77) **biǎomíng** *make clear, demonstrate*]

437

yī
clothes

Radical 衣
6 strokes

---

lid 亠 (25b) + dress 𧘇 (436a) = **clothes 衣**

When this appears as the left-hand side of characters it is squashed into the distorted form 衤 (see 439a below). Originally it was a cloak, but now it can be any piece of clothing.

She lifts the **lid** of the box to reveal a beautiful **dress** — she has never been given **clothes** like this as a present before. / *She doesn't know that the giant is her secret admirer and that he wants to see her looking her best at the Easter parade.*

[大衣(47) **dàyī** *overcoat*]
[洗衣机(139, 10) **xǐyījī** *washing machine*]

438

nóng
farm

Radical 冖
6 strokes

農

---

cover 冖 (82a) + dress 𧘇 (436a) = **farm 农**

This is very easy to mistake for Character 437, to see the difference look at the stroke order diagrams.

She wears overalls to **cover** her **dress** when she is working on the **farm**. / *[DIY pronunciation]*

农业(395) **nóngyè** *agriculture*
农村(104) **nóngcūn** *farming area, countryside*

439a 衤 clothes

This is the form which Character 437 takes when appearing as the left-hand side of characters. Compare this carefully with "sign" 礻 (433a), which is very similar but has one less stroke.

---

439 初 **chū** beginning

Radical 衤
7 strokes

clothes 衤 (439a) + knife 刀(72) = beginning 初

最初(421) **zuìchū** *initially, initial stage*
[初步(378) **chūbù** *initial, tentative*]

The doctors cut away his **clothes** with a **knife** before **beginning** their examination (of the road accident victim). / *The giant tries to stick the clothes together again with chewing gum!*

440a 皮 **pí** skin

Watch the stroke order for this one.

---

440 被 **bèi** by

Radical 衤
10 strokes

clothes 衤 (439a) + skin 皮(440a) = by 被

[被子(17) **bèizi** *quilt, blanket*]

A caveman sees his friend wearing new **clothes** made of animal **skin**. Who were they made **by**? By Ugg? By Zugg? Or by Nugg? / *Actually, by the dwarf who lives down in the basement of his cave.*

---

441 破 **pò** damage

Radical 石
10 strokes

stone 石(115a) + skin 皮(440a) = damage 破

[破产(197) **pòchǎn** *go broke; come to naught*]

Rubbing a **stone** on his **skin** was **damaging** it. / *But the dwarf itched where he had been scratched by the porcupine.*

442 坏 **huài** bad

Radical 土
7 strokes

壊

| 一 | 十 | 土 | 圤 | 坏 | 坏 | 坏 | | |

earth 土(54a) + not 不(9) = **bad** 坏

[破坏(441) **pòhuài** *to damage, vandalise, sabotage*]

(An archaeologist is digging) "This is **not earth** — I've got a **bad** feeling about this." / *At that moment a **ghostly dwarf**, who guards the tombs, appears and unleashes a **hyena** to chase him off.*

443 且 **qiě** "bookcase"

Radical 一
5 strokes

| 丨 | 冂 | 月 | 目 | 且 | | | | |

"Bookcase" is our name for this character which was originally a stand with shelves. Nowadays its meaning is more abstract: "moreover", "yet", "still"; or "while …-ing".

而且(151) **érqiě** *moreover*

/ *They really needed **wheels** to move the heavy **bookcase** but all the **two teddies** could find were **chestnuts** to put underneath it!*

444 姐 **jiě** older sister

Radical 女
8 strokes

| く | 丿 | 女 | 幻 | 如 | 妇 | 姐 | 姐 | |

woman 女(15) + bookcase 且(443) = **older sister** 姐

姐姐 **jiějie** *older sister*
小姐(50) **xiǎojiě** *Miss*
[姐妹(64) **jiěmèi** *sisters*]

"Who's that **woman** cleaning the **bookcase**?" "That's my **older sister**. / *She's cleaning up after the **two teddies** had a **jelly** fight."*

445 助 **zhù** to help

Radical 力
7 strokes

| 丨 | 冂 | 月 | 且 | 且 | 助 | 助 | | |

bookcase 且(443) + power 力(14) = **help** 助

[助手(31) **zhùshǒu** *assistant, aide*]

"We need more man**power** to move the heavy **bookcase** — we need some **help**." / *The **dwarf** takes a swig of his magic **juice** and picks up the bookcase nonchalantly with one hand. (At last, his chance to shine!)*

446 租 zū rent

Radical 禾
10 strokes

`` ´ 二 千 禾 禾 和 和 和 和 租 ``

grain 禾(126a) + bookcase 且(443) = **rent** 租

出租汽车(114, 412, 83) **chūzū qìchē** *taxi*

Some **grain** is left on the **bookcase** every month to pay the **rent**. / *The giant landlord accepts this from his Zulu lodger (but would rather have money).*

447 祖 zǔ ancestor

Radical 礻
9 strokes

`` ` ㇇ 礻 礻 礻 衵 衵 相 祖 ``

sign 礻(433a) + bookcase 且(443) = **ancestor** 祖

祖国(60) **zǔguó** *ancestral land*

(In the library) The **sign** on the genealogy **bookcase** shows where to look for books on the **ancestor**s. / *Teddy dresses up as a Zulu (as he has heard his ancestors came from Africa).*

448 组 zǔ organize

Radical 纟
8 strokes

`` ㇜ ㇜ 纟 纠 纠 细 组 组 ``

thread 纟(233a) + bookcase 且(443) = **organize** 组

组织(255) **zǔzhī** *organize, organization*

You decide to put different colors of **thread** on the shelves of the **bookcase** to **organize** its contents. / *When the thread runs out, Teddy offers to dress up as a Zulu to mark the African section for you.*

449 宜 yí appropriate

Radical 宀
8 strokes

`` ` 丶 宀 宁 宁 宁 宜 宜 ``

house 宀(91a) + bookcase 且(443) = **appropriate** 宜

便宜(400) **piányi** *cheap, inexpensive*

The new **house** has lots of **bookcase**s, and it is going to take a long time to find an **appropriate** place for each book. / *"Easy if you know how," says the fairy as she waves her magic wand.*

450

谚 yì
friendship

Radical 讠
10 strokes

誼

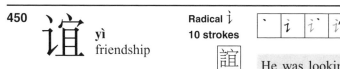

words 讠 (67c) + appropriate 宜(449) = friendship 谊

友谊(53) **yǒuyì** *friendship*

He was looking for a greeting card with **words** which would be **appropriate** to show his **friendship** (but they were all soppy birthday cards). / *The **dwarf** gave up and sent an **email** instead.*

451a

且 "treasure"

Not to be confused with "bookcase" (Character 443) — "treasure" has an extra horizontal stroke inside.

451

直 zhí
straight

Radical 十
8 strokes

ten 十(4) + treasure 且(451a) = straight 直

This means "straight" and can take on related meanings such as "direct", "frank" or "upright".

(The girl has found a map) "At the **cross**roads there is hidden **treasure**! Let's go **straight** there and dig it up **straight** away!" / *The **fairy** says, "Hang on, I'll come too, just give me a minute to get out of the **jacuzzi**."*

一直(1) **yìzhí** *always, all the time*

452

真 zhēn
truly

Radical 十
10 strokes

straight 直(451) + eight 八(20) = truly 真

This means "true", "genuine"; hence "really" or "clearly".

(The octopus pickpocket has been caught red-handed and is being handcuffed by the police: picture them needing four sets of handcuffs …) "I'll go **straight** from now on," the **octopus** says, "**truly** I will." / *[DIY pronunciation]*

真正(29) **zhēnzhèng** *real, genuine*
认真(253) **rènzhēn** *conscientious*
[真理(158) **zhēnlǐ** *truth*]
[真实(250) **zhēnshí** *true, real, authentic*]

453

毛　**máo**
wool

Radical 毛
4 strokes

Compare this with "hand" 手 (Character 31). The hook here has a longer base and goes to the right instead of the left.

The character 毛 means "wool", "fur" or "hair"; and is also a colloquial measure word meaning 1/10 of a yuan.

[羊毛(111)　**yángmáo**　wool]
[毛衣(437)　**máoyī**　(woollen) sweater]

/ *The **fairy** spins **wool** on her spinning **wheel**, to make a pulllover for her pet **mouse**.*

454

笔　**bǐ**
pen

Radical ⺮
10 strokes

筆

| **bamboo** ⺮ (321a) + **wool** 毛(453) = **pen** 笔 |

This can also mean "to write" or (when talking about Chinese characters) "a stroke".

[毛笔(453)　**máobǐ**　writing brush]
[笔记(272)　**bǐjì**　notes (e.g. of meeting)]

A length of **bamboo** with **wool** tied around it (to give a good grip) makes a colorful **pen**. / *Teddy cooks up **beetroot** to make ink for the pen.*

455a

七　"pile of earth"

455

民　**mín**
the people

Radical 乚
5 strokes

| **corpse** 尸(268a) + **pile of earth** 七(455a) = **the people** 民 |

Notice that in this character the last stroke of "corpse" has a barb at the end.

农民(438)　**nóngmín**　farmer, peasant
人民(12)　**rénmín**　the people
[民主(297)　**mínzhǔ**　democracy, democratic]
[民歌(387)　**míngē**　folk song]
[民用(130)　**mínyòng**　for civilian use]

(At the Gettysburg address) Imagine Abraham Lincoln standing among the **corpse**s buried under **piles of earth**, making his famous speech about government "of **the people**, by **the people**, for **the people**." / *A **fairy** records the **minutes** (preserving the words for posterity).*

456a  stake

| pile of earth 弋(455a) + a drop ﹨ (22a) = stake 弋 |

This is like "dagger" (32a) but with a stroke missing.

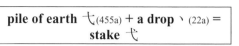

The builders are marking out a building site, using **a drop** of red paint on a small **pile of earth** to indicate where each **stake** should go. / *[No pronunciation needed]*

456 代 **dài** substitute

Radical 亻
5 strokes

| person 亻 (13a) + stake 弋(456a) = substitute 代 |

Harry is playing football and hurts himself by running into a large **stake**, so they have to bring on a **substitute** for him. / *The **dwarf** team manager rolls **dice** to determine who should replace him.*

现代(215) **xiàndài** *modern*
代表(436) **dàibiǎo** *to represent; a delegate*
[时代(105) **shídài** *epoch, age, era*]
[年代(168) **niándài** *a decade (of a century)*]

Test yourself: 牛(384) 千(89) 上(42) 亮(342) 到(74) 音(257) 旧(394)
交(380) 改(359) 信(376) 业(395) 之(121) 懂(408) 爸(370)

Many books give sequences of pictures showing how characters have evolved over thousands of years, from their earliest forms to their current form. An example is the following sequence for "fish" (which we will meet in Chapter 30):

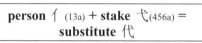

Sometimes knowing how characters have developed tells you something about the character. For example, you may find it interesting to see how the characters for left hand and right hand have developed from primitive pictures of the two hands:

You can then notice, for example, that the intermediate form of "left hand" has the "special" stroke that appears in the character for "send out" (Character 146). Many people find this sort of thing fascinating but we believe that it is not the best way to learn the modern forms of characters when you are starting out. It's like tracing the Latin or Greek roots of English words. It may be interesting to know that the English word "bus" came from "omnibus" (which is Latin for "for all"), but this is not how you would teach a class in English for beginners. These derivations may give some help with remembering the meanings of basic building blocks, but are less use for composites, and give little if any help with pronunciations. In any event, if you are interested in seeing how Chinese characters have developed, there is no shortage of books available covering this topic.

Chapter 26

Another chapter where you already know all the basic building blocks you'll need. As you progress, you will find more and more characters which are made up of building blocks you already know. You have learned about 150 basic building blocks now, which gives a huge number of combinations (even counting just the composite characters which only contain two or three basic building blocks). There are now only 60 or so basic building blocks remaining in this book. After that, you would only need a further 30 or so to get you through the whole of HSK Level B.

457a 舌 shé tongue

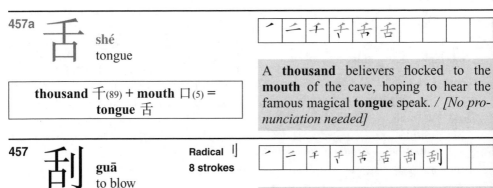

thousand 千(89) + **mouth** 口(5) = **tongue** 舌

A **thousand** believers flocked to the **mouth** of the cave, hoping to hear the famous magical **tongue** speak. / *[No pronunciation needed]*

---

457 刮 guā to blow

Radical 刂
8 strokes

tongue 舌(457a) + **knife** 刂(74a) = **blow** 刮

The young chef runs his **tongue** along the **knife** to lick it clean and then **blows** on it to dry it. / *The ghostly giant, guardian of kitchen cleanliness, excuses this as he loves the taste of garlic too!*

---

458 话 huà speech

Radical 讠
8 strokes

話

words 讠 (67c) + **tongue** 舌(457a) = **speech** 话

会话(59) **huìhuà** *talk (with), conversation*
电话(159) **diànhuà** *telephone*
[对话(154) **duìhuà** *(have a) dialogue*]
[公用电话(119, 130, 159) **gōngyòng diànhuà** *public phone, payphone*]

(In an ancient tomb) The explorer can read the ancient **words** written above the door, but has to get his **tongue** round them, as the door will only open if he recites the whole **speech** in one go. / *The ghostly dwarf guarding the tomb plays the harmonica to put him off.*

459 适 shì suitable

Radical 辶
9 strokes

適

丿　二　千　千　舌　舌　氵舌　活　适

| road 辶(26a) + tongue 舌(457a) = suitable 适 |

合适(347) **héshì** *appropriate*
[适合(347) **shìhé** *to suit, to fit*]
[适当(267) **shìdāng** *suitable, appropriate*]
[适用(130) **shìyòng** *applicable, suitable*]

(The king likes to walk barefoot about his kingdom) He has a team of lackeys to lick the **road** with their **tongues** to check that it is **suitable** for his dainty feet. / *The* **dwarf** *is dismissive, "What a* **charade!**"

---

460 活 huó alive

Radical 氵
9 strokes

丶　冫　氵　氿　汗　汗　活　活

| water 氵(78a) + tongue 舌(457a) = alive 活 |

This also means "lively" or "active".

活儿(21) **huór** *(manual) work, job*
活动(58) **huódòng** *activity, (physical) exercise*
生活(133) **shēnghuó** *a life; to live (a life)*

(In the desert you find someone lying on the sand) You put your last drops of **water** on their **tongue** to revive them, hoping they're still **alive**. / *The* **ghostly fairy** *who guards desert travelers suddenly notices what's going on, and flies up with a magic* **hosepipe** *(to refill your water bottle).*

---

461 术 shù craft

Radical 木
5 strokes

術

一　十　才　木　术

| tree 木(10a) + a drop 丶(22a) = craft 术 |

This also means "skill" or "method".

艺术(414) **yìshù** *art*
[手术(31) **shǒushù** *operation*]
[术语(68) **shùyǔ** *terminology, technical terms*]

She saw **a drop** of rain on the **tree**, and it gave her the idea of making drop-like Christmas-tree decorations to sell at the **craft** fair. / *They draw grudging admiration from the* **dwarf** *selling* **shoes** *at the next stall.*

你(51)   天(76)   牛(384)   北(317)   占(183)

亿(413)   碰(396)   况(360)   史(397)   票(431)

462 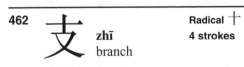 支
zhī
branch

Radical 十
4 strokes

| 一 | 十 | 专 | 支 | | | | | | |

---

ten 十(4) + right hand 又(52) = branch 支

This also means "to prop up", "support" and also acts as a measure word for long, thin things.

At the **cross**roads in the maze the two friends **shake hands** and each chooses a **branch** of the maze to head down. / *The first one to reach the center of the maze where the* **giant** *sits in his* **jacuzzi**, *is the winner.*

[一支笔(1, 454) **yì zhī bǐ** *a pen*]

---

463 技
jì
skill

Radical 扌
7 strokes

| 一 | 亅 | 扌 | 扩 | 扑 | 拄 | 技 | | | |

---

hand 扌(152a) + branch 支(462) = skill 技

技术(461) **jìshù** *technology, skill, technique*

The expert can tell, simply by putting his **hand** on each **branch**, what each type of wood can be used for — a rare **skill**. / *The* **dwarf** *then tells the workers which* **jeep** *to load it on to.*

464a 寺

temple

| 一 | 十 | 土 | 生 | 寺 | 寺 | | | | |

---

earth 土(54a) + inch 寸(104a) = temple 寺

The pilgrims kneel on the **earth** and move forward **inch** by **inch** towards the holy **temple**. / *[No pronunciation needed]*

---

464   等
děng
wait for

Radical 竹
12 strokes

| 丿 | 𠂉 | 𥫗 | 𥫗 | 𥫗 | 竹 | 竺 | 竺 | 竺 | 竺 |
| 等 | 等 | | | | | | | | |

---

bamboo 竹(321a) + temple 寺(464a) = wait for 等

Two other major meanings are "grade" and "etc"; notice that we have sneaked these meanings into the story too.

He takes the **bamboo** to the **temple** but has to **wait for** the chief monk to come and grade it, etc. / *Teddy is bored, and plays in the* **dung**. *(Yuk!)*

[平等(309) **píngděng** *equality, equal status*]
[久等(364) **jiǔděng** *to wait for a long time*]

465  **chí**
maintain

Radical 扌
9 strokes

| 一 | 丨 | 扌 | 扩 | 扩 | 拌 | 拌 | 持 | 持 | |

hand 扌 (152a) + **temple** 寺(464a) =
maintain 持

"We need a **hand** over at the Indian **temple** — we need to do some work to **maintain** it." / The **fairy** conjures up **chapatis** for all those who come to help.

[支持(462) **zhīchí** *to support*]

---

466 **特** **tè**
special

Radical 牛
10 strokes

| 丿 | 一 | 牛 | 牛 | 牛 | 牜 | 牜 | 牜 | 特 | 特 |

cow 牛(384) + **temple** 寺(464a) =
special 特

The **cow** who lived in the **temple** was **special** (a sacred cow!) / The **dwarf's** job is to bring in special **turf** for it each day. ("It's just a cow!" he grumbles).

To write the left-hand part, see the comment for Character 384.

特别(79) **tèbié** *special, especially*

---

467 义 **yì**
just

義

Radical 丶
3 strokes

| 丶 | 丷 | 义 | | | | | | | |

a drop 丶 (22a) + **shears** 乂(25a) = **just** 义

This means "just" in the sense of "right and proper", or "righteous". It can also mean the "meaning or significance" of something.

When one worker asked for **a drop** of oil on his **shears**, they all wanted one, claiming that that would be only **just**. / The **dwarf** supervisor reluctantly agreed, saying, "These days, workers have it too **easy**."

意义(258) **yìyì** *significance*

---

468 风 **fēng**
wind

風

Radical 风
4 strokes

| 丿 | 几 | | | | | | | | |

several 几(7) + **shears** 乂(25a) = **wind** 风

[风力(14) **fēnglì** *wind power, wind force*]

Several pairs of shea_____ _____ tuck in the ground to start making a _____ _____ The **giant** brings some **fungus** to _____ gaps between them.

469a

娄　trouble

| ` | ` | 一 | 半 | 半 | 米 | 米 | 娄 | 娄 |

rice 米(334) + women 女(15) = trouble 娄

(At the wedding) So much **rice** was thrown at the **woman** that she had **trouble** seeing where she was going. / *[No pronunciation needed]*

469

数　shù; shǔ　　　　Radical 攵
　　number; to count　　13 strokes

數

| ` | ` | 一 | 半 | 半 | 米 | 娄 | 娄 | 娄 |
| 数 | 数 | 数 | | | | | | |

trouble 娄(469a) + tap 攵 (190a) = number; count 数

数学(82) **shùxué** *mathematics*
[少数(377) **shǎoshù** *minority*]

 The actor is in **trouble**, and **taps** on the rock face in the cave, furiously trying to get the secret door to work — it is the film set of an "Indiana Jones" movie. But it keeps jamming and the **number** of takes is rising. / *The dwarf is standing behind the door, ready to shoot the hero as he comes through (and is getting fed up at the delay). Teddy jumps up and down and urges him to shoot anyway.* \ He gets so excited that he forgets to **count** the number of takes.

470

楼　lóu　　　　　Radical 木
　　story　　　　13 strokes

樓

| 一 | 十 | 才 | 木 | 术 | 栏 | 栏 | 栏 | 楼 | 楼 |
| 楼 | 楼 | 楼 | | | | | | | |

tree 木(10a) + trouble 娄(469a) = story 楼

This means a multi-story building, or a floor (story) in such a building.

　　　　　lóushàng　u~~~~~
[~~~~~~] ~~~~~

The **tree** is in **trouble** — it has been spotted knocking bricks off the building next door as the workmen are trying to build the latest **story** (which would overshadow the tree). / *The fairy negotiates with the building's owners to use a picture of the tree as their new logo (so then the tree is happy)*

471

层　céng　　　　Radical 厂
　　tier　　　　7 strokes

層

| ⁊ | ⁊ | 尸 | 尸 | 尸 | 层 | 层 |

corpse 尸(268a) + cloud 云(56) = tier 层

[一层楼(1, 470) **yì céng lóu** *the first floor*]

The **corpse** rose up on a **cloud**, carrying it up past each **tier** of the building in turn. / *The fairy flew alongside announcing to the people watching at each level: "This is what happens when you are stung by a killer bee."*

472 室 shì — a room

Radical 宀
9 strokes

| 、 | 丶 | 宀 | 宀 | 宀 | 宏 | 宝 | 宰 | 室 |

house 宀(91a) + **until** 至(74b) = **a room** 室

教室(265) **jiàoshì** *classroom*
办公室(123, 119) **bàngōngshì** *office*

(Searching for a place to stay the night) He went from **house** to **house until** he found **a room** he liked. / The *dwarf* proudly showed off the amenities: "It has a heater, a cooker, a sink — the whole *shebang*."

473 屋 wū — accommodation

Radical 尸
9 strokes

| ㄱ | ㄱ | 尸 | 尸 | 屋 | 屋 | 屋 | 屋 | 屋 |

corpse 尸(268a) + **until** 至(74b) = **accommodation** 屋

Depending on the context (and area of China) this can mean "house" or "room".

屋子(17) **wūzi** *room; house*
同屋(160) **tóngwū** *roommate, flatmate]*

"We'll have to find somewhere to keep the **corpse until** the funeral — and we need to find **accommodation** for all the mourners before we can set a date." / The *giant*, who has been fatally *wounded*, had been very popular...

474 握 wò — grasp

Radical 扌
12 strokes

| 一 | 扌 | 扌 | 扌 | 护 | 护 | 护 | 捏 | 捉 | 捉 |
| 捉 | 握 | | | | | | | | |

hand 扌(152a) + **accommodation** 屋(473) = **grasp** 握

握手(31) **wòshǒu** *shake hands*

In one **hand** he clutched the **accommodation** guide, while the other **grasp**ed the reins of his horse. / "*Whoa!*" shouted the *dwarf*, as his horse trotted straight past all the good hotels.

475 提 tí — carry

Radical 扌
12 strokes

| 一 | 扌 | 扌 | 扌 | 护 | 护 | 护 | 捏 | 捍 |
| 捏 | 提 | | | | | | | |

hand 扌(152a) + **is** 是(30) = **carry** 提

This character means "carry", "lift", "raise"; and also has a range of derived meanings.

"A **hand is** designed to **carry** things." / The *fairy* (giving etiquette lessons) demonstrates by carrying a *tea* cup.

476  **ràng** allow

Radical 讠
5 strokes

讓

words 讠 (67c) + **above** 上 (42) = **allow** 让

[让座 (212) **ràngzuò** *offer seat to; invite guests to be seated*]

The number of **words** in her essay went **above** the **allow**ed limit. / *She would have to **wrangle** with her supervisor the **dwarf**, to see if it would be accepted.*

477a **bèi** sea shell

貝

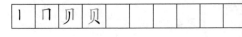

outer limits 冂 (160a) + **person** 人 (12) = **sea shell** 贝

The top part of this character isn't *really* "outer limits" (see Character 214).

This character often has connotations of money (as cowrie sea shells were once used as money).

Harry journeyed to the **outer limits** of the kingdom carrying the magic **sea shell** (for protection against the bandits). / *[No pronunciation needed]*

---

477 **yè** page

Radical 页
6 strokes

頁

thumb tack 丆 (40a) + **sea shell** 贝 (477a) = **page** 页

The small boy tried to use a **thumb tack** to pin the **sea shell** to the **page**. / *The **dwarf** (teacher) said, "I told you **yesterday** that wouldn't work!"*

---

478 **tí** topic

Radical 页
15 strokes

題

is 是 (30) + **page** 页 (477) = **topic** 题

Notice how "is" curls around the bottom of "page" in this character (and is written first, unlike "road" which is written after the part it encloses).

问题 (289) **wèntí** *question*
[题目 (93) **tímù** *(exam) question*]

Teacher to schoolchild: "I told you to write a page, this isn't a page!" "It **is**, it **is** a **page**," said the child, "just not a full page. It's all I can write on this **topic**." *The **fairy** said to the teacher, "You have to admit, there's not a lot you can write about **teaspoons**."*

479 员 yuán member

Radical 口
7 strokes

員

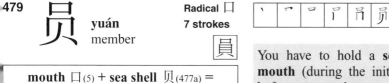

mouth 口(5) + **sea shell** 贝(477a) = **member** 员

You have to hold a **sea shell** in your **mouth** (during the initiation ceremony) before you can become a **member** of the seafood club. / *The **fairy** then gives you a commemoration **yuan** coin.*

This character is often used to mean "employee", or a person performing a role.

[人员(12)   **rényuán**   *staff, personnel*]
[店员(186)   **diànyuán**   *shop assistant*]

---

480 圆 yuán circle

Radical 口
10 strokes

圓

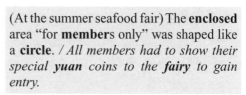

enclosed 口(24a) + **member** 员(479) = **circle** 圆

(At the summer seafood fair) The **enclosed** area "for **member**s only" was shaped like a **circle**. / *All members had to show their special **yuan** coins to the **fairy** to gain entry.*

---

481 高 gāo high

Radical 亠
10 strokes

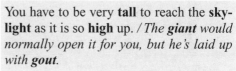

tall 亠(239a) + **skylight** 口(389a) = **high** 高

[提高(475)   **tígāo**   *to raise, increase*
高度(425)   **gāodù**   *altitude; highly*]

You have to be very **tall** to reach the **skylight** as it is so **high** up. / *The **giant** would normally open it for you, but he's laid up with **gout**.*

---

482 搞 gǎo engaged in

Radical 扌
13 strokes

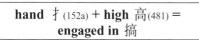

hand 扌(152a) + **high** 高(481) = **engaged in** 搞

搞好(18)   **gǎohǎo**   *make a good job of*]

The doctor held his **hand** up **high**, palm out, to indicate that he was **engaged in** something and couldn't be interrupted. / ***Teddy** didn't want to wait so rolled around on the floor pretending to have **gout**.*

483a
tái
platform

| ㇛ | 厶 | 台 | 台 | 台 | | | |

cocoon 厶(34a) + mouth 口(5) =
platform 台

This character has a number of meanings and at least three traditional forms to go with them. It can refer to things like TV stations; it is used as a measure word; and it is also the "tai" in "Taiwan" and the "ty" in "typhoon".

The ants each brought a **cocoon** to the **mouth** of the cave, where they stacked them up to form a **platform** (for their annual rock concert — they use the cave as it has good acoustics!). / *[No pronunciation needed]*

483
zhì
treat (disease)

Radical 氵
8 strokes

| 丶 | 冫 | 氵 | 氵 | 氵 | 沪 | 治 | 治 |

water 氵(78a) + platform 台(483a) =
treat 治

政治(190) **zhèngzhì** *politics*

(A snake-oil salesman) The colored **water** was ready on the **platform** for the demonstration of how to **treat** diseases. / *His dwarf assistant dipped a wilted geranium in the water, to demonstrate the water's reviving powers.*

484
tái
raise

Radical 扌
8 strokes

| 一 | 亅 | 扌 | 扌 | 扒 | 扮 | 抬 | 抬 |

hand 扌(152a) + platform 台(483a) =
raise 抬

[抬高(481) **táigāo** *to raise prices*]

"Give me a **hand** with the **platform** to **raise** it up" (The parts are lying assembled on the ground). / *The fairy then waves her wand and a magnificent tiger appears on the platform for all to see and admire.*

485
shǐ
start

Radical 女
8 strokes

| 乚 | 乂 | 女 | 女 | 如 | 始 | 始 | 始 |

women 女(15) + platform 台(483a) =
start 始

开始(85) **kāishǐ** *to start; beginning*

A **woman** walks onto the **platform** to **start** the performance (with an operatic aria). / *Teddy (in the audience and impatient to see the main attraction) throws a shallot at her.*

486a 谷 **gǔ** valley

eight 八(20) + tent 人(19b) + mouth 口(5) = valley 谷

The **octopus** climbs on top of his **tent**, but even here the water comes up to his **mouth**. It had been a silly idea to pitch his tent in the **valley**. (It's a strange octopus who doesn't like water!) / *[No pronunciation needed]*

486 容 **róng** tolerate

Radical 宀
10 strokes

house 宀(91a) + valley 谷(486a) = tolerate 容

If you have a **house** in the **valley**, you have to **tolerate** the noise of the air force jets practicing their low level flying. / *The fairy thinks it's wrong. (She can fly quietly, so why can't they?)*

内容(219) **nèiróng** *contents, substance*
容人(12) **róngrén** *broad minded]*

Test yourself: 内(219) 住(298) 正(29) 中(33) 决(404) 次(361) 史(397)

社(433) 写(423) 破(441) 少(377) 东(319) 爬(371) 睡(409)

If you have been looking at the traditional characters, you may have spotted the main methods used to derive simplified characters from the traditional ones. In many cases, the simplified forms were based on widely-used existing abbreviations, which were just given a more official status.

Sometimes the radical was simplified: 詞 ⟶ 词

Sometimes the remainder: 燈 ⟶ 灯

Sometimes both: 錢 ⟶ 钱

Occasionally the same symbol is used as an
abbreviation for several more complicated forms: 難 ⟶ 难
                                                 觀 ⟶ 观

Sometimes there were more drastic changes: 頭 ⟶ 头

Finally, many simpler characters were left unchanged: 本 ⟶ 本

This process of simplification is another reason why the equations "don't make sense". As you can perhaps imagine, it also disrupted some traditional phonetic series (while also creating new ones). Many older books used to admonish you against learning the simplified characters without learning the traditional forms; but learning the simplified ones first is fine, and you can easily pick up the traditional ones later if you want to.

Chapter 27

The picture for "pigeon" on this page, like so many others in this book, does not follow the historical origins of the character — hardly surprising, as the character developed before houses had rooftop TV aerials! But if the picture reminds you, next time you see this basic building block, that its meaning is "pigeon", that's all we need. It doesn't matter that the strokes on the right-hand side originally represented a bird's tail feathers ...

士 scholar	匚 container
虫 shopping basket	束 bundle
亥 pig	隹 pigeon
夊 pursue	疒 illness

487a 士 shì scholar

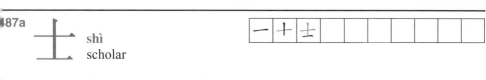

This character differs from "earth" (Character 54a) in that here the first (upper) horizontal stroke is longer than the second (lower) one.

---

487 志 zhì intention   Radical 士   7 strokes

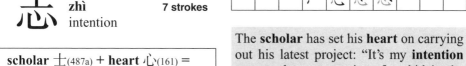

scholar 士(487a) + heart 心(161) = intention 志

This also means "to record" or "a (written) record".

同志(160) **tóngzhì** *comrade*
意志(258) **yìzhì** *(the human) will]*

The **scholar** has set his **heart** on carrying out his latest project: "It's my **intention** to record every species of orchid in the world." / *His assistant the **dwarf** (who thinks if he's going to be dragged around, it might as well be in the sun) says, "Let's start in **Jamaica**."*

"**Tóngzhì**" is rarely used nowadays as a form of address, although it used to be the most common form of address in China.

---

488 声 shēng voice   Radical 士   7 strokes 聲

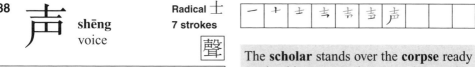

scholar 士(487a) + corpse 尸(268a) = voice 声

大声(47) **dàshēng** *in a loud voice*
声音(257) **shēngyīn** *voice, sound of voices*

The **scholar** stands over the **corpse** ready to give his anatomy lesson — but a **voice** speaks from the corpse and makes him jump! (One of the students has put a small speaker inside it — if you look at the "corpse" you will see the extra stroke that is the microphone). / *[DIY pronunciation]*

489a 壮 zhuàng sturdy 壯

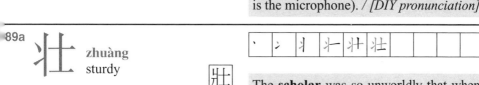

firewood 丬(317a) + scholar 士(487a) = sturdy 壮

The **scholar** was so unworldly that when sent for **firewood** he came back with **sturdy** poles instead of kindling. / *[No pronunciation needed]*

Test yourself: 厂(149) 白(22) 坏(442) 号(424) 哥(386) 省(379) 着(205)
漂(432) 术(461) 使(398) 直(451) 艺(414) 快(403) 飞(410)

489 装 zhuāng — pretend

Radical 衣
12 strokes

丶	冫	刈	爿	壮	壯	壯	芲	芲	裝
芲	裝								

sturdy 壮(489a) + **clothes** 衣(437) = **pretend** 装

[装样子(112, 17) **zhuāng yàngzi** *put on an act, do for appearance sake*]

The children put on **sturdy** boots and warm **clothes** and sneak into the indoor ski slope at night with ropes, so they can **pretend** to be climbing Everest. / *The ghostly giant (guarding the ski slope) jangles his keys to scare them off.*

490a 矢 shǐ — arrow

丿	亡	二	乍	矢					

clouds 宀(124b) + **big** 大(47) = **arrow** 矢

The TV weatherman was given new symbols for **clouds**, but they were so **big** that he hardly had any space left on the map to put the wind **arrow**s. / *[No pronunciation needed]*

490 知 zhī — know

Radical 矢
8 strokes

丿	亡	二	乍	矢	矢勺	知	知		

arrow 矢(490a) + **mouth** 口(5) = **know** 知

知道(145) **zhīdào** *know, be aware of*
知识(256) **zhīshí** *knowledge*

He shoots an **arrow** into the **mouth** of the cave, so that anyone inside will **know** he's there (there are no doorbells on caves). / *The giant appears, complaining, "I was just relaxing in my jacuzzi!"*

491a — container

一	匚								

491 医 yī — heal

Radical 匚
7 strokes

一	丆	工	王	歪	医	医			

container 匚(491a) + **arrow** 矢(490a) = **heal** 医

医生(133) **yīshēng** *doctor*
医院(306) **yīyuàn** *hospital*

The tribal doctor has a **container** full of **arrows** (like acupuncture needles, tipped with various drugs) with which to **heal** his patients. "This won't hurt," he says. / ***Easy for you to say,*** says the **giant**, apprehensively.

492a

串

"shopping basket"

| 丶 | 冖 | 口 | 中 | 虫 | | | | |

492

贵 **guì**
expensive

Radical 贝
9 strokes

貴

| 丶 | 冖 | 口 | 中 | 虫 | 串 | 冉 | 贵 | 贵 |

shopping basket 串 (492a) +
sea shell 贝 (477a) = **expensive** 贵

贵姓 (135) **guìxìng** *(your) family name*

On the beach the girl collects **sea shells** in her **shopping basket** — they'd be **expensive** if bought in the shop. / *The ghostly dwarf who guards the beach sits on the gate (on the path to the beach) watching to make sure she doesn't take too many.*

493

您 **nín**
you (polite)

Radical 心
11 strokes

| 丿 | 亻 | 亻' | 亻" | 竹 | 你 | 你 | 你 | 您 | 您 |
| 您 | | | | | | | | | |

you 你 (51) + **heart** 心 (161) = **you** 您

您贵姓 (492, 135) **nín guìxìng** *what is your surname? (polite)*]

When you say "**you**" and put your **heart** into it, it is a much more polite way of saying "**you**". / *You would use this form of address to a ninja or a fairy (or indeed a fairy ninja!)*

494

束 **shù**
bundle

Radical 木
7 strokes

| 一 | 厂 | 一 | 日 | 申 | 東 | 束 | | |

/ *The dwarf loads bundles of little wheels into his clay-pigeon launcher to practice his shooting.*

495a

敕 **suck**

| 一 | 厂 | 一 | 日 | 申 | 東 | 束 | 敕 | 敕 | 敕 |
| 敕 | | | | | | | | | |

bundle 束 (494) + **tap** 攵 (190a) = **suck** 敕

The magician **tap**ped the **bundle** of rags, and the audience **suck**ed in their breath (gasping at what appears ... use your imagination!). / *[No pronunciation needed]*

495 整 zhěng entire

Radical 止
16 strokes

一	一	一	三	耳	束	束	剌	刺	敕
敕	敕	敕	整	整	整				

suck 敕(495a) + upright 正(29) =
entire 整

[完整(305) **wánzhěng** complete,
  integrated]
[整理(158) **zhěnglǐ** put in order, tidy up]

The fat admiral **suck**s in his tummy and
stands **upright** — and has to hold this
position while the **entire** fleet sails past. /
*Last in line is **Teddy** in his **junk**.*

496a 敕 imperial decree

一	一	一	三	耳	束	束	剌	刺	敕
敕									

bundle 束(494) + lacking 欠(361a) =
imperial decree 敕

The old people complain that they were
lacking their **bundle**s of firewood (which
they are traditionally given each winter).
An **imperial decree** has to be issued to
rectify the situation. / *[No pronunciation
needed]*

496 嗽 sòu cough

Radical 口
14 strokes

丨	口	口	口'	叮	吖	咊	呐	哳	唪
唪	嗽	嗽	嗽						

mouth 口(5) + imperial decree 敕(496a) =
cough 嗽

The town crier opens his **mouth** to pro-
claim the **imperial decree** but can only
cough. / *The **dwarf** thrusts a **soda** into his
hand before he ruins the whole occasion.*

497a 亥 hài pig

、	一	亡	步	岁	亥				

Yet another pig! (See Characters 109a and 263 for the others.)

497 该 gāi ought

Radical 讠
8 strokes

該

、	讠	讠'	讠'	讠'	该	该	该		

words 讠 (67c) + pig 亥(497a) = ought 该

应该(388) **yīnggāi** should, ought to

(In the old church, looking for the famous
tomb) The floor is covered with **words**
carved into the flagstones, and the **pig**
snuffles about. "It **ought** to be here somewhere," he says. / *He asks the **giant** if he
can borrow his **guidebook**.*

498 孩 **hái** youngster

Radical 子
9 strokes

child 子(17) + **pig** 亥(497a) = **youngster** 孩

孩子(17) **háizi** child
小孩儿(50, 21) **xiǎoháir** child

"That **child**'s riding on a **pig**!" "It's OK, he's only a **youngster**." / *The fairy sits on a hydrant, laughing.*

499 咳 **ké** cough

Radical 口
9 strokes

mouth 口(5) + **pig** 亥(497a) = **cough** 咳

咳嗽(496) **késòu** to cough

At the **mouth** of the cave the **pig coughs** discreetly to announce his presence. / *The fairy emerges from behind her curtain to see who it is.*

500 刻 **kè** quarter (hour)

Radical 刂
8 strokes

pig 亥(497a) + **knife** 刂(74a) = **quarter** 刻

This character also means "carve" or "engrave".

立刻(177) **lìkè** at once
刻苦(218) **kèkǔ** hardworking, painstaking]

The **pig** uses a **knife** to cut his lunch apple neatly into **quarters**. / *The dwarf fixes up a curtain round the pigsty (so that passers-by can't see his prissy pig).*

Test yourself: 表(436) 作(207) 意(258) 歌(387) 破(441) 块(402) 吃(415) 代(456) 棵(188) 度(425) 觉(405) 更(399) 步(378) 为(122)

501a 隹 pigeon

This is a picture of a bird, but looks like a composite character made up of "person" plus "lord with an extra stroke". Feel free to make up a story along these lines if you like. (Also, compare this character with "to live in", Character 298).

501

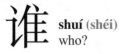 shuí (shéi)
who?

Radical 讠
10 strokes

words 讠 (67c) + pigeon 隹(501a) =
who? 谁

This also has the (colloquial) pronunciation
shéi.

[谁的(23) **shuíde** *whose?*]

(In the dusty tomb) The **pigeon** writes
words in the dust with his beak, asking
"**Who** is in the tomb?" / *The ghostly
fairy who guards the tomb answers, "The
sheikh."*

502

推 **tuī**
push

Radical 扌
11 strokes

hand 扌 (152a) + pigeon 隹(501a) = **push 推**

This can also mean "grind", "to clip",
"deduce", "shirk", "postpone", "elect" or
"esteem"!

[推广(170) **tuīguǎng** *spread; popularize*]
[推动(58) **tuīdòng** *promote, push*]

(She had nursed the wounded pigeon back
to health) She took the **pigeon** in her **hand**
and gave it a **push** to launch it into the air.
/ *The ghostly giant, who would look after
it, attached a piece of colored tape to its
leg (so he could see which one to keep an
eye on).*

503

难 **nán**
difficult

Radical 又
10 strokes

right hand 又(52) + pigeon 隹(501a) =
difficult 难

[难过(106) **nánguò** *sad, grieved*]
[难看(200) **nánkàn** *ugly*]

The toddler tries to **shake hands** with the
pigeon — but is finding it **difficult** as the
pigeon doesn't have hands! / *The fairy
takes the lad back to his nanny.*

504

准 **zhǔn**
accurate

Radical 冫
10 strokes

ice 冫 (360a) + pigeon 隹(501a) =
accurate 准

[准确(419) **zhǔnquè** *accurate, exact*]
[准时(105) **zhǔnshí** *punctual, on time*]

Landing on the **ice**, the **pigeon** slides
neatly to a stop (exactly in the right place);
it has done this so often that it's now very
accurate. / *[DIY pronunciation]*

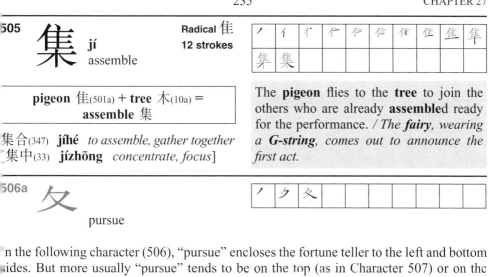

505 集 **jí** assemble

Radical 隹
12 strokes

pigeon 隹(501a) + **tree** 木(10a) = **assemble** 集

集合(347) **jíhé** *to assemble, gather together*
[集中(33) **jízhōng** *concentrate, focus*]

The **pigeon** flies to the **tree** to join the others who are already **assembled** ready for the performance. / *The fairy, wearing a G-string, comes out to announce the first act.*

506a 夂 pursue

In the following character (506), "pursue" encloses the fortune teller to the left and bottom sides. But more usually "pursue" tends to be on the top (as in Character 507) or on the bottom. Compare this with "to tap" (190a), which always appears as the right-hand side of characters. Notice also that "pursue" has 3 strokes while "to tap" has 4.

506 处 **chù (chǔ)** place

Radical 夂
5 strokes

處

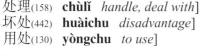

pursue 夂(506a) + **fortune teller** 卜(42a) = **place** 处

Another meaning is "manage" (a business or situation).

好处(18) **hǎochù** *benefit*
[处理(158) **chùlǐ** *handle, deal with*]
[坏处(442) **huàichu** *disadvantage*]
[用处(130) **yòngchu** *to use*]

He **pursues** the **fortune teller** from **place** to **place** (to ask more details about her predictions). / *He asks the dwarf, "Which way did she go?" But the dwarf ignores him and just sits chewing his gum.*

507 各 **gè** each

Radical 夂
6 strokes

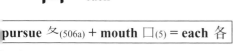

pursue 夂(506a) + **mouth** 口(5) = **each** 各

各种(279) **gèzhǒng** *all kinds of*

The police **pursue** the thieves to the **mouth** of the cave and then stand guard at **each** of the exits. / *The dwarf is determined to retrieve the stolen gherkins!*

508 路 lù path

Radical 足
13 strokes

| ⼀ | ⼝ | ⼝ | ⾜ | ⾜ | ⾜ | ⾜ | ⾜ | ⾜ | 趵 |
| 路 | 路 | 路 | | | | | | | |

foot 足(280) + **each** 各(507) = **path** 路

[道路(145) **dàolù** *road, path*]
[路上(42) **lùshang** *en route*]
[问路(289) **wèn lù** *ask the way*]
[公路(119) **gōnglù** *public road, highway*]
[马路(44) **mǎlù** *street, avenue*]
[路口(5) **lùkǒu** *(road) intersection*]

(At the fork in the road) "If you really can't decide which way to go, try putting a **foot** on **each path**." / *"This is lunatic," says the **dwarf**.*

509 客 kè guest

Radical 宀
9 strokes

| ⼀ | ⼀ | 宀 | 宀 | 灾 | 灾 | 客 | 客 | 客 | |

house 宀(91a) + **each** 各(507) = **guest** 客

The meaning includes "visitor" and "customer".

客气(411) **kèqì** *modest, polite*
[会客(59) **huì kè** *to receive visitors*]
[做客(210) **zuò kè** *to visit, be a guest*]
[客人(12) **kèren** *guest*]
[请客(336) **qǐng kè** *to invite for dinner*]

The old duke has given a **house** to **each** of his children, providing he can stay with each of them as a **guest** whenever he wishes. / *The **dwarf** brings the duke's **curtains** along (so that everywhere he stays, he will feel at home).*

Test yourself: 九(38) 小(50) 快(403) 社(433) 第(322) 态(426) 刮(457)
应(388) 谊(450) 全(416) 道(145) 定(406) 活(460) 农(438)

510a 丙 bǐng third

| ⼀ | ⼀ | 冂 | 丙 | 丙 | | | | | |

one 一(1) + **inside** 内(219) = **third** 丙

When the **unicorn** gets **inside** the Ark he sees that he is only the **third** creature aboard (after Noah and his wife). / *[No pronunciation needed]*

510b 疒

illness

| ⼀ | ⼀ | 广 | 广 | 疒 | | | | | |

Compare this with "shelter", Character 170.

510

病

bìng
disease

Radical 疒
10 strokes

illness 疒(510b) +third 丙(510a) =
disease 病

This can also mean a "fault" or "defect".

After seeing the same mysterious **illness** for the **third** time, he is finally able to diagnose the **disease**. / *"Bingo," says the **dwarf** doctor's assistant sarcastically, "I knew what it was all along."*

看病(200) **kànbìng**   *to see a doctor*
[病人(12) **bìngrén**   *patient, sick person*]
[病房(293) **bìngfáng**   *(hospital) ward*]
[毛病(453) **máobìng**   *problem*]

You may have been wondering how to look up characters in a Chinese dictionary, since there is no "alphabetical order" for characters. Many dictionaries today are organized alphabetically by (pinyin) pronunciation, so if you want to look up a character in a dictionary and you know its pronunciation, then it's easy. But when you don't know the pronunciation of a character, there's a problem.

When you don't know the pronunciation of a character, one way to look it up is to use a radical index — and this is why radicals are useful. To use a radical index you have to know which part of the character is the radical, and you'll also need to be able to count the number of strokes that make up the character. To look up 姓, for example, 女 is the radical (which has 3 strokes) and the remainder 生 has 5 strokes. So first you find the radical 女 amongst the 3-stroke radicals in the radical index. Then, if there are lots of characters under 女, look for 姓 in the subsection which lists all the characters which have 5-stroke remainders. You would also use this method for the more traditional character dictionaries which are organized by radical (instead of by pinyin).

Many dictionaries also have a pure stroke count index (i.e. ignoring the radical). To use this you must count up the strokes in the character as a whole and look the character up under that number (so 姓 would come under the 8-stroke characters). As you can imagine, this type of index can leave you with columns of characters to scan before you find the one you're looking for, so it's usually a last resort!

Dictionaries sometimes use a sub-classification based on the first stroke of the character (whether it is a horizontal stroke or a vertical stroke, etc.) — which is another reason for knowing the correct stroke-orders for characters.

Words (compounds) are often listed under the leading character. But when a dictionary lists words as separate entries, beware that the "pinyin alphabetical order" often works by syllable/character, rather than following "strict" alphabetical order. For example, these words would appear in this order:

... ta ... tamen ... tai ... taiyang ... tan ... tanhua ... tang ...

All these methods have their pitfalls and complications, so recently a completely new way of looking up characters has been devised. The Chinese Character Fast Finder (see the inside back cover) organizes characters purely by their shapes so that you can look up any one of 3,000 characters very quickly without knowing its meaning, radical, pronunciation or stroke-count! The Fast Finder Index at the back of this book is organized using the same principles.

Chapter 28

Once again, we have collected together in one place a number of similar characters so that you can compare them and learn to look for the small details which differ from one to another.

才 only just

水 water

求 request

勿 don't!

昜 sunny

乃 sigh

及 reach

511 杂 zá mixed

Radical 木
6 strokes

雜

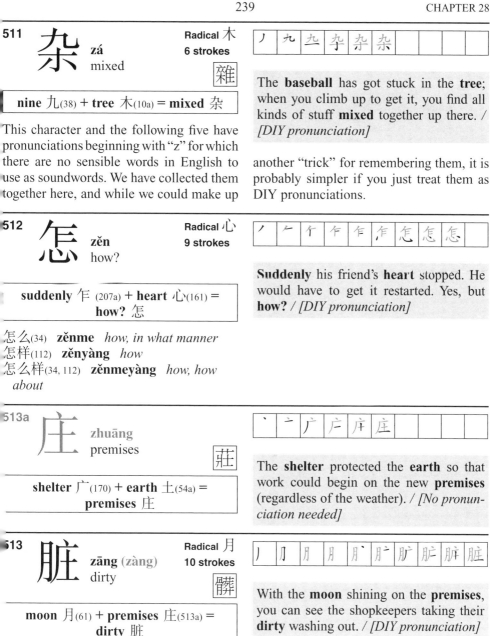

nine 九(38) + tree 木(10a) = mixed 杂

This character and the following five have pronunciations beginning with "z" for which there are no sensible words in English to use as soundwords. We have collected them together here, and while we could make up

The **baseball** has got stuck in the **tree**; when you climb up to get it, you find all kinds of stuff **mixed** together up there. / *[DIY pronunciation]*

another "trick" for remembering them, it is probably simpler if you just treat them as DIY pronunciations.

512 怎 zěn how?

Radical 心
9 strokes

suddenly 乍 (207a) + heart 心(161) = how? 怎

怎么(34) **zěnme** *how, in what manner*
怎样(112) **zěnyàng** *how*
怎么样(34, 112) **zěnmeyàng** *how, how about*

Suddenly his friend's **heart** stopped. He would have to get it restarted. Yes, but **how?** / *[DIY pronunciation]*

513a 庄 zhuāng premises

莊

shelter 广(170) + earth 土(54a) = premises 庄

The **shelter** protected the **earth** so that work could begin on the new **premises** (regardless of the weather). / *[No pronunciation needed]*

513 脏 zāng (zàng) dirty

Radical 月
10 strokes

髒

moon 月(61) + premises 庄(513a) = dirty 脏

This character can also mean an organ of the body when it is pronounced **zàng** (and it then has a different traditional form).

With the **moon** shining on the **premises**, you can see the shopkeepers taking their **dirty** washing out. / *[DIY pronunciation]*

514  总 **zǒng** always

Radical 心
9 strokes

總

horns ⸜ (65a) + mouth 口 (5) +
heart 心 (161) = always 总

This character has a variety of other meanings including "general", "chief", "anyway" and "to sum up".

They hung **horns** above the **mouth** of the cave, and placed an animal's **heart** underneath, in accordance with tradition. "Now we will **always** have enough to eat." / *[DIY pronunciation]*

总适 (459) **zǒngshì** *always*
[总理 (158) **zǒnglǐ** *premier, prime minister*]

515 责 **zé** duty

Radical 贝
8 strokes

責

The prize exhibit at the art gallery is a **plant** growing in a **sea shell**; it's the night watchman's **duty** to top up the water. / *The fairy has given him a zircon-encrusted watering can to use.*

plant 主 (133a) + sea shell 贝 (477a) =
duty 责

516 绩 **jì** achievement

Radical 纟
11 strokes

績

thread 纟 (233a) + duty 责 (515) =
achievement 绩

成绩 (259) **chéngjì** *achievement*

The spider developed a way of making particularly strong **thread** and felt it was his **duty** to teach it to all the other spiders too — a great **achievement**. / *Even so, his whole team could only just make a G-string which did not satisfy the dwarf.*

517 负 **fù** to shoulder

Radical 贝
6 strokes

負

bow ⼓ (51a) + sea shell 贝 (477a) =
shoulder 负

负责 (515) **fùzé** *to be in charge*

The men on the beach **bow** down to pick up **sea shell**s to put in sacks which they then **shoulder**. / *The dwarf has to sample the seafood but gets food poisoning (and takes out his temper on the poor men).*

518
才
cái
only just

Radical 一
3 strokes

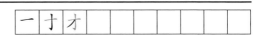

/ The **fairy** has **only just** got brand new **wheels** for her bike — she's proud of them too as they are the latest **style**.

One of the more dramatic simplifications of a traditional character! In its own right 才 also means "ability, talent", and the fragment "talent" (55a) is actually a deformation of this character.

[人才(12) **réncái** *talented person*]
[天才(76) **tiāncái** *genius*]

519
团
tuán
group

Radical 囗
6 strokes

| enclosed 囗(24a) + only just 才(518) = group 团 |

This means a group of people, but also "unite", "ball" or "dumpling".

(An exhibition of precious jewels from the Taj Mahal must be enclosed in a secure glass case; imagine the museum staff scurrying around trying to get everything ready) They **only just** get the jewels **enclosed** when the first **group** of people arrives. / The **ghostly fairy** (who's going to guard the exhibit) complains that it smells of **tandoori**.

520
因
yīn
because

Radical 囗
6 strokes

"He's so **big**, he'll have to be **enclosed**." "Why?" "**Because** he'll frighten everyone." / Poor **giant**, that will upset his **yin**.

| enclosed 囗(24a) + big 大(47) = because 因 |

Be careful not to mix this up with the previous character.

因为(122) **yīnwèi** *because*
[因而(151) **yīn ér** *so, therefore*]

521a
恩
ēn
a favor

Because she has such a kind **heart** she is always doing **favor**s for people. / [No pronunciation needed]

| because 因(520) + heart 心(161) = favor 恩 |

521 ng
eh

Radical 口
13 strokes

mouth 口(5) + favor 恩(521a) = eh 嗯

You open your **mouth** to ask your friend a **favor** but, before you can ask, they say, "So what do you want me to do now? **Eh**?" / *[DIY pronunciation]*

---

522 kùn
difficulty

Radical 口
7 strokes

enclosed 囗(24a) + tree 木(10a) = **difficulty** 困

困难(503) **kùnnán** *difficulty, difficult*

The **tree** doesn't want to be **enclosed** so keeps reaching down with its branches and pulling up the fence. The workers have **difficulty** erecting the fence with this going on! / *The dwarf foreman is **cunning** and brings along his pet canary to sing and calm the tree down.*

---

523 水 shuǐ
water

Radical 水
4 strokes

When this character appears as the left-hand side of other characters, it is abbreviated to the form 氵 which we have already met (78a).

汽水(412) **qìshuǐ** *soft drink*
水果(187) **shuǐguǒ** *fruit*
水平(309) **shuǐpíng** *proficiency; level, standard*

/ *The **water wheel** has stopped and the **ghostly teddy**, who looks after it, is shaking his head — he can't fix it because he's dropped his **shades** in the mechanism (and can't see very well without them).*

---

524 求 qiú
request

Radical 丶
7 strokes

Note that the bottom of this character looks like "water" (Character 523), but all four small strokes are written separately.

要求(101) **yāoqiú** *require, requirement*
[请求(336) **qǐngqiú** *request*]

/ *(In a wheel shop) A **request** comes in for a new **wheel**. The owner chooses **two fairies** wearing sparkling **chokers** to deliver it right away to his best client.*

球 qiú ball

Radical 王
11 strokes

一	二	于	王	王〈	玎	玎	玎	球	球
球									

王(60a) + **request** 求(524) = **ball** 球

(330) **páiqiú**   *volleyball*
(280) **zúqiú**   *football*
(61) **yuèqiú**   *the moon (scientific)*
(54) **dìqiú**   *(the planet) Earth*]

(The king is playing football, but not very well) The **king** has to keep **request**ing the queen to return his **ball** from her private garden. / *She asks her two fairies, wearing sparkling chokers, to deliver it back each time.*

Test yourself: 米(334) 人(12) 去(86) 词(231) 就(239) 找(152) 向(389)

当(267) 义(467) 且(443) 决(404) 祝(434) 市(427) 色(417)

勿 wù don't!

丿	勹	勽	勿				

忽 hū sudden

Radical 心
8 strokes

丿	勹	勽	勿	勿	忽	忽	忽

勿(526a) + **heart** 心(161) = **sudden** 忽

(266) **hūrán**   *suddenly*

The surgeon in the operating theatre shouts, "**Don't** touch the **heart**!" **Sudden**ly blood spurts everywhere. / *The giant comes by with his hoover to clean everything up!*

物 wù thing

Radical 牛
8 strokes

丿	亠	牛	牛	牜	物	物	物

牛(384) + **don't** 勿(526a) = **thing** 物

Remember that "cow" is written with the slanting stroke last (see Character 384).

The **cow** says, "**Don't** touch me — I washed my hair this morning and I can't do a **thing** with it!" / *The dwarf whooped with derision.*

(58) **dòngwù**   *animal*
(158) **wùlǐ**   *physics*
(133) **shēngwù**   *living things*]
(287) **shíwù**   *food*]
动物园(58, 302) **dòngwùyuán**   *zoo*]

528

易 yì
easy

Radical 日
8 strokes

| ㇒ | ㇆ | 冂 | 日 | 日 | 旦 | 圽 | 易 | 易 | | |

---

sun 日(6) **+ don't 勿**(526a) **= easy 易**

容易(486) **róngyì** *easy*

"**Don't** lie in the **sun** for too long — it's **easy** to get sun burnt." / *The **dwarf** decides to put up this warning on an **easel** (as he's fed up of telling everyone).*

529

踢 tī
kick

Radical 足
15 strokes

| ㇒ | ㇐ | 口 | 足 | 乥 | 足 | 尸 | 趸 | 趷 | 趵 |
| 趵 | 踢 | 踢 | 踢 | 踢 | | | | | |

---

foot 足(280) **+ easy 易**(528) **= kick 踢**

[踢球(525) **tī qiú** *to play football*]

The soccer player draws his **foot** back; it is going to be an **easy** shot, and he **kicks** the ball hard into the goal. / *The **giant** cheers the winning **team** (almost deafening everyone around him).*

530a

勿
sunny

| ㇆ | 勹 | 勿 | | | | | | | |

Compare this with "don't" (526a).

530

场 chǎng
site

Radical 土
6 strokes

| ㇐ | 十 | 土 | 圴 | 场 | 场 | | | | |

---

earth 土(54a) **+ sunny 勿**(530a) **= site 场**

机场(10) **jīchǎng** *airport*
[会场 (59) **huìchǎng** *(meeting) venue*]
[广场 (170) **guǎngchǎng** *(city) square*]
[市场 (427) **shìchǎng** *market, marketplace*]
[停车场 (343, 83) **tíngchēchǎng** *parking lot, carpark*]

They look for a patch of **earth** that is **sunny**, for the **site** of their new plantation. / *[DIY pronunciation]*

If you look at the traditional form for Character 530, you will see that 530a is a simplified form of something which looks very like Character 528 (but with an extra line). The same abbreviation happens in the following two characters (531 and 532). Simplified characters usually exhibit this sort of consistency — but not always!

531 汤 **tāng** soup

Radical 氵
6 strokes

湯

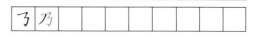

water 氵(78a) + sunny 昜(530a) = soup 汤

[清汤(337) **qīngtāng** *clear soup*]

"Put the **water** in a **sunny** spot (to warm it) before making the **soup**. / *When it's ready make sure to fill the **giant's tankard** first.*"

---

532 扬 **yáng** make known

Radical 扌
6 strokes

揚

hand 扌(152a) + sunny 昜(530a) = make known 扬

表扬(436) **biǎoyáng** *to praise*
[发扬(146) **fāyáng** *develop, carry forward*]

The signaller holds his **hand** aloft where it is **sunny** (so that his mirror catches the sun) to **make known** that the invaders are coming. / *At the next relay station it's cloudy, so the **fairy** has to fly onwards with the message, "The **Yanks** are coming!"*

533a 乃 **nǎi** sigh

---

533 奶 **nǎi** milk

Radical 女
5 strokes

woman 女(15) + sigh 乃(533a) = milk 奶

This character is also used for "breast" or "suckle".

牛奶(384) **niúnǎi** *(cow's) milk*
[奶牛(384) **nǎiniú** *cow*]

The **woman** gives a **sigh** of relief as the baby starts to drink the **milk** (and so stops crying). / *Teddy bounds in with a **nightlight** so the baby can sleep (but trips up, much to the amusement of the baby).*

534a 及 **jí** reach

This means to "reach" or "attain"; also "timely" or "on time".

534 极 jí
extremity

Radical 木
7 strokes

極

一 十 才 朾 朾 极 极

> **tree** 木(10a) + **reach** 及(534a) =
> **extremity** 极

极了(66) **A jíle** *extremely A, very A*
[极其(235) **jíqí** *extremely, highly*]
[北极(317) **běijí** *the North Pole*]

The **tree reach**es out — with the tips of its branches it can just reach the **extremity** of the neighboring tree. / *This is where the fairy has hung her **G-strings** to dry.*

535 级 jí
grade

Radical 纟
6 strokes

級

乚 纟 纟 纴 级 级

> **thread** 纟 (233a) + **reach** 及(534a) =
> **grade** 级

年级(168) **niánjí** *grade (in school)*
[初级(439) **chūjí** *elementary, initial*]
[上级(42) **shàngjí** *a superior, higher authorities*]
[九级风(38, 468) **jiǔjífēng** *10 % off, a 10% discount*]

If the **thread** (from the silkworm) can **reach** across the loom without breaking, it is high **grade** silk. / *They can use the leftovers to make the **fairy** a new **G-string**.*

For Character 535 you can see that simplifying the traditional form consisted of using the simplified form of the radical "thread", and keeping the same right-hand side (534a). In character 534, however, 534a stands in as an abbreviation for something else.

536a 泉
spring

' ′ 白 白 白 宇 皀 泉

> **white** 白(22) + **small** 小(50) = **spring** 泉

This "spring" is a water source, not a season (nor for that matter a piece of coiled metal).

Imagine seeing small dots of **white** in a green alpine meadow. They are edelweiss flowers — but why such a **small** cluster? When you look more closely there is a small **spring** there. (It is also a nice place for a picnic, where you can listen to the sound of the water). / *[No pronunciation needed]*

536 原 **yuán**
original

Radical 厂
10 strokes

一	厂	厂	斤	斤	盾	盾	原	原	原

cliff 厂 (149) + spring 泉 (536a) =
original 原

This also means "a plain" (open country-side).

原来(65) **yuánlái** *former, original*
[平原(309) **píngyuán** *flatland, plain*]
[原因(520) **yuányīn** *a reason*]
[高原(481) **gāoyuán** *highland, plateau*]

The whisky distillery was sited by the **spring** under the **cliff** — the water there gave the whisky its **original** flavor. / *Each bottle carried the trademark picture on the label, of a **fairy** sitting on a **yuan** coin.*

537 愿 **yuàn**
to desire

Radical 心
14 strokes

願

一	丿	厂	斤	盾	盾	盾	原	原	原
原	愿	愿	愿						

original 原(536) + heart 心(161) =
desire 愿

This is usually written in such a way that the "heart" creeps in under the "cliff".

愿意(258) **yuànyì** *be willing; to want*

He realized that the **original** girl he had first lost his **heart** to was the one he now truly **desire**d. / *The **dwarf** wondered sadly if she still had the lucky **yuan** coin he had once given her.*

Test yourself:

页(477) 用(130) 身(107) 气(411) 的(23) 然(266) 懂(408)

度(425) 立(177) 让(476) 组(448) 视(435) 被(440) 广(170)

手(31) 没(169) 成(259) 风(468) 当(267) 带(429) 病(510)

右(213) 表(436) 姐(444) 角(418) 怎(512) 师(428) 真(452)

The simplification process for Character 537 has involved replacing the radical with a different one! This is a bit confusing, but fairly rare.

This is the last comment we shall make about traditional and simplified forms of characters. If you are interested, compare the simplified forms of the characters with their traditional forms as you continue to work through this book.

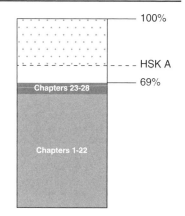

Chapter 29

Another quiz: do you remember the difference between these similar characters and fragments?

重(407)   垂(409a)   目(93)   且(443)   且(451a)

乀(410a)   乙(413a)   廾(85a)   艹(218a)   廿(425a)

538a 吉 jí
auspicious

一 十 士 古 吉 吉

scholar 士(487a) + **mouth** 口(5) = **auspicious** 吉

When the **scholar** (who is normally engrossed in his books in his cave) appears at the **mouth** of his cave, blinking in the sunlight, the villagers take it as an **auspicious** sign. / *[No pronunciation needed]*

---

538 结 jié (jiē)
tie up

Radical 纟
9 strokes

结

纟 纟 纟 纟 纠 纤 纤 结 结

thread 纟 (233a) + **auspicious** 吉(538a) = **tie up** 结

They used the invisible **thread**, produced by the silkworms on the most **auspicious** days, to **tie up** their hair into ornate patterns. / *Two fairies work together to put gel on any stray hairs to stick them down.*

结果(187) **jiéguǒ** *in the end, finally*
团结(519) **tuánjié** *unite, show solidarity*
结束(494) **jiéshù** *terminate*

---

539 喜 xǐ
celebration

Radical 士
12 strokes

一 十 士 吉 吉 吉 吉 吉 壴 喜
喜 喜

auspicious 吉(538a) + **feet** 丷(90a) + **mouth** 口(5) = **celebration** 喜

It's **auspicious** if the first **feet** to enter the **mouth** of your cave at the start of a year are animal feet — when this happens it is a cause for **celebration**. / *Teddy brings a sheep early in the morning to ensure this happens.*

This also means "happy" and has connotations of "to like".

喜欢(363) **xǐhuan** *like, be fond of*
[欢喜(363) **huānxǐ** *joyful*]

540a

"foul mouth"

| 一 | 十 | 土 | 士 | 吉 | 吉 | | | |

---

earth 土 (54a) + **mouth** 口 (5) = **foul mouth** 吉

If you get **earth** on your **mouth**, you get a dirty, or **"foul" mouth**. / *[No pronunciation needed]*

Take care! This character is easily confused with 538a.

---

540 周
zhōu
week

Radical 冂
8 strokes

|) | 几 | 刀 | 用 | 月 | 用 | 周 | 周 | |

---

outer limits 冂 (160a) + **foul mouth** 吉 (540a) = **week** 周

"You will be sent to the **outer limits** if you are **foul mouth**ed and you'll have to stay there for a **week**. / *Even the giant was sent there for telling dirty jokes.*"

This also means, amongst other things, "circuit", "circumference" or "all around".

---

541 调
diào
tune

Radical 讠
10 strokes

调

| ` | 讠 | 讵 | 讵 | 讵 | 调 | 调 | 调 | 调 |

---

words 讠 (67c) + **week** 周 (540) = **tune** 调

(The lyricist for a songwriting team lives on an island where he can concentrate) When the **week**'s quota of **words** is finished, they are ready to have a **tune** written for them. / *The two dwarves collect them each week in their dhow (and take them to his partner, the composer, on the mainland).*

Another character with a range of additional meanings — "mix", "fit in", "mediate", "provoke", "move" and others.

声调 (488) **shēngdiào** *tone (of Chinese character)*

542a 尚
shàng
esteem

| 丨 | ⺌ | ⺌ | 广 | 肖 | 尚 | 尚 | 尚 | |

---

small 小 (50) + **skylight** 冏 (389a) = **esteem** 尚

The double glazing salesman claims, "If you install a **small skylight**, you will be held in great **esteem** by your neighbors." / *[No pronunciation needed]*

When it appears as the top part of other characters this gets somewhat squashed, with the "outer limits" compressed into "cover" (see Characters 543–545 for examples).

542 躺 tǎng lie down

Radical 身
15 strokes

ノ	ノ	イ	勹	自	身	身	身¹	躬
躬	躺	躺	躺	躺				

body 身(107) + **esteem 尚**(542a) = **lie down 躺**

If you hold your **body** in high **esteem**, you will **lie down** for a power nap in the middle of the day. / *Teddy tries this, but bounces about so much that he gets tangled up in the covers.*

543 堂 táng hall

Radical 土
11 strokes

⼀	⼁	⼩	⼩	丛	严	严	严	尚	堂
堂									

esteem 尚(542a) + **earth 土**(54a) = **hall 堂**

食堂(287) **shítáng** *dining hall*

The site of the famous battle that saved the town was an **esteem**ed piece of **earth**, so that's where they built the town **hall**. / *The fairy conjured up a shiny replica tank to sit outside the hall as a memorial.*

544 常 cháng often

Radical 巾
11 strokes

⼀	⼁	⼩	⼩	丛	严	严	严	尚	常
常									

esteem 尚(542a) + **towel 巾**(427a) = **often 常**

常常 **chángcháng** *often (colloq)*
经常(244) **jīngcháng** *often*
非常(328) **fēicháng** *unusual; very*
[平常(309) **píngcháng** *ordinary; normally*]

If you **esteem** the **towel** the king gave you, you will use it **often**. / *[DIY pronunciation]*

545 掌 zhǎng palm (of hand)

Radical 手
12 strokes

⼀	⼁	⼩	⼩	丛	严	严	严	堂	堂
堂	掌								

esteem 尚(542a) + **hand 手**(31) = **palm 掌**

This means a palm (of the hand), and by extension to control something.

掌握(474) **zhǎngwò** *know well, have a good command of*

(Briefing to the recipients at the military medal ceremony) "If the **esteem**ed lady offers you her **hand**, take care to notice if it is **palm** up (shake it) or palm down (kiss it). / *Teddy, holding the medals ready, will jangle them if you look like getting it wrong.*"

546

条 **tiáo**
slip of paper

Radical 夂
7 strokes

條

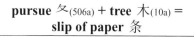

pursue 夂(506a) + **tree** 木(10a) =
slip of paper 条

Also used as a measure word for long, narrow things.

条件(385) **tiáojiàn** *conditions*
[面条儿(313, 21) **miàntiáor** *noodles*]

The squirrels **pursue** one another through the branches of the **tree** until one slips on a **slip of paper** and falls. / *Two fairies stretch a **towel** between them to catch him.*

547

务 **wù**
to work at

Radical 夂
5 strokes

務

pursue 夂(506a) + **power** 力(14) =
work at 务

[业务(395) **yèwù** *(professional) work*]
[医务室(491, 472) **yīwùshì** *clinic*]

He **pursue**d **power** by climbing the corporate ladder, **working at** his desk into the night. / *His rival, the **dwarf**, chose instead to **woo** the CEO's daughter.*

548

备 **bèi**
prepare

Radical 夂
8 strokes

備

pursue 夂(506a) + **field** 田(156a) =
prepare 备

准备(504) **zhǔnbèi** *prepare; preparation*

He **pursue**d the pig round the **field** whilst his wife **prepare**d the other ingredients for the meal. / *They had promised the **dwarf bacon** for dinner.*

549

鱼 **yú**
fish

Radical 鱼
8 strokes

魚

bow 𠂊(51a) + **field** 田(156a) +
one 一(1) = **fish** 鱼

See Character 15 for "pouring rain" stories.

[一条鱼(1, 546) **yì tiáo yú** *a fish*]

  The small boy **bows** to the **unicorn** in the **field**, and proffers the dead **fish** (but the unicorn is unable to revive it). / *The **fairy** holds a burial ceremony and reads a **eulogy** in the pouring rain.*

550  **fù** repeat

Radical 夂
9 strokes

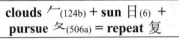

clouds 𠂉(124b) + sun 日(6) + pursue 夂(506a) = repeat 复

This has various shades of meaning — not just to repeat something, but often a sense of responding or replying. It can also mean "complex".

复杂(511) **fùzá** *complex, complicated*
[反复(331) **fǎnfù** *repeatedly*]

(At the fighter pilot training school) The pilots have to fly into the **clouds**, then out again into the **sun**, then **pursue** the instructor's aircraft; and they must **repeat** all this until they get it right every time. / *The dwarf (in charge of the kitchen) grumbles because the food is getting cold.*

551a  **rén** ninth

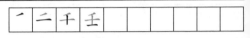

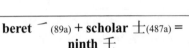

beret 一(89a) + scholar 士(487a) = ninth 壬

Ceremonial **beret**s are given out each year to the top ten **scholars** in the country. Yours has a baseball embroidered on it to show that you came **ninth**. / *[No pronunciation needed]*

---

551  **rèn** whatever

Radical 亻
6 strokes

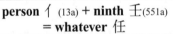

person 亻(13a) + ninth 壬(551a) = whatever 任

This has a range of other meanings including "appoint", "allow", and "despite".

任何(142) **rènhé** *any, whatever*
[任务(547) **rènwu** *mission, assignment*]

Harry is at bat in the **ninth** innings of the baseball match. The coach says, "Do **whatever** it takes!" / *Harry hits the ball and the dwarf calls out, "For goodness' sake, run!"*

---

552 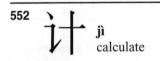 **jì** calculate

Radical 讠
4 strokes

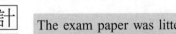

words 讠(67c) + ten 十(4) = calculate 计

[计算(321) **jìsuàn** *to calculate*]

The exam paper was littered with **words** with red **cross**es through them. The examiner used these to **calculate** the final grade. / *The dwarf posted up the GPA scores on the notice board.*

553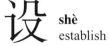
shè
establish

Radical 讠
6 strokes

---

words 讠 (67c) + **strike 殳**(169a) =
establish 设

[设备(548) **shèbèi** *equipment*]
[设计(552) **shèjì** *design*]

(Laying the foundation stone at a hospice) He had to **strike** very hard to etch the **words** into the stone which would mark where the hospice movement was first **established**. / *The dwarf, wearing a bright yellow shirt, was keeping onlookers at a safe distance.*

554
huà (huá)
to plan

Radical 刂
6 strokes

---

dagger 戈(32a) + **knife 刂**(74a) = **plan 划**

Also means to "divide, carve out, delimit". (Pronounced **huá** it can mean "to scratch").

计划(552) **jìhuà** *a plan, to plan*

The actors, one with a **dagger** and one with a kitchen **knife**, carefully **plan** the fight which will be the climax of their play. / *The ghostly dwarf grumpily hands out protective clothing so that he won't get blamed if they come to any harm.*

---

555 或
huò
or

Radical 戈
8 strokes

---

mouth 口(5) + **one 一**(1) +
dagger 戈(32a) = **or 或**

Notice that "one" is written with a pronounced slope and that it is underneath "mouth" this time (compare this with "piled up", 150b).

或者(261) **huòzhě** *or, otherwise*

The dentist uses a small **dagger** to probe the teeth in the **unicorn**'s **mouth**, asking "Which **one** hurts, this one — **or** this one? — **or** this one?" / *The ghostly dwarf, who protects the unicorn, impatiently points out the tooth with the hole in it.*

556a 咸
xián
salty

---

fifth 戊(259a) + **piled up 口**(150b) =
salty 咸

With his **fifth** arm the starfish **piled up** the food he had caught to save for a **salty** snack later. / *[No pronunciation needed]*

556 感 gǎn — feel

Radical 心
13 strokes

一	厂	厂	厈	后	咸	咸	咸	咸
感	感	感						

salty 咸(556a) + **heart 心**(161) = **feel 感**

This can be literal (to "feel", "touch") or metaphorical — "to be moved", "be grateful".

感到(74) **gǎndào** *to feel (e.g. happy)*
感谢(108) **gǎnxiè** *to be grateful*

"All that **salty** food was bad for your **heart**," the doctor said. "But now you've been on that diet, how do you **feel**?" / *Teddy had dressed up as Gandhi (to symbolize frugality and remind the patient that he should eat less salt).*

557 喊 hǎn — shout

Radical 口
12 strokes

丨	叮	口	口	吖	吓	听	咸	咸	喊
喊	喊								

mouth 口(5) + **salty 咸**(556a) = **shout 喊**

[叫喊(354) **jiàohǎn** *to shout*]
[呐喊(220) **nàhǎn** *to shout out*]

(On the beach) Stranded by the high tide at the **mouth** of the cave and surrounded by **salty** water, he **shout**s for help. / *Teddy clambers down the cliff with some drinking water in his handbag!*

558 布 bù — cloth

Radical 巾
5 strokes

一	广	才	右	布				

left hand 广(53a) + **towel 巾**(427a) = **cloth 布**

This character is also used as the simplified form of a traditional character meaning "to spread" or "to arrange".

[一块布(1, 402) **yí kuài bù** *a piece of cloth*]

(At the jeweler's) She tries the ring on her **left hand** and then places it on the **towel** on the counter, and the jeweler cleans it with a **cloth**. / *The dwarf rubs his hands at this boost in his sales.*

559 希 xī — to wish

Radical 巾
7 strokes

丿	乂	亠	产	产	希	希		

shears 乂(25a) + **cloth 布**(558) = **wish 希**

The sheepshearer rubs the magic **shears** with a **cloth** and makes a **wish**. / *And (lo and behold) a giant appears with a sheep for him to practice on!*

Chapter 30

Onward! — with this chapter you will have completed 30 out of the 40 chapters in the book. As you have got this far, you know that your routine is working — so simply keep going and you will be on the final lap before long.

卩 **seal**	巴 **hardship**
乚 **conceal**	雨 **rain**
彡 **hairs**	世 **world**
川 **grain stalks**	亦 **as well**

560a

卩 seal

| 𠃌 | 卪 | or | ⟍ | ⟋ | | | |

This has several variant forms (see 560, 562a and 564a).

It refers to a seal for authenticating documents, which could be carried around and served as a badge of office.

560

节 **jié**
festival

Radical 艹
5 strokes

節

| 一 | 十 | 艹 | 艻 | 节 | | | |

grass 艹(218a) + **seal** 卩(560a) = **festival** 节

In this character the first stroke of "seal" (560a) is lengthened and the vertical stroke starts part-way along it.

The character also means "a node or segment", "an agenda" or "to economize".

节目(93) **jiémù** *(TV, radio) program*
节日(6) **jiérì** *festival day*

Once a year the king allows his **seal** to be hidden in a huge pile of **grass** and the children have to find it — the resulting scrum is the highlight of the **festival**. / *Two fairies prepare a huge jelly for the feast afterwards (picture them having to keep plucking stray pieces of grass out of the jelly).*

561a

却 **què**
despite

卻

| 一 | 十 | 土 | 去 | 去 | 去丁 | 却 | |

go 去(86) + **seal** 卩(560a) = **despite** 却

"I told you to **go** and get me my favorite ornamental **seal**," the king said grumpily. "But **despite** this you've come back with the wrong one." / *[No pronunciation needed]*

561

脚 **jiǎo**
foot

Radical 月
11 strokes

腳

|) | 刀 | 月 | 月 | 月丿 | 月丿 | 脐 | 胠 | 胠 | 胠 |
| 脚 | | | | | | | | | |

moon 月(61) + **despite** 却(561a) = **foot** 脚

[脚步(378) **jiǎobù** *footstep*]
[脚灯(182) **jiǎodēng** *footlights*]

There was a bright **moon**, but **despite** this he kept stubbing his **foot** on the tree roots in the forest. / *At this rate he would be too late to see the two teddies jousting at the secret gathering in the forest.*

Test yourself: 工(147) 产(197) 刀(72) 卖(248) 午(125) 得(118) 破(441)
应(388) 号(424) 将(318) 院(306) 衣(437) 确(419) 推(502)

562a   ruler

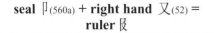

seal ⼘(560a) + right hand 又(52) = ruler 反

As you can see, this ruler is a monarch, not something for measuring things!

Note how the vertical stroke of "seal" extends all the way down the side of "right hand".

(The young prince is instructed) "You must accept the **seal** of state and **shake hands** with the archbishop before you can be enthroned as the new **ruler** of the kingdom." / [No pronunciation needed]

---

562   **bào** to report

Radical 扌
7 strokes

報

hand 扌(152a) + ruler 反(562a) = report 报

[报名(70) **bào míng** to sign one's name]
[报道(145) **bàodào** a news report]

The **ruler** holds out his **hand** for the **report** (on the state of the kingdom). / *The dwarf bows as he gives it to him.*

---

563   **fú** obey

Radical 月
8 strokes

moon 月(61) + ruler 反(562a) = obey 服

This character can also mean "clothes".

服务(547) **fúwù** work for, serve
衣服(437) **yīfu** clothes; garment
服务员(547, 479) **fúwùyuán** waiter, waitress, attendant

At the first full **moon** of his reign, the new **ruler** must pledge to **obey** the traditions of his office. / *The fairy presides over the ceremony sitting on a futon.*

564a   "explosion"

seal マ(560a) + use 用(130) = explosion 甬

The top part of this character is the third, and final, variant of "seal" (560a) — don't confuse this with "cocoon" (34a)

(The assassins are planting a booby trap) When the **seal** is next **used** it will cause an **explosion** and kill the king. / [No pronunciation needed]

564 通 **tōng** pass through

Radical 辶
10 strokes

road 辶(26a) + **explosion** 甬(564a) =
pass through 通

This has a range of other meanings including "connect", "know", "expert", "common" and "whole".

通过(106) **tōngguò** *to pass through; as a result of*
通知(490) **tōngzhī** *to notify; a notice*
[交通(380) **jiāotōng** *traffic, transportation*]

When the **road** was blocked (in a landslip) they used an **explosion** to clear it so that traffic could **pass through**. / *The **giant** used his **tongs** to help remove the rubble.*

565 痛 **tòng** to ache

Radical 疒
12 strokes

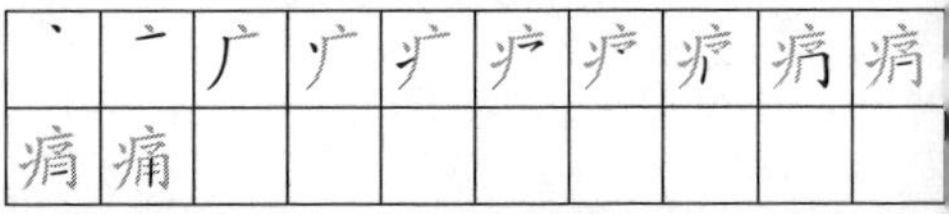

illness 疒(510b) + **explosion** 甬(564a) =
ache 痛

痛快(403) **tòngkuai** *overjoyed*
[痛苦(218) **tòngkǔ** *painful, tortuous*]

"Doctor, the **illness** I had before the **explosion** is gone but now I **ache** all over." / *"My **dwarf** assistant will use special **tongs** to remove the shrapnel, and then you'll be fine," replied the doctor.*

566a 㔾 hardship

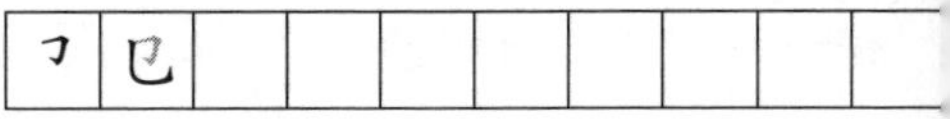

Contrast this with "seal" (560a), and also with "snake" (275a).

566b 厄 **è** "uphill"

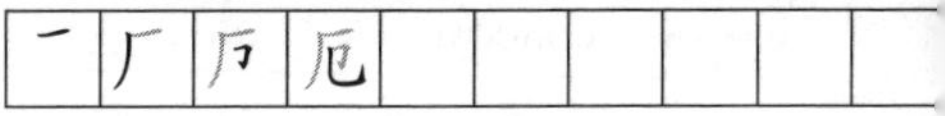

cliff 厂(149) + **hardship** 㔾(566a) =
uphill 厄

There are lots of **hardship**s involved in living on a **cliff**, but it's ideal for someone who likes an **uphill** struggle! / *[No pronunciation needed]*

566
危 wēi
danger

Radical 刀
6 strokes

| ノ | ク | ㇗ | 产 | 危 | 危 | | | | |

bow 宀(51a) + uphill 厄(566b) =
danger 危

[危机(10) wēijī *crisis*]

"If you **bow** to someone you meet as you're going **uphill**, you run the **danger** that they will bow too (and will then fall over on top of you). / *I once had the full weight of the giant on top of me, because of bowing to him like that.*"

567
顾 gù
attend to

Radical 页
10 strokes

顧

| ー | 厂 | 厃 | 厄 | 厄 | 厄' | 厄 | 厄 | 顾 | 顾 |

uphill 厄(566b) + page 页(477) =
attend to 顾

Notice that the hook on "hardship" (566a) in the left-hand side of this character has turned into a "barb". You've seen this happening before (see for example Character 228) and it will happen again (see 570a).

(A reclusive author lives on a hill) The publisher struggles **uphill** with the **pages** of the author's book, so the author can **attend to** the corrections. / *But the dwarf doesn't mind as he is a budding author himself and regards the recluse as his guru.*

[顾客(509) gùkè *customer, client*]

Test yourself: 马(44) 角(418) 开(85) 而(151) 牛(384) 租(446) 准(504)
头(246) 教(265) 代(456) 合(347) 带(429) 风(468) 嘴(420)

568a
L conceal

| L | | | | | | | | | |

Note that this is just one stroke.

568b
亡 wáng
perish

| 丶 | 亠 | 亡 | | | | | | | |

lid 亠(25b) + conceal L (568a) = perish 亡

This can mean "to die" or "to lose".

The mother puts the **lid** on the box of strawberries to **conceal** them from her children — but then forgets about them so they **perish**. (The strawberries, not the children!) / *[No pronunciation needed]*

568 忙 máng busy

Radical 忄
6 strokes

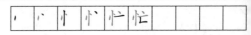

heart 忄 (339a) + **perish** 亡 (568b) = **busy** 忙

Notice that the same two parts ("heart" and "perish") are used to make up this character and the next one. So the order in which they appear in the two equations (and stories) is important for remembering which is which.

Your **heart** will **perish** if you rush around being **busy** all the time. / *The fairy can (magically) see that your arteries are all getting mangled up in there …*

569 忘 wàng forget

Radical 心
7 strokes

perish 亡 (568b) + **heart** 心 (161) = **forget** 忘

[忘记 (272) **wàngjì** *forget*]

(The king dictates a letter to his mistress) "**Perish** the thought that my **heart** will ever **forget** you." / *His retainer, Wang the dwarf, disapproves as he writes all this down. [This is almost a DIY pronunciation; feel free to improve on it if you can — anything that works is OK!]*

570a 朚 "wane"

perish 亡 (568b) + **moon** 月 (61) = **wane** 朚

In some typefaces you will see moon here replaced by its other form (266a).

"That **perish**ing **moon** is on the **wane** again," muttered the farmer (who needed the light for his harvesting). / *[No pronunciation needed]*

570 望 wàng gaze

Radical 王
11 strokes

wane 朚 (570a) + **king** 王 (60a) = **gaze** 望

希望 (559) **xīwàng** *hope, wish*

The old **king**'s health was on the **wane** — all he could do now was to **gaze** out at his kingdom from his balcony. / *Sadly he called for his chancellor Wang the dwarf, to put his affairs in order.*

571 雨　**yǔ**　rain

Radical 雨
8 strokes

It's handy that the character for "rain" needs a "pouring rain" story!

When this appears at the top of other characters, "outer limits" gets compressed into "cover". Remember that the same thing happened for "esteem" (542a).

 / Picture a **wheel** left out in the **rain**: "That **Teddy's** useless — he's always leaving things out in the pouring rain."

雨衣(437)　**yǔyī**　*raincoat*]
下雨(43)　**xià yǔ**　*rain; to rain*]

---

572 雪　**xuě**　snow

Radical 雨
11 strokes

rain 雨(571) + **snout** 彐(267a) = **snow** 雪

雪人(12)　**xuěrén**　*a snowman*]
下雪(43)　**xià xuě**　*to snow*]

The pig slept, dreaming of **rain** falling on his **snout** — but when he woke up it was **snow** (and everything around was white). / *[DIY pronunciation]*

573a 彡　hairs

---

573 参　**cān**　consult

Radical 厶
8 strokes

cocoon 厶(34a) + **big** 大(47) + **hairs** 彡(573a) = **consult** 参

参观(216)　**cānguān**　*visit (a place)*
参加(325)　**cānjiā**　*participate, join in*

The silkworm farmer finds that his **cocoon**s are growing **big hairs**, so takes them along to **consult** the vet. / *The **giant** (working as the vet's assistant) jumps onto a chair saying, "I can't **stand** creepy crawlies!"*

574a 景　**jǐng**　view

sun 日(6) + **capital** 京(239b) = **view** 景

They could see the **sun** glinting on the **capital** in the distance — they knew that this was the right house for them as soon as they saw this **view** from the front porch. / *[No pronunciation needed]*

574  **yǐng** shadow   Radical 彡 15 strokes

丶	冂	冂	日	日	旦	早	昌	景	景
景	景	景'	影	影					

> view 景(574a) + hairs 彡(573a) = shadow 影

He had taken photos of all the **view**s, but **hairs** in the camera had made **shadow**s on all his prints. / *[DIY pronunciation]*

From "shadow" come the additional meanings "image", "photo", "movie".

影响(390) **yǐngxiǎng** *effect; to affect*
电影(159) **diànyǐng** *movie, film*
[影子(17) **yǐngzi** *shadow*]
[合影(347) **héyǐng** *take a group photo*]
[电影院(159, 306) **diànyǐngyuàn** *cinema, movie theater*]

575a "beggar"

丿	勹	勺	勾	匃					

> wrap 勹(23a) + person 人(12) + conceal 匚(568a) = beggar 匃

They **conceal Harry** by **wrap**ping him up in an old cloak, to look like a **beggar**. / *[No pronunciation needed]*

575b  "a drink"

丶	冂	冂	日	尸	弖	昮	曷	曷	

> sun 日(6) + beggar 匃(575a) = a drink 曷

As the **sun** starts to get higher the **beggar** is getting desperate for **a drink**. / *[No pronunciation needed]*

575 **hē** to drink   Radical 口 12 strokes

丶	𠮛	口	叭	叭	吲	吲	咀	喝	喝
喝	喝								

> mouth 口(5) + a drink 曷(575b) = to drink 喝

They leave **a drink** (imagine a glass of beer) by the **mouth** of the cave to see if anyone will come out **to drink** it. / *They're hoping to catch sight of the **giant** who lives there as a **hermit**.*

[喝酒(102) **hējiǔ** *to drink wine/liquor*]
[喝汤(531) **hētāng** *to drink soup*]

576  渇 kě
thirsty

Radical 氵
12 strokes

| ﹅ | ﹀ | 氵 | 氵 | 沪 | 沪 | 汨 | 沪 | 渇 | 渇 |
| 渇 | 渇 | | | | | | | | |

water 氵 (78a) + a drink 曷(575b) =
thirsty 渇

[口渇(5) **kǒukě** *thirsty*]

Watering down the **drinks** in the pub only
works if the customers are **thirsty** (because
then they won't notice). / *Teddy does this
behind a curtain (taking a sip from each
glass and topping it up with water).*

577a   迷
"cut"

| ﹅ | ﹀ | 二 | 半 | 米 | 米 | 迷 | | | |

rice 米(334) + conceal 匚 (568a) = cut 迷

All the farmers in the district **conceal**
some of their **rice** from the government
inspector, in case he decides there's too
much rice and **cut**s the official price. / *[No
pronunciation needed]*

---

577   继 jì
continue

Radical 纟
10 strokes

繼

| ﹅ | 纟 | 纟 | 纟 | 纟 | 纟 | 纟 | 绊 | 继 | 继 |

thread 纟 (233a) + cut 迷(577a) =
continue 继

(In the clothing factory) When the worker
reaches the end of each reel of **thread** he
has to **cut** it off and **continue** straight away
with a new reel. / *The dwarf supervisor
has to check each G-string which has such
a join in it.*

---

578 世 shì
world

Radical 一
5 strokes

| 一 | 十 | 卄 | 世 | 世 | | | | | |

This also means "life", "generation" or
era".

You may like to think of this as "conceal"
(568a) plus "twenty" (425a).

世纪(273) **shìjì** *century*]
去世(86) **qùshì** *pass away*]

/ *After the round the world cycle ride, only
one wheel had lasted the whole trip and
this "world wheel" is now on display in
the town hall, together with a photo of the
dwarf with the "golden shallot" being
presented to him by the French president.*

Test yourself: 常(544)   成(259)   希(559)   或(555)   祖(447)   活(460)   喜(539)

说(67)   部(316)   停(343)   少(377)   高(481)   示(430)   知(490)

579a

丿 "grain stalks"

Notice how this differs from "boy" 儿 (Character 21).

---

579 介 jiè   **Radical** 人
4 strokes
between

tent 人(19b) + grain stalks 丿(579a) =
between 介

The farmer put a **tent** over the **grain stalks**, where the harvest mice had built their nest — so that the harvesters would have to go **between** the tents. / *The two dwarf farmhands were jealous of this treatment (when did the farmer ever show so much consideration for them?)*

---

580 界 jiè   **Radical** 田
9 strokes
boundary

field 田(156a) + between 介(579) =
boundary 界

世界(578) **shìjiè** *the world*

There is a **field between** the two farms, forming a no-man's land so that the **boundary** is disputed. / *The two dwarves (who each own one of the farms) each eye the field jealously.*

581a 亦 yì
as well

When this appears at the top of other characters, the central two lines are truncated int short vertical lines (as in the following character).

---

581 变 biàn   **Radical** 又
8 strokes
transform
變

as well 亦(581a) + right hand 又(52) =
transform 变

变成(259) **biànchéng** *change into*
改变(359) **gǎibiàn** *transformation*
变化(391) **biànhuà** *transformation*

(At the wizard contest) Before starting they had to touch wands **as well** as shake hands. But because they had left their wands activated they **transform**ed one another into slugs. / *The two dwarf stage-hands carried them off on a bench (to the detransforming clinic).*

Chapter 31

As another "quiz", see if you can remember these pairs. This time, each pair has similar meanings rather than being similar in appearance.

较(382) 比(228)   内(219) 里(157)   决(404) 定(406)   能(206) 可(140)

相(163) 互(226)   难(503) 困(522)   妈(46) 母(127)   首(144) 头(246)

582a

夭　die young

| ノ | 二 | 于 | 夭 | | | | |

beret 一 (89a) + **big** 人(47) = **die young** 夭

Notice the subtle difference between this and 天 ("heaven", Character 76).

The child had loved wearing a **beret** which was too **big** for him (he had wanted to grow up to be a commando), but tragically he **died young**. (Picture the beret on the poor lad's coffin at the funeral). / *[No pronunciation needed]*

582

笑　xiào　smile

Radical 𥫗
10 strokes

| ノ | ⺊ | ⺮ | ⺮ | ⺮ | ⺮ | 笡 | 笞 | 竿 | 笑 |

bamboo 𥫗(321a) + **die young** 夭(582a) = **smile** 笑

大笑(47) **dà xiào** *to laugh*]
笑话(458) **xiàohuà** *joke*]
开玩笑(85, 304) **kāiwánxiào** *to play a joke*

(The prince has married the princess from the neighboring kingdom and their first child is born. It is the custom to place a piece of bamboo in the baby's hand) If the baby ignores the **bamboo** it will **die young**, but the baby grasps it — and the parents **smile**. / *The **two dwarf** town criers have to trudge round the two kingdoms **shouting** out the good news.*

583a

乔　qiáo　tall

喬

die young 夭(582a) + **grain stalks** 川(579a) = **tall** 乔

The boy **died young**, while the **grain stalks** were **tall**er than he was. / *[No pronunciation needed]*

583 桥 **qiáo**
bridge

Radical 木
10 strokes

橋

tree 木(10a) + tall 乔(583a) = bridge 桥

They looked for a **tree** that was **tall** enough to make a **bridge** across the river. / *The two fairies on the other side own a restaurant famed for its clam chowder.*

584a 歹 **dǎi**
evil

one 一(1) + evening 夕(69a) = evil 歹

Each **evening** the **unicorn** comes out of the forest to sleep, because he's scared that there are **evil** spirits in there at night. / *[No pronunciation needed]*

584b 列 **liè**
line up

evil 歹(584a) + knife ⺉(74a) = line up 列

The **evil** looking **knife** was confiscated by the police and **lined up** (with the others they have seized) for the TV cameras. / *[No pronunciation needed]*

---

584 例 **lì**
example

Radical 亻
8 strokes

person 亻(13a) + line up 列(584b) = example 例

例如(80) **lìrú** *e.g., such as*
[比例(228) **bǐlì** *percentage*]
[例子(17) **lìzi** *an example*]

Test yourself: 划(554) 给(351) 指(251) 务(547) 嘴(420) 顾(567) 坐(211)
感(556) 忘(569) 坏(442) 它(227) 备(548) 只(254) 脚(561)

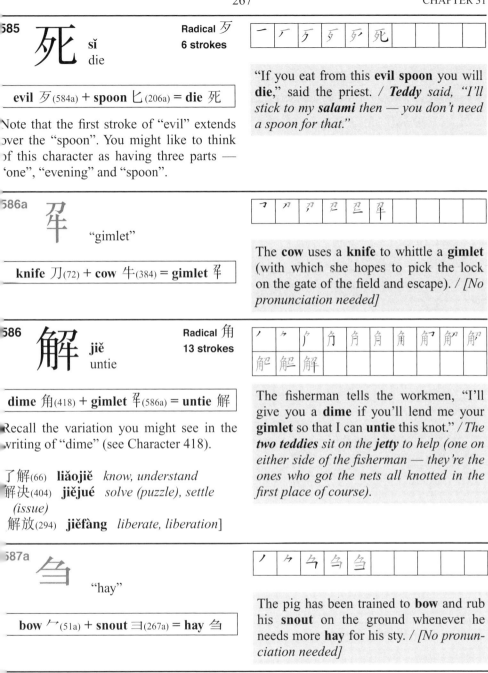

585

死 sǐ
die

Radical 歹
6 strokes

| 一 | 丆 | 歹 | 歹 | 歹 | 死 | | | |

---

evil 歹 (584a) + **spoon** 匕 (206a) = **die** 死

Note that the first stroke of "evil" extends over the "spoon". You might like to think of this character as having three parts — "one", "evening" and "spoon".

"If you eat from this **evil spoon** you will **die**," said the priest. / *Teddy said, "I'll stick to my salami then — you don't need a spoon for that."*

586a

羿

"gimlet"

| 𡕣 | 𡕣 | 𡕣 | 𡳾 | 𡳾 | 羿 | | | |

---

knife 刀 (72) + **cow** 牛 (384) = **gimlet** 羿

The **cow** uses a **knife** to whittle a **gimlet** (with which she hopes to pick the lock on the gate of the field and escape). / *[No pronunciation needed]*

586

解 jiě
untie

Radical 角
13 strokes

| 丿 | 𠂊 | 𠂤 | 刀 | 角 | 角 | 角 | 角 | 解 | 解 |
| 解 | 解 | 解 | | | | | | | |

---

dime 角 (418) + **gimlet** 羿 (586a) = **untie** 解

Recall the variation you might see in the writing of "dime" (see Character 418).

了解 (66) **liǎojiě** *know, understand*
解决 (404) **jiějué** *solve (puzzle), settle (issue)*
解放 (294) **jiěfàng** *liberate, liberation]*

The fisherman tells the workmen, "I'll give you a **dime** if you'll lend me your **gimlet** so that I can **untie** this knot." / *The two teddies sit on the jetty to help (one on either side of the fisherman — they're the ones who got the nets all knotted in the first place of course).*

587a

彑

"hay"

| 丿 | 𠃌 | 彑 | 彑 | 彑 | | | | |

---

bow 𠂆 (51a) + **snout** 彐 (267a) = **hay** 彑

The pig has been trained to **bow** and rub his **snout** on the ground whenever he needs more **hay** for his sty. / *[No pronunciation needed]*

587 急 **jí** urgent

Radical 心
9 strokes

hay 刍(587a) + **heart** 心(161) = **urgent** 急

着急(205) **zháojí** *anxious, worried*
[急忙(568) **jímáng** *hurried, hasty*]

Hay is spilling out of a hole in the scarecrow's coat, and soon his **heart** will be exposed — stopping the leak has become **urgent**. / *The fairy uses her G-string to secure it!*

588a 彦 **yàn** a good man

produce 产(197) + **hairs** 彡(573a) = **a good man** 彦

He decides to **produce hairs** in his factory (to make wigs for bald people) — but he charges nothing as he is **a good man**. / *[No pronunciation needed]*

---

588 颜 **yán** complexion

Radical 页
15 strokes

a good man 彦(588a) + **page** 页(477) = **complexion** 颜

This can mean (a person's) "face", or simply "color".

颜色(417) **yánsè** *color*

The **good man** spends all his time indoors studying the **page**s of his good books — so ends up with a pale **complexion**. / *The fairy casts a spell on him and he suddenly says, "You know, I have a yen to go outside more."*

---

589 许 **xǔ** to permit

Radical 讠
6 strokes

words 讠 (67c) + **noon** 午(125) = **permit** 许

We've gathered together here the four characters pronounced "xu" (for convenience, they're not a phonetic series). Remember to visualize the rain in each story.

许多(69) **xǔduō** *many, much*
也许(8) **yěxǔ** *perhaps*

The **words** on the sign in the street say that from **noon** parking is **permit**ted. / *A parking attendant appears through the pouring rain and Teddy says "Shoo!" in an attempt to chase him off.*

590 需 xū — need

Radical 雨
14 strokes

rain 雨(571) + **and yet** 而(151) = **need** 需

需要(101) **xūyào** *to need; a need*

☔ In the heavy **rain**, the market trader fixes up a makeshift roof for his stall, **and yet** it sags (and collapses with the weight of water) — a proper gutter is what he **need**s. / *The giant fixes up a chute to divert the pouring rain for him.*

---

591 须 xū — have to

Radical 彡
9 strokes

須 鬚

hairs 彡(573a) + **page** 页(477) = **have to** 须

This can also mean "beard" (in which case the second traditional form applies).

必须(162) **bìxū** *must*

☔ He's stuck **hairs** on the **page** to underline certain words (this is in the days before highlighter pens have been invented) but the librarian tells him to remove them. "Do I **have to**?" he wails (wondering how to remove the glue). / *The giant whispers to him, "When my shoelaces got glue on them I just left them to soak in the pouring rain."*

---

592 续 xù — carry on

Radical 纟
11 strokes

續

thread 纟(233a) + **sell** 卖(248) = **carry on** 续

继续(577) **jìxù** *to continue*
[手续(31) **shǒuxù** *formalities*]

☔ The spiders have found that if they produce extra **thread** they can **sell** it — so each day, after making their webs, they **carry on** and produce more thread, which can be sold. / *The dwarf uses it to make waterproof shoelaces, which he tests out in the pouring rain.*

593a 令 lìng — command

combine 亼(59a) + **seal** 卩(560a) = **command** 令

Not to be confused with 今 ("now", Character 166), this character is also used as a respectful way of saying "your".

☔ The emperor simply signs ordinary documents, but when he **combine**s a **seal** with his signature it means that it's a **command**. / *[No pronunciation needed]*

593 **lěng**
cold

Radical 冫
7 strokes

| 丶 | 冫 | 冫 | 冫 | 冫 | 冷 | 冷 | | |

The **ice** queen **command**s it to be **cold**. / *Teddy* complains, "*My **lungs** tickle with the cold air.*"

ice 冫 (360a) + **command** 令(593a) = **cold** 冷

[冷气(411) **lěngqì** *air conditioning*]

---

594 零 **líng**
zero

Radical 雨
13 strokes

| 一 | 厂 | 厂 | 丙 | 雨 | 雨 | 雨 | 雨 | 零 | 零 |
| 零 | 零 | 零 | | | | | | | |

rain 雨(571) + **command** 令(593a) =
zero 零

You will also see "0" used as a symbol for zero, and this is also pronounced **líng**.

[三千零四(3, 89, 24) **sānqiān líng sì** *3004*]

(The trainee wizard is taking his final exams) He tries to **command** that **rain** should fall, but instead the temperature drops to **zero**. / *The **fairy** whispers, "For rain, you should have used **linguini** in your spell.*"

---

595 **lǐng**
to lead

Radical 页
11 strokes

领

| 丿 | 入 | 今 | 今 | 令 | 令 | 令 | 邻 | 领 | 领 |
| 领 | | | | | | | | | |

command 令(593a) + **page** 页(477) =
to lead 领

This means "to lead" or "be in charge"; also "neck" or "collar".

[领导(277) **lǐngdǎo** *lead, guide; leader*]
[本领(174) **běnlǐng** *skill, ability*]

The herald unrolls the **page** and reads out the king's **command** — it says that everyone must **lead** their pets around the town on National Pet Day. / *Teddy* ties a bit of *linguini* to his hamster and brings it along.

596a 召 **zhào**
summon

| ⊃ | 刀 | 刀 | 召 | 召 | | | | |

knife 刀(72) + **mouth** 口(5) = **summon** 召

The sentry looks over the castle walls — and sees a pirate climbing up towards him, a **knife** in his **mouth**. He raises the alarm, crying, "**Summon** the guards!" / *[No pronunciation needed]*

596

绍 **shào** continue

Radical 纟 8 strokes

| 纟 | 纟 | 纟 | 纠 | 纫 | 织 | 绍 | 绍 | | |

thread 纟(233a) + **summon** 召(596a) = **continue** 绍

介绍(579) **jièshào** introduce

(The queen is doing her needlework) She has run out of **thread**, so she **summon**s a servant to fetch more so that she can **continue**. / *The dwarf shouts after him to be quick about it.*

597a

昭 **zhāo** obvious

| 丨 | 冂 | 日 | 日 | 日丁 | 日刀 | 昭 | 昭 | 昭 | |

sun 日(6) + **summon** 召(596a) = **obvious** 昭

On the next day when the **sun** shone brightly, he **summon**ed all his friends to admire his new sundial. One complained, "Why do this on such a hot day?" "Well, isn't it **obvious**?" / *[No pronunciation needed]*

597

照 **zhào** shine

Radical ,,,, 13 strokes

| 丨 | 冂 | 日 | 日 | 日丁 | 日刀 | 昭 | 昭 | 昭 | 昭 |
| 照 | 照 | 照 | | | | | | | |

obvious 昭(597a) + **fire** ,,,,(185a) = **shine** 照

This character has two meanings: "to shine on, illuminate"; and "to look after, care for".

照顾(567) **zhàogù** *look after, care for*
照相(163) **zhàoxiàng** *to take a photo*
[关照(372) **guānzhào** *take care of; notify*]
[照片(353) **zhàopiàn** *photograph*]

The **obvious** way to get the **fire** started is to **shine** focused sunlight onto it. / *The dwarf gets his old jousting shield (and uses the concave side of it as a magnifying mirror).*

598

查 **chá** check up

Radical 木 9 strokes

| 一 | 十 | 才 | 木 | 木 | 杏 | 杏 | 杳 | 查 | |

tree 木(10a) + **dawn** 旦(117a) = **check up** 查

[查对(154) **cháduì** *verify, check*]

(After a storm) He went round the **tree**s at **dawn** to **check up** which ones had survived the night. / *The fairy flew alongside with a chart showing where the trees were supposed to be.*

599a

"conference"

combine 亼(59a) + haul up 业(388a) = conference 金

The delegates **combine** to **haul up** a sign over the convention hall, to announce their **conference**. (Imagine them all lining up along the roof at the front of the building). / *[No pronunciation needed]*

599

 jiǎn
inspect

Radical 木
11 strokes

檢

tree 木(10a) + conference 金(599a) = inspect 检

检查(598) **jiǎnchá** *examine, inspect, check*

When a **tree** arrives at the **conference**, it must be **inspect**ed for contagious diseases. / *If it is genuinely healthy, two teddies will escort it to the conference hall.*

600

 lǐan
face

Radical 月
11 strokes

臉

moon 月(61) + conference 金(599a) = face 脸

[脸红(233) **liǎnhóng** *to blush, get flushed*]

(At a conference of werewolves) When the full **moon** comes up the **conference** delegates have to have their **face**s checked to see if they really are werewolves. / *Two teddies stand on either side of the queue looking out for their friends so they can lend them hairy masks to get past the checks.*

601

 xiǎn
risky

Radical 阝
9 strokes

險

mound 阝(96a) + conference 金(599a) = risky 险

危险(566) **wēixiǎn** *danger, dangerous*

The commandos choose a **mound** to hold their **conference** (because they like to occupy the high ground), and plan how they are going to carry out the final part of their **risky** mission. / *[DIY pronunciation]*

602 验 yàn examine

Radical 马
10 strokes

驗

horse 马(44) + conference 佥(599a) =
examine 验

经验(244) **jīngyàn** *experience*
[实验(250) **shíyàn** *a test, experiment*]

A **horse** with a rare disease has been brought along to the **conference** of vets so that they can **examine** him. / *The dwarf caretaker watches closely as he has always had a yen to be a vet.*

603a 式 shì style

work 工(147) + stake 弋(456a) = **style** 式

He always carries a **stake** to **work**, as he thinks it gives him a certain **style**. (But his teenage son knows better!) / *[No pronunciation needed]*

---

603 试 shì to try

Radical 讠
8 strokes

試

words 讠(67c) + style 式(603a) = **try** 试

[试验(602) **shìyàn** *to test, experiment*]
[试试 **shìshi** *to have a try*]

(Designing a poster for the production of "1001 Nights") The draftsman writes the **words** out in different **style**s, to **try** and see which will work best. / *The dwarf waits until he's finished, and only then points out that he's spelled "Scheherazade" wrong. (You can imagine the ensuing expletives!)*

---

604 考 kǎo to test

Radical 耂
6 strokes

old man 耂(261a) + choke 丂(424a) =
test 考

The first stroke of "choke" has got truncated so that "choke" fits under "old man".

考试(603) **kǎoshì** *to examine; a test*
[考场(530) **kǎochǎng** *exam hall/room*]

The **old man** arrives at the hospital **choking** — but it is just a pretense, to **test** out the hospital's response time. / *Teddy, on reception, rings a cowbell to summon the doctors who come running.*

605a
dòu; dǒu
fight

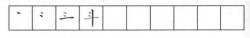

ice crystals ⟨(246a) + **ten** 十(4) = **fight** 斗

The "cross" is rather distorted here to make room for the "ice crystals" — note that the "horizontal" line has a definite slope to it.

Two gangs of boys start throwing **ice crystals** at each other from either side of the **cross**roads — and it soon develops into a full-blown **fight**. / *[No pronunciation needed]*

---

605 科
kē
classification

Radical 禾
9 strokes

grain 禾(126a) + **fight** 斗(605a) =
classification 科

This character is often used for a specialization or field of (academic) study.

The farmers are having a **grain fight** (throwing bags of grain at each other) after the announcement of the grain **classification** results. / *The giant breaks up the fight and imposes a curfew until morning.*

科学(82) **kēxué** *science*
[科长(172) **kēzhǎng** *section chief*]
[科学家(82, 109) **kēxuéjiā** *scientist*]

---

606 研
yán
research

Radical 石
9 strokes

stone 石(115a) + **open** 开(85) =
research 研

[科研(605) **kēyán** *scientific research*]

You are issued with a special **stone** (with an embedded microchip) to **open** the door to the secret **research** lab. (Boffins are always losing normal keys!) / *But the fairy has always had a yen to make the lab's work public, so lets a reporter in to look around.*

Test yourself: 多(69)　干(124)　百(40)　小(50)　九(38)　白(22)　旧(394)

牛(384)　渴(576)　然(266)　足(280)　钟(278)　导(277)　饺(381)

Chapter 32

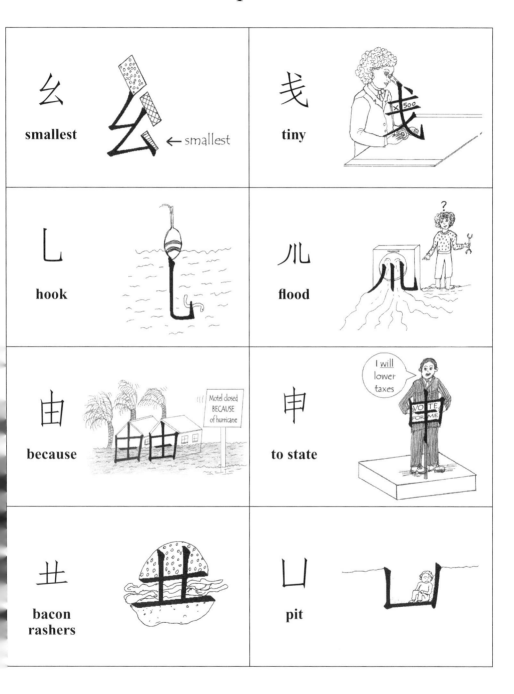

幺
smallest

戋
tiny

乚
hook

儿
flood

由
because

申
to state

丑
bacon rashers

凵
pit

607a

yāo
smallest

| ∠ | 幺 | 幺 | | | | | | |

Used colloquially for "one".

607b

糸 thread

| ∠ | 幺 | 幺 | 糸 | 糸 | 糸 | | | |

> **smallest** 幺(607a) + **small** 小(50) =
> **thread** 糸

The **smallest** of the **small** worms looks just like a piece of **thread**. / *[No pronunciation needed]*

When this character appears as the left-hand side of another character, it is abbreviated to the form 纟 which we already know (233a).

607

系
xì
cluster

Radical 糸
7 strokes

係 繫

| 一 | 纟 | 至 | 玄 | 乎 | 系 | 系 | | |

> **beret** ⌐ (89a) + **thread** 糸(607b) =
> **cluster** 系

A spider has woven a web out of **thread**s in the **beret**, and there is now a **cluster** of eggs there. / *The dwarf wraps it up in a sheet and throws it away.*

This has various senses including "fasten", "system" and "department" (with the traditional forms varying from meaning to meaning).

关系(372) **guānxì** *connection; affect*
联系(374) **liánxì** *train, drill, exercise*
没关系(169, 372) **méiguānxì** *it's OK*
　(reply to 'sorry')

608

累
lèi (lěi)
exhausted

Radical 田
11 strokes

| 丶 | 冂 | 冖 | 田 | 田 | 甲 | 里 | 里 | 累 | 累 |
| 累 | | | | | | | | | |

> **field** 田(156a) + **thread** 糸(607b) =
> **exhausted** 累

Notice that the threads are *under* the field here (compare this with Character 234).

The farmer laid a network of steel **thread**s under the **field** to protect his crops from rabbits — and it worked, as the rabbits rapidly became **exhausted** trying to dig through them. / *The dwarf takes them off and dumps them in the lake.*

609a 戋 tiny

一 二 戋 戋 戋

This is "dagger" (32a) but with an extra stroke.

609 践 jiàn carry out
Radical 足
12 strokes
踐

丶 ㄇ 口 ㅁ 굗 吊 足 趴 趴 趴 践 践

foot 足(280) + tiny 戋(609a) = **carry out** 践

实践(250) **shíjiàn** *put into practice*

(A modern day Cinderella) The old hag slips her **tiny foot** into the slipper, and it fits! Now the prince has to **carry out** his promise (and marry her). / *The two dwarves (who have been carrying the slipper and cushion around) mutter that she can't possibly be the genuine article.*

610 钱 qián money
Radical 钅
10 strokes
錢

ノ ト ㅑ �乍 乍 钅 钅 钅 钱 钱

gold 钅 (278a) + tiny 戋(609a) = **money** 钱

[零钱(594) **língqián** *small change*]

Tiny pieces of **gold** (found in the river beds) were the first **money**. / [DIY pronunciation]

611 浅 qiǎn shallow
Radical 氵
8 strokes
淺

丶 冫 氵 氵 沪 浅 浅 浅

water 氵 (78a) + tiny 戋(609a) = **shallow** 浅

Also means "easy", "low standard".

There was only a **tiny** amount of **water** around so all the ponds were **shallow**. / [DIY pronunciation]

612a 乚 "hook"

乚

612 礼 lǐ gift
Radical 礻
5 strokes
禮

丶 ㇇ 礻 礻 礼

sign 礻 (433a) + hook 乚(612a) = **gift** 礼

礼物(527) **lǐwù** *gift, present*
[礼堂(543) **lǐtáng** *auditorium*]

He sees a **sign** in the sky in the shape of a **hook**. "Aha, the perfect **gift** for my fisherman friend," he thinks. / *Teddy tries his luck fishing, but only catches a leek!*

613

乱 **luàn**
chaotic

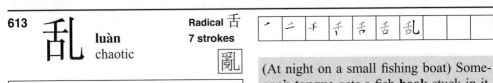

Radical 舌
7 strokes

亂

---

tongue 舌(457a) + hook 乚(612a) =
chaotic 乱

[乱说(67) **luànshuō** *gossip*]
[乱世(578) **luànshì** *turbulent times*]

(At night on a small fishing boat) Some-one's **tongue** gets a fish **hook** stuck in it, and **chaotic** scenes ensue as he thrashes around. / *The **ghostly dwarf** (guardian mascot of the boat) holds a **lantern** while they extract the hook.*

614a

云 new-born baby

---

lid 亠(25b) + cocoon 厶(34a) =
new-born baby 云

The **lid** came off the **cocoon** and out popped a **new-born baby** butterfly. / *[No pronunciation needed]*

614

育 **yù**
nurture

Radical 月
8 strokes

---

new-born baby 云(614a) + moon 月(61) =
nurture 育

教育(265) **jiàoyù** *education, educate*
体育(175) **tǐyù** *sports, P.T.*
[体育场(175, 530) **tǐyùchǎng** *stadium*]

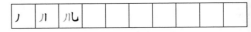 She is over the **moon** about her **new-born baby**, and vows to **nurture** it. / *The **dwarf** grumbles as he has to come out in the pouring rain to read a **eulogy**.*

615a

 儿 flood

You could think of this as "boy" with a "stick", or as "grain stalks" plus "hook".

615b

㐬 birth

---

new-born baby 云(614a) + flood 儿(615a)
= birth 㐬

Picture a mother cradling her **new-born baby** on the roof of a house during a **flood**. This was not how she imagined the **birth** would be! / *[No pronunciation needed]*

---

615 流 liú *to flow* Radical 氵 10 strokes

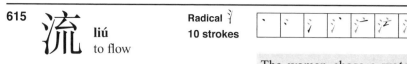

> water 氵(78a) + birth 㐬(615b) = flow 流

[交流(380) **jiāoliú** *to communicate with*]
[流利(132) **liúlì** *fluent*]

The woman chose a **water birth** in the river so that the **flow**ing water would wash the baby clean. / *Two fairies floated lotus blossoms on the water.*

616a 穴 xué *hole*

> house 宀(91a) + eight 八(20) = hole 穴

When this appears at the top of characters, you will sometimes see the legs curl (so that they look like "boy" rather than "eight").

The **house** where the **octopus** lives is so small that he had to make **hole**s in the walls for his tentacles to poke through. / *[No pronunciation needed]*

---

616 究 jiū *investigate* Radical 穴 7 strokes

> hole 穴(616a) + nine 九(38) =
> investigate 究

研究(606) **yánjiū** *research*

In one of the **holes** on the golf course they found a **baseball**, and decided to **investigate** how it had got there. / *It turned out that two giants had been joking around (playing mini-golf and using the baseball as a golf ball).*

---

617 空 kōng (kòng) *empty* Radical 穴 8 strokes

> hole 穴(616a) + work 工(147) = empty 空

空气(411) **kōngqì** *air*
[空间(345) **kōngjiān** *space, room*]
[空中(33) **kōngzhōng** *in the air*]
[太空(48) **tàikōng** *(outer) space*]

Digging the **hole** (for the elephant trap) had been a lot of **work** — but day after day it remained **empty**. / *One day the giant sprained his ankle in it, and was so cross that he filled it in with concrete.*

618 突 tū
prominent

Radical 穴
9 strokes

`、 ⺈ 宀 宀 宂 空 宩 突 突`

> **hole** 穴(616a) + **dog** 犬(238a) =
> **prominent** 突

This also means "sudden".

The **hole** which the **dog** had dug was in a **prominent** position (right in the middle of the front lawn). / *The **giant** (head gardener) used his **toupee** to disguise the hole until he could repair it.*

[突然(266) **tūrán** *sudden, suddenly*]
[突出(114) **tūchū** *prominent; to highlight*]

619a 罙
hearth

`′ ⺈ ⺗ 罒 空 罕 穷 罙`

> **cover** ⼍(82a) + **eight** 八(20) +
> **tree** 木(10a) = **hearth** 罙

(In a game of hide and seek) The **octopus** hides up a **tree** and pulls a **cover** over his head — but still feels cold and wishes he was sitting by a warm **hearth**. / *[No pronunciation needed]*

---

619 深 shēn
deep

Radical 氵
11 strokes

`、 ⺀ 氵 氵 氵 沪 汐 泙 浡 浑 深`
`深`

> **water** 氵 (78a) + **hearth** 罙(619a) = **deep** 深

During the flood, **water** rapidly reached the **hearth** and put the fire out — it was getting really **deep** now. / *This would mean that the **giant** handyman would **shun** the village (until the water receded — he doesn't like getting his feet wet).*

620a  由
yóu
because

`丨 冂 日 由 由`

---

620 抽 chōu
to extract

Radical 扌
8 strokes

`一 ⼅ 扌 扣 扣 扣 抻 抽`

> **hand** 扌(152a) + **because** 由(620a) =
> **extract** 抽

"Hold out your **hand because** it's the only way to **extract** the thorn." / *The **giant** holds out his hand grudgingly, and **chokes** back tears!*

[抽水(523) **chōushuǐ** *to draw (pump) water*]
[抽身(107) **chōushēn** *get away (from work)*]

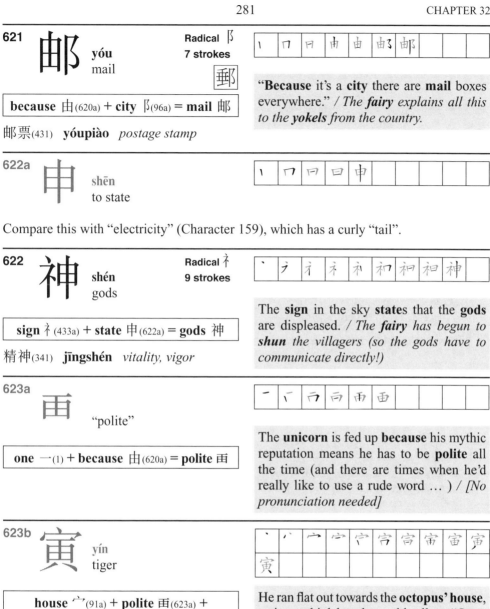

621 邮 **yóu** mail

郵

Radical 阝
7 strokes

because 由 (620a) + city 阝 (96a) = mail 邮

邮票 (431) **yóupiào** *postage stamp*

"**Because** it's a **city** there are **mail** boxes everywhere." / *The **fairy** explains all this to the **yokels** from the country.*

622a 申 **shēn** to state

Compare this with "electricity" (Character 159), which has a curly "tail".

622 神 **shén** gods

Radical 礻
9 strokes

sign 礻 (433a) + state 申 (622a) = gods 神

精神 (341) **jīngshén** *vitality, vigor*

The **sign** in the sky **state**s that the **gods** are displeased. / *The **fairy** has begun to **shun** the villagers (so the gods have to communicate directly!)*

623a 甬 "polite"

one 一 (1) + because 由 (620a) = polite 甬

The **unicorn** is fed up **because** his mythic reputation means he has to be **polite** all the time (and there are times when he'd really like to use a rude word …) / *[No pronunciation needed]*

623b 寅 **yín** tiger

house 宀 (91a) + polite 甬 (623a) + eight 八 (20) = tiger 寅

He ran flat out towards the **octopus' house**, trying to think how he could call out "Open the *** door!" **polite**ly so that he would be let in straight away, before the **tiger** caught up with him. / *[No pronunciation needed]*

623 演 yǎn
perform

Radical 氵
14 strokes

| ` | 冫 | 氵 | 氵 | 氵 | 氵 | 氵 | 氵 | 泸 | 泸 |
| 泸 | 泸 | 演 | 演 | | | | | | |

water 氵 (78a) + **tiger** 寅(623b) =
perform 演

演出(114)　**yǎnchū**　*(theatrical) performance*
表演(436)　**biǎoyǎn**　*perform, performance*
[演员(479)　**yǎnyuán**　*actor, actress*]
[开演(85)　**kāiyǎn**　*to start (movie, etc.)*]

At the finale of the circus act the **tiger** dives into the **water**, drenching the audience. He **perform**s this at every show and it's the big attraction. / *Teddy has a yen to do it too.*

624 黄 huáng
yellow

黄

Radical 艹
11 strokes

| 一 | 十 | 卄 | 艹 | 芏 | 苎 | 苦 | 苗 | 苗 | 黄 |
| 黄 | | | | | | | | | |

grass 艹(218a) + **polite** 甫(623a) +
eight 八(20) = **yellow** 黄

[黄河(141)　**Huánghé**　*the Yellow River*]

If you take your **grass** and are **polite** to the **octopus**, he will sit on it for you until it goes **yellow**. / *The ghostly fairy will then guard it in the aircraft hangar (until it is ready to sell on the black market — it's that sort of grass!)*

625a 丗
"bacon rashers"

| 一 | 卜 | 卅 | 丗 | | | | | | |

625 共 gòng
collectively

Radical 八
6 strokes

| 一 | 卜 | 卅 | 丗 | 共 | 共 | | | | |

bacon rashers 丗 (625a) + **eight** 八(20) =
collectively 共

一共(1)　**yígòng**　*altogther; in all*
[公共(119)　**gōnggòng**　*public*]
公共汽车(119, 412, 83)　**gōnggòng qìchē**　*bus*

One **octopus** was cooking **bacon rashers**, another eggs, and **collectively** they produced a huge breakfast. / *The dwarf sounded a gong when it was ready.*

626a 凵
pit

| ㄴ | 凵 | | | | | | | | |

626 画 huà
drawing

Radical 凵
8 strokes

畫

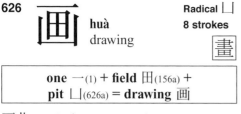

> **one** 一(1) + **field** 田(156a) +
> **pit** 凵(626a) = **drawing** 画

画儿(21) **huàr** *picture, drawing*
[画报(562) **huàbào** *pictorial (magazine)*]

The **unicorn** had fallen into the **pit** in the **field** (that they had dug as an elephant trap). The reporter (in the days before photography) took ages to make a **drawing** of the scene for the local paper. / *The ghostly dwarf guarding the pit suggested attaching a harness to the unicorn to lift him out.*

627 怕 pà
fear

Radical 忄
8 strokes

> **heart** 忄(339a) + **white** 白(22) = **fear** 怕

[可怕(140) **kěpà** *frightening*]
[哪怕(99) **nǎpà** *no matter*]

His **heart** has started pounding and his face has gone **white** — such a look of **fear**! What has he seen? / *It's a dwarf parking attendant bearing down on his parked car …*

628 拍 pāi
clap

Radical 扌
8 strokes

> **hand** 扌(152a) + **white** 白(22) = **clap** 拍

This character can mean "to applaud" or "to beat time", and it can also mean a (ping pong) bat or (tennis) racket.

[拍手(31) **pāishǒu** *to applaud*]
[拍子(17) **pāizi** *bat, racket; to beat time (music)*]

The chef's **hands** are all **white** so he **clap**s them together (to shake off the flour). / *The giant admires the pies (and wonders how many he'll get).*

Test yourself: 文(25) 自(94) 刀(72) 儿(21) 反(331) 家(109) 照(597)

今(166) 事(312) 英(401) 医(491) 任(551) 祖(447) 现(215)

Chapter 33

Yet another chapter where we can further exploit the building blocks we already have, without needing to introduce any more.

629a

吅 cry out

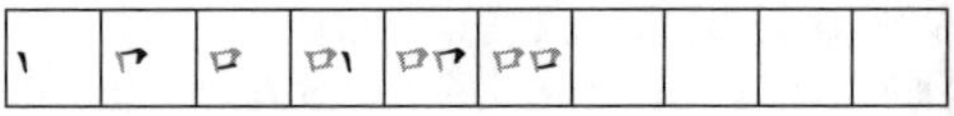

mouth 口(5) + **mouth** 口(5) =
cry out 吅

With **two mouth**s to feed in the nest, they must each **cry out** to get fed (or else the other one will get all the food). / *[No pronunciation needed]*

---

629 哭 **kū** weep

Radical 犬
10 strokes

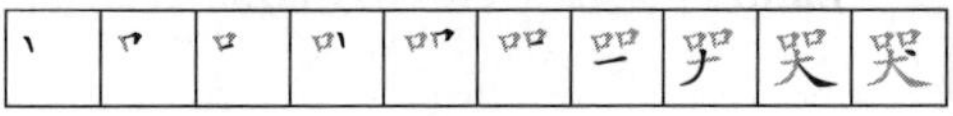

cry out 吅(629a) + **dog** 犬(238a) = **weep** 哭

The child **cried out** as her **dog** was hit by a passing car, and sat **weep**ing at the side of the road. / *The **giant**, who was passing by in his cool new **coupe**, stopped to give them a lift to the vet.*

---

630 器 **qì** utensil

Radical 口
16 strokes

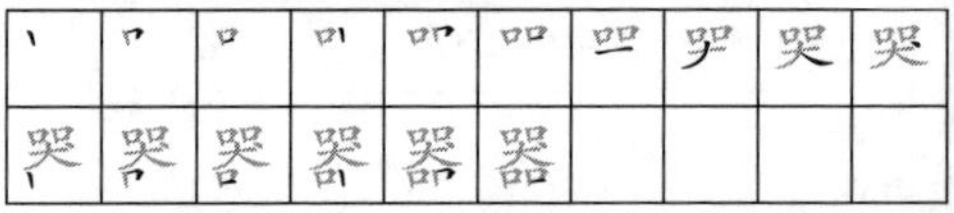

weep 哭(629) + **cry out** 吅(629a) =
utensil 器

机器(10) **jīqì** *machine*

In the kitchen the Chef is **weep**ing, **cry**ing **out** and throwing his **utensils** about in despair. / *He's lost the "Best Restaurant" competition, and reckons that the **dwarf**, his main rival, **cheated** in order to win.*

631a

品 **pǐn** goods

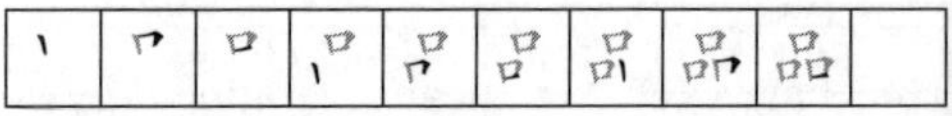

mouth 口(5) + **cry out** 吅(629a) =
goods 品

(The cave dwellers are having a yard sale) At the **mouth** of each cave the owner **cries out** to attract customers for the **goods** they have for sale. / *[No pronunciation needed]*

631b 喿 chirp

丶	丷	口	吕	吕	吕	品	品	品	吕
唄	喿	喿							

goods 品(631a) + **tree** 木(10a) = **chirp** 喿

The magpie steals **goods** from the town and takes them back to his **tree**, where his family welcomes him with a **chirp** each time he brings home something interesting. / *[No pronunciation needed]*

---

631 操 cāo exercise   Radical 扌   16 strokes

一	丨	扌	扌	扩	护	护	护	护	挦
挦	挦	撮	挦	操	操				

hand 扌(152a) + **chirp** 喿(631b) = **exercise** 操

This can mean "to grasp" and hence "to operate" (a machine).

喿场(530) **cāochǎng** *sports ground*

The bird sits on the fitness instructor's **hand** and **chirp**s to set the tempo for the **exercise**s. / *The giant has joined the class because he is getting too stout.*

---

632 澡 zǎo bathe   Radical 氵   16 strokes

丶	丷	氵	氵	氵	沪	沪	沪	沪	沪
沪	沪	温	淖	澡	澡				

water 氵(78a) + **chirp** 喿(631b) = **bathe** 澡

先澡(139) **xǐzǎo** *take a bath, shower*

The bird sees the **water** and gives a delighted **chirp** — it can **bathe** at last! / *[DIY pronunciation]*

---

633 早 zǎo early   Radical 日   6 strokes

丿	冂	冂	日	旦	早				

sun 日(6) + **ten** 十(4) = **early** 早

This can also mean "morning", "before" or "long ago".

早饭(332) **zǎofàn** *breakfast*
早上(42) **zǎoshàng** *morning*

As the car approaches the **cross**roads the rising **sun** is directly in the driver's eyes — if only he didn't have to get to work so **early**! / *[DIY pronunciation]*

634 章 zhāng badge

Radical 立
11 strokes

stand 立(177) + **early** 早(633) = **badge** 章

文章(25) **wénzhāng** *essay, article*

"If you **stand** there **early** you will get a **badge**. / *You'll know the giant is coming with the badges when you hear them jangling together.*"

635 草 cǎo straw

Radical ⺾
9 strokes

grass ⺾(218a) + **early** 早(633) = **straw** 草

[草地(54) **cǎodì** *lawn*]
[草原(536) **cǎoyuán** *steppe, pasture*]

If you cut the **grass early** in the morning it will make the best **straw**. / *Teddy decides to watch, declaring, "I'm too stout to help with cutting grass."*

636 包 bāo parcel

Radical 勹
5 strokes

wrap 勹(23a) + **snake** 巳(275a) = **parcel** 包

面包(313) **miànbāo** *bread*
[钱包(610) **qiánbāo** *purse, wallet*]
[包子(17) **bāozi** *steamed bun*]
[书包(176) **shūbāo** *school bag*]

(Before the birthday party) They **wrap** up the multicolored toy **snake** to make a long thin **parcel**. / *The giant has to bow down low to pick it up before he sets off to deliver it.*

637 饱 bǎo replete

Radical 饣
8 strokes

飽

food 饣(288a) + **parcel** 包(636) = **replete** 饱

This means "full", "satisfied" or "to eat one's fill".

(At the birthday party) The **food** and **parcels** look so colorful on the table. The children eat quickly until they are all **replete**. / *The birthday boy then opens the first parcel, and out jumps Teddy, who then gives a deep bow.*

638

抱 bào
     embrace

Radical 扌
8 strokes

| 一 | 丁 | 扌 | 扩 | 扚 | 抅 | 抱 | 抱 | | |

hand 扌(152a) + **parcel** 包(636) =
embrace 抱

The latecomer to the birthday party has the **parcel** in her **hand** when the birthday boy opens the door, and they hug in a fond **embrace**. / *The dwarf butler tactfully stays bowing until the embrace is over.*

639

跑 pǎo
     run

Radical 足
12 strokes

| 丿 | 口 | 口 | 甲 | 甲 | 足 | 足 | 足 | 趵 | 跑 |
| 跑 | 跑 | | | | | | | | |

foot 足(280) + **parcel** 包(636) =
run 跑

步(378) **pǎobù** *jogging*
跑道(145) **pǎodào** *runway*]

In the crowded airport he doesn't see the **parcel** until his **foot** hits it (and there's the sound of breaking glass) — he decides to **run** away before anyone sees him. / *But Teddy is curious and looks inside, sneezes, and gets covered in fine white powder from the parcel.*

640a

冋   "porthole"

| 丿 | 冂 | 冂 | 冂 | 冋 | 冋 | 冋 | | | |

skylight 冋(389a) + **eight** 八(20) =
porthole 冋

The **octopus** is trying to squeeze through a **skylight**. "This should be easy — I've got through many a **porthole**," he says. / *[No pronunciation needed]*

Again in this character you will sometimes see the legs curl (so that they look like "boy" rather then "eight").

640

商 shāng
     trade

Radical 亠
11 strokes

| 丶 | 一 | 亠 | 立 | 产 | 产 | 商 | 商 | 商 | 商 |
| 商 | | | | | | | | | |

stand 立(177) + **porthole** 冋(640a) =
trade 商

Once again (see Characters 197, 295) the final stroke of "stand" has merged into the character below.

店(186) **shāngdiàn** *shop, store*
商业(395) **shāngyè** *commerce, business*]
商场(530) **shāngchǎng** *shopping mall*]
商人(12) **shāngrén** *businessman*]

Imagine **stand**ing, looking out through a **porthole** as your ship comes into port, and seeing all the possibilities for **trade**. / *But when you get ashore, the giant sitting on the quayside advises, "I'd set up in Shanghai if I were you."*

641a 佰 bǎi "$100 check"

person 亻 (13a) + **hundred** 百 (40) = **$100 check** 佰

This is the form of "100" used on checks, banknotes, etc. to prevent alterations.

Harry buys a pet centipede with a **hundred** legs and has to write out a **$100 check**. (At a dollar a leg, it gets quite expensive, he muses). / *[No pronunciation needed]*

641 宿 sù stay overnight

Radical 宀
11 strokes

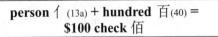

house 宀 (91a) + **$100 check** 佰 (641a) = **stay overnight** 宿

[食宿 (287) **shísù** *board and lodging*]

At the manor **house** they write a **$100 check** to **stay overnight**. / *They've arrived just in time for the evening meal — the* ***dwarf*** *head chef is just dishing out the* ***soup***.

642a 予 yǔ bestow

seal 卩 (560a) + **nail** 丁 (81b) = **bestow** 予

Notice that the first stroke of "nail" has a hook on it (a sign that we're cheating slightly again!)

If the proclamation with the king's **seal** is **nail**ed to your door, this **bestows** special status on your house. / *[No pronunciation needed]*

642 预 yù in advance

Radical 页
10 strokes

bestow 予 (642a) + **page** 页 (477) = **in advance** 预

[预备 (548) **yùbèi** *prepare, get ready*]

 The authors of this book **bestowed** a sample **page** on their publisher **in advance**, to show them the design. / *The* ***dwarf*** *sub-editor said it was* ***useless***, *and threw the manuscript out the window into the pouring rain!*

643 舍 shè
shed

Radical 人
8 strokes

捨

tent 人(19b) + dry 干(124) +
mouth 口(5) = shed 舍

宿舍(641) sùshè hostel, dormitory

The explorer pitches his **tent** on the **dry** ground by the **mouth** of the cave — and only then spots a **shed** nearby. / *A **dwarf sherpa** lives there (who will act as his guide — for a fee of course).*

644 舒 shū
spread out

Radical 人
12 strokes

shed 舍(643) + bestow 予(642a) =
spread out 舒

舒服(563) shūfu comfortable

The duke **bestow**s a **shed** on the cobbler so that he has space to **spread out** his patterns on the floor. / *He's started making **shoes** for the **giant** so he needs lots of space.*

645 兴 xìng (xīng)
excited

Radical 八
6 strokes

興

haul up 丷 (388a) + eight 八(20)
= excited 兴

高兴(481) gāoxìng happy, delighted

The fishermen **haul up** the **octopus** into their boat — they get very **excited** at this rare catch (which will fetch a good price). / *On the shore they sell it to a **dwarf** fishmonger — but the octopus revives and escapes, throwing up **shingle** everywhere as he makes a dash for the sea.*

646a 矛 máo
spear

bestow 予(642a) + slide ╱(34b) = spear 矛

This is easily confused with "bestow" (Character 642a) so it seems best to draw attention to the difference by adding "slide" (even though "slide" is not usually joined to anything).

(Imagine the king playing on the children's slide — whee!) The king decides to **bestow** the royal warrant on the **slide** by scratching his initials on it with his bodyguard's **spear**. / *[No pronunciation needed]*

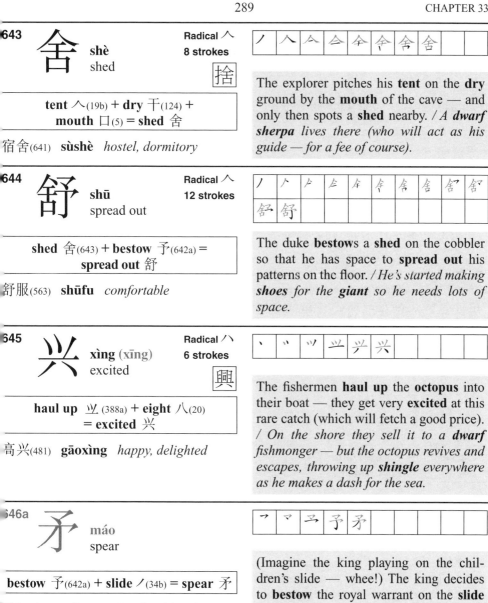

646b 矞 stab

㇇	㇖	亍	予	矛	矛	矞	矞	矞	矞
矞	矞								

spear 矛(646a) + porthole 冏(640a) =
stab 矞

The Viking poked his **spear** through the **porthole** to **stab** the surprised guard. / *[No pronunciation needed]*

---

646 橘 jú tangerine

Radical 木
16 strokes

一	十	才	木	木'	术	杉	杉	杉	杉
橘	橘	橘	橘	橘	橘				

tree 木(10a) + stab 矞(646b) =
tangerine 橘

 A party game: all stand around the **tree**, and the first one to **stab** a **tangerine** is the winner. / *The **fairy** takes the **juice** outside into the pouring rain, to dilute it.*

Time for some more "pouring rain" stories — we have collected together the five remaining characters with pronunciation "ju".

橘子(17) **júzi** *tangerine*

---

647 桔 jú tangerine

Radical 木
10 strokes

一	十	才	木	木	朴	杜	桔	桔	桔

 In the palace grounds there is a **tree**, from which, on a certain **auspicious** day, you are allowed to pick a **tangerine** to eat. / *The **fairy** takes the **juice** outside into the pouring rain, to dilute it.*

tree 木(10a) + auspicious 吉(538a) =
tangerine 桔

This is simply an alternative character (to the previous one) for tangerine.

桔子(17) **júzi** *tangerine*

---

648 举 jǔ to raise

Radical 丶
9 strokes

舉

丶	㇒	㇒'	兴	兴	兴	兴	举	

 The **criminal** is **excited** as he **raises** his head carefully out of the prison escape tunnel he has dug. / *Teddy runs up in the pouring rain, shouting, "I've got you some **juice**!" (and almost gives the game away).*

excited 兴(645) + criminal 卅(130a) =
raise 举

[举行(81) **jǔxíng** *to hold (meeting etc)*]

649

句 **jù**
sentence

Radical 勹
5 strokes

| ノ | 勹 | 勽 | 句 | 句 | | | | |

mouth 口(5) + wrap 勹(23a) =
sentence 句

句子(17) **jùzi** *sentence (of text)*

☂ They are fed up of his grumbling, so **wrap** something round his **mouth** before he can speak another **sentence**. / *But the dwarf is a judo expert and escapes, running out into the pouring rain.*

650

局 **jú**
office

Radical 尸
7 strokes

| ┐ | ⁊ | 尸 | 月 | 局 | 局 | 局 | | |

corpse 尸(268a) + sentence 句(649) =
office 局

Notice that "sentence" here is fused onto "corpse". An alternative breakdown for this character might be "corpse" plus "blade" plus "mouth".

邮局(621) **yóujú** *post office*
局长(172) **júzhǎng** *bureau chief]*

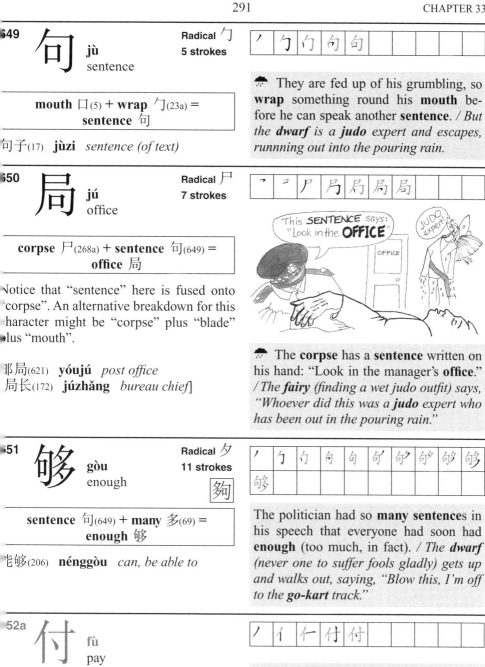

☂ The **corpse** has a **sentence** written on his hand: "Look in the manager's **office**." / *The fairy (finding a wet judo outfit) says, "Whoever did this was a judo expert who has been out in the pouring rain."*

651

够 **gòu**
enough

Radical 夕
11 strokes

夠

| ノ | 勹 | 勽 | 句 | 句 | 句 | 句 | 够 | 够 |
| 够 | | | | | | | | |

sentence 句(649) + many 多(69) =
enough 够

能够(206) **nénggòu** *can, be able to*

The politician had so **many sentence**s in his speech that everyone had soon had **enough** (too much, in fact). / *The dwarf (never one to suffer fools gladly) gets up and walks out, saying, "Blow this, I'm off to the go-kart track."*

652a

付 **fù**
pay

| ノ | 亻 | 仁 | 什 | 付 | | | | |

person 亻(13a) + inch 寸(104a) = pay 付

(At the fairground ride) **Harry** was an **inch** too tall, so had to **pay** the adult fare. / *[No pronunciation needed]*

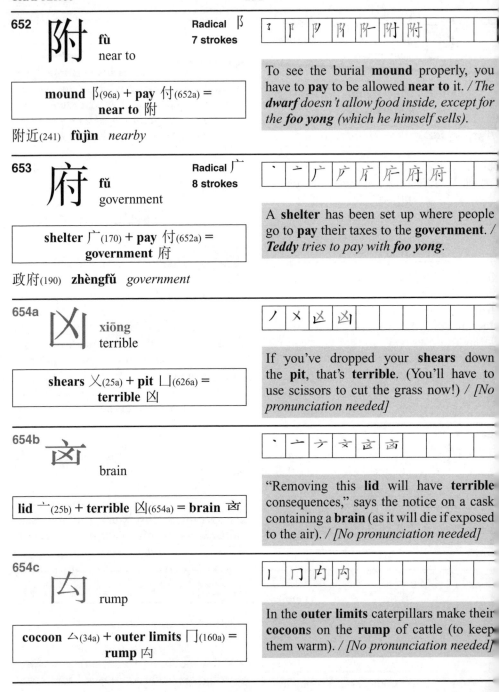

652 附 **fù**
near to

Radical ß
7 strokes

mound ß(96a) + pay 付(652a) =
near to 附

To see the burial **mound** properly, you have to **pay** to be allowed **near to** it. / *The dwarf doesn't allow food inside, except for the foo yong (which he himself sells).*

附近(241) **fùjìn** *nearby*

653 府 **fŭ**
government

Radical 广
8 strokes

shelter 广(170) + pay 付(652a) =
government 府

A **shelter** has been set up where people go to **pay** their taxes to the **government**. / *Teddy tries to pay with foo yong.*

政府(190) **zhèngfŭ** *government*

654a 凶 **xiōng**
terrible

shears ㄨ(25a) + pit 凵(626a) =
terrible 凶

If you've dropped your **shears** down the **pit**, that's **terrible**. (You'll have to use scissors to cut the grass now!) / *[No pronunciation needed]*

654b 卤
brain

lid 亠(25b) + terrible 凶(654a) = brain 卤

"Removing this **lid** will have **terrible** consequences," says the notice on a cask containing a **brain** (as it will die if exposed to the air). / *[No pronunciation needed]*

654c 内
rump

cocoon 厶(34a) + outer limits 冂(160a) =
rump 内

In the **outer limits** caterpillars make their **cocoon**s on the **rump** of cattle (to keep them warm). / *[No pronunciation needed]*

654

离 **lí**
distant from

Radical 亠
10 strokes

| 丶 | 亠 | 亣 | 文 | 立 | 卨 | 离 | 离 | 离 | 离 |

brain 卨 (654b) + **rump** 内 (654c) =
distant from 离

This also means "to depart".

"The **brain** and **rump** of a giraffe are very **distant from** each other." / *To demonstrate, the fairy pokes the giraffe in the rump with her wand. "Now let's see how long he takes to leap up in surprise."*

离开 (85) **líkāi** *to depart*
[离别 (79) **líbié** *bid farewell*]

655a

禺
monkey

| 丿 | 冂 | 曰 | 日 | 甼 | 禺 | 禺 | 禺 | 禺 |

field 田 (156a) + **rump** 内 (654c) =
monkey 禺

Notice how the vertical stroke carries through into "rump" so that the "cocoon" part of this character gets slightly altered.

Out in the **field** the cow plonks her **rump** down — but there's a squeal and she discovers she's sat on a **monkey** (who is now looking rather squashed). / *[No pronunciation needed]*

655

遇 **yù**
encounter

Radical 辶
12 strokes

| 丿 | 冂 | 曰 | 日 | 甼 | 禺 | 禺 | 禺 | 禺 | ㇏禺 |
| 禺 | 遇 | | | | | | | | |

road 辶 (26a) + **monkey** 禺 (655a) =
encounter 遇

遇到 (74) **yùdào** *encounter*

As a rite of passage, each young **monkey** has to walk along the **road** near the jungle, where they **encounter** various tests. / *The first test is to sneak past the dwarf playing his ukulele without him noticing — the trick is to do it when it's pouring with rain.*

656

脱 **tuō**
undress

Radical 月
11 strokes

| 丿 | 刀 | 月 | 月 | 肜 | 肜 | 肜 | 肜 | 肜 | 肜 |
| 脱 | | | | | | | | | |

moon 月 (61) + **convert** 兑 (67b) =
undress 脱

This character also refers to removing shoes, a hat, etc.

Whenever the **moon** comes out it **converts** him into a werewolf. Each time he must quickly **undress** before his clothes get ripped. / *The ghostly giant guards his clothes and gives him a toga to wear for the duration.*

Chapter 34

Another quiz, where we've put together groups of characters which have very similar meanings:

不(9) 没(169) 非(328)　　　　　数(469) 第(322) 号(424)

化(391) 变(581) 成(259) 改(359)　　　使(398) 用(130) 拿(348) 以(120)

见(214) 望(570) 视(435) 观(216) 看(200)　　查(598) 验(602) 检(599) 究(616) 考(604)

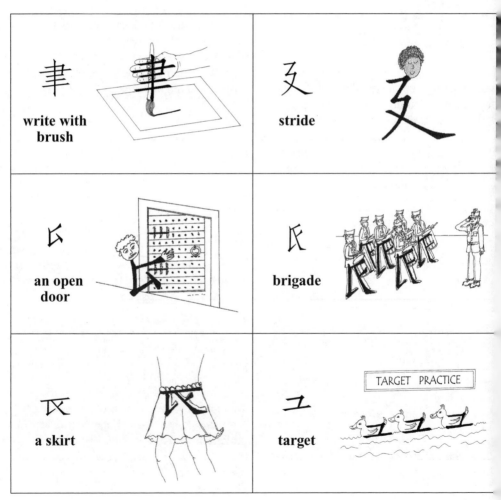

write with brush	stride
an open door	brigade
a skirt	target

657a 聿   "write with brush"

We've treated this as a basic building block, but if you like you can think of it as "dexterity" plus "two" (or even "dexterity" plus "criminal") and make up a story accordingly.

657b 廴   stride

---

657 建   jiàn   build

Radical 廴
8 strokes

stride 廴(657b) + **write with brush**
聿(657a) = **build** 建

Like "road" (26a), "stride" is written last, after the fragment it encloses.

On the building site the foreman **strides** about **writing** on the ground **with a brush**, to mark out where they should **build** the walls. / *Two dwarf building inspectors come round to check there'll be enough room for the generator.*

建设(553) **jiànshè** *build, install*
[建立(177) **jiànlì** *set up, build*]

---

658 健   jiàn   strong

Radical 亻
10 strokes

person 亻 (13a) + **build** 建(657) = **strong** 健

[健儿(21) **jiàn'ér** *good athlete*]

Harry is helping to **build** the floors of the new building, which have to be **strong** enough to take a lot of weight. / *The two dwarf building inspectors will try to find fault with the floor of the generator room.*

659a 廷   tíng   court

stride 廴(657b) + **ninth** 壬(551a) = **court** 廷

This is a feudal court rather than a modern judicial court.

The youngest member of the royal family **strides** arrogantly about the palace with a baseball bat — although he is only **ninth** in line to the throne. Everyone is waiting for him to get his comeuppance when he gets to **court**. / *[No pronunciation needed]*

659  庭 **tíng** courtyard

Radical 广
9 strokes

`丶 一 广 广 庐 庄 庄 庭 庭`

shelter 广(170) + court 廷(659a) = courtyard 庭

家庭(109) **jiātíng** *family*

They need a **shelter** to house the overflowing **court**, so build one over the **courtyard** outside. / *The fairy administers tincture (to ward off colds for those stuck outside in the cold weather).*

660 挺 **tǐng** exceptionally

Radical 扌
9 strokes

`一 扌 扌 扩 扩 拝 挺 挺`

hand 扌(152a) + court 廷(659a) = exceptionally 挺

The head guard holds up his **hand** to stop people entering the **court** — only **exceptionally** does he let someone in. / *Teddy gets in because he is carrying the king's tincture (and is likely to spill it if he has to hold it for long).*

This is often just used to mean "very"; it also means "erect", "straight" or "firm".

[挺立(177) **tǐnglì** *to stand upright; to stand firm*]

661a 肖 **xiào** resemble

`丿 丶 丷 丬 肖 肖 肖`

small 小(50) + moon 月(61) = resemble 肖

The **small moon** (of the planet) **resemble**s a potato. / *[No pronunciation needed]*

661 消 **xiāo** vanish

Radical 氵
10 strokes

`丶 丶 氵 氵 氵 沪 沪 消 消 消`

water 氵(78a) + resemble 肖(661a) = vanish 消

The enchanted **water resemble**s lemonade and is used to make things **vanish**. / *The **two giants** take a **shower** in it (but then keep bumping into each other as they are both now invisible).*

[取消(88) **qǔxiāo** *to cancel*]
[消化(391) **xiāohuà** *to digest*]

Test yourself: 九(38) 水(523) 火(181) 子(17) 民(455) 页(477) 痛(565)

难(503) 助(445) 办(123) 姓(135) 支(462) 容(486) 扬(532)

662 息 xī stop

Radical 心
10 strokes

self 自(94) + heart 心(161) = stop 息

消息(661) **xiāoxī** *news*

The surgeon is trying to do a **heart** operation on him**self**. "**Stop!**" cry the other doctors. / *The giant brings a shield to use as a stretcher (to take him to the proper operating theater).*

663a 匕 "an open door"

663b 匂 "barred"

an open door 匕(663a) + knife 刀(72) = barred 匂

Returning to your apartment you find **an open door** and see an intruder inside with a **knife**. You quickly lock the door from the outside so that he is **barred** from escaping. / *[No pronunciation needed]*

---

663 留 liú remain

Radical 田
10 strokes

barred 匂(663b) + field 田(156a) = remain 留

This also means to "detain" or "keep".

留念(167) **liú niàn** *keep as a souvenir*
留学生(82, 133) **liúxuéshēng** *international students (in a university)*

(Cows were escaping from the field) The farmer **barred** the gate to the **field** so that the cows who had not yet escaped would have to **remain** in the field. / *The two fairies set out to tempt the escaped cows back with lotus leaves.*

664a 氏 "brigade"

Compare this with "dress" 衣 (436a).

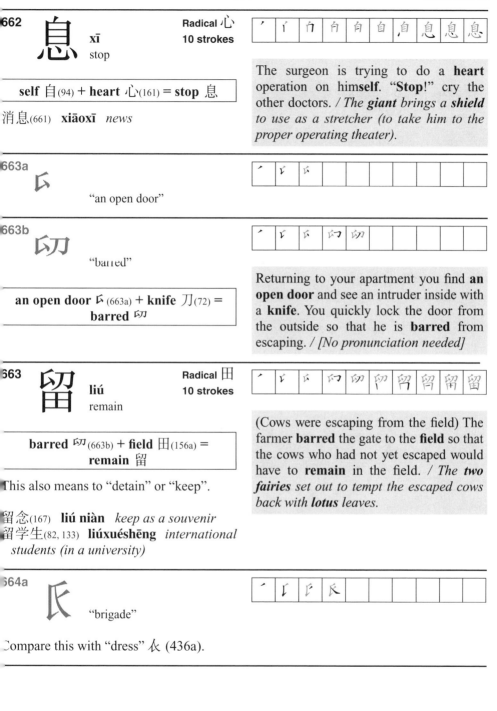

664b

 辰 tributary

drag 厂(150a) + **brigade** 辰(664a) = **tributary** 辰

The commanding officer **drag**s his **brigade** miles to the river, but when they get there it's just a **tributary** (he's got the navigation wrong again). / *[No pronunciation needed]*

664

派 **pài** group

Radical 氵
9 strokes

water 氵 (78a) + **tributary** 辰(664b) = **group** 派

This is generally a group of people in the sense of a faction or school of thought.

The **water** in the **tributary** is particularly good and only a privileged **group** is allowed to fish there. / *The **dwarf** objects to this because he thinks there's plenty of **pike** for everyone.*

[派别(79) **pàibié** *group, school, faction*]
[派系(607) **pàixì** *faction (in a political party)*]
[派头(246) **pàitóu** *style (as in "doing something in style")*]

Test yourself:　方(291)　复(550)　科(605)　设(553)　高(481)　钱(610)　笔(454)

志(487)　城(260)　页(477)　因(520)　租(446)　定(406)　法(87)

665a

 "a skirt"

This is the bottom part of "dress" (436a), suspended from a horizontal line (which you can think of as a belt).

665b

 gown

grass 艹(218a) + **a skirt** 衣(665a) = **gown** 裳

Imagine sewing sheaves of **grass** together to make the **skirt** for a **gown**. / *[No pronunciation needed]*

Although this looks like "grass" plus "skirt", if you look closely you can see that the grass is actually joined on, as it is in "bacon rashers" (625a).

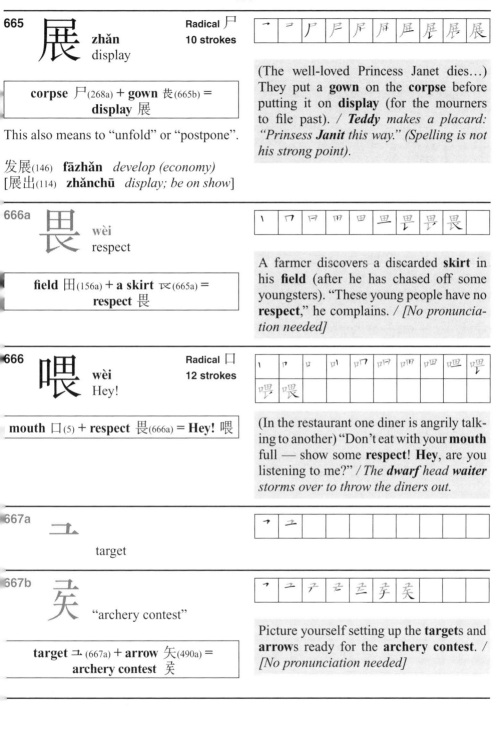

665 展 zhǎn display

Radical 尸
10 strokes

corpse 尸(268a) + gown 㠱(665b) =
display 展

This also means to "unfold" or "postpone".

发展(146) **fāzhǎn** *develop (economy)*
[展出(114) **zhǎnchū** *display; be on show*]

(The well-loved Princess Janet dies…) They put a **gown** on the **corpse** before putting it on **display** (for the mourners to file past). / *Teddy makes a placard: "Prinsess **Janit** this way." (Spelling is not his strong point).*

666a 畏 wèi respect

field 田(156a) + a skirt 𧘇(665a) =
respect 畏

A farmer discovers a discarded **skirt** in his **field** (after he has chased off some youngsters). "These young people have no **respect**," he complains. / *[No pronunciation needed]*

666 喂 wèi Hey!

Radical 口
12 strokes

mouth 口(5) + respect 畏(666a) = **Hey!** 喂

(In the restaurant one diner is angrily talking to another) "Don't eat with your **mouth** full — show some **respect**! **Hey**, are you listening to me?" / *The dwarf head waiter storms over to throw the diners out.*

667a 㠯 target

667b 㚑 "archery contest"

target 㠯 (667a) + arrow 矢(490a) =
archery contest 㚑

Picture yourself setting up the **target**s and **arrow**s ready for the **archery contest**. / *[No pronunciation needed]*

667c

仴

"man with stick"

person 亻 (13a) + **stick** │ (19a) =
man with stick 仴

This hardly needs a story … / *[No pronunciation needed]*

667

候　hòu
wait for

Radical 亻
10 strokes

man with stick 仴 (667c) + **archery
contest** 矦 (667b) = **wait for** 候

This means "to await" but also appears as
the second half of various compounds.

时候(105) **shíhòu** *(the) time*
有时候(63, 105) **yǒu shíhòu** *sometimes*
[气候(411) **qìhòu** *climate*]

Who's the **man with a stick** at the **archery
contest**? He's **waiting for** a new string for
his bow. / *His **dwarf** manservant must go
back to the **hotel** to fetch one.*

668

齐　qí
tidy

Radical 文
6 strokes

齊

culture 文 (25) + **grain stalks** 丿(579a) =
tidy 齐

整齐(495) **zhěngqí** *in good order*
[一齐(1) **yìqí** *together*]

In one particular **culture** the **grain stalks**
must be **tidy** after the harvest. / *The **fairy**
then flies off to get the tribal **chief** to come
and make his inspection.*

669

挤　jǐ
squeeze

Radical 扌
9 strokes

擠

hand 扌 (152a) + **tidy** 齐 (668) =
squeeze 挤

[挤奶(533) **jǐ'nǎi** *to milk (a cow)*]

The mother tells her teenage daughter,
"Give me a **hand** to **tidy** up all these
clothes — see if you can **squeeze** them all
into those drawers." / *Meanwhile **Teddy**
has found a **G-string** (and is twanging it
until it is snatched away from him).*

670 济 jì
bring relief

Radical 氵
9 strokes

濟

| ` | 冫 | 氵 | 汀 | 汇 | 汶 | 泫 | 浐 | 济 | |

water 氵 (78a) + **tidy** 齐 (668) =
bring relief 济

(After the flood) The **water** had receded, but before they could **tidy** up they needed to **bring relief** supplies to the stranded people. / *The **dwarf** directed operations from his amphibian **jeep**.*

经济 (244)   **jīngjì**   *(country's) economy*

671a 吅
"kiss"

| ` | 冖 | 叮 | 吅 | | | | |

mouth 口 (5) + **mouth** 口 (5) = **kiss** 吅

Use your imagination! / *[No pronunciation needed]*

You can tell from the stroke order that these are not "really" two mouths glued together (see also 629a), but we liked the idea of being able to use "kiss" in a few stories!

671b 罒
"windowpane"

| ` | 冖 | 叮 | 叩 | 罒 | 罒 | | |

kiss 吅 (671a) + **horns** `/ (65a) =
windowpane 罒

The two deer met for a **kiss** but they were too near the hut and their **horns** smashed the **windowpane**. / *[No pronunciation needed]*

Note the stroke order, here and in the following character.

---

671 黑 hēi
black

Radical 黑
12 strokes

| ` | 冖 | 叮 | 罒 | 罒 | 罒 | 甲 | 里 | 黒 | 黑 |
| 黑 | 黑 | | | | | | | | |

windowpane 罒 (671b) + **earth** 土 (54a) +
fire 灬 (185a) = **black** 黑

You throw **earth** at the upstairs **window-pane** to alert the occupants that their house is on **fire** — they run out unharmed but they're **black** with soot. / *The **giant** lets them stay in his **hayloft** while their house is rebuilt.*

The top part of this is often handwritten 里 ("in", Character 157), where the "horns" are replaced by a single horizontal stroke.

黑板 (333)   **hēibǎn**   *blackboard*]
黑市 (427)   **hēishì**   *black market*]
黑白 (22)   **hēibái**   *black and white; right and wrong*]

672a

曾 céng; zēng
used to be

丶	ﾂ	丷	亠	丗	丗	丗	曽	曽	曾
曽	曾								

horns ⌄ (65a) + windowpane 罒 (671b) + sun 日 (6) = used to be 曾

The old stag looks at his **horns** in the **windowpane** as the **sun** goes down. They **used to be** magnificent, he sighs. / *[No pronunciation needed]*

672

增 zēng
to increase

Radical 土
15 strokes

一	十	土	圹	圹	圹	圹	圹	圹	增
增	增	增	增	增					

earth 土 (54a) + used to be 曾 (672a) = increase 增

增加 (325) **zēngjiā** *to increase*
[增长 (172) **zēngzhǎng** *to increase, grow*]

(A farmer looks at a handful of soil) The **earth used to be** arid and barren, but he's enriched it and **increase**d the crop yield tremendously. / *[DIY pronunciation]*

673a

免 miǎn
avoid

丿	夕	亇	台	召	夕	免			

bow ⌐ (51a) + kiss 口 (671a) + boy 儿 (21) = avoid 免

Although the middle of this character looks like "kiss", you will see from the stroke order diagrams that you draw a box (like "mouth") and then the first stroke of "boy" divides this in two on its way down.

The aunt **bow**s down to **kiss** the **boy** — but he ducks away to **avoid** her (as he hates sloppy kisses from relatives). / *[No pronunciation needed]*

673

晚 wǎn
evening

Radical 日
11 strokes

丨	冂	日	日	日'	日⁷	日⁷	晘	晗	晚
晚									

sun 日 (6) + avoid 免 (673a) = evening 晚

This can either mean "to be late for something", or late in the day, i.e. "evening".

晚饭 (332) **wǎnfàn** *supper*
晚上 (42) **wǎnshang** *evening*
晚会 (59) **wǎnhuì** *soiree, evening party*

The albino animal has to **avoid** the **sun**, so only comes out in the **evening**. / *[DIY pronunciation]*

674a 象 xiàng
elephant

---

bow 宀 (51a) + **kiss** 口 (671a) +
pig 豕 (109a) = **elephant** 象

The top part is similar to "avoid" (673a), but the bottom is now "pig" (but note that the pig has lost its first horizontal stroke).

The character also means "shape" and

The princess **bows** down to **kiss** the **pig** — who promptly turns into a handsome … **elephant**! / *[No pronunciation needed]*

is often used as a simplified form of the following character (674) if there is no room for confusion.

---

674 像 xiàng
likeness

Radical 亻
13 strokes

---

person 亻 (13a) + **elephant** 象 (674a) =
likeness 像

好像 (18) **hǎoxiàng** *be like, similar to*

Harry pointed at his **elephant** and then at its passport photo, and said, "But — it's a good **likeness**!" / *The two dwarf immigration officers at **Shanghai** are dubious — each takes one end of the elephant but neither end looks like the passport photo …*

675a 夬 wonderful

---

bow 宀 (51a) + **center** 央 (401a) =
wonderful 夬

Note the difference between this character and "avoid" (673a). By now you are probably pretty good at spotting details like this.

(At the bowing master class) The bowing expert stood in the **center** of the arena and demonstrated the perfect **bow**. "**Wonderful**," they all cried. / *[No pronunciation needed]*

---

675 换 huàn
exchange

Radical 扌
10 strokes
换

---

hand 扌 (152a) + **wonderful** 夬 (675a) =
exchange 换

(At the sculpture class) "That **hand** is **wonderful** — would you give it to the art college, in **exchange** for extra lessons? / *The ghostly dwarf will guard it as part of our **hand** collection."*

Chapter 35

鸟 bird

虫 insect

舟 boat

匚 a vise

氏 surname

夫 held in the hands

丶 splinter

676a 冈 gāng
ridge

冈

| 丨 | 冂 | 冈 | 冈 | | | | | |

outer limits 冂(160a) + shears ㄨ(25a) =
ridge 冈

This character means the ridge of a hill.
Don't confuse it with 风 ("wind",
Character 468).

In the **outer limits** they use **shears** to trim the hedges on the **ridge** of the hill, so that they can peer over into the neighboring kingdom. / *[No pronunciation needed]*

676 刚 gāng
barely

Radical 刂
6 strokes

剛

| 丨 | 冂 | 冈 | 冈 | 冈丨 | 刚 | | | |

ridge 冈(676a) + knife 刂(74a) =
barely 刚

刚才(518) **gāngcái** *a short while ago*
[刚刚 **gānggāng** *only just, barely*]

Imagine crawling up to the **ridge** (at dusk, to investigate a suspicious noise), **knife** at the ready, but there's **barely** enough light to see what's going on. / *When you peer over you see the giant and his gang making camp.*

677 钢 gāng
steel

Radical 钅
9 strokes

鋼

| 丿 | 𠂉 | 𠂉 | 𠂉 | 钅 | 钅 | 钢 | 钢 | 钢 |

gold 钅(278a) + ridge 冈(676a) = steel 钢

钢笔(454) **gāngbǐ** *fountain pen*

You take **gold** up to the **ridge** to trade it for **steel**. / *The giant and his gang are well known for making the best steel around.*

Test yourself: 宜(449) 话(458) 数(469) 物(527) 题(478) 知(490) 周(540)
明(77) 技(463) 毛(453) 母(127) 集(505) 床(171) 树(155)

678a 鸟 niǎo
bird

鳥

| 丿 | 𠃌 | 𠃌 | 鸟 | 鸟 | | | | |

There are two characters for "bird": this one and the one we have called "pigeon" (501a). Traditionally these are said to apply to long-tailed birds and short-tailed birds respectively.

678 鸡 **jī**
chicken

Radical 又
7 strokes

鷄

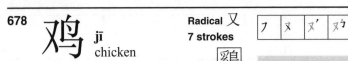

right hand 又(52) + **bird** 鸟(678a) =
chicken 鸡

[一只鸡(1, 254) **yì zhī jī** *a bird*]

The farmer's daughter solemnly **shakes hands** with each **bird** before it leaves — no **chicken** is allowed to go for slaughter until she has done this. / *The* ***giant*** *loads them onto his* ***jeep*** *to drive them away.*

679a 虫 **chóng**
insect

蟲

This character also applies to other very small animals, including worms.

---

679 虽 **suī**
although

Radical 口
9 strokes

雖

mouth 口(5) + **insect** 虫(679a) =
although 虽

虽然(266) **suīrán** *although*

The exhausted **insect** (imagine a cute furry caterpillar) crawls into the **mouth** of the cave, **although** he has heard that it is haunted. / *The* ***ghostly giant***, *who guards the cave, rushes out brandishing his* ***saber*** *(until he realises that the poor, frightened caterpillar is not a threat).*

680a 舟 **zhōu**
boat

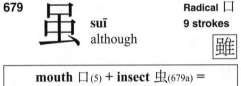

When it is used as a part of other characters, "boat" has sometimes evolved into "moon" (月, Character 61). Look at "canoe" (90b) and see if you get an "aha" feeling.

---

680 般 **bān**
a sort

Radical 舟
10 strokes

boat 舟(680a) + **strike** 殳(169a) = **sort** 般

This means a sort of, or type of, something.

一般(1) **yìbān** *average, commonplace*

At the launching ceremony they **strike** the **boat** with a bottle, but what **sort** of bottle depends on what **sort** of boat it is. / *The* ***giant*** *strikes up the* ***band*** *as the boat is launched.*

681  **bān**
move

Radical 扌
13 strokes

一	扌	扌	扩	扜	扚	捛	捛	捛
捛	搬	搬						

---

hand 扌 (152a) + **sort** 般(680) = **move** 搬

This generally means to move house.

[搬家(109) **bānjiā** *to move house*]

"We need a **hand**." "What **sort** of hand?" "Any sort we can get, to help us **move** house." / *The **giant** brings his **band** of helpers (and they finish the move in no time).*

682a "a vise"

´	𠃌							

Compare this with "open door" (663a).

682b 卬 aspire

´	𠃌	𠂎	卬					

a vise 𠃌 (682a) + **seal** 卩(560a) = **aspire** 卬

He uses the **vise** in his shed to hold the **seal** while he fashions an intricate design on it, worthy of the chief scribe which he **aspire**s one day to be. / *[No pronunciation needed]*

---

682 迎 **yíng**
greet

Radical 辶
7 strokes

´	𠃌	𠂎	卬	卬	讪	迎		

road 辶(26a) + **aspire** 卬(682b) = **greet** 迎

欢迎(363) **huānyíng** *welcome*
[迎接(203) **yíngjiē** *to meet, greet*]

The **road aspire**d to be declared a Boulevard, so **greet**ed each car effusively to ingratiate itself to everyone. / *[DIY pronunciation]*

683a 氏 **shì**
surname

一	𠂉	斤	氏					

You can probably see "vise" and "pile of earth" here; feel free to make up a story for this if you like.

683

 zhǐ
paper

Radical 纟
7 strokes

thread 纟 (233a) + **surname** 氏 (683a) =
paper 纸

[报纸(562) **bàozhǐ** *newspaper*]

It is customary when finishing a piece of embroidery to use **thread** to sign your **surname** at the bottom — but it is best to work out the design on **paper** first. / *Teddy jumps onto the embroidery frame (using it as a trampoline), and cries out,* **"Geronimo!"**

684a

 "settle down"

surname 氏 (683a) + **a drop** 丶 (22a) =
settle down 氏

In some typefaces you will see the older form of this character where the dot is replaced by a (very) short horizontal line.

Her fiancé has been a playboy, so she will only marry him if he will sign his **surname** in **a drop** of his own blood, to swear that he is now ready to **settle down**. / *[No pronunciation needed]*

684

 dī
low

Radical 亻
7 strokes

person 亻 (13a) + **settle down** 氏 (684a) =
low 低

[低调(541) **dīdiào** *low-key*]

Harry plans to **settle down** somewhere quiet where he can keep a **low** profile. / *He finds the perfect place in the corner of the* **giant's** *estate and the giant kindly gives him the* **deeds** *so that he will never have to leave.*

685

 yǒng
forever

Radical 丶
5 strokes

a drop 丶 (22a) + **water** 水 (523) =
forever 永

永远(303) **yǒngyuǎn** *forever*

"Put **a drop** of this elixir in your drinking **water** and you will live **forever**." / *Teddy asks, "Will it keep me looking* **young?"** *and takes a swig.*

686 泳 yǒng
swim

Radical 氵
8 strokes

丶 丶 氵 汀 汀 汈 泳 泳

water 氵(78a) + forever 永(685) = swim 泳

She wanted to stay in the **water forever**, now that she had learnt to **swim**. / *Teddy said, "You're never too young to learn!" as he jumped in, feet first.*

Test yourself: 七(37) 见(214) 世(578) 累(608) 邮(621) 海(129) 民(455)
真(452) 楼(470) 体(175) 刻(500) 问(289) 提(475) 肉(221)

687a 㫃
banner

丶 二 亍 方 方 㫃

direction 方(291) + clouds 𠂉(124b) = banner 㫃

He looks to see what **direction** the **clouds** are coming from, so that he can work out where to hang the **banner** (for the fete, so that it won't be torn down by the wind). / *[No pronunciation needed]*

This combination occurs together in several characters (such as the following two; and also Character 755). However, the combination is not a radical, and dictionaries simply classify these characters under "direction" (Character 291).

---

687 族 zú
clan

Radical 方
11 strokes

丶 二 亍 方 方 㫃 㫃 旅 族
族

banner 㫃(687a) + arrow 矢(490a) = clan 族

民族(455) **mínzú** *nationality, ethnic group*

The African tribe have a **banner** with an **arrow** painted on it, as the symbol of their **clan** (to match the arrows they have painted on their faces). / *They asks the fairy to fly aloft with it to scare off the neighboring Zulus.*

688a 斿
roam

丶 二 亍 方 方 㫃 㫃 斿

banner 㫃(687a) + child 子(17) = roam 斿

A **banner** went up (announcing that the circus was in town), and the young **child** ran to see these fascinating people who **roam**ed from place to place. / *[No pronunciation needed].*

688 游 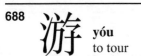 yóu — to tour

Radical 氵
12 strokes

water 氵 (78a) + roam 斿 (688a) = tour 游

This also means "to swim".

游泳(686) **yóuyǒng** *swim*

The sailing enthusiast said, "We love **roam**ing about on the **water**, and it's an easy way for us to **tour** the world — and it has the added benefit that we can swim whenever we want to. / *We even get the* **fairy** *to come along to give us* **yoga** *lessons on board."*

689 冬 dōng — winter

Radical 夂
5 strokes

pursue 夂 (506a) + ice crystals 冫(246a) = winter 冬

冬天(76) **dōngtiān** *winter*

A keen photographer likes to **pursue** unusual **ice crystals** — although he can only indulge this hobby in **winter**. / *The* **giant** *brings his* **donkey** *along to carry things (in winter the donkey is free from his summer job of giving rides on the beach).*

690 疼 téng — ache

Radical 疒
10 strokes

illness 疒 (510b) + winter 冬 (689) = ache 疼

[头疼(246) **tóuténg** *headache*]

The **illness** doing the rounds that **winter** caused various parts of the body to **ache**. / *The* **fairy** *could diagnose it by looking at the color of people's* **tongues**.

691 图 tú — diagram

Radical 囗
8 strokes

圖

enclosed 囗 (24a) + winter 冬 (689) = diagram 图

[地图(54) **dìtú** *map*]

The planned **winter** garden is **enclosed** by a wall, and attached to the wall is a **diagram** showing the planned layout. / *The* **fairy** *flies around putting* **toothpaste** *on the trees so that people can see what it will look like in the snow.*

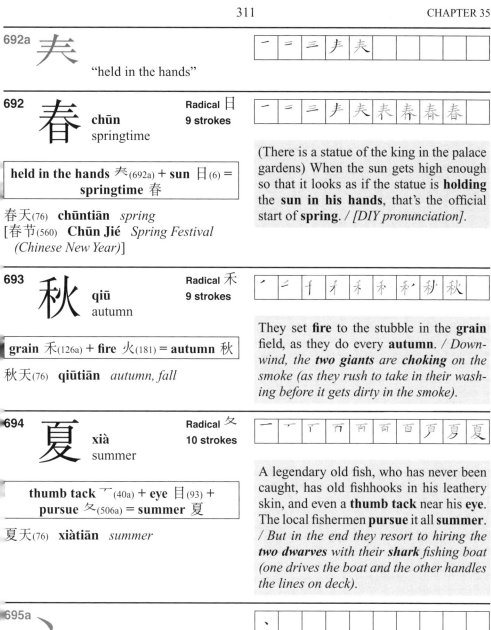

692a 夫
"held in the hands"

692 春 **chūn** springtime
Radical 日
9 strokes

held in the hands 夫(692a) + sun 日(6) = springtime 春

春天(76) **chūntiān** *spring*
[春节(560) **Chūn Jié** *Spring Festival (Chinese New Year)*]

(There is a statue of the king in the palace gardens) When the sun gets high enough so that it looks as if the statue is **holding the sun in his hands**, that's the official start of **spring**. / *[DIY pronunciation].*

693 秋 **qiū** autumn
Radical 禾
9 strokes

grain 禾(126a) + fire 火(181) = autumn 秋

秋天(76) **qiūtiān** *autumn, fall*

They set **fire** to the stubble in the **grain** field, as they do every **autumn**. / *Downwind, the two giants are choking on the smoke (as they rush to take in their washing before it gets dirty in the smoke).*

694 夏 **xià** summer
Radical 夂
10 strokes

thumb tack ⼀(40a) + eye 目(93) + pursue 夂(506a) = summer 夏

夏天(76) **xiàtiān** *summer*

A legendary old fish, who has never been caught, has old fishhooks in his leathery skin, and even a **thumb tack** near his **eye**. The local fishermen **pursue** it all **summer**. / *But in the end they resort to hiring the two dwarves with their shark fishing boat (one drives the boat and the other handles the lines on deck).*

695a
"splinter"

This is a short stroke which crosses another stroke, as in the following character.

695b 丸 wán — pellet

nine 九(38) + **splinter** 丶(695a) = **pellet** 丸

A youngster is sitting idly in the sun carving **splinter**s off an old **baseball**, until what is left is just a **pellet**. / *[No pronunciation needed]*

695c 执 zhí — hold on to

執

hand 扌(152a) + **pellet** 丸(695b) = **hold on to** 执

The dead man had a **pellet** in his **hand** — he was **hold**ing **on to** it as if it was important. (Perhaps it's a clue to a homicide!) / *[No pronunciation needed]*

This also means "to manage", in the sense of managing a business.

695 热 rè — hot

Radical ,,,,
10 strokes

熱

hold on to 执(695c) + **fire** ,,,,(185a) = **hot** 热

You **hold on to** the metal poker while stoking the **fire**, but it becomes so **hot** that you drop it. / *The dwarf growls, "Rrr... rug! You've burnt a hole in my rr..rug!"*

You will see from the following list of compounds that this can literally mean "hot" (high temperature) or, more metaphorically, "warm" to give meanings such as "ardent".

热情(339) **rèqíng** *enthusiasm*
[热点(185) **rèdiǎn** *hot-spot*]
[热爱(365) **rè'ài** *to love deeply*]
[热带(429) **rèdài** *the Tropics*]
[热心(161) **rèxīn** *enthusiastic; warm-hearted*]

696a 享 xiǎng — enjoy

tall 亠(239a) + **child** 子(17) = **enjoy** 享

You would think that the **tall child** would **enjoy** basketball (but no — it's no challenge and he gets bored). / *[No pronunciation needed]*

696b 孰
cooked

`	亠	亠	古	古	言	亨	享	郭	孰
孰									

enjoy 享(696a) + pellet 丸(695b) = cooked 孰

Your cat **enjoy**s **pellet**s because they are **cooked** — she much prefers them to raw meat like mice. / *[No pronunciation needed]*

696 熟
shú
familiar

Radical 灬
15 strokes

`	亠	亠	古	古	言	亨	享	郭	孰
孰	孰	孰	熟	熟					

cooked 孰(696b) + fire 灬(185a) = familiar 熟

[成熟(259) **chéngshú** *mature, ripe*]
[面熟(313) **miànshú** *to look familiar*]

The boy scouts **cooked** food on the **fire** — but overdid it. "It looks **familiar**," said the scoutmaster, bravely tucking into the charred remains. / *The **fairy** tried it and pulled a face. "It tastes like **shoe** leather," she said.*

Test yourself: 页(477)   事(312)   神(622)   往(300)   半(131)   西(100)   心(161)

适(459)   安(91)   对(154)   加(325)   脏(513)   员(479)   处(506)

东(319)   布(558)   画(626)   行(81)   始(485)   声(488)   贵(492)

重(407)   愿(537)   层(471)   奶(533)   等(464)   易(528)   念(167)

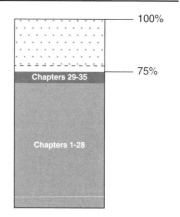

Chapter 36

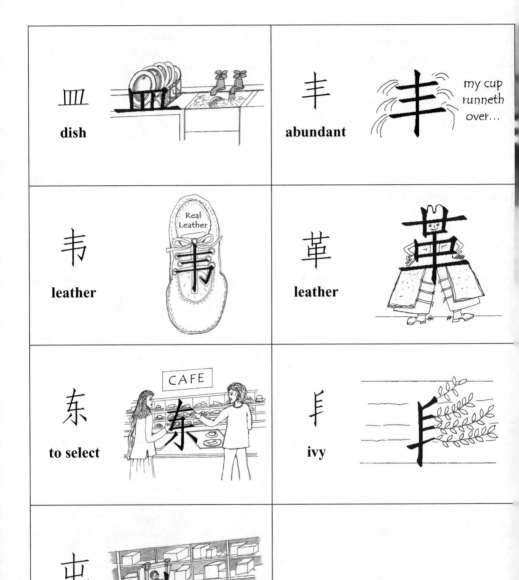

皿

dish

丰

abundant

my cup
runneth
over...

韦

leather

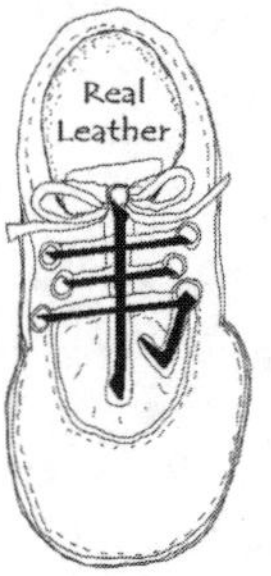
Real
Leather

革

leather

东

to select

CAFE

⺺

ivy

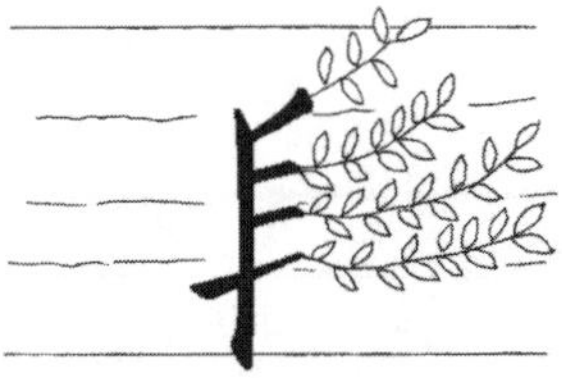

屯

to store

697a 川 "two sticks"

stick | (19a) + stick | (19a) = two sticks 川

Another fragment which hardly needs a story! / *[No pronunciation needed]*

697b 収 firm

two sticks 川 (697a) + right hand 又 (52) = firm 収

This also means "firm" in the sense of "strict" (but not in the sense of a business corporation).

At the start of the hockey match the two center-forwards hold their **two sticks** and **shake hands** — the umpire will insist on a **firm** handshake. / *[No pronunciation needed]*

697 坚 jiān resolute

Radical 土
7 strokes

堅

firm 収 (697b) + earth 土 (54a) = resolute 坚

坚持 (465) **jiānchí** *uphold, persist in*
坚决 (404) **jiānjué** *resolute, determined*]

(Awards are being given for bravery after a landslide) "You both stood **firm**, holding back the **earth** and **resolute**ly protecting the village." / *The two giants were proud that the general himself had come (to present them with medals for saving the village).*

698 紧 jǐn tight

Radical 糸
10 strokes

緊

firm 収 (697b) + thread 糸 (607b) = tight 紧

紧张 (173) **jǐnzhāng** *nervous, tense*
要紧 (101) **yàojǐn** *important, urgent*]
不要紧 (9, 101) **bú yàojǐn** *Do not ...*]

He takes a **firm** hold on the **thread** and pulls it **tight**. / *Teddy then steps gingerly onto it and edges along (thinking that perhaps he's not cut out for tightrope walking after all!)*

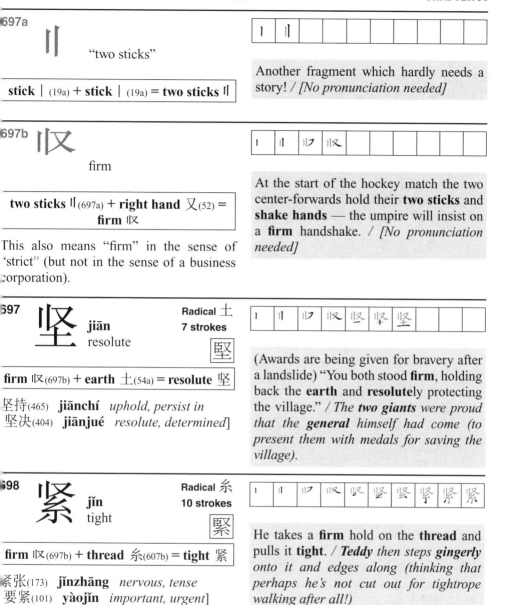

699a

仳 "prostrate"

two sticks ‖ (697a) + **(half) bamboo** ⺮ (321a) = **prostrate** 仳

(Visiting the emperor, everyone is waiting in the antechamber) When the emperor approaches, a court official uses **two sticks** to beat loudly on a drum, "Bam! Bam!" — and everyone falls **prostrate**. (Notice that we've cheated here and used "bam" to stand for half of "bamboo"!) / *[No pronunciation needed]*

699

览 **lǎn** to view

Radical 见
9 strokes

覽

prostrate 仳 (699a) + **see** 见 (214) = **view** 览

展览 (665) **zhǎnlǎn** *exhibit, exhibition*
[游览 (688) **yóulǎn** *tour, sightsee*]

You lie **prostrate** to see if you can **see** any mouse holes in the skirting board — you do this every time you **view** a room you might rent. / *Teddy says, "Why not just ask the landlord?"*

700a

皿 dish

700b

监 **jiān** supervise

監

prostrate 仳 (699a) + **dish** 皿 (700a) = **supervise** 监

The head chef in the palace kitchen is the only one who can **prostrate** himself while holding a **dish** and not spill the contents; which is why he gets to **supervise** the other chefs (rather than because of his culinary skills). / *[No pronunciation needed]*

700

蓝 **lán** blue

Radical ⺾
13 strokes

藍

grass ⺾ (218a) + **supervise** 监 (700b) = **blue** 蓝

[蓝图 (691) **lántú** *blueprint*]

The **grass** he was supposed to **supervise** overnight had turned **blue**. / *This had been caused by the fairy's magic lantern (and neither of them had noticed).*

701 篮 **lán**
basket

Radical 竹
16 strokes

籃

| ノ | ⺊ | ⺭ | ⺮ | ⺮ | 笃 | 竹 | 竹 | 筲 | 筲 |
| 筲 | 筲 | 笆 | 篮 | 篮 | 篮 | | | | |

bamboo 竹 (321a) + supervise 监 (700b) =
basket 篮

篮球 (525)   **lánqiú**   *basketball*

The **bamboo** he has to **supervise** tonight
is going to be made into a **basket**. / *This
is for the* ***fairy*** *to keep her magic* ***lantern***
*in (so that it won't turn the grass blue any
more!)*

702a 畐
plenty

| 一 | ⼀ | 冖 | 曰 | 畐 | 畐 | 畐 | 畐 | | |

piled up 口 (150b) + field 田 (156a) =
plenty 畐

Picture potatoes **piled up** in the corner of
every **field** — there's **plenty** for everyone.
/ *[No pronunciation needed]*

---

702 福 **fú**
blessing

Radical 衤
13 strokes

| ⺀ | ㇇ | 衤 | ⻂ | ⻂ | 衤 | 衤 | 福 | 福 | 福 |
| 福 | 福 | 福 | | | | | | | |

sign 衤 (433a) + plenty 畐 (702a) =
blessing 福

Along with characters for "peace" and
"longevity", this is a very popular Chinese
character, seen on many necklaces and
earrings in the West. It has the general sense
of "good fortune".

幸福 (308)   **xìngfú**   *happy, fortunate*

A farmer points out to his son a **sign** of
plenty in the sky, "It is a **blessing** on us. /
The ***fairy*** *is promising that we will always
have* ***food*** *to eat."*

---

703 富 **fù**
wealthy

Radical 宀
12 strokes

| ⺀ | 宀 | 宀 | 宀 | 宁 | 宫 | 宫 | 宫 | 宫 | 富 |
| 富 | 富 | | | | | | | | |

house 宀 (91a) + plenty 畐 (702a) =
wealthy 富

"In that **house** they always have **plenty**,
they're really **wealthy**. / *They even have a*
dwarf *who brings* ***food*** *to them whenever
they want it."*

Test yourself: 马 (44)   青 (335)   斤 (240)   的 (23)   爱 (365)   冷 (593)   系 (607)

今 (166)   圆 (480)   汉 (78)   胜 (134)   书 (176)   您 (493)   特 (466)

704 丰 **fēng** abundant

Radical |
4 strokes

豐

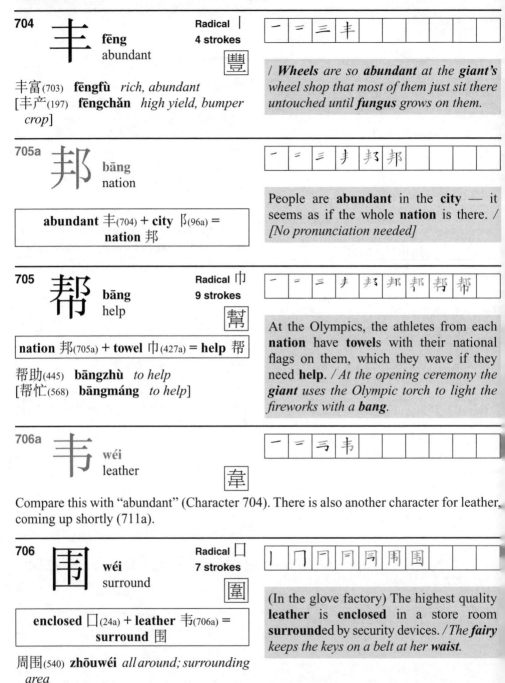

丰富(703) **fēngfù** *rich, abundant*
[丰产(197) **fēngchǎn** *high yield, bumper crop*]

/ *Wheels* are so **abundant** at the **giant's** *wheel shop that most of them just sit there untouched until **fungus** grows on them.*

705a 邦 **bāng** nation

abundant 丰(704) + **city** 阝(96a) = **nation** 邦

People are **abundant** in the **city** — it seems as if the whole **nation** is there. / *[No pronunciation needed]*

705 帮 **bāng** help

Radical 巾
9 strokes

幫

nation 邦(705a) + **towel** 巾(427a) = **help** 帮

帮助(445) **bāngzhù** *to help*
[帮忙(568) **bāngmáng** *to help*]

At the Olympics, the athletes from each **nation** have **towels** with their national flags on them, which they wave if they need **help**. / *At the opening ceremony the **giant** uses the Olympic torch to light the fireworks with a **bang**.*

706a 韦 **wéi** leather

韋

Compare this with "abundant" (Character 704). There is also another character for leather, coming up shortly (711a).

706 围 **wéi** surround

Radical □
7 strokes

圍

enclosed □(24a) + **leather** 韦(706a) = **surround** 围

周围(540) **zhōuwéi** *all around; surrounding area*

(In the glove factory) The highest quality **leather** is **enclosed** in a store room **surround**ed by security devices. / *The **fairy** keeps the keys on a belt at her **waist**.*

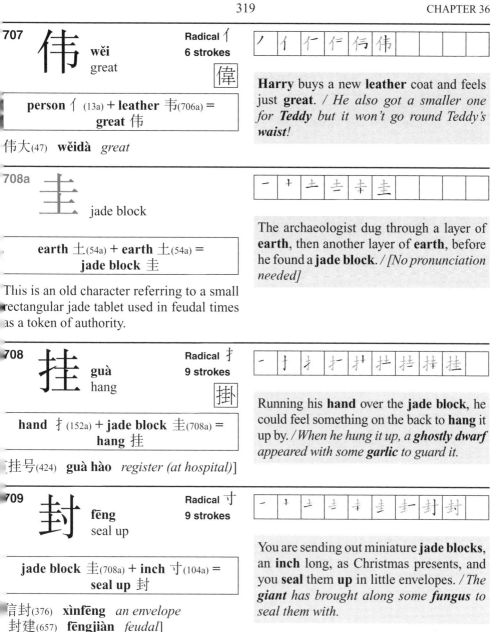

707 伟 **wěi** great

Radical 亻
6 strokes

偉

person 亻 (13a) + leather 韦(706a) = great 伟

伟大(47) **wěidà** *great*

Harry buys a new **leather** coat and feels just **great**. / *He also got a smaller one for Teddy but it won't go round Teddy's waist!*

708a 圭 jade block

earth 土(54a) + earth 土(54a) = jade block 圭

This is an old character referring to a small rectangular jade tablet used in feudal times as a token of authority.

The archaeologist dug through a layer of **earth**, then another layer of **earth**, before he found a **jade block**. / *[No pronunciation needed]*

708 挂 **guà** hang

Radical 扌
9 strokes

掛

hand 扌 (152a) + jade block 圭(708a) = hang 挂

挂号(424) **guà hào** *register (at hospital)*]

Running his **hand** over the **jade block**, he could feel something on the back to **hang** it up by. / *When he hung it up, a **ghostly dwarf** appeared with some **garlic** to guard it.*

709 封 **fēng** seal up

Radical 寸
9 strokes

jade block 圭(708a) + inch 寸(104a) = seal up 封

信封(376) **xìnfēng** *an envelope*
封建(657) **fēngjiàn** *feudal*]
封里(157) **fēnglǐ** *inside front cover/ inside back cover (of a book)*]

You are sending out miniature **jade blocks**, an **inch** long, as Christmas presents, and you **seal** them **up** in little envelopes. / *The **giant** has brought along some **fungus** to seal them with.*

710 街 jiē
street

Radical 彳
12 strokes

step forward 彳(81a) + **jade block** 圭(708a)
+ **footstep** 亍(81c) = **street** 街

Although this looks to be made up of three parts, it actually comes from combining 圭 (708a) with 行 (Character 81).

He **steps forward** to pick up the **jade block**, but hears a **footstep** behind him, and he quickly looks up and down the deserted **street**. / *Two giants appear, one at each end of the street, each armed with a jellyfish!*

[街道(145) **jiēdào** *street*]

[大街(47) **dàijiē** *(main) street*]

711a 革 gé
leather

This also means "to expel".
You'll remember that we just met another character for "leather" (706a).

---

711 鞋 xié
shoe

Radical 革
15 strokes

leather 革(711a) + **jade block** 圭(708a) =
shoe 鞋

[脱鞋(656) **tuō xié** *take off one's shoes*]
[鞋带(429) **xié dài** *shoelace*]

SHOES

The cobbler rubs the **leather** with a **jade block** to soften it up to make the best **shoes**. / *When each pair is made, two fairies fly up and arrange them on a shelf.*

---

712 双 shuāng
pair

Radical 又
4 strokes

雙

right hand 又(52) + **right hand** 又(52) =
pair 双

We've made an exception here and used "two right hands" instead of "shaking hands".

Someone who has **two right hands** is shopping for gloves. "We only sell them as a **pair**," all the shops tell him. / *"Try the ghostly giant of Shangri-La. He looks after people who have special requirements."*

[双方(291) **shuāngfāng** *both sides*]
[双号(424) **shuānghào** *an even number*]

[一双鞋(1, 711) **yì shuāng xié** *a pair of shoes*]

713a

东 to select

Compare this with 东 ("east", Character 319). The difference is the small horizontal line at the beginning of the third stroke.

The traditional forms of "east" and "select" are also very similar. The traditional form of "east" (see the entry for Character 319) can be thought of as the "sun" rising behind a "tree". The traditional form of 713a can be seen in the following two entries — here the "sun" looks more like "windowpane" (671b).

713

炼 liàn smelt

Radical 火
9 strokes

煉

fire 火(181) + select 东(713a) = smelt 炼

The **fire** had to be fed with carefully **select**ed wood so that it could be used to **smelt** the iron. / *It took **two dwarves** to lift the cauldron of **lentil** soup for the workers at the ironworks.*

714

练 liàn to train

Radical 纟
8 strokes

練

thread 纟(233a) + select 东(713a) = train 练

熟练(696) **shúliàn** *skilled, skilful]*

"You must learn how to **select** the correct **thread** if you want to **train** to become a dressmaker." / ***Two dwarves** come round with a selection of things to test the students' skills, including **lentils** (in place of sequins) to sew onto dresses.*

715a

耳 ivy

715

段 duàn piece

Radical 殳
9 strokes

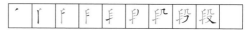

ivy 耳(715a) + strike 殳(169a) = piece 段

手段(31) **shǒuduàn** *means, measure]*

Vandals attack the **ivy** — they **strike** it and leave only a single **piece** in place. / *The king calls in the **ghostly dwarf** to guard his special **dandelion** (so that it doesn't meet the same fate).*

716 锻 duàn forge

Radical 钅
14 strokes

鍛

gold 钅(278a) + piece 段(715) = forge 锻

锻炼(713) **duànliàn** *do physical exercise*

The king donates a **gold piece** to be **forged** into a gift. / *He gives it to the **ghostly dwarf** as a reward for guarding his special dandelion.*

717a 屯 tún to store

You might prefer to think of this as "seven" plus "pit"; if so, feel free to make up a story accordingly.

717 顿 dùn session

Radical 页
10 strokes

頓

store 屯(717a) + page 页(477) = session 顿

[三顿饭(3, 332) **sān dùn fàn** *three meals*]

You are writing a book and **store** the **pages** you have produced at the end of each **session**. / *The **ghostly dwarf** who guards the pages thinks it's such drivel that he keeps a **dunce's** cap on top of them as a paperweight.*

718 烦 fán bother

Radical 火
10 strokes

煩

fire 火(181) + page 页(477) = bother 烦

[烦劳(324) **fánláo** *trouble*]

He's trying to light a **fire** with a **page** torn from the newspaper — but keeps burning his fingers on the matches. "**Bother!**" he cries. "Bother, bother, bother!" / *The **fairy** offers to **fan** the flames with her wings.*

Test yourself: 可(140)　米(334)　早(633)　舍(643)　银(285)　须(591)　联(374)

附(652)　建(657)　各(507)　相(163)　字(92)　睡(409)　持(465)

工(147)　天(76)　小(50)　举(648)　局(650)　处(506)　喜(539)

请(336)　踢(529)　卡(198)　室(472)　束(494)　切(230)　总(514)

Chapter 37

As you review the characters you learned way back in the earliest chapters, there will be many which you instantly recognize, and others where you have to think for a while, and recall the story in your head. Of course, there are also bound to be many characters which you have tried to learn a few times but keep forgetting. Often the thing to do with these is to go back to the story and really explore the setting, imagine yourself as part of the action and embellish the story with more details. If all else fails, make a list of the characters you find particularly problematic, and teach them to somebody else (one of your fellow students, or even a friend who is not studying Chinese). Teaching something is a very effective way of learning it yourself — we've both been teachers so we know!

719a

斥 chì
drive out

axe 斤(240) + splinter 丶(695a) = drive out 斥

In some typefaces the splinter doesn't reach all the way across the vertical stroke.

The gang use an **axe** to chop **splinter**s out of the door of anyone they want to **drive out** of the neighborhood. / *No pronunciation needed*

719

诉 sù
tell

Radical 讠
7 strokes

訴

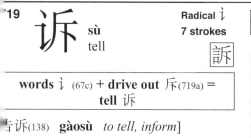

words 讠 (67c) + drive out 斥(719a) = tell 诉

告诉(138) **gàosù** *to tell, inform*]

The lurid **words** scrawled on the wall urge people to **drive out** any foreigners; the authorities have asked people to **tell** the police if they know who was responsible. / *The **dwarf** police official will be stationed at the **supermarket** (ready to take reports).*

720a

约 yuē
approximate

約

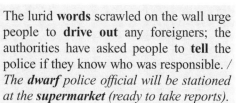

thread 纟 (233a) + ladle 勹(23b) = approximate 约

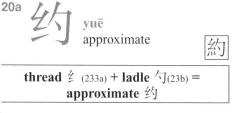

This also means to make an appointment or come to an agreement.

In the palace kitchens they hang a **ladle** from a **thread** and use it as a makeshift pendulum (to time the boiled eggs) — a traditional method, but only **approximate**! / *[No pronunciation needed]*

720

药　yào
medicine

Radical ⁺⁺
9 strokes

藥

一　十　艹　艻　艻　荳　药　药　药

grass ⁺⁺(218a) **+ approximate** 约 (720a) **=
medicine** 药

[药房(293)　**yàofáng**　*pharmacy*]
[药片(353)　**yàopiàn**　*pill, tablet*]

The sick cow has eaten poisonous plants which looked **approximately** like **grass**, and so now has to take some **medicine**. / *But as the **dwarf** assistant reaches for the medicine, the cow stands on his foot and he yells out, "**Yeow!**"*

721a

争　zhēng
contend

ノ　ク　グ　刍　刍　争

bow ⼂(51a) **+ dexterity** ⺕(312a) **=
contend** 争

This character can mean "argue (about)" or "compete (for)". You may see an older form of this character which has "claw" (365b) instead of "bow".

(In the pickpocket's master-class) The expert demonstrates his skill by **bow**ing to the volunteer and, with great **dexterity**, simultaneously picking his pocket without being noticed. "I **contend**, ladies and gentlemen," he says, "that this is the ultimate skill." / *[No pronunciation needed]*

721

净　jìng
clean

Radical ⺡
8 strokes

丶　冫　冫　氵　汃　浄　浄　净

ice ⺡ (360a) **+ contend** 争(721a) **= clean** 净

干净(124)　**gānjìng**　*clean (adjective)*

The tour guide in the arctic points to the **ice** and says, "I **contend** that this is the most pure and **clean** water in the world." / *The **dwarf** in charge of the husky sledge for transport **jingles** the sledge bells impatiently (he's heard it all before and wants to move on).*

722

静　jìng
calm

Radical 青
14 strokes

一　二　丰　主　青　青　青　青　青

静　静　静　静

blue-green 青(335) **+ contend** 争(721a) **=
calm** 静

安静(91)　**ānjìng**　*quiet, peaceful*
[平静(309)　**píngjìng**　*calm, quiet*]

(Two people are arguing over the color of a book in the library) "I **contend** it's **blue**!" "I **contend** it's **green**!" "**Calm** down!" says their friend. / *The **dwarf** librarian **jingles** his bell for quiet.*

723a 卓 *daybreak*

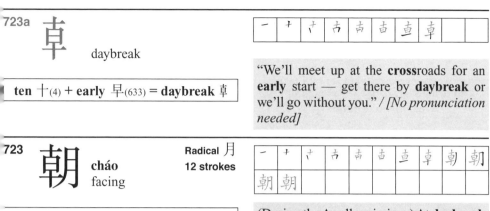

ten 十(4) + early 早(633) = daybreak 卓

"We'll meet up at the **cross**roads for an **early** start — get there by **daybreak** or we'll go without you." / *[No pronunciation needed]*

---

723 朝 **cháo** *facing*

Radical 月
12 strokes

daybreak 卓(723a) + moon 月(61) = facing 朝

朝阳(96) **cháoyáng** *sunny aspect, exposed to the sun*]

(During the Apollo missions) At **daybreak** the **moon** had set in the USA, so they had to swap to an Australian ground station which was now **facing** the moon. / *The fairy had produced chowder to wake the Australians up.*

724a 卓 **zhuō** *eminent*

fortune teller 卜(42a) + early 早(633) = eminent 卓

The **fortune teller** got to her tent **early** that day, to prepare for an **eminent** client (picture her polishing up her crystal ball, etc.) / *[No pronunciation needed]*

This is easy to confuse with "daybreak" 723a).

---

724 掉 **diào** *to drop*

Radical 扌
11 strokes

hand 扌(152a) + eminent 卓(724a) = drop 掉

用掉(130) **yòngdiào** *to use up*]
卖掉(248) **màidiào** *to sell out*]
忘掉(569) **wàngdiào** *to forget*]

The **eminent** surgeon holds out his **hand** for the scalpel, but promptly **drop**s it! / *The two dwarf clinical assessors exchange glances — they have doubts about the surgeon's competence (however eminent he is).*

Test yourself: 酒(102) 谁(501) 和(126) 研(606) 车(83) 多(69) 情(339)
派(664) 整(495) 别(79) 嗯(521) 房(293) 目(93) 者(261)

725

zhuō
table

Radical 木
10 strokes

| 丶 | 广 | 疒 | 占 | 占 | 占 | 直 | 卓 | 卓 | 桌 |

fortune teller 卜 (42a) + **sun** 日 (6) +
tree 木 (10a) = **table** 桌

桌子 (17)　**zhuōzi**　*table, desk*

The **fortune teller** sets up her stall out of the **sun** under the shade of the **tree**, and puts her crystal ball on a **table**. / *The ghostly giant watches over her to dissuade anyone from making a joke of her.*

726a

"earring"

| 乛 | 一 | 子 | 于 | 耳 | 耳 | 耳 |

knee 乛 (166a) + **ear** 耳 (88a) = **earring** 耳

The bit on top of the "ear" is sometimes written like "nail" instead of "knee", although it's actually derived from "work" (Character 147)!

"Put your **ear** here on my **knee** and I will fix your **earring** for you." / *[No pronunciation needed]*

726

gǎn
dare

Radical 攵
11 strokes

| 乛 | 一 | 子 | 于 | 耳 | 耳 | 耳 | 耳 | 耳 | 敢 |
| 敢 | | | | | | | | | |

earring 耳 (726a) + **tap** 攵 (190a) = **dare** 敢

[不敢当 (9, 267)　**bùgǎndāng**　*Thank you (polite, modest reply to compliment)*]

(At the pirates' lair in the creek, the door is in the shape of a giant pirate's head) You **tap** on the **earring** to gain entry — and a voice booms out, "Who **dares** to enter here?" / *But actually it's only Teddy on a gantry behind the door (speaking into a megaphone).*

727

xīu
leisure

Radical 亻
6 strokes

| 丿 | 亻 | 仁 | 什 | 休 | 休 |

person 亻 (13a) + **tree** 木 (10a) = **leisure** 休

休息 (662)　**xīuxi**　*(take a) rest*

Harry always goes to sit high up in the **tree** whenever he has **leisure** time. / *Today he's watching the two giants put on a show.*

728 退 tuì
retreat

Radical 辶
9 strokes

| ⁊ | ⁊ | ⁊ | ⼍ | ⼍ | ⼍ | `⼍ | 退 | 退 |

road 辶(26a) + stubborn 艮(281a) =
retreat 退

[退休(727) tuìxiū *to retire*]

On the single-track **road** the two drivers sit, both **stubborn**ly waiting for the other to **retreat**. / *The ghostly dwarf, who guards the stretch of road, gets out his **tape** measure (to see who would have to reverse the least distance).*

729 腿 tuǐ
leg

Radical 月
13 strokes

| ⼅ | ⼅ | 月 | 月 | 月⁊ | 月⁊ | 月⁊ | 肥 | 肥 | 腿 |
| 腿 | 腿 | 腿 | | | | | | | |

moon 月(61) + retreat 退(728) = leg 腿

[大腿(47) dàtuǐ *thigh*]

(The Apollo astronauts had finished their moonwalk) They had to leave the **moon** and make a rapid **retreat** into their spacecraft (before their oxygen ran out), but one trapped his **leg** in the airlock. / *Back inside the lunar module the **ghostly teddy** who looked after the astronauts measured the leg with a **tape** measure (to see if it was all there!)*

730a 豆 dòu
bean

| 一 | ⼍ | ⼍ | 口 | 百 | 豆 | 豆 | | | |

piled up 口(150b) + feet ⼍(90a) = bean 豆

The pilgrims **piled up** their gifts at the **feet** of the statue — each pilgrim had brought a tin of holy **bean**s. / *[No pronunciation needed]*

730 短 duǎn
brief

Radical 矢
12 strokes

| ⼃ | ⼂ | ⼂ | 乞 | 矢 | 矢⁊ | 知 | 知 | 知 | 短 |
| 短 | 短 | | | | | | | | |

arrow 矢(490a) + bean 豆(730a) = brief 短

[短期(236) duǎnqī *short-term*]

William Tell could shoot an **arrow** to hit a **bean** on his son's head, after only a **brief** glance to judge the distance. / *The ghostly teddy who protects the son suggests putting the bean on a pile of **dandruff** (to give him more room for error)!*

731a

吴   shout out

> **mouth** 口(5) + **heaven** 天(76) = **shout out** 吴

丶 丆 口 口 旦 导 吴

"Turn your **mouth** to the **heaven**s and **shout out** your message," the preacher tells his congregation. / *[No pronunciation needed]*.

731

误   wù   mistake

Radical 讠
9 strokes

誤

> **words** 讠 (67c) + **shout out** 吴(731a) = **mistake** 误

丶 讠 讠 讠 讠 误 误 误

(Monks are poring over a piece of calligraphy) Looking over the beautiful **words**, they **shout out** whenever they spot a **mistake**. / *The dwarf, who wrote it, is wounded by their criticism (and goes off in a huff).*

This also means "to miss" (e.g. a train, by arriving too late).

[误会(59) **wùhuì** *misunderstand*]
[误点(185) **wùdiǎn** *late, overdue, behind schedule*]

732a

采   cǎi; cài   pick

採

> **claw** 爫 (365b) + **tree** 木(10a) = **pick** 采

丿 爫 爫 爫 平 平 采 采

With her **claw**-like hand the old crone reaches up to the **tree** to **pick** the apple. / *[No pronunciation needed]*

Try not to confuse this with "claw marks" (734a) — at first glance they look almost identical.

732

彩   cǎi   colorful

Radical 彡
11 strokes

> **pick** 采(732a) + **hairs** 彡(573a) = **colorful** 彩

丿 爫 爫 平 平 采 采 彩 彩
彩

The hairdresser **pick**s out individual **hairs** to highlight, producing a **colorful** effect. / *Teddy wants a whole new style!*

精彩(341) **jīngcǎi** *thrilling, exciting*
[彩色(417) **cǎisè** *multi-colored*]

733

菜 cài
vegetable

Radical ⁺⁺
11 strokes

一	十	艹	艹	艺	芒	苎	苹	荬	荬
菜									

> **grass** ⁺⁺(218a) + **pick** 采(732a) =
> **vegetable** 菜

[白菜(22) **báicài** *cabbage*]
[做菜(210) **zuòcài** *to cook*]
[饭菜(332) **fàncài** *food*]
[点菜(185) **diǎncài** *to choose (items from
a menu)*]

The greengrocer knows the best **grass** to
pick, and uses it to display his **vegetable**s
to best effect. / *But the **dwarf** owner always
dictates the exact **style** of the display.*

734a

"claw marks"

一	⺅	⼞	⺬	平	平	采			

> **beret** 一(89a) + **rice** 米(334) =
> **claw marks** 采

This is very easy to confuse with "pick"
(732a).

The palaeontologist fills his **beret** with
rice and pours it into the fossilized **claw
marks** to measure their volume — each
claw mark takes up a whole beret-full
of rice. (So it must have been quite a
dinosaur!) / *[No pronunciation needed]*

734b

番 fān
a time

一	⺅	⼞	⺬	平	平	采	采	番	番
番	番								

> **claw marks** 采(734a) + **field** 田(156a) =
> **a time** 番

Picture huge **claw marks** scarring the
field. They have tried **time** after **time** to
catch the beast which makes them, without
success. / *[No pronunciation needed]*

734

播 bō
to sow

Radical 扌
15 strokes

一	扌	扌	扩	扩	护	护	押	押	採
採	播	播	播	播					

> **hand** 扌(152a) + **a time** 番(734b) = **sow** 播

广播(170) **guǎngbō** *broadcast*

He has to dip his **hand, time** after **time**,
into the bag as he walks up and down
sowing the seeds. / *The **giant** is finding this
boring (even though he can do it in half
the time it would take most people ...)*

735

习 xí
to practice

Radical 冫
3 strokes

習

| 丁 | 习 | 习 | | | | | | |

ice 冫 (360a) + blade 刁 (231a) = **practice** 习

Notice that "ice" is usually on the left-hand side but here it is enclosed by "blade".

He uses an **ice blade** to **practice** his fencing skills. / *The fairy conjures up an insulated sheath to keep it in.*

学习(82) **xuéxí** *to study, learn*
复习(550) **fùxí** *review (a lesson)*
练习(714) **liànxí** *to practice*
预习(642) **yùxí** *preview, prepare*

736a

羽 yǔ
feather

| 丁 | 习 | 习 | 羽 | 羽 | 羽 | | | |

practice 习(735) + **practice** 习(735) = **feather** 羽

You would have to **practice** and **practice** before you could balance a **feather** on your nose (without sneezing!) / *[No pronunciation needed]*

736

翻 fān
turn over

Radical 羽
18 strokes

| 一 | 丿 | 亚 | 平 | 乎 | 采 | 采 | 番 |
| 番 | 番 | 番 | 番 | 番 | 翻 | 翻 | 翻 |

a time 番(734b) + **feather** 羽(736a) = **turn over** 翻

Every **time** the **feather** (on the ground) moves in the breeze, it **turns over**. / *The giant is creating the breeze with his fan (on a nearby hill).*

[翻新(243) **fānxīn** *recondition, renovate*]
[翻跟头(283, 246) **fān gēntou** *turn somersaults; loop the loop*]

Test yourself:
会(59)　几(7)　走(275)　前(90)　点(185)　就(239)　般(680)
族(687)　道(145)　高(481)　调(541)　特(466)　屋(473)　极(534)

737a

卒
watch over

| 丁 | 又 | 圣 | 圣 | 圣 | | | | |

right hand 又(52) + **criminal** 辛(130a) = **watch over** 卒

In the prison at each shift change, the new warder **shakes hands** with the notorious **criminal** as he arrives to **watch over** him. / *[No pronunciation needed]*

---

737 译 **yì** translate

Radical 讠
7 strokes

譯

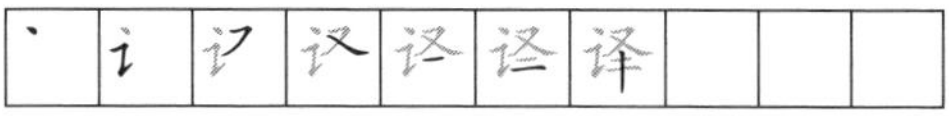

words 讠(67c) + **watch over** 圣(737a) = **translate** 译

翻译(736) **fānyì** *translate, interpret*

(A crime scene: the dead man, a foreigner, has managed to write something on the floor beside him) The police have to **watch over** the **words** until someone arrives to **translate** them. / *The **dwarf** police inspector is impatient — he wants to **e-mail** for a translation instead.*

738a 余 **yú** surplus

餘

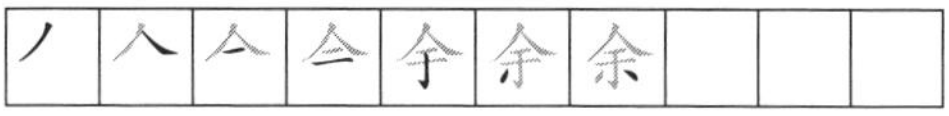

tent 𠆢(19b) + **work** 工(147) + **small** 小(50) = **surplus** 余

We have cheated a bit here by breaking the lower part of this character into "work" and "small".

The **tent** they are **work**ing in is very **small**, so you can tell which one it is by the pile of **surplus** equipment outside. / *[No pronunciation needed]*

---

738 除 **chú** to remove

Radical 阝
9 strokes

mound 阝(96a) + **surplus** 余(738a) = **remove** 除

除了(66) **chúle** *except, besides*

The **mound** of **surplus** office equipment has grown so big that the council has told them to **remove** it. / *The **fairy** wants to **choose** some things for herself first.*

---

739 茶 **chá** tea

Radical 艹
9 strokes

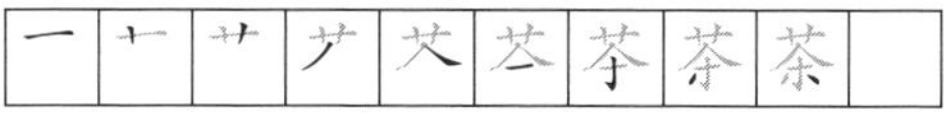

grass 艹(218a) + **tent** 𠆢(19b) + **tree** 木(10a) = **tea** 茶

Note that the bottom part of this character is *not* "surplus" (738a). Also note that the last two strokes of "tree" have become slightly detached.

[红茶(233) **hóngchá** *black tea*]
[茶杯(11) **chábēi** *tea cup*]

They set up their **tent** on the **grass** underneath the **tree** and the first thing they do is make some **tea**. / *The **fairy** relaxes, saying, "This is a nice cup of **cha**."*

740a 奇 qí; jī
strange

big 大(47) + may 可(140) = strange 奇

The extra **big may**pole is for the most senior students; it's really **strange** to see them dancing round it like small children. / *[No pronunciation needed]*

740 骑 qí
ride

Radical 马
11 strokes

騎

horse 马(44) + strange 奇(740a) = ride 骑

That **horse** may be very **strange**-looking, but it's wonderful to **ride**. / *The fairy streaks along on it, explaining, "That's because it's half cheetah."*

This character means to ride an animal (or bicycle) which you sit astride. Riding in a bus or car is different (see 783a).

[骑马(44) **qí mǎ** *to ride a horse*]

741 椅 yǐ
chair

Radical 木
12 strokes

tree 木(10a) + strange 奇(740a) = chair 椅

椅子(17) **yǐzi** *chair*

The **tree** is a **strange** shape and part of it has been carved into a **chair**. / *Picture Teddy sitting on it, munching his chocolate Easter egg.*

742 寄 jì
send

Radical 宀
11 strokes

house 宀(91a) + strange 奇(740a) = send 寄

[寄件人(385, 12) **jìjiànrén** *sender (of letter)*]

"The **house** is really **strange**," she pleads, "Please don't **send** me there. / *The dwarf who lives there is weird, even if he is a genius."*

Chapter 38

We hope that you've enjoyed writing the characters at the same time as you've been learning them. Writing Chinese characters can be fun and satisfying, even if you have no interest in being particularly artistic about it. If you are interested in calligraphy, however, Chinese characters are a fascinating subject and there are many books available. To do it properly you will need a writing brush and thick black ink. The Chinese themselves hold calligraphy in high esteem, ranking it alongside, if not above, painting, sculpture and poetry.

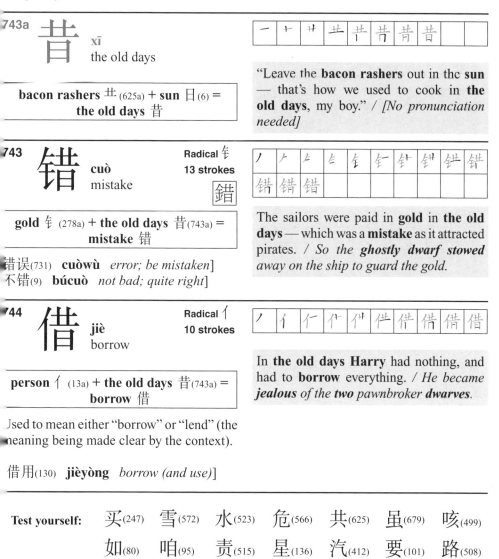

743a 昔 xī
the old days

| 一 | 十 | 艹 | 䒑 | 共 | 昔 | 昔 | 昔 | | |

bacon rashers 龶 (625a) + sun 日 (6) = the old days 昔

"Leave the **bacon rashers** out in the **sun** — that's how we used to cook in **the old days**, my boy." / *[No pronunciation needed]*

743 错 cuò
mistake
Radical 钅
13 strokes
錯

| 丿 | 𠂉 | 𠂆 | 钅 | 钅 | 钅 | 针 | 钳 | 铁 | 错 |
| 错 | 错 | 错 | | | | | | | |

gold 钅 (278a) + the old days 昔 (743a) = mistake 错

错误 (731) **cuòwù** *error; be mistaken*]
不错 (9) **búcuò** *not bad; quite right*]

The sailors were paid in **gold** in **the old days** — which was a **mistake** as it attracted pirates. / *So the ghostly dwarf stowed away on the ship to guard the gold.*

744 借 jiè
borrow
Radical 亻
10 strokes

| 丿 | 亻 | 仁 | 仕 | 供 | 供 | 借 | 借 | 借 | 借 |

person 亻 (13a) + the old days 昔 (743a) = borrow 借

Used to mean either "borrow" or "lend" (the meaning being made clear by the context).

借用 (130) **jièyòng** *borrow (and use)*]

In **the old days Harry** had nothing, and had to **borrow** everything. / *He became jealous of the two pawnbroker dwarves.*

Test yourself: 买 (247) 雪 (572) 水 (523) 危 (566) 共 (625) 虽 (679) 咳 (499)
如 (80) 咱 (95) 责 (515) 星 (136) 汽 (412) 要 (101) 路 (508)

745a 昔

"midnight feast"

| 一 | 十 | 卄 | 生 | 芒 | 昔 | 昔 | 昔 | | |

---

bacon rashers 卄 (625a) + **moon** 月 (61) =
midnight feast 昔

Compare this with "the old days" (743a above).

They took **bacon rashers** into the **moon**lit forest for a **midnight feast**. / *[No pronunciation needed]*

---

745 散 sàn disperse   **Radical** 攵 **12 strokes**

| 一 | 十 | 卄 | 生 | 芒 | 昔 | 昔 | 昔 | 昔 | 昔 |
| 散 | 散 | | | | | | | | |

midnight feast 昔 (745a) + **tap** 攵 (190a) =
disperse 散

散步 (378) **sànbù** *a stroll; to stroll*

At the **midnight feast** in the forest they are eating hungrily when the lookout **tap**s out a warning on the tree and they all **disperse** quickly. / *When the dwarf arrives, all he finds is a pile of abandoned sandwiches.*

746a 凸 ravine

| 丿 | 几 | 几 | 凸 | 凸 | | | | | |

several 几 (7) + **mouth** 口 (5) = **ravine** 凸

From the air, what looked like a string of **several mouth**s in the landscape, was actually a deep **ravine**. / *[No pronunciation needed]*

---

746 船 chuán ship   **Radical** 舟 **11 strokes**

| 丿 | 丿 | 刀 | 月 | 舟 | 舟 | 舟 | 舟 | 舟 | 船 |
| 船 | | | | | | | | | |

boat 舟 (680a) + **ravine** 凸 (746a) = **ship** 船

[汽船 (412) **qìchuán** *steamship*]
[船场 (530) **chuánchǎng** *shipyard*]
[船员 (479) **chuányuán** *sailor; crew*]
[船票 (431) **chuánpiào** *boat ticket*]

They sailed the **boat** down the **ravine** until it opened out, and there on the lake was a beautiful golden **ship**. / *Beyond the lake the ghostly fairy waited to guide them through the next dangerous channel.*

747 铅　qiān
lead

Radical 钅
10 strokes

鉛

gold 钅 (278a) + **ravine** 凸 (746a) = **lead** 铅

This is lead, the metal (not "lead" as in "to lead the way").

The pirates store their **gold** in the **ravine**, because there (in the gloom) it looks like **lead**. / [DIY pronunciation]

铅笔(454)　**qiānbǐ**　*pencil*

Test yourself:　饭(332)　火(181)　厂(149)　市(427)　户(269)　空(617)　嗽(496)

看(200)　困(522)　握(474)　级(535)　装(489)　单(344)　自(94)

748a 疋
bolt of cloth

cap 乛 (247a) + **stop** 龰 (30a) = **bolt of cloth** 疋

This character is easy to mistake for 'upright' (30b).

The stall-holder whips off his **cap** when he realizes that it's the princess who has **stop**ped at his stall — and he quickly produces his finest **bolt of cloth** for her inspection. / [No pronunciation needed]

---

748 蛋　dàn
egg

Radical 疋
11 strokes

bolt of cloth 疋 (748a) + **insect** 虫 (679a) = **egg** 蛋

鸡蛋(678)　**jīdàn**　*(hen's) egg*

The **bolt of cloth** has been invaded by **insect**s, who have laid tiny white **egg**s in it. / *The dwarf (a market trader selling the cloth) tells his customers it's only dandruff.*

749a 林　lín
a wood

tree 木 (10a) + **tree** 木 (10a) = **a wood** 林

It takes **two trees** to make a **wood** (and three to make a forest). / [No pronunciation needed]

749 楚   **chǔ**   clear   Radical 疋   13 strokes

一	十	才	木	术	术	材	林	梺	梺
梺	梺	楚							

> **a wood** 林(749a) + **bolt of cloth** 疋(748a) = **clear** 楚

清楚(337) **qīngchu** *clear (image, speech)*

For the picnic they took a **bolt of cloth** to the **wood**s and had to **clear** a space to spread it out. / *When they opened the picnic basket, they found **Teddy** inside **chewing** on a sausage!*

---

750 麻   **má**   hemp   Radical 麻   11 strokes

`	一	广	广	庁	庈	床	床	床	麻
麻									

> **shelter** 广(170) + **a wood** 林(749a) = **hemp** 麻

You will sometimes see this character with "detached final strokes of trees" (see Character 739).

麻烦(718) **máfán** *to bother; trouble*
[麻药(720) **máyào** *anesthetic*]
[麻烦您(718, 493) **máfan nín** *Would you mind …?*]

They build a **shelter** in the **wood** to hide their **hemp** crop. / *When it is ready the **fairy** takes it to **market**.*

---

751 嘛   **ma**   surely   Radical 口   14 strokes

丨	口	口	口`	口一	吖	吋	咹	咹	喢
嗞	嘛	嘛	嘛						

> **mouth** 口(5) + **hemp** 麻(750) = **surely** 嘛

"You need some **hemp** in your **mouth** — you'll **surely** feel the effects." / *"Let's send the **robot** to get some from the **market** — nobody will suspect him!"*

752a 隶   **lì**   subordinate

⁊	彐	彐	聿	聿	聿	聿	隶		

> **dexterity** 聿(312a) + **water** 水(523) = **subordinate** 隶

This is cheating slightly as the bottom half isn't really "water" (see also Character 524); the same applies to Character 753 below.

On the oil rig out at sea, fixing the pipes under **water** calls for **dexterity**, but it's tedious work so it's a job that is always given to the **subordinate**s. / *[No pronunciation needed]*

752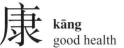

康 **kāng**
good health

Radical 广
11 strokes

`	一	广	广	广	户	序	序	唐	康
康									

shelter 广 (170) + **subordinate** 隶 (752a) = **good health** 康

健康 (658) **jiànkāng** *health, healthy*

The manager wants to build a **shelter** for his **subordinate**s to keep them in **good health**. / *The giant workman comes to build it — with a kangaroo assistant who keeps the tools in her pouch.*

753

录 **lù**
to record

Radical ⺕
8 strokes

録

⼀	⼆	⺕	子	寻	寻	录	录

snout ⺕ (267a) + **water** 水 (523) = **record** 录

Note that the final stroke of "snout" (267a) is extended here.

录音 (257) **lùyīn** *(sound) recording*
[记录 (272) **jìlù** *to record, a record*]

Each time the pig dips his **snout** in the **water**, the naturalist excitedly **record**s it. / *His dwarf assistant thinks this obsession is ludicrous.*

754

绿 **lǜ**
green

Radical 纟
11 strokes

綠

⼁	⼂	纟	纟	纟	纩	纾	纾	绿
绿								

thread 纟 (233a) + **record** 录 (753) = **green** 绿

[红绿灯 (233, 182) **hónglǜdēng** *traffic light, stoplight*]

☁ **Thread**-work (like the Bayeux tapestry) is often used to **record** important events or stories. Picture the story of Robin Hood being stitched — and they keep running out of **green** thread. / *The dwarf had to go out in the pouring rain to get luminous green thread (to do the night scenes).*

755

旅 **lǚ**
travel

Radical 方
10 strokes

`	二	方	方	方	扩	旅	扩	旂	旅

banner 扩 (687a) + **brigade** 氏 (664a) = **travel** 旅

旅行 (81) **lǚxíng** *travel*
[旅客 (509) **lǚkè** *passenger; hotel guest*]

☁ The **brigade** are looking for their **banner** as they are about to **travel** (and want to fly it over their new barracks). / *They find Teddy taking a bath in the pouring rain with a loofah (and he's pinched the banner to use as a bath towel).*

756a **俞** yú "catamaran"

combine 合 (59a) + canoe 刖 (90b) = catamaran 俞

He **combined** two **canoe**s together to make a **catamaran**. / *[No pronunciation needed].*

---

756 **愉** yú happy

Radical 忄
12 strokes

heart 忄 (339a) + catamaran 俞 (756a) = happy 愉

愉快 (403) **yúkuài** *happy; pleasant*

He had set his **heart** on a **catamaran** so is really **happy** when he finally gets one. / *The fairy comes out in the pouring rain to write the name "Eureka" on the side of the boat with her wand (which fortunately conjures up waterproof paint).*

---

757 **输** shū lose

Radical 车
13 strokes

輸

car 车 (83) + catamaran 俞 (756a) = lose 输

The **car** has a race with the **catamaran** but in the end it **lose**s. / *Halfway round it had crashed into the **giant's shoe**.*

This means "to lose a game" (*not* "to mislay something") and also "transport".

[运输 (57) **yùnshū** *transport, carry, transportation*]
[输出 (114) **shūchū** *emit; export*]
[输家 (109) **shūjiā** *the loser (in a game)*]

---

758 **凉** liáng cool

Radical 冫
10 strokes

ice 冫 (360a) + capital 京 (239b) = cool 凉

凉快 (403) **liángkuai** *(pleasantly) cool*

Ice covers the **capital** and finally **cool**s it down after the sweltering summer. / *The **two fairies**, who had been **languishing** in the heat, come to life again.*

759 谅 liàng
forgive

Radical 讠
10 strokes

諒

`、 讠 讠 讠 讠 讠 讠 谅 谅 谅`

words 讠 (67c) + capital 京(239b) =
forgive 谅

原谅(536) **yuánliàng** *to excuse, forgive*

The peace activists have painted **words** on walls all over the **capital**: "**Forgive** your *?#* enemies" is the message. / *The **two dwarves** object to the uncouth **language** (and take it in turns to remove the words).*

760a
turn in one's sleep

`丿 ㄅ 夕 夗 夗`

evening 夕(69a) + hardship 巳(566a) =
turn in one's sleep 夗

If you spend all **evening** dwelling on your **hardship**s you will **turn in your sleep** all night. / *[No pronunciation needed]*

760b wǎn
winding

`、 ㇐ 宀 宀 宁 㝀 㝀 宛`

house 宀(91a) + turn in one's sleep
夗(760a) = winding 宛

Once again the **house** had appeared in his dreams, and he **turned in his sleep** with a groan, knowing that the endless **winding** path would be next. / *[No pronunciation needed]*

---

760 碗 wǎn
bowl

Radical 石
13 strokes

`一 丆 丆 石 石 石 矿 砑 砑 砑 砑 砕 碗`

stone 石(115a) + winding 宛(760b) =
bowl 碗

[饭碗(332) **fànwǎn** *rice bowl; livelihood*]
[两碗饭(222, 332) **liǎng fàn wǎn** *two bowls of rice*]

The children roll small **stone**s down the **winding** marble-run and the stones clatter into a **bowl** at the bottom. / *[DIY pronunciation]*

Test yourself: 北(317) 共(625) 元(301) 找(152) 连(84) 满(225) 搞(482)
阳(96) 都(262) 打(153) 万(296) 告(138) 场(530) 绩(516)

761

香 **xiāng**
fragrant

Radical 禾
9 strokes

一 二 千 千 禾 禾 香 香 香

---

grain 禾(126a) + **sun** 日(6) = **fragrant** 香

The **grain** drying in the **sun** gives off a **fragrant** smell. / *The two giants from Shanghai agree that they have never smelled anything like it.*

This character appears in the name **Xiānggǎng**, 香港, "Hong Kong" — the other character (港, "harbor") is not an HSK A character.

[香水(523) **xiāngshuǐ** *perfume, scent*]
[香精(341) **xiāngjīng** *essence (of plant)*]
[香气(411) **xiāngqì** *aroma, sweet smell*]
[香客(509) **xiāngkè** *pilgrim*]
[香火(181) **xiānghuǒ** *burning incense, etc. (in a temple)*]

762a

 nú
slave

丨 刁 女 如 奴

---

women 女(15) + **right hand** 又(52) = **slave** 奴

When the **woman shakes hands** with him he notices the mark on her wrist which marks her out as a **slave**. / *[No pronunciation needed]*

762

努 **nǔ**
exert oneself

Radical 力
7 strokes

丨 刁 女 如 奴 奴 努

---

slave 奴(762a) + **power** 力(14) = **exert oneself** 努

努力(14) **nǔlì** *make great efforts; try hard*

They used **slave power** to build the pyramids — the foremen made sure that the slaves **exerted themselves** to the full. / *Nowadays it's just a ruin and Teddy sits on it eating his noodles.*

763a

焦 **jiāo**
scorched

丿 亻 亻 仁 仁 仨 隹 隹 隹
焦 焦

---

pigeon 隹(501a) + **fire** 灬(185a) = **scorched** 焦

The **pigeon** sat by the **fire** for too long and **scorched** his tail feathers. / *[No pronunciation needed]*

763 蕉 **jiāo** [banana] **Radical** 艹 **15 strokes**

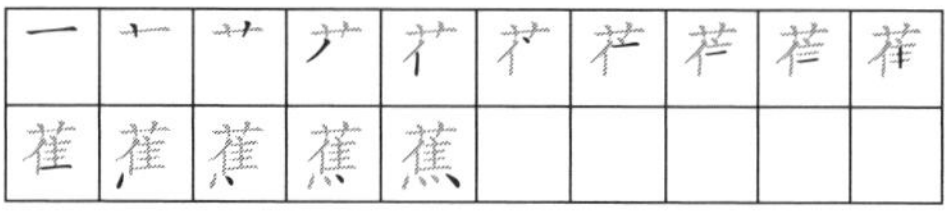

grass 艹(218a) + **scorched** 焦(763a) = **banana** 蕉

香蕉(761) **xiāngjiāo** *banana*

The **grass** had been **scorched** by the fire, but the **banana**s on the trees were undamaged. / *The **two giants** (who owned the banana plantation) had been off at a **jousting** match (and were relieved that their crop was alright).*

764a 肀 "rude"

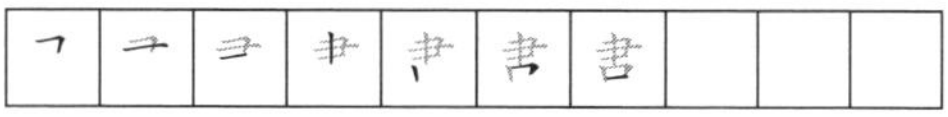

dexterity 聿(312a) + **mouth** 口(5) = **rude** 肀

Notice how the bottom part of "dexterity" has been truncated.

He displayed great **dexterity** with his **mouth** to make faces — many of which were **rude**! / *[No pronunciation needed]*

764b 唐 **táng** Tang

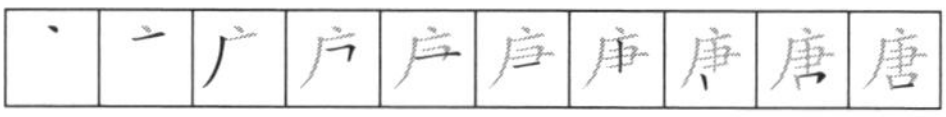

shelter 广(170) + **rude** 肀(764a) = **Tang** 唐

This is "Tang" as in the name of the Tang dynasty.

They had to build a **shelter** to hide the **rude** statues from sensitive eyes, particularly those from the **Tang** dynasty. / *[No pronunciation needed]*

---

764 糖 **táng** sugar **Radical** 米 **16 strokes**

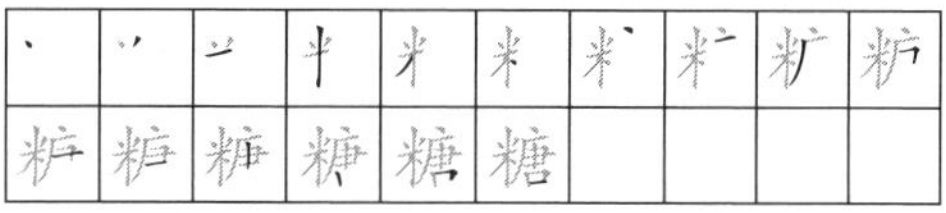

rice 米(334) + **Tang** 唐(764b) = **sugar** 糖

[糖果(187) **tángguǒ** *candy, sweets*]
[糖衣(437) **tángyī** *sugar-coating, sugar-coated*]
[一块糖(1, 402) **yí kuài táng** *a lump of sugar*]

Rice from the **Tang** period was as sweet as **sugar**. / *But only the **fairy** can conjure up **Tang** rice nowadays.*

765a hesitate

| ㇀ | ㄙ | ㄙ | 亠 | 夂 | 夅 | 夋 | | | |

cocoon ㄙ(34a) + eight 八(20) +
pursue 夂(506a) = hesitate 夋

The butterfly emerges from the **cocoon** and the first thing it sees is an **octopus**, which it **pursue**s, thinking the octopus is its mother — but when it gets closer it **hesitate**s. (Would its mum have *quite* so many legs?) / *[No pronunciation needed]*

765 suān
sour

Radical 酉
14 strokes

| 一 | 丆 | 丏 | 酉 | 西 | 酉 | 酉 | 酉 | 酉 | 酉 |
| 酉 | 酸 | 酸 | 酸 | | | | | | |

whisky bottle 酉(102a) + hesitate 夋(765a)
= sour 酸

[酸牛奶(384, 533) **suānniúnǎi** *yogurt; sour milk*]

The alcoholic picked up the **whisky bottle** but **hesitate**d — the last drink had tasted very **sour**. / *The ghostly giant (from Alcoholics Anonymous) had tampered with his liquor by steeping his sandals in it!*

766a wěi
entrust

| ㇐ | 二 | 千 | 禾 | 禾 | 委 | 委 | 委 | | |

grain 禾(126a) + women 女(15) =
entrust 委

The first bag of **grain** from the harvest was carried proudly on her head by the **woman** who had been **entrust**ed to present it to the king. / *[No pronunciation needed]*

766 ǎi
short

Radical 矢
13 strokes

| ノ | ㇡ | 上 | 手 | 矢 | 矢 | 矢 | 矫 | 矫 | 矮 |
| 矮 | 矮 | 矮 | | | | | | | |

arrow 矢(490a) + entrust 委(766a) =
short 矮

[矮子(17) **ǎizi** *dwarf; short person*]

The apprentice Cupid takes the **arrow**s he has been **entrust**ed with. For his first solo mission he is only allowed to bewitch **short** people! / *Teddy skips about marking likely targets with iodine to identify them.*

Test yourself: 页(477) 头(246) 喂(666) 间(345) 阴(97) 拉(179) 原(536)
全(416) 课(189) 酒(102) 还(199) 治(483) 该(497) 屋(473)

Chapter 39

Only two more chapters to go!

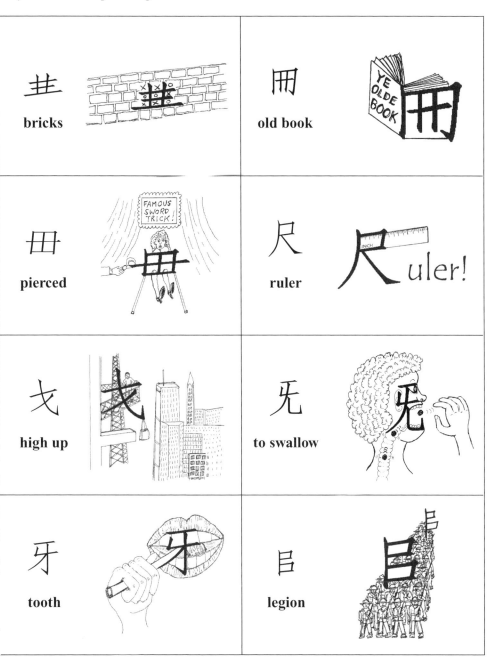

丑 bricks

冊 old book

毌 pierced

尺 ruler

戈 high up

旡 to swallow

牙 tooth

㠯 legion

767a cōng
[chimney]

| ′ | ⺁ | ⺁ | 匇 | 匇 | 肉 | 囱 | | |

> **a drop** 丶 (22a) + **enclosed** 囗 (24a) + **pursue** 夂 (506a) = **chimney** 囱

In some typefaces "pursue" gets changed to a leaned-over version of "criminal".

At the zoo, the mother monkey feels **a drop** of rain so **pursue**s the baby monkey round the **enclosure** — but the baby monkey climbs up the **chimney** out of reach. / *[No pronunciation needed]*

---

767 窗 chuāng
window

Radical 穴
12 strokes

| 丶 | ⼍ | 宀 | 宀 | 穴 | 宋 | 窏 | 窏 | 窗 | 窗 |
| 窗 | 窗 | | | | | | | | |

> **hole** 穴 (616a) + **chimney** 囱 (767a) = **window** 窗

窗户 (269) **chuānghù** *window*

Imagine making a **hole** in the **chimney** above your fireplace and installing a small **window** (so that you can watch the smoke going up it — a nice talking point for your visitors). / *[DIY pronunciation]*

768a
"bricks"

| 一 | 二 | ⺀ | 卝 | 圭 | | | | |

768b
to block up

| 丶 | ⼍ | 宀 | 宀 | 宀 | 宔 | 审 | 窜 | 寒 | 寒 |

> **house** 宀 (91a) + **bricks** 卝 (768a) + **eight** 八 (20) = **block up** 寒

The **octopus** built his **house** out of **bricks** and **block**ed up his chimney (to stop the wolf coming down — he'd read the story!) / *[No pronunciation needed]*

---

768 寒 hán
freezing

Radical 宀
12 strokes

| 丶 | ⼍ | 宀 | 宀 | 宀 | 宔 | 审 | 窜 | 寒 | 寒 |
| 寒 | 寒 | | | | | | | | |

> **block up** 寒 (768b) + **ice crystals** 冫 (246a) = **freezing** 寒

All the pipes in the house are **blocked up** with **ice crystals** in the **freezing** weather. / *The fairy pulls lengths of lagging from her handbag (to wrap round the pipes).*

769 賽 sài — compete

Radical 宀
14 strokes

賽

| ` | ` | 宀 | 宀 | 宁 | 宁 | 审 | 宲 | 実 | 実 |
| 寒 | 寒 | 賽 | 賽 | | | | | | |

block up 実 (768b) + **sea shell** 贝 (477a) = **compete** 賽

比賽 (228) **bǐsài** *competition*
[賽跑 (639) **sàipǎo** *a (running) race*]

They had to **block up** a big trench on the beach with **sea shell**s so that they could **compete** in the sand-yacht races. / *The dwarf sounded the siren to start each race.*

770a 冊 old book

| ` | 冂 | 冃 | 冊 | 冊 | | | | | |

770b 扁 biǎn; piān — flat

| ` | ` | ⼾ | 户 | 户 | 启 | 启 | 扁 | 扁 | |

door 户 (269) + **old book** 冊 (770a) = **flat** 扁

They propped the **door** open with an **old book**. But it slammed in the wind and knocked the book **flat**. / *[No pronunciation needed]*

770 遍 biàn — everywhere

Radical 辶
12 strokes

| ` | ` | ⼾ | 户 | 户 | 启 | 启 | 扁 | 扁 | 扁 |
| 谝 | 遍 | | | | | | | | |

road 辶 (26a) + **flat** 扁 (770b) = **everywhere** 遍

This also means "times" as in "I've been there three times."

[三遍 (3) **sānbiàn** *three times*]

In Holland the **road**s are all **flat** — **everywhere**, there are no hills at all. / *Two dwarves sit on a bench bemoaning this (they can't get a good view anywhere).*

771 篇 piān — piece of paper

Radical ⺮
15 strokes

| ⼃ | ⼂ | ⺯ | 竻 | 竻 | 竹 | 竻 | 笁 | 笁 | 笁 |
| 笁 | 笁 | 篇 | 篇 | 篇 | | | | | |

bamboo ⺮ (321a) + **flat** 扁 (770b) = **piece of paper** 篇

Imagine pounding slivers of green **bamboo flat** and joining them together to make a primitive **piece of paper**. / *The two giants each make you something to write with — one makes a pen and the other a pencil so you can try them out.*

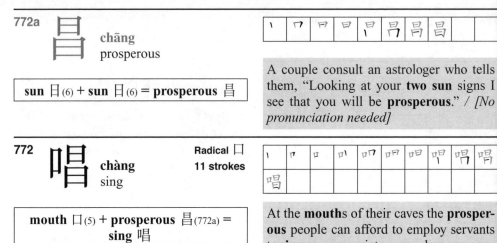

772a 昌 chāng
prosperous

sun 日(6) + sun 日(6) = **prosperous** 昌

A couple consult an astrologer who tells them, "Looking at your **two sun** signs I see that you will be **prosperous**." / [No pronunciation needed]

772 唱 chàng
sing
Radical 口
11 strokes

mouth 口(5) + prosperous 昌(772a) = **sing** 唱

[合唱(347) **héchàng** *chorus*]

At the **mouth**s of their caves the **prosperous** people can afford to employ servants to **sing** an appropriate song when someone approaches (instead of having doorbells). / [DIY pronunciation]

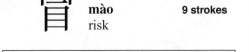

Test yourself: 忙(568) 千(89) 前(90) 系(607) 初(439) 后(150) 思(165)
求(524) 客(509) 那(98) 数(469) 发(146) 躺(542) 姑(192)

773a 冂 hood

outer limits 冂(160a) + two 二(2) = **hood**

When flying his **biplane** in the **outer limits** the pilot is so cold he has to put his coat **hood** up (over his flying helmet). / [No pronunciation needed]

When it is part of a composite character, this is easily mistaken for "sun" (日, Character 6) unless you look closely.

773 冒 mào
risk
Radical 日
9 strokes

hood 冂(773a) + eye 目(93) = **risk** 冒

Another major meaning is "emit" or "give off".

感冒(556) **gǎnmào** *catch a cold*

The thief is so well-known that even with his **hood** pulled down over his **eye**s he runs the **risk** of people recognizing him. / *The dwarf security guard spots him anyway, as he recognizes the thief's mouth.*

774 帽 **mào** — hat

Radical 巾
12 strokes

towel 巾 (427a) + risk 冒 (773) = hat 帽

帽子 (17) **màozi** *hat, cap*

(At the boxing match) One trainer threw a **towel** into the ring, as there was a **risk** his boxer could get badly injured — the other trainer threw his **hat** in the air triumphantly. / *Unfortunately the hat hit the **dwarf** referee in the **mouth** (which started another fight).*

775a 辰 **chén** — heavenly body

cliff 厂 (149) + one 一 (1) + a skirt 𧘇 (665a) = heavenly body 辰

The **unicorn**, standing on the **cliff**, sees a **skirt** round one of the stars. "It's a planet with rings, or some other **heavenly body**." / *[No pronunciation needed]*

775 晨 **chén** — morning

Radical 日
11 strokes

sun 日 (6) + heavenly body 辰 (775a) = morning 晨

早晨 (633) **zǎochén** *(early) morning*

When the **sun** rises and the other **heavenly bodies** dim, it is **morning**. / *[DIY pronunciation]*

776a 毌 — pierced

Writing this one often catches people out! It is derived from "mother" (Character 127) and has the same "sloping" appearance. Contrast the stroke order with, for example, the stroke order for "field" (156a). The stroke-count for this fragment is 4, not 5!

776b 贯 **guàn** — pierce

貫

pierced 毌 (776a) + sea shell 贝 (477a) = pierce 贯

Finding a **pierced sea shell** on the beach, she thinks, "I could **pierce** lots of shells and string them together to make necklaces!" / *[No pronunciation needed]*

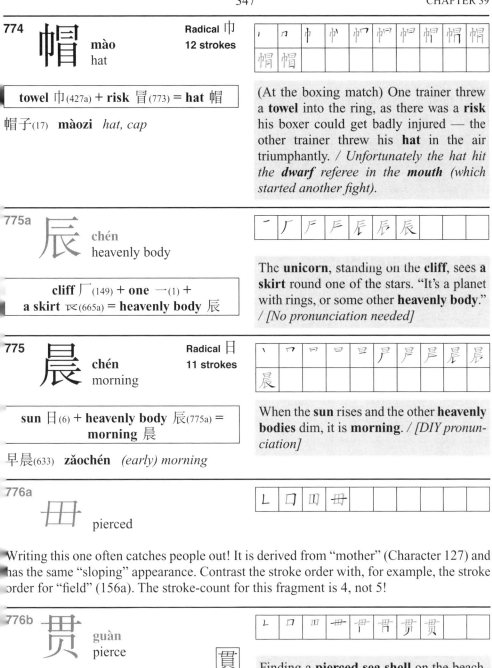

776  **guàn**
habitual

Radical 忄
11 strokes

heart 忄 (339a) + pierce 贯 (776b) =
habitual 惯

习惯 (735) **xíguàn** *habit; be used to*

Cupid flies around the neighborhood **piercing** the **hearts** of the **habitual** criminals (in the hope that this will reform them). / *The ghostly dwarf, who protects the neighborhood, sits on a gantry, directing who to shoot at.*

777a **chǐ**
ruler

This time the ruler is not a monarch, but a ruler for measuring things. A "meter", the unit of length, is 公尺 (**gōngchǐ**) although a more colloquial character for meter is 米 (**mǐ**, Character 334).

777 **chí**
late

Radical 辶
7 strokes

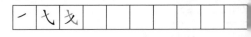

road 辶 (26a) + ruler 尺 (777a) = **late** 迟

迟到 (74) **chídào** *be late (for meeting)*

Some small boys are playing with a **ruler** on the **road** (measuring out a hopscotch pitch) — and they're going to be **late** for school. / *The fairy chases them off, and wipes the chalk marks off the road with a chapati.*

778a
high up

Keep this distinct in your mind from 七 ("pile of earth", 455a) and from 戈 ("dagger", 32a).

778b **yáo**
Chieftain Yao

high up 尧 (778a) + pedestal 兀 (301a) =
Chieftain Yao 尧

Yao was a legendary emperor who lived a little over 4000 years ago.

High up on a **pedestal** stands a statue of the legendary **Chieftain Yao** (who was in fact so legendary that he had his own Chinese character!) / *[No pronunciation needed]*

778 烧 **shāo**
burn

燒

Radical 火
10 strokes

| 丶 | ⺀ | ⺌ | 火 | 火 | 灼 | 烧 | 烧 | 烧 | 烧 |

fire 火(181) + Chieftain Yao 尧(778b) =
burn 烧

发烧(146) **fā shāo** *run a fever*

The villagers lit a **fire** beside **Chieftain Yao**'s statue, but it got out of hand and started to **burn** the statue and its surroundings. / *Luckily the **giant** had been taking a **shower**, and directed the spray at the fire to put it out.*

779a 旡 to swallow

| 一 | 二 | 尹 | 旡 |

Compare this with "tooth" (780a below). The distinguishing feature is that "to swallow" has a hook.

779b 既 **jì**
since

| 7 | ⺕ | ⺕ | 𠃌 | 艮 | 𠂤 | 旡 | 旣 | 既 |

stubborn 艮(281a) + swallow 旡(779a) =
since 既

The elderly man **stubborn**ly refused to **swallow** the pills, saying, "**Since** I've never swallowed a pill, I'm not going to start now." / *[No pronunciation needed]*

One of the strokes of "stubborn" is missing here (see 281a). This is the form which "stubborn" takes whenever there is something else to its right in a composite character.

---

779 概 **gài**
summary

Radical 木
13 strokes

| 一 | 十 | 才 | 木 | 机 | 杛 | 杚 | 柷 | 根 | 柮 |
| 概 | 概 | 概 | | | | | | | |

tree 木(10a) + since 既(779b) =
summary 概

大概(47) **dàgài** *probably; more or less*

"The **tree** has been there **since** ancient times, and must be saved," the **summary** stated (although there was a huge report with all the details). / *The **dwarf** will be in charge of attaching **guy** ropes to support the tree.*

780a 牙 **yá**
tooth

| 一 | 二 | 于 | 牙 |

Compare this with "swallow" (779a above).

780

呀   yā (ya)   Radical 口
       oh!   7 strokes

丶	丆	口	口⁻	吖	呀	呀		

mouth 口(5) + **tooth** 牙(780a) = **oh!** 呀

At the end of a phrase, this character can take a neutral tone (see Character 143 for another example of this happening).

The dentist looks into the **mouth**, sees a colored **tooth** and cries, "Oh!" / *The **giant** had tied colored **yarn** round the tooth when he was trying to pull it out.*

781

穿   chuān   Radical 穴
       penetrate   9 strokes

丶	宀	宀	宀	穴	空	空	穿	穿

hole 穴(616a) + **tooth** 牙(780a) = **penetrate** 穿

There was a **hole** in the **tooth** so the dentist had to **penetrate** it with his drill. / *The **ghostly giant** had protected his friend's root **channel** until he got to the dentist. (We know you normally say "root canal", but work with us here!)*

Test yourself: 然(266)   实(250)   回(202)   示(430)   老(264)   谁(501)   抬(484)

孩(498)   负(517)   色(417)   汤(531)   哪(99)   次(361)   园(302)

782a

異   different

丶	冂	冃	用	田	甲	罒	甼	甼	異
異									

field 田(156a) + **collectively** 共(625) = **different** 異

Imagine each member of your family owning a **field**, and farming them **collectively**, even though each person has a **different** crop. / *[No pronunciation needed]*

782b

戈   wound

一	十	士	戈	戈	戈			

earth 土(54a) + **dagger** 戈(32a) = **wound** 戈

Another "fused" character — "earth" and "dagger" share a stroke. Compare this with "I" (Character 32) all the way back in Chapter 3.

(In a self-defense class) "I want everyone to plunge their **daggers** into the **earth** before we start; I don't want anyone getting **wound**ed like in the last session." / *[No pronunciation needed]*

782 戴 dài to wear

Radical 戈
17 strokes

| 一 | 十 | 土 | 圭 | 吉 | 吉 | 吉 | 吉 | 吉 |
| 吉 | 吉 | 吉 | 吉 | 戴 | 戴 | 戴 | | |

different 異(782a) + **wound** 戈(782b) = **wear** 戴

[穿戴(781) **chuāndài** *apparel, dress*]

In the hospital the patients with **different** types of **wound** have to **wear** different colored gowns (a red gown for arm wounds, a green gown for leg wounds, etc.) / *The dwarf grumbles as he has to dye all the gowns.*

783a 乘 chéng ride

| 一 | 二 | 千 | 千 | 千 | 千 | 乖 | 乖 | 乘 | 乘 |

grain 禾(126a) + **north** 北(317) = **ride** 乘

An unusual combination, where "north" is fitted around "grain" rather than just being placed above, below, or to the side of it.

This is to ride in a vehicle (remember that in Character 740 we had another sort of "ride", which involved sitting astride something, like a horse or a bicycle).

The **north** wind blows through the vast fields of **grain** — you gaze at this vista as you **ride** on the train through the Canadian prairies. / *[No pronunciation needed]*

783 剩 shèng residue

Radical 刂
12 strokes

| 一 | 二 | 千 | 千 | 千 | 千 | 乖 | 乖 | 乘 | 乘 |
| 乘 | 剩 | | | | | | | | |

ride 乘(783a) + **knife** 刂(74a) = **residue** 剩

Imagine **riding** on a train, using a **knife** to make sandwiches for your lunch — from the **residue** of last night's supper. / *[DIY pronunciation]*

784a 𠂤 legion

| 丨 | 𠂤 | 𠂤 | 𠂤 | 𠂤 | | | | |

784b 官 guān an official

| 丶 | 宀 | 宀 | 宁 | 宁 | 官 | 官 | 官 | 官 |

house 宀(91a) + **legion** 𠂤(784a) = **an official** 官

The **house** to be allocated to each member of the **legion** is decided by the town **official**. / *[No pronunciation needed]*

784   馆   guǎn   public building

Radical 饣
11 strokes

館

| ノ | ⺈ | 饣 | 饣 | 饣 | 饣 | 饣 | 饣 | 饣 | 馆 |
| 馆 | | | | | | | | | |

food 饣 (288a) + an official 官 (784b) =
public building 馆

图书馆 (691, 176)   **túshūguǎn**   *library*

(After an earthquake) **Food** is handed out by an **official** at the **public building**. / *The **ghostly teddy** dressed up as **Gandhi** is supposed to guard the food but larks about instead.*

Test yourself: 开 (85)   年 (168)   去 (86)   结 (538)   才 (518)   堂 (543)   从 (103)

医 (491)   球 (525)   江 (148)   病 (510)   讨 (201)   最 (421)   长 (172)

We have given you stories all the way through this book rather than stopping halfway through and saying "the rest is up to you". However, for other characters beyond those included in this book, you will have to make up your own stories. How do you do this? Let's expand on what we said at the end of Chapter 7.

Suppose you are trying to make a story for "hand" + "sigh" = "throw", for example. As a starting point, take the parts of the character (in this case, "hand" and "sigh") and see what your mind comes up with. The best bet is often to use the first thing that comes into your head as the basis for the story, because that is what you will naturally think of again, the next time you see "hand" plus "sigh".

Next, link the target ("throw") to "hand" and "sigh", with a story in which these three parts *interact* — they should not just be "standing around" in the story.

Make a list of soundwords for the required syllable and pick one which gives the most memorable story (you can easily list all the ones we used in this book by looking up the characters with that pronunciation in the pronunciation index). With some syllables you will find there are lots of soundwords to choose from, but for others you have very little choice, and you just have to do the best you can. Again, make the second part of the story interact with the first part if you can.

The best stories are those that are vivid — try to bring in details which catch your interest, that are quirky and fun. Make the story unusual, by making it out of the ordinary, or rude: at the very least, exaggerate things. A good thing to do at times is to bring in your other senses (imagine sounds or smells). Finally, try to personalize your story: include people, places and things that have particular significance for you personally. (This is one aspect we couldn't include in our stories — for obvious reasons — the best we could do was sometimes to suggest that you yourself are in the story). You don't have to do all of these things for every story; these are just ways of "spicing up" a story to make it more memorable. The only rule is, if it works (in that you remember the character) then it's fine!

Creating memorable stories is not easy (although you will improve with practice), but time spent thinking up a really memorable story will be repaid many times over by all the rote-learning you *don't* have to do!

Chapter 40

This is the last page of character pictures in this book. We hope you've found them useful (and that you had as much fun with them as we did!) — but, as we have said before, if a different character picture works better for you, then use that instead. Sometimes, if you look at a basic building block for a few moments, often letting your mind wander a bit, the shape will suddenly suggest something which is familiar to you in your own life, which can form the basis for a "personal" character picture.

If you decide to go on and learn more characters, then it would be a good idea to practice making up character pictures for yourself. Don't worry if they aren't "perfect" in some way — the very fact that you have dreamed them up yourself will mean that they are memorable to *you* — which is all you need.

So this is it — the final chapter!

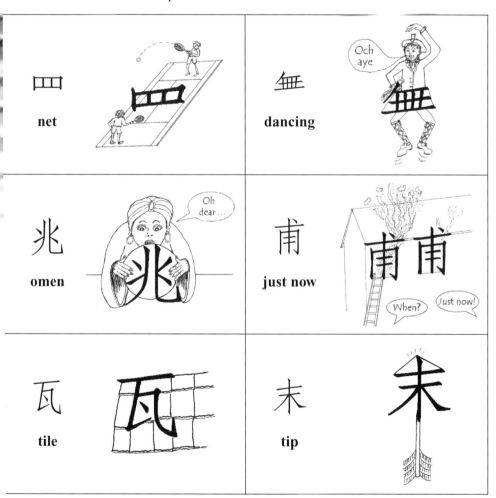

net

dancing

omen

just now

tile

tip

785a 罒
net

| 丶 | 冖 | 罒 | 罒 | 罒 | | | | | |

785b 曼
màn
graceful

| 丶 | 冖 | 冖 | 日 | 戶 | 骨 | 骨 | 骨 | 冒 | 曼 |
| 曼 | | | | | | | | | |

sun 日 (6) + **net** 罒(785a) +
right hand 又(52) = **graceful** 曼

(The princess comes to award national fisherman's prizes to the fishermen in the village) They drape a **net** over poles to shield her from the **sun** while she **shakes hands** with the winners; they are all captivated by how **graceful** she is. / *[No pronunciation needed]*

785 慢
màn
slow

Radical 忄
14 strokes

| 丶 | 丶 | 忄 | 忄 | 忄 | 忄 | 忄 | 忄 | 悍 | 悍 |
| 愠 | 愠 | 愠 | 慢 | | | | | | |

heart 忄 (339a) + **graceful** 曼(785b) =
slow 慢

[慢车(83) **mànchē** *slow train*]
[慢慢 **mànmàn** *gradually, slowly*]

He has set his **heart** on the **graceful** woman — but he's just too **slow** to attract her attention. / *The dwarf (running a dating agency) suggests that he learns to play a mandolin to serenade her.*

786a 罢
bà
stop

罷

| 丶 | 冖 | 冖 | 罒 | 罒 | 罒 | 罘 | 罘 | 罘 | 罢 |

net 罒(785a) + **go** 去(86) = **stop** 罢

You watch the fishermen pick up their **nets** to **go** fishing — but you see one of the nets has snagged on a rock and shout, "**Stop!**" / *[No pronunciation needed]*

786 摆
bǎi
arrange

Radical 扌
13 strokes

擺

| 一 | 扌 | 扌 | 扌 | 扌 | 扌 | 扌 | 扌 | 扌 | 扌 |
| 摆 | 摆 | 摆 | | | | | | | |

hand 扌 (152a) + **stop** 罢(786a) =
arrange 摆

[摆设儿(553, 21) **bǎisher** *ornaments*]

The child reaches out her **hand** to the flowers and her mother calls out, "**Stop** right there, I've spent hours **arranging** those!" / *But just then Teddy comes by on his bike and crashes into them anyway.*

787a 舛 opposing

| ノ | ク | タ | タ− | タヒ | 舛 | | | |

evening 夕 (69a) + surpass 中 (168a) = opposing 舛

The **evening**'s debate **surpass**ed everyone's expectations: the highlight was the speech given by the **opposing** team's captain. / *[No pronunciation needed]*

787b 無 dancing

| ノ | ⌐ | ⌐⌐ | 仁 | 午 | 缶 | 缶 | 無 | |

787 舞 wǔ dance

Radical ノ
14 strokes

| ノ | ⌐ | ⌐⌐ | 仁 | 午 | 缶 | 缶 | 無 | 無 | 無 |
| 舞 | 舞 | 舞 | 舞 | | | | | | |

dancing 無 (787b) + opposing 舛 (787a) = dance 舞

At the **dancing** competition the **opposing** teams compete to produce the best **dance**. / *Teddy retires **wounded** in the first round (when someone stands on his paw with a stiletto heel).*

788a 兆 zhào omen

| ノ | ノ | ノノ | 兆 | 兆 | 兆 | | | |

Compare this with "north" (Character 317).

788 跳 tiào jump

Radical 足
13 strokes

| ⌐ | ⌐ | 口 | ⌐ | ⌐ | ⌐ | 足 | 趴 | 趴 | 趴 |
| 趴 | 跳 | 跳 | | | | | | | |

foot 足 (280) + omen 兆 (788a) = jump 跳

兆舞 (787) **tiàowǔ** *to dance*
跳高 (481) **tiào gāo** *high jump*]

You find a bird's **foot** in the road — this is an **omen** and you know that what you have to do is **jump** over it. / *Two dwarf bureaucrats from the **town** hall arrive to make sure the omen sighting is documented in duplicate.*

789a 甫 fǔ just now

| ⌐ | 丆 | 厈 | 冋 | 冐 | 甫 | 甫 | | |

Make up a story involving "ten", "moon" and "drop" if you wish.

789 辅 fǔ — assist

Radical 车
11 strokes

一	㇅	二	车	车	轩	轩	轩	辅	辅
辅									

car 车(83) + **just now 甫**(789a) = **assist 辅**

辅导(277) **fǔdǎo** *tutor; tutorial*

(Talking to the police after your car has been stolen) "The **car** was here **just now**, officer, but I don't know where it's gone. I'd like to be able to **assist** you, really I would." / *But Teddy has been fooling around (and has hidden the car in your garage, but then gives himself away by hitting the horn).*

790a 甫 — spread over

一	厂	冂	冂	甶	甫	甫	車	専	専

just now 甫(789a) + **inch 寸**(104a) = **spread over 専**

Note that the bottom part of "just now" is truncated somewhat here.

"There's a puddle of green liquid on the kitchen floor — and it's an **inch** bigger than it was **just now**! If we don't do something it will **spread over** the whole floor." / *[No pronunciation needed]*

790 傅 fù — teacher

Radical 亻
12 strokes

丿	亻	仁	仁	佢	佢	佢	俌	傅	傅
傅	傅								

person 亻(13a) + **spread over 専**(790a) = **teacher 傅**

师傅(428) **shīfù** *master worker*

Harry spread the icing carefully **over** the cake, to impress his cookery **teacher**. / *The dwarf teacher thinks teaching food classes is beneath him (and would much rather be teaching car maintenance).*

791a 并 bìng — actually

丶	丷	丷	兰	羊	并			

horns 丷(65a) + **open 开**(85) = **actually 并**

This is easy to mistake for "well" (Character 357a).

The character has several other meanings including "combine" or "side by side".

The old bull is trying to **open** the gate by hooking his **horns** under it to pull it open; the (smart-ass) young bull comes across and says, "**Actually**, all you need to do is push it." / *[No pronunciation needed]*

791b 瓦 wǎ; wà tile

| 一 | 厂 | 瓦 | 瓦 | | | | |

This means a (roof) tile or, more generally, earthenware.

791 瓶 píng bottle

Radical 瓦
10 strokes

| ` | ` | 丷 | 兰 | 羊 | 并 | 并 | 瓶 | 瓶 | 瓶 |

actually 并(791a) + **tile** 瓦(791b) = **bottle** 瓶

[瓶子(17) **píngzi** *bottle*]
[花瓶(392) **huāpíng** *vase*]

(The archaeologist is pontificating during a lecture) "This may look like a roof **tile**, but **actually** it's a fragment from a huge earthenware **bottle**." / *In the audience, the fairy whispers to her neighbor, "Actually, it's a bit of old pot I painted pink."*

792a 夕又 "Druid"

| ` | 勹 | 夕 | 夕 | 夕' | 夕又 | | |

moon 夕(266a) + **right hand** 又(52) = **Druid** 夕又

Notice the truncation of "right hand".

(At Stonehenge) At the full **moon** the cloaked figures gather, **shake hands**, and wait for the **Druid** to appear and conduct the ceremony. / *[No pronunciation needed]*

792b 祭 jì worship

| ` | 勹 | 夕 | 夕 | 夕' | 夕又 | 怒 | 怒 | 祭 | 祭 |
| 祭 | | | | | | | | | |

Druid 夕又(792a) + **sign** 示(430) = **worship** 祭

(At Stonehenge again) The **Druid** waits for a **sign** (to appear in the sky) before the **worship** can begin. / *[No pronunciation needed]*

792c 察 chá inspect

| ` | ` | 宀 | 宀 | 宀 | 宀 | 宀 | 宀 | 突 | 宓 |
| 宓 | 窣 | 察 | 察 | | | | | | |

house 宀(91a) + **worship** 祭(792b) = **inspect** 察

If you want to set up your **house** as a place of **worship**, you have to get it **inspect**ed. / *[No pronunciation needed]*

792 擦 cā
wipe

Radical 扌
17 strokes

hand 扌(152a) + inspect 察(792c) =
wipe 擦

The doctor asks for help: "Give me a **hand** to **inspect** this patient — we'll have to give him a good **wipe** down first though." / *He pulls back the curtain to reveal ... the giant standing there starkers!*

You will perhaps have noticed that there are a lot of gray characters and fragments in this final chapter, and most of these are only used once. That is why they are here: if they were useful for many common characters they would have been introduced earlier in the book. However, that is not to say that they won't crop up again (beyond HSK Level A) so don't be too dismissive of them!

793a 末 mò
tip

Here the first stroke is longer than the second; compare this with "not yet" (64a).
The character means an extremity, the tip or end of something.

---

793 袜 wà
socks

Radical 衤
10 strokes

襪

clothes 衤(439a) + tip 末(793a) = socks 袜

袜子(17) **wàzi** *sock, stocking*

The **clothes** are hung up to dry on the branches of the tree, and fitted over the **tips** of the branches are the **socks**. / *The dwarf has been left to look after the baby who is crying "Waaah!" (the baby is cold: it has no clothes as they are all being washed).*

Test yourself: 洗(139) 杂(511) 忽(526) 结(538) 校(383) 位(178) 远(303)
所(270) 故(191) 常(544) 想(164) 票(431) 记(272) 团(519)

794a 丝 "teeny weeny"

smallest 幺(607a) + smallest 幺(607a) =
teeny weeny 丝

The **smallest** of the **smallest** is **teeny weeny**! / *[No pronunciation needed]*

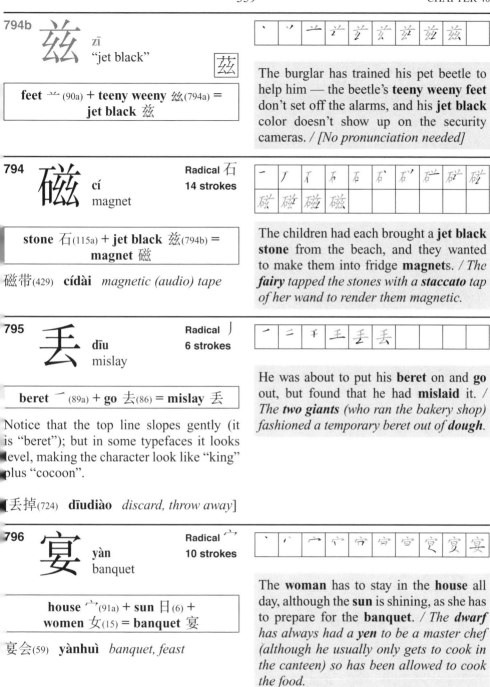

794b

兹 zī

"jet black"

兹

feet ⵗ (90a) + teeny weeny 丝 (794a) = jet black 兹

The burglar has trained his pet beetle to help him — the beetle's **teeny weeny feet** don't set off the alarms, and his **jet black** color doesn't show up on the security cameras. / *[No pronunciation needed]*

794

磁 cí

magnet

Radical 石
14 strokes

stone 石 (115a) + jet black 兹 (794b) = magnet 磁

磁带 (429) **cídài** *magnetic (audio) tape*

The children had each brought a **jet black stone** from the beach, and they wanted to make them into fridge **magnets**. / *The fairy tapped the stones with a staccato tap of her wand to render them magnetic.*

795

丢 diū

mislay

Radical 丿
6 strokes

beret ⁻ (89a) + go 去 (86) = mislay 丢

Notice that the top line slopes gently (it is "beret"); but in some typefaces it looks level, making the character look like "king" plus "cocoon".

[丢掉 (724) **diūdiào** *discard, throw away*]

He was about to put his **beret** on and **go** out, but found that he had **mislaid** it. / *The two giants (who ran the bakery shop) fashioned a temporary beret out of dough.*

796

宴 yàn

banquet

Radical ⁸⁻
10 strokes

house 宀 (91a) + sun 日 (6) + women 女 (15) = banquet 宴

宴会 (59) **yànhuì** *banquet, feast*

The **woman** has to stay in the **house** all day, although the **sun** is shining, as she has to prepare for the **banquet**. / *The dwarf has always had a yen to be a master chef (although he usually only gets to cook in the canteen) so has been allowed to cook the food.*

And so we've arrived at the last page! We've left these four rather splendid characters until last. In each case note the odd strokes. We haven't even attempted to come up with stories for them. You might enjoy having a go at writing equations according to how you feel these characters break up into parts, and devising stories to go with them. After that, no other Chinese character should pose any problems for you. (Alternatively, you can chicken out, like us, and try remembering them by rote).

797 夜　yè　night　　Radical 亠　8 strokes

[夜里(157)　**yèli**　*at night*]
[半夜(131)　**bànyè**　*midnight*]

798 假　jià (jiǎ)　vacation　　Radical 亻　11 strokes

放假(294)　**fàngjià**　*to be on holiday*
请假(336)　**qǐng jià**　*to ask for leave*
寒假(768)　**hánjià**　*winter vacation*

799 墙　qiáng　wall　　Radical 土　14 strokes　牆

[爬墙(371)　**páqiáng**　*to climb a wall*]

800 赢　yíng　win　　Radical 亠　17 strokes　贏

[赢利(132)　**yínglì**　*profit, gain*]

The final progress diagram: this completes HSK Level A. If you didn't think you'd ever get to the end of the book — well, neither did we when we were writing it! We reckon we all deserve a break to celebrate.

再见!

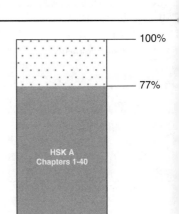

100%

77%

HSK A
Chapters 1-40

APPENDIX: Soundwords

Soundwords are the words we use in the stories to indicate the pronunciation of a character. The first *syllable* of the English soundword has a similar sound to the pronunciation of the Chinese character. So for the pronunciation **ma** we could use the soundwords market or marbles because **ma** is pronounced somewhat like the "mar" sound at the start of these words. The tables in this appendix give you all the pronunciations of Chinese characters you need for HSK Level A, along with an example of a soundword that could be used for each of them. (For a full explanation of how we use soundwords, along with archetypes to represent tones, see the User Guide). Again we must stress that the purpose of the soundwords is to help you remember the pronunciations of each of the 800 characters; it is not to mimic exactly the sounds of Chinese.

Here is a *very* brief description of the sounds of Chinese — as mentioned in the User Guide, you really need to hear Chinese spoken to appreciate fully the correct sounds.

Consonants

b, p, m, f, d, t, n, l, s, r, g, k, h are pronounced similarly to how they are in English.
(Although b and d are more like "soft" versions of p and t respectively).
z is pronounced like the "ds" in adds and **c** like the "ts" in tsunami.
Because English does not use these sounds at the beginning of words, we had to cheat with the soundwords here (it was that or declare them "DIY" which we have tried to avoid whenever possible). If you look at Table 1 you'll see that for "z" we simply use soundwords beginning with "z", and for "c" we use soundwords beginning with "st" (not "ts").
zh, ch, sh are pronounced like the "j" in jar, the "ch" in chart, and the "sh" in shark respectively.
j, q, x are pronounced like the "j" in jeep, the "ch" in cheat, and the "sh" in sheet respectively.
The difference between zh & j, ch & q and sh & x is that for zh, ch and sh the tongue is curled back against the roof of the mouth to say the sound, and for j, q and x the tip of the tongue is pressed against the lower teeth. For soundwords we just use English words beginning with j, ch and sh regardless. Happily this does not cause any confusion because, as you will see in the tables, if zh has an entry in a particular vowel column then j does not and vice versa. The same applies to the other two pairs (ch & q and sh & x).

Vowels

a, o, e, u are pronounced as indicated by the soundwords in the relevant columns in Table 1.
(But when "e" has neutral tone, it is pronounced closer to the "u" in huh).
i can be pronounced in two ways:
After most consonants it is pronounced like the "i" in Fiji. But after some consonants (z, c, s, zh, ch, sh, r; see the final column in Table 1) it is as if the "i" is hardly there at all. It seems to just modify the consonant sound slightly. The closest we could get to this sound is to use English soundwords where the first syllable is unstressed, so for **zhi** we use jacuzzi. (For this reason, in all other soundwords we have chosen, the stress is on the first syllable).
ü is pronounced like "ü" in German or the "u" in the French tu.
Say "oo", and then, keeping your lips in the same position, try and say "ee". Rather confusingly the two dots are only written above the u for **nü** and **lü** (to distinguish them from **nu** and **lu**), otherwise they are omitted (see the ü column of Table 1). "Pouring rain" is used in the stories to indicate ü pronunciations (see Character 15).
When vowels are on their own (with no consonant in front of them), the pinyin system sometimes inserts a "y" or a "w" before the vowel. So instead of "i", "u" and "ü" we write **yi**, **wu** and **yu** respectively (see the final row of the tables).
In the tables you will see that we have listed the consonants down the left-hand side and the vowels along the top. The table entries give the pinyin spelling and an example soundword for each combination of consonant and vowel we need. For some combinations there is no reasonable

soundword in English — these are the "DIY pronunciations" and they are indicated in the table by "DIY". Blanks indicate combinations not used in HSK Level A.

Remember that it is the *sound* of the soundword that is important, not its English spelling. So the soundwords herb, shirt and lurk all appear in the "e" column of Table 1 because they all have the same vowel *sound* even through their English spellings use three different vowels.

Table 1 shows the simplest Chinese syllables, which are just a consonant followed by a vowel.

Table 1: simple syllables

	a	o	e	u	ü	i	-i
b	**ba** bar	**bo** board		**bu** boot		**bi** bee	
p	**pa** park	**po** port				**pi** pea	
m	**ma** market		**me** mermaid	**mu** moon		**mi** meat	
f	**fa** farm			**fu** food			
d	**da** dart		**de** dervish	**du** doodle		**di** diesel	
t	**ta** tart		**te** turkey	**tu** toupe		**ti** tea	
n	**na** narcissus		**ne** nerd	**nu** noodles	**nü** noodles	**ni** needle	
l	**la** lava		**le** lurk	**lu** loop	**lü** loop	**li** leap	
z	**za** DIY		**ze** zircon	**zu** zoo			**zi** zapata
c	**ca** star						**ci** statistics
s			**se** surf	**su** soup			**si** sedate
zh			**zhe** jerk	**zhu** juke box			**zhi** jacuzzi
ch	**cha** chart		**che** church	**chu** chew			**chi** chapati
sh			**she** shirt	**shu** shoe			**shi** cheroot
r			**re** rrrr	**ru** ruby			**ri** relinquish
g			**ge** girder	**gu** goose			
k	**ka** carpet		**ke** curtain	**ku** coupon			
h	**ha** harp		**he** herb	**hu** hoop			
j					**ju** juke box	**ji** jeep	
q					**qu** chew	**qi** cheetah	
x					**xu** shoe	**xi** sheet	
-	**a** arm		**e** eh	**wu** wound	**yu** eulogy	**yi** easy	

Table 2 shows how the syllables which have two vowels are spelled and pronounced.

Table 3 shows how the endings "-n" or "-ng" can be added to some of the syllables in Tables 1 and 2. Note that it is still the first syllable of the soundword that indicates the pronunciation. Notice too that the English ending "nk" contains an "ng" sound, so the stories for the Chinese syllable **bang** might use either of the English soundwords bang or bank. For this reason, the soundwords we use for the syllables in Tables 1 and 2 never contain these "n" or "ng" sounds.

Table 2: two vowels

	ai	ei	ai	ou
b	**bai** bike	**bei** baby	**bao** bow	
p	**pai** pie		**pao** powder	
m	**mai** mitre	**mei** mail	**mao** mouse	
f		**fei** face		
d	**dai** dice	**dei** daisy	**dao** douse	**dou** dodo
t	**tai** tie		**tao** tower	**tou** toe
n	**nai** nightie	**nei** nail		
l	**lai** light	**lei** lake	**lao** loud	**lou** locust
z	**zai** xylophone		**zao** DIY	**zou** zodiac
c	**cai** sty		**cao** stout	
s	**sai** siren			**sou** soap
zh			**zhao** joust	**zhou** joke
ch			**chao** chowder	**chou** choker
sh			**shao** shower	**shou** show
r				**rou** rope
g	**gai** guy	**gei** gate	**gao** gout	**gou** goat
k	**kai** kite	**kei** cow	**kao**	**kou** coat
h	**hai** hive	**hei** halo	**hao** house	**hou** hose
-	**ai** island			

Table 3: -n and -ng endings

	an	en	in	un	ang	eng	ong	ing
b	**ban** band	**ben** bun			**bang** bang			**bing** bingo
p						**peng** puncture		**ping** pingpong
m	**man** mansion	**men** money	**min** mint		**mang** mango			**ming** mink
f	**fan** fan	**fen** funnel			**fang** fang	**feng** fungus		
d	**dan** dandelion				**dang** dangle	**deng** dungarees	**dong** donkey	**ding** dinghy
t	**tan** tannoy				**tang** tank	**teng** tongue	**tong** tongs	**ting** tingle
n	**nan** nanny		**nin** ninja			**neng** DIY	**nong** DIY	
l	**lan** lantern					**leng** lung		**ling** linger
z	**zan** Zanzibar	**zen** DIY			**zang** DIY	**zeng** DIY	**zong** DIY	
c	**can** stand					**ceng** stung	**cong** DIY	
s	**san** sand						**song** song	
zh	**zhan** janitor	**zhen** junta			**zhang** jangle	**zheng** jungle	**zhong** jonquil	
ch	**chan** channel	**chen** chunter			**chang** DIY	**cheng** chunk		
sh	**shan** shandy	**shen** shun			**shang** Shanghai	**sheng** DIY		
r	**ran** ransom	**ren** runway			**rang** rank		**rong** wrong	
g	**gan** gantry	**gen** gun			**gang** gang	**geng** gunk	**gong** gong	
k	**kan** candle				**kang** kangaroo		**kong** conga	
h	**han** hand	**hen** hunter			**hang** hangar		**hong** honk	
j			**jin** gin					**jing** jingle
q			**qin** chin					**qing** chink
x			**xin** shin					**xing** shingle
-	**an** ant		**yin** yin	**yun** DIY				**ying** DIY

The vowel "i" sometimes gets inserted between the consonant and another vowel. When this happens the "i" takes on a "y" sound and is called an on-glide. The syllables that arise this way are shown in Table 4. Unfortunately English has virtually no words that begin with the necessary sounds for these pronunciations. Instead of making them all "DIY" pronunciations we use soundwords in the stories that ignore the i on-glide but we introduce *two* of the appropriate archetype instead of one (as explained following the entry for Character 38). For example when there are two teddies in a story with the soundword lava then you know that the character is pronounced **lia**, not **la** (and with tone 3).

An oddity is that "ian" is pronounced like "yen", not "yan", and hence **bian** uses bench as a soundword (with a double archetype). But "iang" is pronounced "yang", and so **liang** uses language as a soundword (with a double archetype).

Just to confuse things, if there is no initial consonant, the "i" is written "y". Thus "ia" on its own is written "ya", and so on. For this reason, and because there *are* English words available for these sounds, we simply use soundwords beginning with "y" and there is no need for double archetypes.

Table 4: i on-glides (double archetype)

	ia	iao	ie	iou	ian	iang	iong
b		biao bow	bie bed		bian bench		
p		piao powder			pian pen		
m					mian menu		
d		diao douse		diu dodo	dian dent		
t		tiao tower			tian tennis		
n				niu nose	nian DIY	niang DIY	
l	lia lava	liao loud		liu locust	lian lend	liang language	
j	jia jar	jiao joust	jie jelly	jiu joke	jian generator	jiang jangle	
q		qiao chowder	qie chest	qiu choker	qian DIY	qiang DIY	
x	xia shark	xiao shower	xie shed	xiu show	xian DIY	xiang Shanghai	
-	ya yard	yao yowl	ye yeti	you yoga	yan yen	yang yankee	yong young

Using a device, such as having two archetypes, underlines the fact that the role of the soundwords is not to teach pronunciation, but to work as a memory system. Although we match the pronunciations approximately (close enough so that you remember the pinyin spelling for the character), we also deliberately use additional tricks and coding devices (such as having two archetypes, a ghostly archetype, or a pouring rain story). These devices help with the memory system but it does mean that the soundword on its own, taken in isolation and forgetting the device, is not an exact guide to the Chinese pronunciation.

The "u" on-glide is similar to the "i" on-glide except that the "u" takes on a "w" sound and is signalled in the stories by a ghostly archetype (as explained in the comment following Character 59).

If there is no initial consonant, the "u" is written "w". Thus "ua" on its own is written "wa", and so on. In this case we simply use soundwords beginning with "w" (and there is no need for the archetype to be ghostly).

Table 5: u on-glides (ghostly archetype)

	ua	uo	uai	uei	uan	uen	uang
d		duo dodo		dui daisy	duan dandelion	dun dunce	
t		tuo toe		tui tail	tuan tannoy		
n					nuan nanny		
l					luan lantern	lun London	
z		zuo zodiac		zui DIY			
c		cuo stove				cun stunt	
s		suo soap		sui sail	suan sand		
zh		zhuo joke				zhun DIY	zhuang jangle
ch				chui chain	chuan channel	chun DIY	chuang DIY
sh		shuo show		shui shave			shuang Shanghai
g	gua garden	guo goat		gui gate	guan gantry		guang gang
k			kuai kite			kun cunning	kuang kangaroo
h	hua harp	huo hose	huai hive	hui halo	huan hand		huang hangar
-	wa wah	wo woe	wai white	wei waiter	wan DIY	wen wonderful	wang wangle

Table 6 shows the syllables where "ü" acts as an on-glide. There are only a few such syllables, which are mostly treated as "DIY" pronunciations, and in these the two dots on the ü are not actually written (so that "jüe" is written "jue", etc.). If there is no consonant, the "ü" is written "yu", thus "üe" is written "yue".

Table 7 shows two syllables which are exceptions and don't fit into the general pattern.

Table 6: ü on-glides

	üa	üan
j	jue DIY	
q	que DIY	quan DIY
x	xue DIY	
-	yue DIY	yuan yuan

Table 7: exceptions

er	ng
earth	uncle

PRONUNCIATION INDEX

This index gives the serial numbers of all the 800 HSK Level A characters. Where a character has more than one (HSK Level A) pronunciation, it has a separate entry for each of those pronunciations.

Pinyin	Char	No.		Pinyin	Char	No.		Pinyin	Char	No.		Pinyin	Char	No.		Pinyin	Char	No.
ā	啊	143		bìng	病	510		chuān	穿	781			弟	323		fēi	飞	410
a	啊	143		bō	播	734		chuán	船	746			第	322			非	328
ǎi	矮	766		bù	不	9		chuāng	窗	767		diǎn	点	185			啡	329
ài	爱	365			步	378		chuáng	床	171			典	232		fēn	分	73
ān	安	91			布	558		chuī	吹	362		diàn	电	159		fēng	风	468
bā	八	20			部	316		chūn	春	692			店	186			丰	704
bǎ	把	369		cā	擦	792		cí	词	231		diào	调	541			封	709
bà	爸	370		cái	才	518			磁	794			掉	724		fū	夫	49
ba	吧	368		cǎi	彩	732		cì	次	361		dìng	定	406		fú	服	563
bái	白	22		cài	菜	733		cóng	从	103		dīu	丢	795			福	702
bǎi	百	40		cān	参	573		cūn	村	104		dōng	东	319		fǔ	府	653
	摆	786		cāo	操	631		cuò	错	743			冬	689			辅	789
bān	班	113		cǎo	草	635		dá	答	352		dǒng	懂	408		fù	父	367
	般	680		céng	层	471		dǎ	打	153		dòng	动	58			负	517
	搬	681		chá	茶	739		dà	大	47		dōu	都	262			附	652
bǎn	板	333			查	598		dài	大	47		dū	都	262			复	550
bàn	半	131		chà	差	204			代	456		dú	读	249			富	703
	办	123		chǎn	产	197			带	429		dù	度	425			傅	790
bāng	帮	705		cháng	长	172			戴	782		duǎn	短	730		gāi	该	497
bāo	包	636			常	544		dān	单	344		duàn	段	715		gǎi	改	359
bǎo	饱	637		chǎng	厂	149		dàn	但	117			锻	716		gài	概	779
bào	抱	638			场	530			蛋	748		duì	对	154		gān	干	124
	报	562		chàng	唱	772		dāng	当	267		dùn	顿	717		gǎn	敢	726
bēi	杯	11		cháo	朝	723		dāo	刀	72		duō	多	69			感	556
běi	北	317		chē	车	83		dǎo	导	277		è	饿	288		gàn	干	124
bèi	倍	315		chén	晨	775			倒	75		ér	儿	21		gāng	刚	676
	备	548		chéng	成	259		dào	到	74			而	151			钢	677
	被	440			城	260			倒	75		èr	二	2		gāo	高	481
běn	本	174		chī	吃	415			道	145		fā	发	146		gǎo	搞	482
bǐ	比	228		chí	持	465		dé	得	118		fǎ	法	87		gào	告	138
	笔	454			迟	777		de	的	23		fān	翻	736		gē	哥	386
bì	必	162		chōu	抽	620			地	54		fán	烦	718			歌	387
biān	边	41		chū	出	114			得	118		fǎn	反	331		gè	个	19
biàn	变	581			初	439		děi	得	118		fàn	饭	332			各	507
	便	400		chú	除	738		dēng	灯	182		fāng	方	291		gěi	给	351
	遍	770		chǔ	楚	749		děng	等	464		fáng	房	293		gēn	根	282
biǎo	表	436			础	115		dī	低	684		fǎng	访	292			跟	283
bié	别	79		chù	处	506			地	54		fàng	放	294		gèng	更	399

me	么	34	péng	朋	62	qù	去	86		使	398	tái	抬	484
méi	没	169	pèng	碰	396	quán	全	416		始	485	tài	太	48
měi	每	128	pī	批	229	què	确	419	shì	示	430		态	426
mèi	妹	64	pí	啤	356	rán	然	266		世	578	tán	谈	422
mén	门	27	piān	篇	771	ràng	让	476		是	30	tāng	汤	531
men	们	28	pián	便	400	rè	热	695		市	427	táng	堂	543
mǐ	米	334	piàn	片	353	rén	人	12		适	459		糖	764
miàn	面	313	piào	票	431		认	253		试	603	tǎng	躺	542
mín	民	455		漂	432	rèn	任	551		视	435	tǎo	讨	201
míng	名	70	píng	平	309	rì	日	6		室	472	tè	特	466
	明	77		评	311	róng	容	486		事	312	téng	疼	690
mǔ	母	127		苹	310	ròu	肉	221	shōu	收	355	tī	踢	529
mù	目	93		瓶	791	rú	如	80	shǒu	手	31	tí	提	475
ná	拿	348	pò	破	441	sài	赛	769		首	144		题	478
nǎ	哪	99	qī	七	37	sān	三	3	shū	书	176	tǐ	体	175
nà	那	98		期	236	sàn	散	745		舒	644	tiān	天	76
	呐	220	qí	其	235	sè	色	417		输	757	tiáo	条	546
na	哪	99		齐	668	shān	山	110	shú	熟	696	tiào	跳	788
nǎi	奶	533		骑	740	shāng	商	640	shǔ	数	469	tīng	听	242
nán	男	156	qǐ	起	276	shàng	上	42	shù	术	461	tíng	停	343
	难	503	qì	气	411	shāo	烧	778		束	494		庭	659
	南	307		汽	412	shǎo	少	377		数	469	tǐng	挺	660
ne	呢	268		器	630	shào	绍	596		树	155	tōng	通	564
nèi	内	219	qiān	千	89	shè	社	433	shuāng	双	712	tóng	同	160
néng	能	206		铅	747		设	553	shuí	谁	501	tòng	痛	565
ng	嗯	521	qián	前	90		舍	643	shuǐ	水	523	tóu	头	246
nǐ	你	51		钱	610	shēn	身	107	shuì	睡	409	tū	突	618
nián	年	168	qiǎn	浅	611		深	619	shuō	说	67	tú	图	691
niàn	念	167	qiáng	墙	799	shén	什	35	sī	思	165	tuán	团	519
niáng	娘	286	qiáo	桥	583		神	622	sǐ	死	585	tuī	推	502
nín	您	493	qiě	且	443	shēng	生	133	sì	四	24	tuǐ	腿	729
niú	牛	384	qiè	切	230		声	488	sòng	送	373	tuì	退	728
nóng	农	438	qīn	亲	196	shěng	省	379	sòu	嗽	496	tuō	脱	656
nǔ	努	762	qīng	轻	245	shèng	胜	134	sù	宿	641	wà	袜	793
nǚ	女	15		青	335		剩	783		诉	719	wài	外	71
nuǎn	暖	366		清	337	shī	师	428	suān	酸	765	wán	玩	304
pá	爬	371	qíng	晴	338	shí	十	4	suàn	算	321		完	305
pà	怕	627		情	339		识	256	suī	虽	679	wǎn	晚	673
pāi	拍	628	qǐng	请	336		时	105	suì	岁	116		碗	760
pái	排	330	qiū	秋	693		拾	349	suǒ	所	270	wàn	万	296
pài	派	664	qiú	求	524		实	250	tā	他	13	wǎng	往	300
páng	旁	295		球	525		食	287		她	16		忘	569
pǎo	跑	639	qǔ	取	88	shǐ	史	397		它	227		望	570

MEANING INDEX

This index gives the serial numbers of all the characters and fragments used in this book.

As in the main text, we use the following two conventions. A meaning in "quotes" is simply our name for a fragment which might not have a true meaning of its own. A meaning in [brackets] means that you are only ever likely to see this character in a compound which has this meaning.

Meaning	Character	Page		Meaning	Character	Page
	峃	542a		gift	礼	612
even more	更	399		"gimlet"	钅	586a
evening	晚	673		give back	还	199
	夕	69a		glowing	芐	324a
every	每	128		go through	经	244
everywhere	遍	770		go	去	86
evil	歹	584a			往	300
examine	验	602		gods	神	622
example	例	584		going to	将	318
exceptionally	挺	660		gold	钅	278a
exchange	换	675		good fortune	幸	308
excited	兴	645		good health	康	752
exclamation	啦	180		good man	彦	588a
exercise	操	631		good	好	18
exert oneself	努	762			良	286a
exhausted	累	608		goods	品	631a
exit	出	114		government	政	190
expensive	贵	492			府	653
experience	历	393		gown	丧	665b
"explosion"	甬	564a		graceful	曼	785b
extract	抽	620		grade	级	535
extremity	极	534		grain	禾	126a
eye	目	93		"grain stalks"	川	579a
	眼	284		gram	克	194
face	面	313		grasp	握	474
	脸	600		grass	艹	218a
facing	朝	723		great	伟	707
factory	厂	149		green	绿	754
fall short	差	204		greet	迎	682
familiar	熟	696		ground	地	54
farm	农	438		group	团	519
father	父	367			派	664
favor	恩	521a		guest	客	509
fear	怕	627		guide	导	277
feather	羽	736a		habitual	惯	776
feel	觉	405		hairs	彡	573a
	感	556		half	半	131
"feet"	丷	90a		hall	堂	543
festival	节	560		halt	停	343
few	少	377		Han Chinese	汉	78
	些	314		hand down	严	365c
field	田	156a		hand	手	31
fifth	戊	259a			扌	152a
fight	斗	605a		handle	把	369

Meaning	Character	Page		Meaning	Character	Page
filial piety	孝	265a		hands		82b
fine weather	晴	338		reaching down	丷	82b
finish	完	305		hang	挂	708
fire	火	181		happy	愉	756
	灬	185a		hardship	巳	566a
"firewood"	彐	317a		hat	帽	774
firm	収	697b		"haul up"	业	388a
fish	鱼	549		have	有	63
five	五	36		have to	须	591
flat	扁	770b		"hay"	彐	587a
flood	巛	615a		he	他	13
flow	流	615		head	头	246
flower	花	392			首	144
fly	飞	410		heal	医	491
food	食	287		hear	闻	290
	饣	288a		heart	心	161
foot	足	280			忄	339a
	𧾷	280		hearth	朵	619a
	脚	561		heaven	天	76
footstep	丁	81c		heavenly body	辰	775a
for	为	122		heavy	重	407
	给	351		"held in the hands"	夫	692a
forever	永	685		help	助	445
forge	锻	716			帮	705
forget	忘	569		hemp	麻	750
forgive	谅	759		hero	英	401
former	故	191		heron	隽	420a
fortune teller	卜	42a		hesitate	燚	765a
"foul mouth"	吉	540a		hey!	喂	666
foundation	基	237		hidden	阴	97
four	四	24		high	高	481
fragrant	香	761		high up	戈	778a
freezing	寒	768		history	史	397
friend	友	53		hit	打	153
friendship	谊	450		hold on to	执	695c
from	从	103		hole	穴	616a
fruit	果	187		hood	冂	773a
full	满	225		"hook"	乚	612a
furs	月	98a		horns	丷	65a
garden	园	302		horse	马	44
gate	门	27		hot	热	695
gaze	望	570		house	宀	91a
"gazebo"	亠	342a			房	293
get	导	118a		household	家	109

FAST FINDER INDEX

Use this index when you see a character and want to find it in this book, but you don't know its pronunciation or meaning. This index uses the appearance of the character directly, and how the character splits up into parts. This is the same method as used in the book "Chinese Character Fast Finder" (see the inside back cover), which enables you to find any of the 3,000 characters in all four HSK Levels A — D rapidly, without knowing their meanings, pronunciations, radicals or stroke-counts.

Most characters split left-right or top-bottom into parts:

Take the simpler component (or the one you recognize) and look up the character in the appropriate section, depending on whether this part is the left, right, top or bottom part of the character:

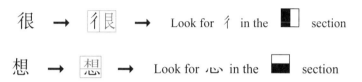

You will find all such characters (for example, all the characters which have 亻 as the left-hand side) listed together, and by scanning along the charaters listed you should be able to quickly find the one you want.

For some characters, instead of a left-right or top-bottom split, one part of the character encloses another on two or more sides. For such cases, use the enclosing part to look up the character:

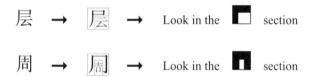

Finally, many simple characters are "indivisible" — they do not break down into parts:

本 → 本 → Look in the ■ section

So this index is similar to a radical index, except that you don't need to count strokes. You also don't need to decide which part is the "proper" radical. For example:

和 appears under 禾 in the ■ section, and also under 口 in the ■ section.

If the character is printed in gray, you were not really looking for it in the right place: never mind, at least you have found it! Taking a close look at these gray characters will help you to distinguish between similar and easily-confused characters and fragments.

The numbers given refer to serial numbers in the book.

丶	小	心	必	办	火	为			
	50	161	162	123	181	122			

丿	牛	午	年	生	久				
	384	125	168	133	364				

丿	八	儿	从	片					
	20	21	103	353					

忄	快	忙	怕	情	惯	慢	愉	懂	
	403	568	627	339	776	785	756	408	

火	灯	烦	炼	烧					
	182	718	713	778					

丬	将	北							
	318	317							

讠	认	记	计	让	许	评	讲		
	253	272	552	476	589	311	357		
	访	该	谅	谊	请	读	说	谈	
	292	497	759	450	336	249	67	422	
	论	识	设	误	语	课	译	话	
	252	256	553	731	68	189	737	458	
	谁	谢							
	501	108							
	诉	讨	试	词	调				
	719	201	603	231	541				

冫	次	决	况	凉	冷	净	准	习	头
	361	404	360	758	593	721	504	735	246

氵	江	汉	浅	汤	酒				
	148	78	611	531	102				
	注	法	洗	泳	消	济	流	演	清	满
	299	87	139	686	661	670	615	623	337	225
	治	汽	海	深	活	没	渴	澡	漂
	483	412	129	619	460	169	576	632	432
	湖								
	193								
	河	游	派						
	141	688	664						

丨	旧	门	师	以					
	394	27	428	120					

亻	亿	化	代	什	件	伟	作		
	413	391	456	35	385	707	207		
	休	体	你	他	使	便	俩		
	727	175	51	13	398	400	224		
	位	住	倍	信	停	傅	借		
	178	298	315	376	343	790	744		
	但	任	低	像					
	117	551	684	674					
	们	例	做	假	倒	候	何	健	
	28	584	210	798	75	667	142	658	

彳	行	往	街	很	得				
	81	300	710	281	118				

扌	打	找	扬	把	抽				
	153	152	532	369	620				
	拍	拉	技	持	挂	挤	接	掉	搞	擦
	628	179	463	465	708	669	203	724	482	792
	指	拾	抬	换	提	操	摆	播	
	251	349	484	675	475	631	786	734	
	推	排	批	搬					
	502	330	229	681					
	报	握	挺	抱					
	562	474	660	638					

牛	物	特							
	527	466							

车	轻	较	辆	输	辅				
	245	382	223	757	789				

礻	礼	社	神	祖	祝	视	福		
	612	433	622	447	434	435	702		

衤	初	袜	被						
	439	793	440						

方	放	族	旅						
	294	687	755						

(page 2 / 2)

刂	划 554	利 132	刻 500	刮 457	别 79	到 74	倒 75	例 584	刚 676	剩 783
门	门 27	们 28	词 231	翻 736	切 230	初 439				
丁	打 153	灯 182	可 140	河 141	何 142	啊 143				
寸	讨 201	对 154	时 105	封 709	树 155	谢 108	村 104	的 23		
比	北 317	比 228	批 229	化 391						
力	助 445	动 58	切 230							
欠	次 361	欢 363	吹 362	歌 387						
攵	收 355	改 359	政 190	做 210	放 294	故 191	教 265	数 469	散 745	敢 726
又反	汉 78	双 712	取 88	饭 332	板 333					
卜亍	外 71	处 506	行 81	街 710						
十中	计 552	什 35	钟 278	种 279						
乚立	礼 612	乱 613	亿 413	拉 179	啦 180					
不巴	坏 442	杯 11	吧 368	把 369	爬 371					
人马	认 253	从 103	以 120	吗 45	妈 46					
工彡	江 148	红 233	彩 732	影 574						
己也	记 272	纪 273	起 276	他 13	地 54	她 16				

口	如 80	加 325	知 490	和 126	咖 327			
日	旧 394	阳 96						
且	姐 444	租 446	祖 447	组 448	相 163			
月	明 77	阴 97	朋 62	期 236	朝 723	湖 193		
阝	邮 621	那 98	都 262	部 316	哪 99			
斤	听 242	所 270	新 243	诉 719				
殳	没 169	设 553	段 715	般 680				
见	现 215	观 216	视 435					
页	须 591	烦 718	顿 717	预 642	领 595	顾 567	颜 588	题 478
隹	准 504	谁 501	难 503	推 502				
艮	很 281	根 282	眼 284	跟 283	银 285	娘 286		
戈	找 152	我 32	成 259	城 260	或 555	戴 782	代 456	
戋	浅 611	践 609	钱 610					
other	叫 354	非 328	化 391	让 476	社 433	代 456	科 605	研 606	班 113
	切 230	机 10	好 18	秋 693	妹 64	袜 793	联 374	钢 677
	相 163	脚 561	鸡 678	的 23	句 649	包 636		
	就 239	舒 644	瓶 791	起 276	建 657	解 586	能 206	静 722

丶	义	户	永	主	之	术	发	或	感
	467	269	685	297	121	461	146	555	556

	广	书	尤	求	心	必	门	为	集
	170	176	238	524	161	162	27	122	505

丿	向	白	自	息	身
	389	22	94	662	107

丷	羊	弟	单	总	关	首	前	半	米
	111	323	344	514	372	144	90	131	334

丷	当	堂	常	掌	半	米	火
	267	543	544	545	131	334	181

	觉	举	兴	学
	405	648	645	82

八	公	分	父	爸	少	省
	119	73	367	370	377	379

人	个	介	全	今	念	会	合	舍	拿	食
	19	579	416	166	167	59	347	643	348	287

亠	文	六	方	立	交	衣	言	夜	齐	主
	25	39	291	177	380	437	375	797	668	297

	齐	市	忘	变	育	亮	高	离	赢
	668	427	569	581	614	342	481	654	800

	辛	亲	音	章	意	产	旁	商
	195	196	257	634	258	197	295	640

宀	它	安	字	家	实	定	宜	宿	农
	227	91	92	109	250	406	449	641	438

	完	室	客	寄	富	寒	赛	宴
	305	472	509	742	703	768	769	796

	究	空	突	穿	容	窗
	616	617	618	781	486	767

卜	卡	占	点	桌
	198	183	185	725

十	支	克	直	真	南	卖	喜	先
	462	194	451	452	307	248	539	137

士	去	走	幸	志	声	喜
	86	275	308	487	488	539

丰	责	青	表
	515	335	436

一	二	三	云	元	示	画	买	写	死	哥
	2	3	56	301	430	626	247	423	585	386

	下	不	干	平	天	开	万	正	西	两
	43	9	124	309	76	85	296	29	100	222

一	而	面	页	百	夏
	151	313	477	40	694

一	千	系	香	爱	重	丢	么
	89	607	761	365	407	795	34

厂	午	气	年	每	复	怎	舞
	125	411	168	128	550	512	787

勹	色	负	危	鱼	角	急	包	句
	417	517	566	549	418	587	636	649

夂夕	冬	条	务	各	备	名	多
	689	546	547	507	548	70	69

廿	艺	节	苹	花	药	共
	414	560	310	392	720	625

	茶	菜	蕉	黄	劳	苦	英	草	蓝
	739	733	763	624	324	218	401	635	700

	带
	429

⺮	笑	笔	第	答	等	简	算	篮	篇
	582	454	322	352	464	346	321	701	771

大山	太	态	岁	出
	48	426	116	114

口品	只	号	足	员	虽	哭	器
	254	424	280	479	679	629	630

日	星	最	易	早	晨	是	冒
	136	421	528	633	775	30	773

田	男	思	累	界	里	果
	156	165	608	580	157	187

西雨	要	票	雪	需	零
	101	431	572	590	594

other	么	见	共	写	买	步	录	希	导	哥
	34	214	625	423	247	378	753	559	277	386

	先	杂	忽	蛋	集	参	贵	查	冒	舞
	137	511	526	748	505	573	492	598	773	787

丶冫	太 冬 寒
	48 689 768

八贝	六 兴 只 共 典 黄 真 其
	39 645 254 625 232 624 452 235
	页 负 员 责 贵 赛
	477 517 479 515 492 769

刂	齐 介 界 开
	668 579 580 85

儿见	元 先 克 完 亮 见 觉 览
	301 137 194 305 342 214 405 699

小糸	示 票 系 紧 累
	430 431 607 698 608

灬	点 黑 热 熟 然 蕉 照
	185 671 695 696 266 763 597

心	志 忘 怎 忽 急 态 思
	487 569 512 526 587 426 165
	息 总 您 想 念 意 感 愿
	662 514 493 164 167 258 556 537

一	二 三 鱼 查 些
	2 3 549 598 314

土	里 坐 坚 堂 基 在 室 全 望
	157 211 697 543 237 55 472 416 570

十	干 千 午 辛 早 草 章 单 举
	124 89 125 195 633 635 634 344 648

木	果 亲 杂 条 茶 菜 桌 集 米
	187 196 511 546 739 733 725 505 334

大	天 关 哭 笑 突 英 实 卖
	76 372 629 582 618 401 250 248

乂	义 父 文 交
	467 367 25 380

又	变 支 友 爱
	581 462 53 365

夕夂	岁 多 夏 复
	116 69 694 550

女	安 宴 要
	91 796 101

口	占 告 各 名 合 舍
	183 138 507 70 347 643
	苦 答 客 容 言 喜 右 可 句
	218 352 509 486 375 539 213 140 649

日	白 百 音 香 春
	22 40 257 761 692

目	自 省 首 冒 看 宜
	94 379 144 773 200 449

田	备 留 富
	548 663 703

月	青 育 有 角
	335 614 63 418

皿	蓝 篮
	700 701

工	左 空
	209 617

厶	云 去 会 公 离
	56 86 59 119 654

力	男 务 劳 努 分 究
	156 547 324 762 73 616

力	万 方 房 旁
	296 291 293 295

彐子	当 雪 字 学
	267 572 92 82

巾皿	市 布 带 常 帮 而 需
	427 558 429 544 705 151 590

衤衣	衣 农 表 装 晨
	437 438 436 489 775

辶足	走 足 是 定 楚
	275 280 30 406 749

other	个 卡 少 今 气 艺 它
	19 198 377 166 411 414 227
	出 求 分 究 举 节 穿 蛋 驾 哥
	114 524 73 616 648 560 781 748 326 386
	望 整 楚 掌 等 零 器 爸 包
	570 495 749 545 464 594 630 370 636

厂

厂 厂	历 原 愿 反 后 厂
	393 536 537 331 150 149
广	床 店 应 座 度 康 府 麻 庭 广
	171 186 388 212 425 752 653 750 659 170
疒	疼 病 痛
	690 510 565
𠂇	友 左 右 有 布 在
	53 209 213 63 558 55
尸	层 屋 展 局 民
	471 473 665 650 455
耂	老 考 者 差 着
	264 604 261 204 205
方	放 族 旅
	294 687 755
other	在 发 死 名 危 房 看
	55 146 585 70 566 293 200

辶

辶	边 还 近 迟 过 进 连 退 迎
	41 199 241 777 106 358 84 728 682
	这 运 远 送 适 道 通 遇 遍
	26 57 303 373 459 145 564 655 770
other	处 爬 建 起 题 也 世
	506 371 657 276 478 8 578
	习 可 句 包 或 戴
	735 140 649 636 555 782
	头
	246
	问 间 闻 同 周 风 门 几
	289 345 290 160 540 468 27 7
	向 内 肉 见
	389 219 221 214
	医
	491
	回 四 园 团 因 困 围 国 图 圆
	202 24 302 519 520 522 706 60 691 480
	班 街 解 能 静 舒
	113 710 586 206 722 644

■

亠	十 上 丰 书 牛 生 山 出
	4 42 704 176 384 133 110 114
	中 本 束 来
	33 174 494 65
	七 长 电
	37 172 159
	才 小 水 求 事
	518 50 523 524 312
丿	人 力 九 女 车 东 史 内 肉 农
	12 14 38 15 83 319 397 219 221 438
	大 夫 火 尤 太 久 午 年
	47 49 181 238 48 364 125 168
	之 广 门 义 户 术 主 永 发 身
	121 170 27 467 269 461 297 685 146 107
	为 心 必 羊 半 米 弟 头
	122 161 162 111 131 334 323 246
凵	八 儿 片 世 也 其 业 非
	20 21 353 578 8 235 395 328
一	一 下 不 万 天 干 平 开 两 西
	1 43 9 296 76 124 309 85 222 100
	工 五 互 正 雨 再 更 死
	147 36 226 29 571 217 399 585
	厂 几 又
	149 7 52
	刀 了 子 己 已 飞 马
	72 66 17 271 274 410 44
	口 日 目 且 月 用 母
	5 6 93 443 61 130 127
丆	千 手 毛 斤 乐 重
	89 31 453 240 320 407